1996

University of St. Francis
GEN 111 O621
Onny Graham.

W9-AES-561

Ontological arguments and belief in God

Ontological arguments and belief in God

GRAHAM OPPY
Australian National University

CAMBRIDGE
UNIVERSITY PRESS

Published by the Press Syndicate of the University of Cambridge
The Pitt Building, Trumpington Street, Cambridge CB2 1RP
40 West 20th Street, New York, NY 10011-4211, USA
10 Stamford Road, Oakleigh, Melbourne 3166, Australia

© Cambridge University Press 1995

First published 1995

Printed in the United States of America

Library of Congress Cataloguing-in-Publication Data applied for.

A catalog record for this book is available from the British Library

ISBN 0-521-48120-1 Hardback

111
0621

$54.72

Publication

6-17-96

156,818

In memory of my mother
Jean Oppy

Contents

Contents

Contents

Preface

THIS book is part of a larger work, which seeks to expound and defend an agnostic stance on theistic matters. The larger work, most of which remains to be written, is intended to have four parts:

i.   an examination of conceptions of deities, including a discussion of the consistency and mutual compatibility of allegedly divine attributes, and an examination of the structure and function of religious vocabulary;
ii. an examination of traditional arguments for and against the existence of various deities, including: ontological arguments, cosmological arguments, teleological arguments, arguments from evil, moral arguments, arguments from revelation, arguments from authority, arguments from religious experience, and arguments from miracles;
iii. an examination of formulations of agnosticism, including a comparative evaluation of formulations of theism and atheism; and
iv. an investigation of the epistemological merits of agnosticism, including a somewhat qualified defense.

Obviously, the present work is one subpart of part (ii). Not surprisingly, the main thesis that is defended in it is that ontological arguments do not provide an agnostic with any good reason to change her view – that is, to give up her agnosticism. One of the projected themes of the larger work is that the most fruitful approach to arguments in philosophy of religion is to ask: Do these arguments embody reasons for agnostics – atheists, theists – to change their views? That is, do these arguments embody considerations that reasonable and reflective agnostics – atheists, theists – must recognize as providing motivating reasons for them to change their views? Or can there be reasonable and reflective agnostics – atheists, theists – who are quite reasonably unmoved by the considerations adduced in the arguments?[1]

The present work has four main components. First, there is a survey of the main events in the history of the discussion of ontological arguments. Second, there is an analysis of different kinds of ontological arguments, together with an application of that analysis to the major historical arguments. Third, there is an assessment of attempts to show that no ontological arguments can succeed, including (i) an examination of the question of whether existence is a predicate, and (ii) a look at the significance of various proposed parodies of ontological arguments. Finally, there is an examination of the uses that ontological arguments might be thought to have by theists and atheists, including a discussion of the idea that ontological arguments can be used to demonstrate the rationality of belief in the conclusions of those arguments.

There is a large appendix to the text, entitled "Literature Notes." It is primarily a survey of the vast recent literature on ontological arguments. Although decisions about where to locate material are to some extent arbitrary, I have tried to limit detailed examination of secondary sources to this appendix. Joint use of the index and the bibliography should facilitate the extraction of information from these pages.

Since judgments about what is reasonably believed play a large role in this work, a few remarks about this topic are in order.[2] I assume that there is a *procedural* or *dispositional* sense in which there can be reasonable theists, atheists, and agnostics: Such people are disposed to revise their beliefs when they are shown how their view can be improved – for example, simplified, unified, rendered more coherent, or rendered less inconsistent. Further, I assume that all parties interested in ontological arguments will concede this much; one could hardly suppose that one has an opponent with whom it is appropriate to *argue* unless one concedes that the person in question is dispositionally rational. Moreover, the main thesis for which I wish to argue is this: that ontological arguments do not give dispositionally reasonable agnostics – theists, atheists – a reason to change their views.

---

1 See Oppy (1994) for a more detailed sketch of the general position that I endorse here.
2 These remarks were prompted by much appreciated comments from an anonymous reader at Cambridge University Press.

More controversially, I also hold that ontological arguments should be located in a dialectical framework in which views are presumed innocent until convicted; in particular, I hold that there should be a *pro tem* presumption that there can be reasonable acceptance of theism – atheism, agnosticism – by sensitive, reflective, and informed persons. This *systematic* sense of reasonableness leaves room for the view that agnosticism – atheism, theism – is inconsistent, incoherent, intolerably convoluted, *ad hoc,* and so on, and so leaves room for the view that it could come to be the case that agnosticism – atheism, theism – cannot reasonably be believed by sensitive, reflective, and informed persons; and it also leaves room for the view that there can be reasonable acceptance of inconsistent – incoherent, intolerably complex, and *ad hoc* – views by subjects who are not suitably informed. Consider Russell and Whitehead's belief in the complete, recursive axiomatizability of arithmetic. At the time, their view was reflective and informed; but now one who held this view would not count as suitably informed, at least in those cases in which one is culpably ignorant of Godel's work. Clearly, more needs to be said about the notion of being "suitably informed" – and about the related notion of "epistemic responsibility" – but, as this is not a treatise on epistemology, I shall not attempt to do so here.

Of course, some people will simply disagree with my judgments about the systematic reasonableness of agnosticism – theism, atheism – because they disagree with my *pro tem* judgment that reflective and sensitive supporters of this doctrine can be suitably informed, that is, epistemically responsible. I do not suppose that such people are unreasonable, though I do find this stance unacceptable. I have friends who are theists, friends who are atheists, and friends who are agnostics; and I feel that it would be offensive and disloyal to some of them to hold that they are systematically irrational even though I know of no argument that on pain of conviction of procedural irrationality, should make them change their minds. However, for my purposes, nothing very important hangs on these questions about systematic rationality; none of the judgments in question affects the point that there is nothing in ontological arguments that should bring a procedurally reasonable agnostic – theist, atheist – to think that he has been systematically irrational.

Since many of the primary sources for the arguments that I discuss are historically significant philosophical and theological texts, some further remarks about my use of these texts may also be in order.[3]

Throughout, my main interest is in the collection, classification, and analysis of arguments that sensitive, reflective, and informed persons do, or might, take to encode *a priori* reasons for the adoption of particular stances on questions about the existence of various deities. Consequently, my interest in historical texts is solely concerned with their use as sources of such arguments, or as sources of criticisms of such arguments, quite independent of the question whether the texts are *best* interpreted as sources of these kinds. If the texts must be misread in order to generate the arguments, that need be no concern of mine. As it happens, however, I think that – except in cases where I make explicit claims to the contrary – my readings actually do no violence to the texts in question; but aside from references to contemporary philosophical authorities, I make little or no attempt to substantiate this contention. Moreover, I do not claim that the value of these texts is exhausted by the use I make of them; that is, I claim no more than that part of what is on offer in these texts is arguments of the kind that I wish to investigate. Thus, for example, I have no quarrel here with one who wants to insist that the initial sections of St. Anselm's *Proslogion* provide much insight into the nature of God, or at least a particular Christian conception of God; my interest is solely in the question whether arguments generated from that text encode *a priori* reasons for me, or anyone else, to embrace that conception of God and/or to make judgments about the rationality of the various stances that I, or anyone else, could take with respect to that conception.

Some people will have further reservations about this "ahistorical, acontextual" approach to ontological arguments; for example, on one popular view, the historical context of an argument is an integral constituent of a proper analysis of that argument: Arguments are partly constituted by their function in the texts in which they appear and their place in the wider projects that they serve. I don't need to dispute the claim that a *complete* analysis of a part of a historical text must attend to the function which that part plays in the total text, the global project which that text is intended to serve, the historical context in which the text was written, and so on. However, as should already be clear, I have no interest in the project of providing a complete account of "ontological arguments" in this sense. My project involves merely the conceptual analysis of arguments – that is, sets of

---

3   These remarks were prompted by much appreciated comments from another anonymous reader at the press.

sentences[4] in which one sentence is claimed to follow logically from the rest – not the complete analysis of written texts. By my lights, if a piece of text cannot be massaged into the form of an argument – that is, a set of sentences, one of which is claimed to follow logically from the rest – then it is simply incorrect to say that that text contains an argument. If you apply the term 'ontological argument' to pieces of text that cannot be massaged into the form of an argument, then we shall simply be talking at cross-purposes. Of course, as I have already suggested, it is important not to lose sight of the functions that arguments can serve; but these functions – which concern the rational revision of belief – need have nothing to do with the historical contexts of any texts that played a role in the construction of the arguments.

4 Strictly speaking, this talk of 'sets of sentences' is shorthand for more convoluted talk about sets of standardly interpreted sentences, i.e., sets of what are sometimes, perhaps misleadingly, called *statements* or *propositions*. The difficulty here is to make a more accurate claim that does not suggest a perhaps undesirable commitment to the existence of abstract entities associated with utterances or inscriptions of sentence-tokens.

Acknowledgments

This book was written while I held an Australian Research Council Postdoctoral Fellowship in the Research School for the Social Sciences at the Australian National University. I am indebted to the Australian Department of Employment, Education, and Training for awarding me this fellowship, and to the RSSS at ANU for the facilities that they made available. The Philosophy Department in RSSS is one of the best places in the world to do philosophy; I am grateful to all of the staff, students, and visitors who helped to make this the case during the time that I was writing this book. In particular, I should thank Nick Agar, David Armstrong, Michael Ayers, John Bishop, Simon Blackburn, David Braddon-Mitchell, Stuart Brock, John Broome, Mark Colyvan, Tim Dare, Michael Devitt, Brian Garrett, Moira Gatens, Tim van Gelder, Phillip Gerrens, Andrew Gleason, Alan Hajek, Kelly Hite, Dominic Hyde, Cathy Legg, Doug MacLean, Peter Menzies, Alex Miller, Joe Mintoff, Kevin Mulligan, Karen Neander, Graham Nerlich, John O'Leary-Hawthorne, Phillip Pettit, Ian Ravenscroft, Georges Rey, Denis Robinson, Judith Sellars, Jack Smart, Barry Taylor, Debbie Trew, Caroline West, Kevin Wilkinson, Susan Wolf, Tamara Zutlevics, and, especially, Frank Jackson and Michael Smith. Daniel Nolan read a near-final version of the manuscript; I am greatly indebted to him for his helpful critical comments and advice, which led to numerous improvements of the text. Audiences at RSSS, Wollongong and Sydney, also provided helpful critical comments; in particular, in addition to those already mentioned, I thank Susan Dodds, Robert Dunn, Stephen Gaukroger, Adrian Heathcote, George Molnar, Huw Price, Lloyd Reinhardt, Michael Shepanski, David Simpson, and Suzanne Uniacke. Thanks, too, to Ed Zalta for bringing Oppenheimer and Zalta (1991) to my attention.

Much of this book contains criticism of the work of others. However, it would be remiss of me not to record my debt to the writings of many philosophers on the subject of ontological arguments. In particular, I have been greatly influenced by the excellent work of Robert Adams, John Barnes, William Forgie, David Lewis, George Mavrodes, Alvin Plantinga, Nathan Salmon, Michael Tooley, and Peter van Inwagen. A passing remark in Plantinga (1974b:86) provided part of the motivation for the book, namely, "I do not believe that any philosopher has ever given a cogent and conclusive refutation of the ontological argument in its various forms." One *aim* of this book is to provide such a "refutation"; how far it falls short of that aim I leave to the reader to judge.

I could not have written this book without the love and support of my family: my father, Ted; my brother, Ian; my sisters, Joan and Linda; and, especially, my wife, Camille, and my sons, Gilbert and Calvin.

Ontological arguments and
belief in God

Introduction

THE following is a discussion of certain kinds of arguments for the existence of God. The distinctive feature of the arguments – at least according to the traditional Kantian method of classification – is that they proceed from premises which at least some defenders of the arguments allege can all be known *a priori*. Consequently, it would be most appropriate to call these arguments '*a priori* arguments for the existence of God'. However, following Kant, it has been established practice to call these kinds of arguments "ontological arguments," and I see no urgent reason to depart from this tradition. Many things have well-established but inappropriate names – for example, the Holy Roman Empire, which, as Voltaire pointed out, was neither holy, nor Roman, nor an empire.[1]

I shall divide the arguments that I consider into six classes, namely, (i) *definitional arguments*, whose premises invoke certain kinds of definitions; (ii) *conceptual arguments*, whose premises advert to the possession of certain kinds of concepts or ideas; (iii) *modal arguments*, whose premises advert to certain possibilities; (iv) *Meinongian arguments*, whose premises invoke a distinction between different categories of existence; (v) *experiential arguments*, whose premises include the assumption that the concept of God is only available to those who

---

1 In my view, a better characterization of ontological arguments than the traditional Kantian characterization given in the text is as follows: Ontological arguments are arguments that proceed from considerations that are entirely internal to the theistic worldview. Other theistic arguments proceed from facts, or putative facts that are at least *prima facie* independent of the theistic worldview – for example, the presence of nomic, causal, or spatiotemporal order in the universe; the presence and nature of complex living structures in the universe; the presence and nature of conscious and intelligent agents in the universe. But ontological arguments are concerned solely with a domain or theory that is *in dispute* between theists and their opponents.

1

have had veridical experiences of God; and (vi) *"Hegelian" arguments*, which, at least in my view, bear some relation to the philosophy of Hegel. This division will not be mutually exclusive; that is, some arguments may belong to more than one category. Moreover, it may not be exhaustive. However, I do not know of any *a priori* arguments for the existence of God that do not belong to at least one of these categories.

For each of these categories of argument, I propose to do two things. First, I shall exhibit some arguments that belong to the category in question. And, second, I shall explain why none of the arguments that I exhibit provides me with a convincing reason to believe in God. The explanation of why I find the arguments unconvincing is different for each of the six categories of argument – and, indeed, this is the main rationale for the division that I make.[2]

There are various other tasks that will remain to be undertaken. The objections that I propose to give are mostly ones that I have been unable to find in the literature – though they usually bear some close relation to objections that have appeared there. In many cases, it will be useful to explain why the objections that have been formulated hitherto are not perfectly satisfactory. In particular, I shall consider the question of the relevance, and correctness, of the claim that existence is not a predicate, and I shall also evaluate the claim that it is possible to parody *a priori* arguments for the existence of God in ways that show that those arguments are unacceptable.

Throughout the first part of this work, I shall mostly be considering the arguments from the standpoint of an agnostic – that is, from the standpoint of someone who is committed neither to the existence, nor to the nonexistence, of the deities whose existence the arguments purport to establish. My interest is in whether the arguments provide such a person with good reasons to accept the conclusions of those

---

2 Peter van Inwagen (1977:375) discusses what I shall call 'modal ontological arguments involving necessity'. He claims that "every well-known 'version of the ontological argument' is either (i) essentially the same as one of the arguments called ontological herein, or (ii) invalid or outrageously question-begging, or (iii) stated in language so confusing it is not possible to say with any confidence just what its premises are or what their conclusion is supposed to be." My discussion shows that this is mistaken: Modal ontological arguments involving necessity are no clearer, and no better, than, e.g., conceptual ontological arguments, or Meinongian ontological arguments, or modal ontological arguments involving actuality – and yet these kinds of arguments are clearly distinct from modal ontological arguments involving necessity.

arguments. In the last part of the work, I shall take up the question whether the arguments have some value for those who are anteced-ently convinced of the truth of their conclusions.

I have not bothered to give formalizations of the arguments that I discuss. This is not because I think that there is no value in the formalization of intuitive arguments; on the contrary, I think that there is much to be learned from the formalization of intuitive arguments. However, I do not think that anything would have been added to the discussion that I give by the formalization of the arguments.[3]

Also, I have not worried about niceties concerning quotation: cor-ner quotes, use versus mention, and so on. Readers who care will be able to work out for themselves which uses of single quotes are really uses of corner quotes – for example, those in which schematic letters appear.

Finally, I occasionally refer to modal logics – K, T, B, S4, S5, and so on – by their standard (Hughes and Cresswell: 1968) names without giving any further information about them. Readers who want to know more about them should consult one of the standard texts on modal logics listed in the bibliography.

---

3 For those who are interested, for most of the arguments discussed, I have provided references to works in which they have been formalized.

Chapter 1

Some historical considerations

I BEGIN with a synoptic history of ontological arguments. In the remaining part of this chapter, I shall discuss the works of some of the more prominent historical figures – St. Anselm, Descartes, Leibniz, Hume, and Kant – in more detail. Then, in the following chapters, I shall provide analyses of different kinds of ontological arguments, and show how these analyses relate to the historically important arguments.

(1) HISTORICAL SYNOPSIS

Ontological arguments have been "found" in ancient Greek philosophy,[1] in St. Augustine[2] and other early Christians, and in the work of

---

1 Hartshorne (1965) attempts to locate an anticipation of St. Anselm's ontological argument in the writings of Plato – and he also discerns related anticipations in Aristotle, Philo, and Ikhnaton. Similar attempts have been made by Ferguson (1953), Johnson (1963), and Paullin (1906). As Barnes (1972:18) notes, these attempts are mostly not very convincing. However, following Ferguson, Barnes suggests that there is an ontological argument in the writings of Zeno of Cition, as reported by Sextus Empiricus: "A man can properly honour the gods; a man cannot properly honour what does not exist; therefore the gods exist." But, while this argument bears some relation to, e.g., the Cartesian ontological argument, it seems doubtful that this argument qualifies as an ontological argument. In particular, it is doubtful that it should be allowed that one could reasonably hold that the first premise is knowable *a priori*.

Slattery (1969) claims that ontological arguments were invented by Parmenides. However, while it is clear that there are affinities between Parmenides' "way of truth" and Spinoza's "ontological argument," it seems to me that the title 'ontological argument' should be reserved for arguments that purport to demonstrate the existence of a *deity*. And, moreover – the views of Spinoza notwithstanding – it seems clear to me that it is a mistake to suppose that the universe, or the Universal Substance, is a deity. Those who see no difficulty in the view that the universe is God should take the present paragraph to record a terminological decision; for,

4

Jewish and Islamic philosophers prior to the eleventh century.[3] However, it can be reasonably contended that the first clear statement of an ontological argument is that of St. Anselm, archbishop of Canterbury, in the eleventh century. St. Anselm's argument was much discussed throughout the succeeding centuries. Many prominent medieval thinkers accepted St. Anselm's argument – or modified versions of it – including Duns Scotus and St. Bonaventure. However, other significant medieval thinkers, including St. Thomas Aquinas and William of Occam, rejected the argument. One of the most important objections to St. Anselm's argument was provided by one of his contemporaries, the monk Gaunilo.

Ontological arguments received a fresh defense in the work of Descartes. It is not clear how much of Descartes' arguments were original with him – in particular, the nature and extent of his acquaintance with the work of St. Anselm is controversial – though the use to which he put the arguments in his philosophical system was undeniably his own work. The replies to Descartes' *Meditations* – the work of some of his prominent contemporaries – collected together a number of valuable objections to his versions of the arguments. Many of these objections were unduly neglected during the succeeding centuries.

Leibniz defended Descartes' arguments. In particular, he attempted to defend one of the assumptions upon which the arguments seem to depend, namely, that the notion of an absolutely perfect being is coherent. Malebranche, Spinoza, Baumgarten, and Wolff also accepted ontological arguments, generally in their Cartesian form. On the other hand, Berkeley noted: "Absurd to Argue the Existence of God from his Idea. . . . we have no Idea of God. 'tis impossible!"[4] And Locke,

despite my reservations, I do discuss Spinoza's argument – c.f. Section 4 in the literature notes.

2   For the claim that St. Anselm's argument is anticipated by St. Augustine, see Malcolm (1960:n4) and Maloney (1980:13n4). As Copleston (1950:70) notes, it is plausible to think that St. Anselm was influenced by the words of St. Augustine – e.g., by St. Augustine's claim that "all concur in believing God to be that which excels in dignity all other objects" (*De gratia et libero arbitrio ad valentinum*); however, this is hardly evidence that St. Augustine actually produced an ontological argument.

3   For the claim that St. Anselm's argument is anticipated by Islamic theologians, see Morewedge (1970), who claims that there is a modal ontological argument in ibn Sina.

4   *Philosophical Commentaries*, 782. Sillem (1957:44) claims that Berkeley "never discussed the ontological argument, nor even suggested that it might have any value or interest. He referred to it but once, and then only in a curt note [cited in the main text]." This isn't quite correct, since there are clear references to ontological argu-

while refusing to take a stand on the question whether the Cartesian arguments constitute proofs, observed that "It is an ill way of establishing [God's existence] and silencing atheists."[5]

Hume provided what he took to be a simple and decisive refutation of all *a priori* arguments for the existence of God.[6] This "simple and decisive refutation" was taken over by Kant, who provided it with various embellishments. It has been the opinion of many subsequent philosophers, including some current ones, that the Kantian form of the Humean objection is absolutely decisive.

Hegel held that "the ontological argument" provided the sole sound demonstration of the existence of God; this view was taken over by many subsequent Hegelians – for example, Collingwood.[7] On the other hand, Schopenhauer held that ontological arguments involved a "charming joke."[8]

As a young man, Bertrand Russell (1946b:10) came to believe in the existence of God as the result of some Hegelian ontological reasoning:

I remember the precise moment, one day in 1894, as I was walking along Trinity Lane, when I saw in a flash (or thought I saw) that the ontological argument is valid. I had gone out to buy a tin of tobacco; on my way back, I suddenly threw it up in the air, and exclaimed as I caught it: "Great Scott, the ontological argument is sound."

Later, Russell (1946a:568) came to the view that "the argument does not, to a modern mind, seem very convincing, but it is easier to feel

ments in *Alciphron*. Nonetheless, speaking very roughly, we can say that it is characteristic of the British empiricist tradition to hold ontological arguments in low esteem – and that it is characteristic of the continental rationalist tradition to hold a much more respectful attitude toward them.

5   Locke (1964/1690:4, IX, 7).
6   Under this category, Hume included both ontological and cosmological arguments, even though the latter are not, strictly speaking, *a priori* arguments.
7   Ontological arguments were very important for both the British and U.S. idealists. On the British side, ontological arguments are defended by Stout, Bosanquet, the Cairds, and many others. And on the U.S. side, ontological arguments are defended by Royce, Hocking, Sheldon, and, ultimately, Hartshorne. Perhaps some of the arguments that these authors call 'ontological' are badly named. For example, the argument defended by Sheldon (1923) (1924) (1929) – from and for the extraordinary, but barely intelligible hypothesis that the basic principle that governs the world is that all possibilities are realized equally in the long run – is only dubiously *a priori*. For further references to the idealist literature, see Bandas (1930) and the works referred to therein.
8   Schopenhauer (1897), excerpted in Plantinga (1965:65–7). Subsequent citations of Schopenhauer are from this text.

convinced that it must be fallacious than it is to find out precisely where the fallacy lies." In fact, Russell thought that his philosophy of language – in particular, his theories about quantification, definite descriptions and proper names – showed just where ontological arguments go wrong. This view was shared by many of Russell's contemporaries and successors – for example, Frege, Moore, and Ryle – during the heyday of linguistic analysis. Somewhat similar views were held by the logical positivists, who maintained that a proper theory of meaning revealed that all "religious" talk is meaningless.

From the late 1950s, the tide began to turn against the positivists and linguistic analysts, at least narrowly construed. Work in modal logic – especially that of Kripke – prompted a revival of metaphysics. One of the products of this revival was a renewed interest in ontological arguments. Hartshorne (1941) (1962) (1965) and Malcolm (1960) – and later, though in a quite different way, Plantinga (1974a) – defended modal ontological arguments. Moreover, Plantinga (1967) objected strenuously to the suggestion that Kant had provided a definitive refutation of nonmodal ontological arguments. Once the dam was broached, there was a steady stream of defenses of different ontological arguments. Of course, these articles generated a similar stream of responses and attempted refutations. One important aim of the present book is to describe and assess this recent work.

So much for the potted history. I turn now to a slightly more detailed account of some of the most important work referred to in this sketch.

(2) ST. ANSELM'S ARGUMENTS

St. Anselm (c. 1033–1109) produced two famous theological works in 1077 and 1078, during the time that he was prior of the Abbey of Bec in Normandy. The first of these, the *Monologion,* was a lengthy meditation on the Christian understanding of God. St. Anselm was dissatisfied with its complexity and entered into a search for a single premise that would serve as the foundation for a proof of the existence and nature of God. When he finally discovered what he took to be a suitable principle, he recorded his discovery in a work entitled *Proslogion.* This work consists of twenty-six chapters; most subsequent attention has focused on chapters 2–4.

There is little about the *Proslogion* that is completely uncontroversial. Some theologians have gone so far as to deny that in it St. Anselm intended to put forward any proofs of the existence of God. Moreover, among those who agree that St. Anselm did intend to prove the existence of God, there is considerable disagreement about its method. Some hold that chapter 2 contains the main argument, and that chapter 3 is supplementary to it. Others argue that the main argument is in chapter 3. I am not interested in pursuing these tiresome exegetical questions. Since St. Anselm's text can be read as an attempt to prove the existence of God, and since it has been interpreted by many readers in this way ever since it first appeared, I see no reason why I should not read the text in this way. Moreover, I shall pay serious attention to any *prima facie* plausible ontological argument that can be derived from it. In particular, I shall suppose that there are distinct arguments in chapters 2 and 3 and that these arguments deserve separate treatment.

The first difficulty that confronts a reader of the *Proslogion* is to find a clear and precise statement of its arguments. I shall begin with a consideration of the argument in chapter 2.

(a) *Chapter 2 of the* Proslogion

The crucial passage from *Proslogion* 2 may be translated as follows:

Thus even the fool is convinced that something than which nothing greater can be conceived is in the understanding, since when he hears this, he understands it; and whatever is understood is in the understanding. And certainly that than which a greater cannot be conceived cannot be in the understanding alone. For if it is even in the understanding alone, it can be conceived to exist in reality also, which is greater. Thus if that than which a greater cannot be conceived is in the understanding alone, then that than which a greater cannot be conceived is itself that than which a greater can be conceived. But surely this cannot be. Thus without doubt something than which a greater cannot be conceived exists, both in the understanding and in reality.[9]

There are a number of ways in which this argument can be reconstructed, depending upon the interpretation that one is prepared to put upon the crucial expressions 'can be conceived' and 'exists in the understanding'. Some of these reconstructions do severe violence to the original argument – that is, they are best considered as arguments inspired by certain aspects of St. Anselm's writing; nonetheless, I shall give them consideration here.

9 Mann (1972:260–1). For alternative translations, see, among others, Barnes (1972), Campbell (1976), Charlesworth (1965), Deane (1962), Hopkins (1986), Hopkins and Richardson (1974), and Schufrieder (1978).

As a first attempt at exhibiting the structure of the argument, I suggest the following:[10]

1a. When the fool hears the expression 'a being than which no greater can be conceived', the fool understands these words.

1b. If an expression 'X' is understood by a person Y, then X exists in the understanding of Y.

1c. (Hence) When the fool hears the expression 'a being than which no greater can be conceived', a being than which no greater can be conceived exists in the fool's understanding.

1. A being than which no greater can be conceived exists in the understanding. (Premise, supported by 1a, 1b, 1c)

2. A being than which no greater can be conceived does not exist in reality. (Assumption for *reductio*)

3. If a being than which no greater can be conceived does exist in the understanding but does not exist in reality, then a being than which no greater can be conceived that exists both in the understanding and in reality is greater than a being than which no greater can be conceived. (Premise)

4. A being than which no greater can be conceived that does exist both in the understanding and in reality is greater than a being than which no greater can be conceived. (From 1, 2, 3)

5. No being is greater than a being than which no greater can be conceived. (Premise, supported by the meaning of the expression 'being than which no greater can be conceived')

6. (Hence) A being than which no greater can be conceived does exist in reality. (From 2, 4, 5, by *reductio*)

One important feature of this presentation of the argument is 3. This premise just concerns a being than which no greater can be conceived – that is, it does not enunciate a general connection between greatness and existence in reality. There are a number of principles connecting greatness and existence in reality that have been attributed to St. Anselm and/or that have been discussed in connection with this argument. Among these principles are the following:

1a. Any being that exists in reality is greater than every being that exists only in the understanding.

1b. For some (specified) kind K, any being of kind K that exists

---

10 Most of the subsequent discussion will focus only on the second part of the argument – i.e., 1–6.

in reality is greater than every being that exists only in the understanding.

1c. Any being that exists in reality is greater than every being of kind K that exists only in the understanding.

2a. For any kind K, any being of kind K that exists in reality is greater than every being of kind K that exists only in the understanding.

2b. For some (specified) kind K, any being of kind K that exists in reality is greater than every being of kind K that exists only in the understanding.

3a. For any being that exists only in the understanding, if there is a being that is just like it except that it also exists in reality, then that latter being is greater.

3b. For any kind K, for any being of kind K that exists only in the understanding, if there is a being of kind K that is just like it except that it also exists in reality, then that latter being is greater.

3c. For some (specified) kind K, for any being of kind K that exists only in the understanding, if there is a being of kind K that is just like it except that it also exists in reality, then that latter being is greater.

4a. For any being that exists only in the understanding, there is a greater being that is just like it, except that it also exists in reality.

4b. For any kind K, for any being of kind K that exists only in the understanding, there is a greater being of kind K that is just like it, except that it also exists in reality.

4c. For some (specified) kind K, for any being of kind K that exists only in the understanding, there is a greater being of kind K that is just like it, except that it also exists in reality.

5a. Some being that exists in reality is greater than every being that exists only in the understanding.

5b. For some (specified) kind K, some being of kind K that exists in reality is greater than every being that exists only in the understanding.

5c. Some being that exists in reality is greater than every being of kind K that exists only in the understanding.

It seems that some more general principle – perhaps to be chosen from the list that I have given – is required to support, or supplant, premise 3. After all, there seems to be no good reason to suppose that existence in reality is a great-making property solely in the case of a being than which no greater can be conceived. Consider, for instance, any being than which only a few greater can be conceived. Surely, if existence in reality is a great-making property of a being than which no greater can be conceived, then it will also be a great-making property of a being than which only a few greater can be conceived. Consider, for example, a being than which no greater can be conceived except that it has forgotten a name that it bestowed upon itself last Tuesday. Such a being is less than omniscient and less than omnipotent. But there seems to be no good reason to say that existence in reality would not be a great-making property for it. Perhaps it might be objected that the notion of a being than which no greater can be conceived except that it has forgotten a name that it bestowed upon itself last Tuesday is incoherent – for example, on the grounds that a being than which no greater can be conceived must be atemporal. This is a dangerous strategy: for it is far from clear that, in the relevant sense, the notion of a being than which no greater can be conceived is coherent. Moreover, the objection can be repaired so that it will apply to an atemporal being: consider, instead, a being than which no greater can be conceived except that it knows nothing about transfinite arithmetic.

Some of the principles that I have listed clearly must be rejected: For example, 4a and 4b have obviously unacceptable ontological commitments. However, once these are rejected, there is still a large menu from which to choose. It seems clear to me that, no matter which principle is chosen, it will be permissible for a reasonable agnostic or atheist to reject it. However, it also seems to me that it will not be unreasonable for some theists to accept one or more of these remaining principles. Since the main criticisms that I wish to make of ontological arguments will be independent of this point, I do not propose to pursue the issue further.[11]

Another important feature of the preceding presentation of St. Anselm's argument is that it preserves his talk of 'existence in the understanding' and 'that which can be conceived'. It is not clear how these expressions are best understood, and many modern commentators have chosen to translate them into a more favored idiom – and, in particular, the idiom of 'logical possibility'. I suggest that there are three promising candidates for arguments that can be constructed as interpretations of St. Anselm's argument. First, there are those arguments that I call 'modal ontological arguments involving actuality': These arguments result from the interpretation of 'existence in the understanding' and 'that which can be conceived' as 'that which

---

11   But cf. the discussion, in Chapter 10, of the question whether existence is a predicate, for some relevant considerations.

is logically possible'. Second, there are those arguments that I call 'Meinongian ontological arguments', in which 'existence in the understanding' and 'that which can be conceived' are taken to refer to a special category of existence involving a special kind of entity. And, third, there are those arguments that I call 'conceptual ontological arguments' in which 'exists in the understanding' is interpreted to mean 'is conceived of', and the whole argument is construed in terms of propositional attitude ascriptions. This last kind of argument could be construed as a version of either of the other two, depending upon the semantics that one is inclined to give for modality and propositional attitude ascriptions. However, there are accounts of the semantics of propositional attitude ascriptions on which this third approach is quite distinct. Moreover, I shall suggest that this kind of argument can be given a satisfactory analysis without worrying about any of the details of the underlying semantic theory.

(b) *Chapter 3 of the* Proslogion

The argument of *Proslogion 3* has been much discussed in relatively recent times. Hartshorne (1962) and Malcolm (1960), among others, have claimed to find a modal ontological argument in *Proslogion 3* that is distinct from, and better than, the nonmodal ontological argument of *Proslogion 2*. As a matter of interpretation, I think that this claim is implausible: St. Anselm did not take himself to be providing an independent argument for the existence of God in *Proslogion 3*; rather, he took himself to be discovering one of the attributes of the being whose existence he took himself to have demonstrated in *Proslogion 2*. Nonetheless, it is possible to read *Proslogion 3* as a presentation of an independent argument for the existence of a being whose nonexistence is inconceivable – and the resulting argument is deserving of attention.

The crucial part of *Proslogion 3* is the following:

[A being than which no greater can be conceived] assuredly exists so truly that it cannot be conceived not to exist. For it is possible to conceive of a being which cannot be conceived not to exist; and this is greater than one which can be conceived not to exist. Hence, if that than which nothing greater can be conceived, can be conceived not to exist, it is not that, than which nothing greater can be conceived. But this is an irreconcilable contradiction. There is, then, so truly a being than which nothing greater can be conceived to exist, that it cannot even be conceived not to exist.[12]

---

12   Deane (1962:8–9).

We may represent the independent argument, for the existence of a being than which no greater can be conceived and that cannot even be conceived not to exist, that is claimed to be contained in this passage, as follows:

1. It is conceivable that there is a being than which no greater can be conceived to exist, and that cannot be conceived not to exist. (Premise)
2. A being than which no greater can be conceived to exist, and that cannot be conceived not to exist, does not exist. (Assumption for *reductio*)
3. It is conceivable that a being that cannot be conceived not to exist does not exist. (From 2)
4. It is inconceivable that a being that cannot be conceived not to exist does not exist. (Premise)
5. (Hence) A being than which no greater can be conceived to exist, and that cannot be conceived not to exist, exists both in the understanding and in reality. (From 2, 3, 4, by *reductio*)

In this formulation of the argument, I have avoided St. Anselm's talk of "existence in the understanding"; however, the argument could have been formulated in those terms.

Most interest in this argument focuses on an interpretation in which 'conceivability' is taken to mean 'broadly logical possibility'.[13] Under this interpretation, the argument reduces to a particularly simple form, namely:

1. It is logically possible that there is a greatest possible and necessarily existent being.
2. (Hence) There is a greatest possible and necessarily existent being.

As we shall see in our discussion of modal ontological arguments involving necessity, there are versions of this argument that are unde-

---

13   In the subsequent discussion, I shall drop the qualification 'broadly'; however, at no point do I mean to refer to narrowly logical possibility, which admits, for example, that it is possible that $2 = 3$. Broadly logical necessity requires (i) metaphysical necessity and (ii) *a priori* knowability; hence, it is to be distinguished from mere metaphysical necessity, which may also involve *a posteriori* considerations about origins, constitution, and so forth. Often, defenders of ontological arguments have wished to interpret the necessity that figures in their arguments as mere metaphysical necessity. Since it does no harm to the case that I wish to make, I shall sometimes conflate broadly logical necessity with mere metaphysical necessity in the following pages.

niably valid; moreover, it is precisely this form of the argument that is defended by Hartshorne (1941) (1962) (1965) and Plantinga (1974a). Malcolm (1960) also defends an argument of this form; but he does not unequivocally defend the view that 'necessity' should be interpreted as 'broadly logical necessity'.

(c) *Further chapters of the* Proslogion

There are further chapters of the *Proslogion* that contain arguments that might be construed as independent ontological arguments. In particular, *Proslogion 15* contains an interesting passage, namely:

> Therefore, Lord, not only are you that than which a greater cannot be thought, but you are also something greater than can be thought. For, since it is possible to think that there is such a one, then, if you are not this same being something greater than you can be thought – which cannot be.[14]

We might represent the independent argument that is "implicit" in this passage as follows:

1. It is conceivable that there is a being that is greater than any being that can be conceived. (Premise)
2. A being that is greater than any being that can be conceived does not exist. (Assumption for *reductio*)
3. A being that is greater than any being that can be conceived and that exists is greater than a being that is greater than any being that can be conceived but that does not exist. (Premise)
4. It is conceivable that there is a being that is greater than any being that can be conceived. (From 1, 2, 3)
5. It is inconceivable that there is a being that is greater than a being that is greater than any being that can be conceived. (Premise)
6. A being that is greater than any being that can be conceived exists. (From 2, 4, 5, by *reductio*)

It is clear that this argument confronts more difficulties than the arguments in *Proslogion 2* and *Proslogion 3*. In particular, one might wonder how the first premise could possibly be true: How can it be intelligible to claim that one can conceive of a being of which it is impossible to conceive, that is, greater than any being of which one can conceive? Paradox seems to threaten: For isn't this just like the

---

14   Charlesworth (1965:137).

claim, to which Russell first drew attention, that there is a village in which there is a barber who shaves all and only those members of the village who do not shave themselves? As soon as one asks the question 'Who shaves the barber?' one realizes that there can be no such village. But don't similar considerations show that there can be nothing that would count as conceiving of a being of which it is impossible to conceive?

A natural response at this point would be to draw a distinction between different kinds of conceivings, namely, positive conceivings and negative conceivings. Using this distinction, we might recast the argument as follows:

1. It is negatively conceivable that there is a being that is greater than any being that can be positively conceived. (Premise)
2. A being that is greater than any being that can be positively conceived does not exist. (Assumption for *reductio*)
3. A being that is greater than any being that can be positively conceived and that exists is greater than a being that is greater than any being that can be positively conceived but that does not exist. (Premise)
4. It is negatively conceivable that there is a being that is greater than a being that is greater than any being that can be positively conceived. (From 1, 2, 3)
5. It is not negatively conceivable that there is a being that is greater than a being that is greater than any being that can be positively conceived. (Premise)
6. A being that is greater than any being that can be positively conceived exists. (From 2, 4, 5 by *reductio*)

The air of paradox now seems to have been dispelled, but only if we can provide some account of the distinction between positive conceiving and negative conceiving. One likely suggestion – which is consistent with doctrines to which St. Anselm himself might have subscribed – is the following: in order to have a *negative* conception of something, all that one requires is possession of a form of words that one takes to refer, and which, as a matter of fact, does refer to that thing, *even if that form of words attributes no positive characteristics to the thing*. Thus, the mere possession of the form of words 'being than which no greater can be conceived' suffices for a negative conception of a being than which no greater can be conceived, provided that there is a being than which no greater can be conceived to which these words can refer, even though one cannot form any positive conception of the attributes of such a being. On the other hand, in order to have a *positive* conception of some thing one is required to have a positive conception of the attributes of that thing – that is, one is required to have an understanding of the attributes of that thing.

Clearly, more needs to be said in defense of the required distinction. In particular, since the proffered explanation relies on the notion of 'understanding of the attributes of a thing', the explanation simply runs in a circle. I doubt that the distinction can be properly explained; but, for the sake of argument, let us grant that the distinction is primitive, and that there are no more difficulties that the attempt to draw the distinction must surmount. Will the argument then go through?

No. There is nothing in this new argument that rules out the possibility that there might be a hierarchy of beings, each greater than the next, all of which are incapable of being positively conceived, at least by beings like us – that is, there is nothing that guarantees that premise 5 is true. But it is hard to see how this possibility can be ruled out, once one grants that one is talking about beings whose attributes are ones that one cannot understand. Moreover, it is unclear why we should suppose that the least being of which we are incapable of forming a positive conception – hence, *the* being of which we are incapable of forming a positive conception, if there is only one such being – is a being of religious significance. For it is not clear that, in the relevant sense, we can form a positive conception of, for example, particularly large numbers or particular objects forever outside our light cone.

Even if we waive the worries already raised, there are further reasons to think that the argument is unsuccessful. Whether we interpret the argument in terms of conceivability, or existence in the understanding, or logical possibility, it turns out to be either invalid or else possessed of premises that an atheist or agnostic can reasonably reject. However, the proof of this contention is in the subsequent chapters of this book.[15]

---

15   Actually, it is hard to reconstrue this argument in terms of logical possibility. As Matthews (1961) notes, it seems that the formula 'being greater than any which can be conceived' is not well interpreted as 'being greater than any which is logically possible' – for that seems to entail that the being in question is not logically possible. This provides one part of the support for the claim that 'is conceivable' is not well interpreted in St. Anselm's work by 'is logically possible'.

(d) *Gaunilo's objection and St. Anselm's reply*

The first response to St. Anselm's arguments was provided by one of his contemporaries, the Marmoutier monk Gaunilo. In a pamphlet "In Behalf of the Fool," Gaunilo tried to show that there must be something wrong with St. Anselm's argument because it could be readily adapted to prove the existence of all kinds of things in which it seems it would be absurd to believe:

Consider this example: Certain people say that somewhere in the ocean there is a "Lost Island" . . . which is more abundantly filled with inestimable riches and delights than the Isles of the Blessed. . . . Suppose that one was to go on to say: You cannot doubt that this island, the most perfect of all lands, actually exists somewhere in reality, because it undoubtedly stands in relation to your understanding. Since it is most excellent, not simply to stand in relation to the understanding, but to be in reality as well, therefore this island must necessarily be in reality. . . . If, I repeat, someone should wish by this argument to demonstrate to me that this island truly exists and is no longer to be doubted, I would think he were joking.[16]

In a work customarily referred to as the *Responsio editoris,* St. Anselm responded to Gaunilo's attack, and in particular, he provided the following response to the argument involving the lost island:

[I] promise confidently that if any man shall devise anything existing either in reality or in concept alone (except that than which no greater can be conceived) to which he can adapt the sequence of my reasoning, I will discover that thing, and will give him his lost island, not to be lost again.[17]

This is very disappointing. Gaunilo purports to be able to adapt St. Anselm's argument to "prove" the existence of an island than which no greater island can be conceived – that is, his claim is that he *has* adapted St. Anselm's sequence of reasoning to something other than a being than which no greater can be conceived. It is not enough for St. Anselm simply to assert that Gaunilo's argument does not parallel his own argument for the existence of a being than which no greater can be conceived.

We might represent the argument that Gaunilo is inviting us to consider as follows:

1. An island than which no greater island can be conceived exists in the understanding. (Premise, supported by 1a, 1b, 1c)

16 Hick and McGill (1967:22–3).
17 Deane (1962:158).

2. An island than which no greater island can be conceived does not exist in reality. (Assumption for *reductio*)
3. If an island than which no greater island can be conceived does exist in the understanding but does not exist in reality, then an island than which no greater island can be conceived that exists both in the understanding and in reality is greater than an island than which no greater island can be conceived. (Premise)
4. An island than which no greater island can be conceived that does exist both in the understanding and in reality is greater than an island than which no greater island can be conceived. (From 1, 2, 3)
5. No island is greater than an island than which no greater island can be conceived. (Premise, supported by the meaning of the expression 'island than which no greater island can be conceived')
6. (Hence) An island than which no greater island can be conceived does exist in reality. (From 2, 4, 5, by *reductio*)

This argument is certainly parallel in form to St. Anselm's argument – that is, it is valid iff St. Anselm's argument is valid. Consequently, if St. Anselm has an objection to this argument, it can only be to one of the premises. But which?

Perhaps St. Anselm might have followed the lead of St. Bonaventure:

Against the objection of an island that which nothing better or greater can be conceived, we must say that . . . 'island' refers to a defective being, while the predicate designates the most perfect of beings. Therefore, since there is a direct opposition here, this island is conceived irrationally, and in thinking it the mind is divided against itself. It is no wonder, therefore, that we cannot infer that this island exists in reality. It is otherwise, however, in the case of 'being' or 'God', since this is not repugnant to the predicate.[18]

But this won't do. In general, 'being' refers to defective things: It is only 'being than which no greater can be conceived' that refers to something that is not defective. So, by parity, even if 'island' refers to defective things, why shouldn't it be the case that 'island than which no greater island can be conceived' refers to something that is not

---

18 *Quaestio disputata de mysterio Trinitatis* Q.1, a.1, sol. opp. 6, translated by A. Daniels, cited in Hick and McGill (1967:24n12).

defective?[19] While it may be true that islands are essentially defective, it is hard to see how there could be a non-question-begging argument for this contention. And more important, Gaunilo's objection could be recast using other cases that are plainly not open to St. Bonaventure's response – compare Chapter 11, Section three, this volume.

Perhaps St. Bonaventure's objection is better rephrased as a doubt about the coherence of the notion of an island than which no greater island can be conceived – that is, as a doubt about the truth of premise 1. There are a number of ways in which this objection can be developed; I shall discuss them in Chapter 11. However, as I noted earlier, there should be an at least *pro tem* suspicion that this is a dangerous line to take. For there are very similar doubts about the coherence of the notion of a being than which no greater can be conceived.

Chapter 3 of the *Responsio* also contains a reworking of the claims that were made in *Proslogion 2* and *Proslogion 3*:

If anyone say that he conceives this being [a being than which no greater can be conceived] not to exist, I say that at the time when he conceives of this either he conceives of a being than which no greater can be conceived, or he does not conceive at all. If he does not conceive, he does not conceive of the non-existence of that of which he does not conceive. But if he does conceive, he certainly conceives of a being which cannot even be conceived not to exist. ... He, then, who conceives of this being conceives of a being which cannot be even conceived not to exist; but he who conceives of this being does not conceive that it does not exist; else he conceives what is unconceivable. The non-existence, then, of that than which no greater can be conceived is inconceivable.[20]

We might formulate this argument as follows:

1. The fool says that he believes that there is no being than which no greater can be conceived. (Premise)
2. When the fool says that he believes this, either (i) he conceives of a being than which no greater can be conceived, or else (ii) he does not conceive of a being than which no greater can be conceived. (Excluded middle)

19 Perhaps St. Bonaventure's objection is stronger against its intended target, namely: the idea of an island than which no greater being can be conceived. But, whatever Gaunilo's intentions may have been, this intended target is not the strongest form of Gaunilo's argument.
20 Deane (1962:159).

3. If (ii) – that is, if he does not conceive of a being than which no greater can be conceived – then he does not believe that there is no being than which no greater can be conceived, since he doesn't even conceive of a being than which no greater can be conceived. (Premise)

4. If (i) – that is, if he does conceive of a being than which no greater can be conceived – then he conceives of a being that cannot even be conceived not to exist, and hence does not believe that there is no being than which no greater can be conceived. (Premise)

5. (Hence) The fool is mistaken: The nonexistence of that than which no greater can be conceived is unbelievable because inconceivable. (From 2, 3, 4)

There are some suppressed premises that are invoked in the statement of premises 3 and 4. In 3, it is taken for granted that one cannot have a belief about an entity X unless one possesses the concept of X. Moreover, it is also taken for granted that possession of the concept of X requires that one has a concept of X in which one thinks of X as X. Perhaps – though this is less clear – it is also taken for granted that one can only have a thought about X if X is an existent object. Similarly, in premise 4, it is taken for granted that one cannot believe something that is inconceivable. Moreover, it is also taken for granted that possession of 'the concept of X' requires that one has a concept of X in which one thinks of X as X; and perhaps – though this is again less clear – it is also taken for granted that one can only have a thought about X if X is an existent object. The analysis of this argument is quite complex; we shall discuss the relevant issues in the chapter on conceptual ontological arguments.

(3) DESCARTES' ARGUMENTS

Rene Descartes (1596–1650) is often considered to be the "father" of modern philosophy. As with most intellectuals of his time, Descartes was a polymath: He made important contributions to geometry, optics, and so on. His most famous philosophical work is his *Meditations on the First Philosophy*, which provides an elegant synopsis of his philosophical thought. However, discussion of ontological arguments is scattered throughout his other writings, including the *Discourse on the Method* and *The Principles of Philosophy*.

There are two distinct arguments for the existence of God in the *Meditations*. The first of these arguments – which is concerned with the possible origins of the idea of God – I shall treat as a kind of cosmological argument.[21] The other argument – from *Meditation V* – is a distant cousin of St. Anselm's argument which begins from the idea of a most perfect being.

The ontological argument from *Meditation V* is contained in the following passage:

I find in myself an infinity of ideas of certain things which cannot be considered as pure nothing, although perhaps they have no existence outside my thought, and which are not invented by me, although it may be in my power to think or not to think them, but possess their own true and immutable natures. As, for example, when I imagine a triangle, although there may not perhaps be, and never has been, in any place in the world outside my thought such a figure, yet it remains true that there is a certain determined nature or form or essence of this figure, immutable and eternal, which I have not invented, and which does not depend in any way on my mind. . . .

[I]f from the fact alone that I can draw from my thought the idea of a thing, it follows that all that I recognize clearly and distinctly as belonging to that thing does indeed belong to it, cannot I derive from this an argument and a proof demonstrating the existence of God? It is certain that I no less find the idea of God in me, that is to say, the idea of a supremely perfect being, than that of any figure or number whatsoever. And I know no less clearly and distinctly that an actual and eternal existence belongs to his nature, than that all I can demonstrate of any figure or number truly belongs to the nature of that figure or number. . . .

[T]here is no less contradiction in conceiving a God, that is to say, a supremely perfect being, who lacks existence, that is to say, who lacks some particular perfection, than in conceiving a mountain without a valley.[22]

This argument is difficult to encapsulate; the following is merely a first attempt:

1. I possess the idea of God. (Premise)
2. The idea of God includes the idea of existence – that is, the idea that God exists. (Premise)

---

21 It is not clear whether one ought to say that it is an argument that proceeds from premises all of which are alleged to be knowable *a priori*. Since the argument takes as a datum the *fact* of the possession of an idea of God, I shall suppose that one of the crucial premises of the argument draws on the deliverance of *inner* experience. In this respect, it is quite different from other ontological arguments, including the one that Descartes subsequently defends. In Descartes' ontological argument, the only relevant datum is the *content* of the idea of God.

22 Descartes (1968/1637:143ff.).

3. The idea of God is the idea of a true and immutable nature. (Premise)
4. Whatever belongs to a true and immutable nature may be truly affirmed of it. (Premise)
5. Existence belongs to the true and immutable nature of God. (From 2, 3, 4)
6. (Hence) I may truly affirm of God that God exists. (From 1, 5)
7. (Hence) God exists. (From 6)

It is not clear that Descartes provides an unequivocal understanding of premise 1. On the one hand, he sometimes writes as though the idea of God is the idea of a thing; on the other hand, he also sometimes writes as though the idea of God is the idea of a nature or form or essence. The difference between these two interpretations of 1 is considerable, since Descartes himself acknowledges the distinction between things and their natures or forms or essences; things are *substances* – though perhaps of a kind that have no mind-independent existence – which *possess* natures or forms or essences.

A natural thought is that we should try to recast Descartes' argument using one or another of the unequivocal readings of the first premise. When we do this, we obtain something like the following two versions of the argument:

1. I possess the idea of supreme perfection. (Premise)
2. The idea of supreme perfection includes the idea of existence – that is, the idea that supreme perfection is existent. (Premise)
3. The idea of supreme perfection is the idea of a true and immutable nature. (Premise)
4. Whatever belongs to a true and immutable nature may be truly affirmed of it. (Premise)
5. Existence belongs to the true and immutable nature of supreme perfection. (From 2, 3, 4)
6. (Hence) I may truly affirm of supreme perfection that existence belongs to it. (From 1, 5)
7. (Hence) Supreme perfection is existent – that is, God exists. (From 6)

1. I possess the idea of a supremely perfect being. (Premise)
2. The idea of a supremely perfect being includes the idea of existence – that is, the idea that a supremely perfect being exists. (Premise)

3. The idea of a supremely perfect being is the idea of a being with a true and immutable nature. (Premise)
4. Whatever belongs to the true and immutable nature of a being may be truly affirmed of it. (Premise)
5. Existence belongs to the true and immutable nature of a supremely perfect being. (From 2, 3, 4)
6. (Hence) I may truly affirm of a supremely perfect being that it exists. (From 1, 5)
7. (Hence) A supremely perfect being exists. (From 6)

As we shall see in our discussion of definitional arguments and conceptual arguments, the main difficulty that confronts the first version of the argument is that there is no justification for the move from premise 6 to 7. Given the distinction between beings and natures, the fact that the nature of supreme perfection includes existence does nothing at all toward showing that there is a being that possesses the nature of supreme perfection.

The main focus of our subsequent discussion of the second version of the argument will be premise 1. In what sense is it true that I possess the idea of a supremely perfect being? For the purpose of the argument, it *seems* that all that Descartes ought to suppose is that he can form an idea as of a supremely perfect being – that is, a mental item that can be characterized as such in terms of its intrinsic, nonreferential properties. However, he *seems* to make the stronger supposition that there is *something* to which the mental item refers – though he does not make the surely question-begging further assumption that the thing to which the mental item refers is an actually existent thing.[23] Consequently, there are two distinct interpretations of this argument: one that invokes an ontology of 'subsistent beings' – that is, beings that do not, or at least may not, actually exist, and yet that cannot absolutely be said not to exist – and one that does not.

On the version of the argument that invokes an ontology of subsistent beings, we end up with an example of what I call a Meinongian ontological argument; and on the version of the argument that does not invoke an ontology of subsistent beings, we end up with an

23 For example, "I find in myself an infinity of ideas of certain things which cannot be considered as pure nothing, although perhaps they have no existence outside my thought, and which are not invented by me, although it may be in my power to think or not to think them, but possess their own true and immutable natures" (Descartes 1968/1637:143).

example of what I call a conceptual ontological argument. I am not sure which of these arguments is the one that Descartes intended; and, for present purposes, I don't care.[24]

(4) LEIBNIZ'S CONTRIBUTION TO THE ARGUMENTS

Gottfried Leibniz (1646–1716) was a brilliant mathematician and philosopher. Ontological arguments are discussed in many of his works, including *Monadology* (1714), *Theodicy* (1710), and *New Essays Concerning Human Understanding* (c. 1709).

Leibniz thought that the Cartesian ontological argument was promising but incomplete. In particular, he thought that the argument would be shown to be valid if it were shown that the idea of a most perfect being is coherent, that is, if it were shown that it is possible that there is a most perfect being. His main contribution to the history of ontological arguments is an attempted demonstration of the coherence of the idea of a most perfect being.

The following is a relevant passage from Leibniz's writings:

I call every simple quality which is positive and absolute, or expresses whatever it expresses without any limits, a perfection. But a quality of this sort, because it is simple, is therefore irresolvable or indefinable, for otherwise, either it will not be a simple quality but an aggregate of many, or, if it is one, it will be circumscribed by limits and so be known through negations of further progress contrary to the hypothesis, for a purely positive quality was assumed.

From these considerations it is not difficult to show that all perfections are compatible with each other or can exist in the same subject. For let the proposition be of this kind:

A and B are incompatible

(for understanding by *A* and *B* two simple forms of this kind or perfections, and it is the same if more are assumed like them), it is evident that it cannot be demonstrated without the resolution of the terms *A* and *B*, of each or both; for otherwise their nature would not enter into the ratiocination and the

---

24 One important advocate of the Meinongian interpretation of the Cartesian argument is Kenny (1968b). The case that he makes is not decisive. When Descartes says that he possesses "ideas of certain things which cannot be considered as pure nothing," it seems possible to interpret this as an insistence on the evident facts that the ideas in question are contentful, and yet not as an insistence on the further, controversial fact that for an idea to be contentful, there must be an existent of some kind that is its content.

incompatibility could be demonstrated as well from any others as from themselves. But now (by hypothesis) they are irresolvable. Therefore this proposition cannot be demonstrated from these forms.[25]

We can encapsulate the reasoning of this passage as follows:

1. By definition, a perfection is a simple quality that is positive and absolute. (Definition)
2. A simple quality that is positive and absolute is irresolvable or indefinable. (Premise – capable of further defense)
3. *A* and *B* are perfections whose incompatibility can be demonstrated. (Hypothesis for *reductio*)
4. In order to demonstrate the incompatibility of *A* and *B*, *A* and *B* must be resolved. (Premise)
5. Neither *A* nor *B* can be resolved. (From 2)
6. (Hence) It cannot be demonstrated that *A* and *B* are incompatible. (From 3, 4, 5 by *reductio*)

There are two major difficulties that face this argument. First, even if it succeeded in showing that all simple, positive, absolute qualities are compatible, it seems that there would still be a hole in the Cartesian argument – for nothing in this argument shows that there is even one simple, positive, absolute quality. If there are no simple, positive, absolute qualities, then there cannot be a being that possesses all and only simple, positive, absolute qualities. Moreover, given the nature of simple, positive, absolute qualities, there seems to be an epistemological problem about the possibility of reasonable belief in their existence: What grounds could one have for thinking that there are simple, positive, absolute qualities? There may only be the appearance of a problem here, since it seems reasonable to allow that reasonable belief need not require grounds. However, this problem does appear to threaten the dialectical value of the demonstration; it certainly seems that one could reasonably believe that there are no simple, positive, absolute qualities.

Second, it is clear that the argument fails to reach the conclusion that is required. It is one thing to show that it cannot be demonstrated that *A* and *B* are incompatible; it is quite another thing to show that *A* and *B* are in fact compatible. Again, it could be argued that a demonstration that it cannot be shown that *A* and *B* are incompatible suffices

---

25   Leibniz (1896/1709:714–15).

156, 8/8

to show that it could be reasonable to hold that *A* and *B* are compatible. But, once more – even if this dubious contention were granted – it is clear that the dialectical force of the demonstration is completely undermined.[26]

It should also be noted that if one grants that there are simple, positive, absolute qualities, the question can be raised whether existence *is* a simple, positive, absolute quality. Why should we suppose that existence is relevantly different from color attributes: say, blueness and redness? As the post-Tractarian Wittgenstein discovered, it is plausible to think that color terms cannot be simple, positive, absolute quantities – for it is plausible to think, for instance, that no surface can be simultaneously blue all over and red all over. But why should we think that existence is a better candidate for the status of a simple, positive, absolute quality, given that there are other incompatible candidates – for example, being imaginary, being a creature of fiction, being an impossible item, being a denizen of a merely possible world?

(5) HUME'S OBJECTIONS

David Hume (1711–1776) is one of the great figures in philosophy. His treatment of such topics as causation, necessity, morality, and action – especially in his *Treatise of Human Nature* – is still essential reading for philosophers. However, despite its influence, Hume's discussion of ontological arguments in Part IX of the *Dialogues Concerning Natural Religion* is not one of the high points of his philosophy.

Hume's *Dialogues* were written some time in the decade before 1761, but they were not published until three years after his death, in 1776. There are three main characters who participate in the dialogues: Philo, Cleanthes, and Demea; and there is also a narrator – Pamphilus – who introduces the dialogues and also provides an evaluation of the upshot of the discussion. Very roughly (i) Cleanthes is a representative of the main currents of eighteenth-century natural theology, that is, a defender of teleological arguments for the existence of God; (ii) Demea is a representative of both orthodox rationalism, that is a defender of ontological and cosmological arguments for the existence

---

26 Perhaps Leibniz supposed that impossibility is finitely demonstrable inconsistency. In that case, the objection is not that Leibniz's argument fails to reach the desired conclusion, but rather that it relies upon a highly contentious conception of modality, which – at least as things stand – can clearly be reasonably rejected.

of God, and of traditional fideism, that is of that kind of theism that is content to place its reliance on faith even at the expense of reason; and (iii) Philo is a representative of philosophical and religious skepticism, and hence is opposed equally to the positions espoused by Cleanthes and Demea. By and large, it seems reasonable to suppose that Philo comes closest to representing Hume's own opinions – even though many characteristically Humean arguments are propounded by Cleanthes. The interpretation of the *Dialogues* is still controversial; but we needn't enter into those controversies here:

In Part IX of the *Dialogues,* the following argument is put into the mouth of Cleanthes:

> I shall begin with observing that there is an evident absurdity in pretending to demonstrate a matter of fact, or to prove it by any arguments *a priori.* Nothing is demonstrable unless the contrary implies a contradiction. Nothing that is distinctly conceivable implies a contradiction. Whatever we conceive as existent, we can also conceive as non-existent. There is no being, therefore, whose non-existence implies a contradiction. Consequently there is no being whose existence is demonstrable. I propose this argument as entirely decisive, and am willing to rest the whole controversy upon it.[27]

Despite the fact that this argument is given by Cleanthes, it seems reasonable to think that it expresses Hume's own considered views about *a priori* arguments – and certain *a posteriori* arguments involving very general premises, that is, cosmological arguments – for the existence of God. At any rate – at least for ease of exposition – I shall henceforth assume that this argument does express Hume's considered opinion.

Hume's argument may be schematized as follows:

1. *A* can be demonstrated iff not-*A* implies a contradiction. (Premise)
2. *A* is distinctly conceivable iff *A* does not imply a contradiction. (Premise)
3. For any *x*, if *x* can be distinctly conceived as existent, then *x* can be distinctly conceived as nonexistent. (Premise)
4. (Hence) For any *x*, the nonexistence of *x* does not imply a contradiction. (From 2, 3)
5. (Hence) For any *x*, the existence of *x* is not demonstrable. (From 1, 4)

---

27 Hume (1948/1779:58).

As it stands, the argument is formally invalid: Conclusion 4 does not follow from premises 2 and 3. In order to remedy this defect in the proof, we might replace 3 with:

3'. For any x, x can be distinctly conceived as nonexistent.

A natural objection is that there are things that cannot be distinctly conceived not to exist – for example, Descartes' *cogito* can be construed as an argument in favor of the claim that *I* cannot distinctly conceive that *I* do not exist; and it seems highly doubtful that it is distinctly conceivable that an existent lion does not exist. However, it might be replied that this response relies upon a mistaken substitutional interpretation of the quantifier in 3': While it is true that I cannot think, of myself, in the usual first-personal way – that I do not exist – I can think of myself, under other modes of presentation, that I do not exist; and likewise, while I cannot think, of an existent lion, under the mode of presentation 'existent lion', that it does not exist, I can certainly think this under other modes of presentation. On an objectual interpretation of the quantifier, premise 3' will be true provided that, for any x, there is at least one mode of presentation under which it can be distinctly conceived to be nonexistent. Unfortunately, there is an obvious problem with this reply, namely, that all that will follow from 1, 2, and 3' is that, for any x, there is some mode of presentation under which the existence of x is not demonstrable. But it is compatible with this that for at least some x, there are modes of presentation under which the existence of x is demonstrable. For example, while it might be true that God, when distinctly conceived as 'St. Anselm's favorite being', can be distinctly conceived to be nonexistent, it does not follow from this that God's existence cannot be demonstrated when he is distinctly conceived as 'a being than which no greater can be conceived.'

Clearly, more could be said – especially about Hume's use of the terms 'demonstrable', 'contradiction', and 'distinct conception', and the consequent status of premises 1 and 2. In particular, one might wonder whether the role of axioms and theorems in demonstrations undermines premise 1; and one might wonder whether the nonsubstitutional reading required for the interpretation of 3' undermines 2. However, we have already done enough to expose the frailty of Hume's argument.

Despite the weakness of the argument, Hume's opinion has been immensely influential. Many people have thought that his "objection" deals a fatal blow to ontological arguments. One person of whom this seems to be true is Kant. As we shall now see, Kant took up Hume's objection and elaborated upon it in a number of different ways – though without making any substantial addition to it.[28]

(6) KANT'S OBJECTIONS

Immanuel Kant (1724–1804) is another of the greatest figures in philosophy. He lived a quiet academic life in Konigsberg, where he lectured in philosophy at the local university. It is said that he led a highly regulated existence – to the extent that neighbors set their clocks by the time that he left for his evening walk. His great works – including *The Critique of Pure Reason, The Critique of Practical Reason, The Critique of Judgement* and *Groundwork for the Metaphysics of Morals* – were all written in the latter part of his life, after he passed fifty years of age.

In *The Critique of Pure Reason*, Kant provides a discussion of "the ontological argument." The argument in question is, more or less, the argument defended by Descartes.[29] Kant's discussion is not easy to understand, but I think that there are three distinct objections to "the ontological argument" that he provides. There are (i) the objection that no existence claims are analytic, (ii) the objection that existence is not a predicate, and (iii) the objection that negative existentials are never self-contradictory.

(a) *No existence claims are analytic*

The weakest objection that Kant makes – the one that is most clearly taken over from Hume – is based on his distinction between analytic and synthetic judgments. According to Kant, simple subject/predicate judgments of the form '*A* is *B*' – where '*A*' is the subject of the judgment, and '*B*' is the predicate – divide into two nonoverlapping categories: *analytic* judgments, in which 'The predicate *B* belongs to the subject *A* as something which is (covertly) contained in this concept *A*' (A7B11); and *synthetic* judgments, in which '*B* lies outside the

---

28 Kant also introduced an objection of his own that does provide a non-question-begging reason to reject certain ontological arguments – that is, he didn't *merely* take over the Humean opinion.

29 I am not sure that Kant actually read any of Descartes' own formulations of the proof; it is at least possible that Kant only heard about them secondhand, from his contemporaries in Germany. In particular, Kant was certainly familiar with the arguments through the writings of Christian Wolff.

concept A, although it does stand in connection with it' (A7B11).[30] As an example of an analytic judgment, Kant offers 'All bodies are extended'; and as an example of a synthetic proposition, he offers 'All bodies are heavy'. In the light of modern physics, these examples seem not to be well chosen: For (i) if point objects – electrons, perhaps – are not extended, then it is not true that all bodies are extended; and (ii) if enough of general relativity is *a priori* – and, in particular, if it is *a priori* that only those particles that travel at limiting velocity have zero rest mass *and* that these particles have finite relativistic mass – then it is *a priori*, and hence (?) analytic, that all bodies are heavy. This points to an important worry about the Kantian distinction between analytic and synthetic judgments, namely, that it is quite unclear what it means to say, 'A predicate is contained in a concept'. It is also unclear how the Kantian account is to be extended to more complex kinds of judgments. But we need not concern ourselves with these difficulties here.

Kant applies his distinction between analytic and synthetic judgments to the claim that God exists. Given that the distinction is exclusive and exhaustive, this claim must be either analytic or synthetic. But, on the one hand, it cannot be analytic:

If we admit, as every reasonable person must, that all existential propositions are synthetic, how can we profess to maintain that the predicate of existence cannot be rejected without contradiction? This is a feature which is found only in analytic propositions, and is precisely what constitutes their analytic character. (A598B626)

And on the other hand, since it is thus synthetic,

There is already a contradiction in introducing the concept of existence – no matter under what title it may be disguised – into the concept of a thing which we profess to be thinking solely in reference to its possibility. (A597B625)

In other words, no existential proposition can be analytic; and no synthetic proposition can be given a purely logical proof. So no ontological proof of the existence of God is possible.

The problem with this argument – even waiving the difficulties involved in the formulation of the distinction between analytic and synthetic judgments – is that it ignores the apparent counterargument that is provided by "the ontological argument" itself. It is true, as Kant observes, that a proponent of "the ontological argument" will

---

30   Kant (1933/1787). All subsequent excerpts are from this source.

insist that there are descriptions – concepts – of God that guarantee that God exists; but such a person also claims that "the ontological argument" itself shows that at least in this case, there is an existential proposition – that is, a proposition that proclaims the existence of an object – that is analytically true. Clearly, the mere assertion that there are, and can be, no nonmathematical existential propositions contributes nothing at all to the project of undermining the position of a defender of "the ontological argument." Perhaps it might be replied that an agnostic or atheist could rest content with the unsupported claim that there can be no nonmathematical existential propositions that are analytically true. After all, it surely is the case that one can reasonably believe that there are no nonmathematical existential propositions that are analytically true. However, this seems unsatisfactory, for the recalcitrant data provided by "the ontological argument" is then simply being ignored. At the very least, an opponent of "the ontological argument" needs to explain why it lends no support to the claim that there is at least one existential proposition that is analytically true.

Furthermore, as Mackie (1982) and Plantinga (1967) both note, there do seem to be existential propositions in, for example, arithmetic, that are analytically true. Consider, for instance, the claim that there is a prime number between seventeen and twenty. Kant himself thought that the propositions of arithmetic are synthetic; but, given that one accepts a distinction between analytic and synthetic judgments, it seems more reasonable to suppose – with Ayer (1948/1930) – that the claims of arithmetic are actually analytic. However, one could still try to save Kant's position by arguing that there aren't any real existence propositions in arithmetic – for it is widely agreed that the ontological status of numbers is far from clear. Do we really want to say that numbers *exist?* If they do exist, what is the mechanism by which we come to have knowledge of their properties? Since it would involve a large digression to pursue this topic further, I shall just note that there is a potential problem here for Kant.

In any case, in view of the previous objections, I conclude that, in its intended form – that is, as an objection that any rational being ought to accept – the first Kantian objection fails. Even if the analytic–synthetic distinction can be made out, and even if other purported cases of analytic existential propositions can be dismissed, it is dubious that there is a good reason for some theists to give up the belief that one existential proposition – namely, that which asserts the existence of God – is analytic. On the other hand though, at least for all that has been said so far, it seems that an atheist could reasonably believe that the claim that God exists is not analytically true. If one is reasonably antecedently committed to the contention that no existence claims are analytic, then that antecedent commitment will provide one with a reason to reject the relevant ontological arguments. And if one is reasonably agnostic about the contention that there are analytic existence claims, then – at least for all that has been said so far – one will reasonably be agnostic about the conclusions of the relevant ontological arguments.

(b) *Existence is not a predicate*

The most famous of Kant's objections to "the ontological argument" is summed up in the slogan 'Existence is not a predicate'. As Plantinga (1967:27) notes, there are many philosophers who have been prepared to dismiss ontological arguments by citing this slogan – but it is far from clear what they have in mind when they do so, other than that they mean to refer to Kant's own account of the backing for the slogan:

'*Being*' is obviously not a real predicate; that is, it is not a concept of something which could be added to the concept of a thing. It is merely the positing of a thing, or of certain determinations, as existing in themselves. Logically, it is merely the copula of a judgement. The proposition 'God is omnipotent' contains two concepts, each of which has its object – God and omnipotence. The small word 'is' adds no new predicate, but only serves to posit the predicate *in its relation* to the subject. If, now, we take the subject (God) with all its predicates (among which is omnipotence), and say 'God is' or 'There is a God', we attach no new predicate to the concept of God, but only posit the subject itself with all its predicates, and indeed, posit it as an *object* that stands in relation to my *concept*. The content of both must be one and the same; nothing can have been added to the concept, which expresses merely what is possible, by my thinking its object (through the expression 'it is') as given absolutely. Otherwise stated, the real contains no more than the merely possible. A hundred real thalers do not contain the least coin more than a hundred possible thalers. For as the latter signify the concept and the former the object and the positing of the concept, should the former contain more than the latter, my concept would not, in that case, express the whole object, and would not therefore be an adequate concept of it. My financial position, however, is affected very differently by a hundred real thalers than it is by the mere concept of them (that is, of their possibility). For the object, as it actually is, is not analytically contained in my concept, but is added to my concept (which is a determination of my state) synthetically; and yet the conceived hundred thalers are not themselves in the least increased through thus acquiring existence outside my concept. By whatever and however many predicates we may think a thing – even if we completely determine it – we do not make the least addition to the thing when we further declare that this thing is. Otherwise, it would not be exactly the same thing that exists, but something more than we thought in the concept; and we could not, therefore, say that the exact object of my concept exists. If we think in a thing every feature of reality except one, the missing reality is not added by my saying that this defective thing exists. (A598B626–A600B628)

It can hardly be said that the meaning of this passage is transparent. It seems clear enough that Kant is claiming that there is something special about the predicate 'exists' and allegedly related words such as 'being'. But what, exactly?

One suggestion that is sometimes made is that Kant's claims should be understood in terms of the Frege–Russell theory of naming and quantification. Of course, such an understanding is extremely anachronistic: Kant was one of the most vehement advocates of the Aristotelian logic that the theory of Frege and Russell supplanted. Nonetheless, it might be worthwhile to try to interpret Kant's argument in this light.

Superficially, it certainly seems that the term 'exists' functions as a predicate in sentences like 'God exists', 'Ronald Reagan exists', 'This chair exists', and 'Mickey Mouse does not exist'. However, it is possible to argue – and to take Kant to be arguing – that, in fact, the term 'exists' does not function in the same way as the predicates 'is omnipotent', 'is no longer governor of California', 'is green', and 'adores Pluto' function in the sentences 'God is omnipotent', 'Ronald Reagan is no longer governor of California', 'This chair is green', and 'Mickey Mouse adores Pluto'.[31]

According to the view in question, an existentially generalized sentence of the form 'Fs exist' or 'There are Fs' must be symbolized as '$\exists x F x$,', where '$\exists x$' is an existential quantifier, and 'x' is a variable of quantification. As John Mackie (1982:46) puts it, "To yield a well-formed sentence, the existential quantifier '$\exists x$' – or 'There is' or 'There are' – must be attached to a predicate expression or general description; and what the sentence will then say is that the collection of features indicated by the predicate expression is realised or instantiated."

31 Note that I have claimed that 'is omnipotent' is a predicate, whereas Kant claims (i) that 'omnipotent' is a predicate and (ii) that 'is' functions as "the copula of a judgement." This already marks a point of departure, of the Frege–Russell theory, from Kant's own conception of the logic of predication.

However, while it is correct to say that the existential quantifier must be attached to a predicate or general description, it is unclear how this is meant to show that existence isn't a predicate. For, as Mackie points out, as things now stand, it seems that the Frege–Russell theory is simply unable to formalize sentences like 'God exists' or 'Ronald Reagan exists' – and yet these sentences are obviously both grammatically well formed and meaningful. Surely the correct way to formalize these sentences will be to introduce a predicate '$E!$' for 'exists', and then render them as '$E!$(God)' and '$E!$(Ronald Reagan)', respectively.

Russell would have disagreed, for his theory of the meaning of proper names can be invoked to support the claim that a correct rendition of these sentences will involve existential quantifiers that attach only to predicates or general descriptions. According to this theory – first introduced in Russell (1905) – proper names are actually just abbreviations for, or disguised forms of, definite descriptions; and definite descriptions are themselves terms that should be analyzed in terms of existential quantifiers, predicates, and general descriptions. Thus, for example, the sentence 'Aristotle is intelligent' (Ia) should first be taken as shorthand for something like 'The philosopher who is a pupil of Plato and teacher of Alexander the Great is intelligent' ($I(\iota x)(Px\&PPx\&TAGx)$); and then this in turn should be taken as shorthand for 'There is one and only one philosopher who is a pupil of Plato and a teacher of Alexander the Great, and that one is intelligent' – which involves an existential quantifier – $(\exists x)(\forall y)((Py\&PPy\&TAGy)\leftrightarrow y=x)\&Ix)$.

The problem with this, as Kripke (1980) famously argues, is that it does not seem to be true that names are abbreviations of – or shorthand for, or disguised versions of – definite descriptions. In particular, it often seems to be the case that ordinary speakers use names to refer to objects when either (i) there are no definite descriptions of those objects that the speakers would be prepared to offer as substitutes for those names and that do not ride piggyback on the names; or else (ii) the definite descriptions that those speakers would be prepared to offer as substitutes for those names do not actually pick out the objects that are referred to by those names. Although this issue is still somewhat controversial, it seems to me to be reasonable to insist that many proper names are not merely abbreviations for definite descriptions – and hence to insist that the claim that the existential quantifier attaches only to predicates and general names does not establish that it is incorrect to formalize the sentence 'God exists' as '$E!$(God)'.

In his discussion of this matter, Mackie fails to point out that there is a standard way of formalizing sentences like 'God exists' in Frege–Russell notation – namely, in the form '$(\exists x)x = $ God'.[32] But, given this formulation, what is there to prevent us from introducing a predicate '$E!$' – for 'exists' – that is such that '$E!a$' is equivalent to '$(\exists x)x = a$'? And, moreover, what is there to prevent us from reading the sentence '$(\exists x)x = a$' as an attribution of the property of singular existence to the object a? Surely one could think that while, in general, sentences of the form '$(\exists x)(\ldots x \ldots)$' do not attribute a singular property, existence, to a particular object, nonetheless, sentences of the form '$(\exists x)x = a$' do attribute a singular property, existence, to the object a. While this is probably not a compulsory understanding of the matter, it certainly seems reasonable – and hence suggests that the Frege–Russell notation really provides no barrier to the supposition that existence *is* a predicate.

Of course, there are complications. In particular, in the standard – classical – version of the Frege–Russell account, it is taken for granted that there are no empty names – that is, '$(\exists x)x = a$' is a theorem of the logic. This is problematic, if we want to read '$E!a$' as 'a exists'. In particular, since it is a theorem of the classical version of the Frege–Russell theory that '$(\exists x)x = $ God', it follows – even without the equivalence to '$E!$(God)' – that God exists. This is the shortest – but also the most worthless – attempted proof of the existence of God.[33]

What is required is an amendment of the classical theory in which there can be empty names. *Free logics* seek to provide such amendments. There are many such logics around. In one typical version, '$E!a$' is introduced as definitionally equivalent to '$(\exists x)x = a$', and empty singular terms, for which '$-E!a$' is true, are permitted. In order to accommodate these terms, other changes are made to the rules of inference governing the quantifiers. Moreover, even though there is a sense in which '$E!$' is not expressible independent of the apparatus of quantification, it is hard to see that Kant provides any reason to deny that it is not a real predicate.

Within free logics, it may still be possible to find a sense in which '$E!$' is not a *real* predicate – that is, a sense in which '$E!$' is different from other predicates.[34] However, in order to show this, one would need to provide an entirely new kind of argument – that is, the considerations

32 It should be pointed out that while Mackie (1982) fails to note that there is a standard way of formalizing sentences of the form 'a exists' in the Frege–Russell theory of quantification, this point is noted in Mackie (1976).
33 Cf. the caustic remarks in Routley (1980:132ff.) about "Quine's sixth way."
34 See Bencivenga (1980) for one attempt to provide such a sense.

that have been advanced thus far would do nothing at all toward showing that existence is not a real predicate. Consequently, we should conclude that this attempt to interpret the Kantian argument is a failure. Not only does the interpretation produce an argument to which Kant himself would not have been able to assent, but the argument as thus construed is a hopeless failure. So is there some other way of construing what Kant is on about that is more successful?

What I think that Kant could have in mind is something like this.[35] Suppose that we draw up two lists. On one, we list all of the properties that are possessed by a given object; and on the other, we list all of the properties that are attributed to that object by a *complete* concept of the object.[36]

Now, consider the relationship between a complete concept of an object and that object – that is, consider the case in which an object exists and in which someone has – or, perhaps, rather, in which there is – a complete concept of that object. For each *real* property of the object, there is a representation of that property in the complete concept of the object. The question that we wish to answer is, Is existence such a property – that is, is existence a property that is attributed to the object by the complete concept of the object? Kant thinks not; he claims that, instead, the existence of the object is a matter of its being related in a suitable way to the complete concept of it.

Even if the existence of an object is a matter of its being related in a suitable way to the complete concept of that thing, how does that show that existence is not a real property? If one thought that the real properties of an object are to be identified with the intrinsic – that is, nonrelational – properties of that object, then acceptance of the claim that existence is a relational property would provide one with reason to reject the claim that existence is a real property. Perhaps this is what motivates Kant's rejection of the claim that existence is a real property – but it seems a rather egregious error for such a sophisticated thinker. Could there be another motivation?

Perhaps, instead, Kant thinks that the allegedly relational nature of existence gives rise to the threat of regress. Suppose that we grant that the existence of an object is a matter of its being related in a suitable

---

35 Perhaps this suggestion is implausible; certainly, it doesn't have a lot of textual support. But it seems as promising as any interpretation that I know of.

36 The notion of a complete concept requires explanation: The idea is (roughly) that a complete concept is the kind of concept that God would have – i.e., a concept in which every property that is possessed by an object is represented. More needs to be said; but this should be enough to get on with.

way to the complete concept of that thing, but allow that relational properties can be real properties of things. Then how can the fact that the concept stands in a certain relation to an external thing be represented as part of the concept – that is, how can the concept in question be taken to be complete? Suppose that C is the complete concept of C*, where C* is an existing object. Can it be the case that one of the properties that C attributes to any object that falls under it is the property of falling under C? Surely not. For, when we add the property of falling under C to the concept C, we have specified a new concept, C', say – that is, we have specified a concept that is distinct from C. Now consider C'. Can it be the case that one of the properties that C' attributes to any object that falls under it is the property of falling under C' Again, surely not. For, when we add the property of falling under C' to the concept C', we have specified a new concept, C", say – that is, we have specified a concept that is distinct from C'. The argument iterates: Whenever we add to a concept K the further property of possessing the property of falling under K, we produce a new concept. Consequently, we can never construct a complete concept C that attributes the property of falling under C.

Of course, this argument is completely specious. A defender of the claim that existence is a real predicate can reasonably object that it is simply question begging to suppose that the property of falling under K must be *added* to K in order to obtain a new concept in which there is an attribution of existence. Rather, the idea is going to be that a complete concept can involve an attribution of 'the property of falling under this very concept' – that is, it can already involve an attribution of the property of existence. It is true that whether or not there is something that falls under the concept is a relational question: It depends upon whether there is a suitably related object in the world. But that the question is relational does not show that it cannot be part of the concept to claim that there is an appropriate relatum.

It should be clear that this response also shows that it would be a mistake to agree with Kant that the existence of an object is a matter of its being related in a suitable way to the complete concept of that thing. That there is something that falls under a certain concept is a relational matter in the sense that it concerns a relation between two things: a concept and an object. But the *existence* of the object is an independent matter – that is, it does not depend upon the existence of the concept. In particular, it does not depend upon the possession of the concept, by me or by anyone else. To suppose otherwise is to lapse into Kantian idealism. And, notwithstanding Kant's own views on the matter, many will quite reasonably hold that embracing Kantian idealism is a very high price to pay for a knockdown refutation of ontological arguments.

I conclude that the Kantian dictum that existence is not a real predicate is not adequately defended by the arguments that Kant provides, or, at least, that I have not been able to find a construal of those arguments on which they provide an adequate defense for the dictum.[37]

(c) *No negative existentials are self-contradictory*

The final objection that Kant makes is also tersely and eloquently expressed:

If in an identical proposition, I reject the predicate while retaining the subject, contradiction results; and I therefore say that the former belongs necessarily to the latter. But if we reject subject and predicate alike, there is no contradiction; for nothing is then left to be contradicted. To posit a triangle, and yet to reject its three angles, is self-contradictory, but there is no contradiction in rejecting the triangle together with its three angles. The same holds true of the concept of an absolutely necessary being. If its existence is rejected, we reject the thing itself with all its predicates; and no question of contradiction can then arise. There is nothing outside it that would then be contradicted, since the necessity of the thing is not supposed to be derived from anything external; nor is there anything internal that would be contradicted, since in rejecting the thing itself we have at the same time rejected all its internal properties. 'God is omnipotent' is a necessary judgement. The omnipotence cannot be rejected if we posit a Deity, that is, an infinite being; for the two concepts are identical. But if we say, 'There is no God', neither the omnipotence nor any other of its predicates is given; they are one and all rejected together with the subject; and there is therefore not the least contradiction in such a judgement. (A595B623)

About this passage, Plantinga (1967:32) says that it appears to be a lot of "fancy persiflage" and that it is no more than an "elaborate and confusing way of asserting that no existential propositions are necessary." However, I think that there is something a little more charitable to be said for it.

It is possible to construe the claim that Kant is making as a claim about the presuppositions that are made by atheists and agnostics. Atheists and agnostics will agree that 'existence' is part of the defini-

---

37   We shall return to this topic in Chapter 10.

tion, or concept, of God – 'that than which no greater can be conceived', 'the most perfect being'. Similarly, they will agree that 'having three angles' is part of the definition, or concept, of the largest triangle. But, since atheists and agnostics do not share the theist's presupposition that God exists, they will just take the fact about definition, or concept, to show that, according to the definition, or concept, God exists. But, of course, to agree to this falls far short of assent to the claim that God exists – since, as the agnostic will insist, for all they know there is no God. Similarly, they might concede that, according to the definition, the largest triangle has three angles, while refusing to accept the unqualified claim that the largest triangle has three angles – on the grounds that, for all they know, there is no largest triangle.

There is more to be said about this line of argument; but I shall reserve that discussion for Chapter 2, on definitional arguments. The important point to be noted here is that it may be possible to salvage something from Kant's discussion – though it must be admitted that the suggested operation does rather extend the bounds of charity. Even if this interpretation could be justified, it should be noted that it was missed by generations of subsequent philosophers.

(7) THE LOGICAL POSITIVIST CRITIQUE

In the early decades of the twentieth century, the logical positivists – Ayer, Carnap, Schlick, and others – mounted a concerted attack on the intelligibility, or meaningfulness, of 'metaphysical' language. Since they included religious claims within the domain of the metaphysical, the logical positivists contended that the claim that God exists is, strictly speaking, meaningless. But if this is correct then there cannot be a sound argument to the conclusion that God exists, since no meaningless claim can be true. Hence, if the contention of the logical positivists is correct, then no ontological argument can succeed.

Prima facie, it seems implausible to claim that religious claims are, strictly speaking, meaningless. As Mackie (1982:2) emphasizes, it seems that we can imagine – conceive of – what it would be like for God to exist, for people to have a future disembodied existence, and so on. But that we take ourselves to be able to do these things is evidence that the claims in question – that God exists, that there is life after death – are intelligible, and hence meaningful. Anyone who wishes to deny that these claims are meaningful will surely need to provide a quite powerful argument.

Ayer (1930) provides one characteristic logical positivist response to this kind of difficulty, namely, he formulates a criterion of meaning-fulness for language that entails that all metaphysical claims are mean-ingless. This *verification principle* has had an interesting subsequent history; we shall consider just a few of the salient features here.

First, it has proved very difficult to find a version of the principle that is not immediately subject to counterexample. The initial formula-tion of it by Ayer is roughly as follows: A statement is literally meaningful iff it is either analytic or empirically falsifiable.[38] In order to understand this claim, we need to understand the vocabulary in which it is couched.

Following Hempel, let us define the notion of an *observation state-ment* as follows: An observation statement is any statement that – correctly or incorrectly – asserts of one or more specifically named or described objects that they have, or that they lack, some specified observable characteristics. Further, although this is far from unprob-lematic, we shall follow Ayer in our definition of an *analytic statement*: A statement is analytic iff it is true solely in virtue of the words that are used to make it. Finally, we need to define the notion of an *empirically falsifiable statement*. This turns out to be rather difficult.

A first suggestion might be that a statement is falsifiable iff there is some finite and consistent set of observation statements that entails its denial. This suggestion would entail the following formulation of the verification principle: a statement is meaningful iff either (i) it is analytic or (ii) there is some finite and consistent set of observation statements that entails its denial. But this won't do. Consider the obviously meaningful claim that every raven is the same color as some other raven. No finite series of observations can falsify this claim – since it is always possible that further observations will find mates for ravens that thus far seem to be unique in color.

A second suggestion might be that a statement is falsifiable if there is some finite and consistent set of observation statements that entails its denial. There are a number of versions of the verification principle that might be derived from this definition. If the verification principle is formulated as follows: a statement is meaningful iff either (i) it is analytic, or (ii) it is falsifiable, or (iii) it is verifiable – that is, its negation is falsifiable, then it is refuted by the same example as before. If the verification principle is formulated as follows: a statement is

---

38 Strictly, Ayer formulated his criterion in terms of verifiability rather than in terms of the cognate notion of falsifiability; however, for ease of exposition, I shall over-look this point.

meaningful iff either (i) it is analytic, or (ii) it is falsifiable, or (iii) it is verifiable, or (iv) it is a logical consequence of a statement that is meaningful, then it is (also) subject to a new difficulty, namely, that it entails that there are no meaningless statements. To see this, consider a putatively meaningless statement, N. We can conjoin N with a falsifiable statement S to form the statement $(S\&N)$. By our criterion, $(S\&N)$ is meaningful – since any observation statements inconsistent with S will be inconsistent with $(S\&N)$ – and, moreover, $(S\&N)$ entails N. So, by our criterion, N is meaningful.

A third suggestion might be that a statement is falsifiable if there is some finite and consistent set of observation statements that relevantly entails its denial. This suggestion would allow us to formulate the following version of the verification principle: A statement is meaningful iff either (i) it is analytic, or (ii) it is falsifiable, or (iii) it is verifiable, or (iv) it is relevantly entailed by statements that are meaningful. There are relevance logics on which N is not entailed by $(S\&N)$; if we choose one of these logics, then we can avoid the preceding counterexample – that is, we won't be able to use the preceding argument to show that this criterion entails that all statements are meaningful.[39] However, our first counterexample is still with us: The principle currently under consideration still entails that the claim that every raven is the same color as some other raven is meaningless.

A fourth suggestion might be that a statement is falsifiable if there is some consistent set of observation statements that relevantly entails its denial. If we combine this suggestion with the preceding formulation of the verification principle, then it might seem that we could evade the initial counterexample – for won't there be sufficiently large sets of observation statements that do entail the denial of the claim that every raven is the same color as some other raven? In particular, won't some sets of observation statements that cover *all* of the ravens have this entailment? No; as Russell (1918) inter alia pointed out, the further claim that these are all of the ravens would need to be added to the set of observation sentences before the entailment can be said to hold. But this claim is not an observation statement; nor is *it* entailed by any sets of observation statements.

---

39 For discussion of relevance logics, see Anderson and Belnap (1975) and Routley (1982). Throughout most of this book, I shall simply take classical logic for granted. This is not because I am committed to the view that relevance logics are wrong, or useless, or whatever; rather, it's just that questions about the validity of the arguments under consideration seem to be quite independent of the debate between relevantists and their rivals.

There are many further suggestions that we could consider.[40] However, there is an argument due to David Lewis (1988) that suggests that no formulation of the verification principle can avoid collapse into triviality. As Lewis notes, there are two separate principles that seem to be required in any formulation of the verification principle: (i) There is an *entailment principle*, which says that any statement that entails a verifiable statement is itself verifiable; and (ii) there is a *compositional principle*, which says that any first-order sentence that is composed entirely of verifiable statements is either analytic or verifiable. Neither principle is sufficient on its own: With just the entailment principle, statements like 'Every raven is the same color as some other raven' are not verifiable; and with just the compositional principle, no statement that contains nonobservational vocabulary is verifiable. But with both principles together, we get collapse. For suppose that V is a (noncontradictory) verifiable statement. Then not-V is verifiable, by the compositional principle. Moreover, for any statement S, each of $(S\&V)$ and $(S\&not-V)$ entails a verifiable statement, and hence is verifiable. So the disjunction $(S\&V)$ or $(S\&not-V)$ is either analytic or verifiable (by the compositional principle). Hence, by the entailment principle, S is either analytic or verifiable. Thus, any statement S that is not analytic is verifiable.

As Wright (1989) notes, there is one possible loophole in Lewis's argument: Lewis takes for granted that the entailment principle is stated in terms of classical entailment. But might there not be some nonclassical notion of entailment that can be used to rescue the verification principle? Wright suggests the following: Say that an entailment $\{A_1, \ldots, A_n, S\} \Rightarrow B$ is *S-compact* iff it is subject to disruption by uniform replacement of any nonlogical constituent in S. Then we can formulate the verification principle as follows:

S is verifiable iff S is not analytic and either:

(i) S is an atomic observation statement; or
(ii) S is a negation, disjunction, or existential generalization of verifiable statements; or
(iii) Some verifiable T is S-compactly entailed by the union of S with some set $\langle S_1, \ldots, S_n \rangle$ of verifiable statements, and S has no compact equivalent S^* for which the entailment of T by $S^* \cup \langle S_1, \ldots, S_n \rangle$ is non-S^* compact; or

40 Crispin Wright (1986:263ff.) provides an interesting account of the "puncture and patch" industry that centered on attempts to find a plausible version of the verification principle.

(iv) *S* is entailed by some verifiable statement and contains only vocabulary occurring in statements that may be established by appeal only to (i)–(iii) or in correct definitions of vocabulary that so features.

This formulation seems to avoid collapse into triviality. However, it is not clear that it does not exclude statements that intuitively count as verifiable. Wright suggests that if there are *analytic bridge principles* that connect observational and nonobservational vocabulary, then there is no reason to suppose that any statements that intuitively count as verifiable are excluded. But I doubt that there is good reason to suppose that there are always such principles. In particular, I doubt that such principles can be found for highly theoretical scientific vocabulary – for example, the vocabulary of string theory. Moreover, it also seems that appeal to such bridge principles will undermine the use of the verification principle as a criterion of meaningfulness. For it is not at all clear that science and metaphysics differ in their entitlements to bridge principles of the kind in question.[41]

I conclude that it is very unlikely that anyone will ever be able to formulate an unproblematic version of the verification principle. Any version of the principle that does not collapse into triviality is subject to hard questions about its content. Thus ends the discussion of the first difficulty that I find with Ayer's formulation of the verification principle.

The second difficulty is that even if we could find a plausible formulation of the verification principle, it is not clear how the principle could be justified. In particular, it seems doubtful that a justification of the principle could be given that did not violate the content of the principle. According to the principle, every meaningful statement is either analytic or verifiable. Consequently, the principle itself must be either analytic or verifiable. But (i) it seems doubtful that the principle is verifiable, and (ii) it seems equally doubtful that the principle is analytic. Ayer himself claimed that the principle was 'like a definition', and hence analytic. But, on any intuitive account of

41 Wright seems to equate 'analytic principles' with 'principles about conceptual connections'. But this is not very far from 'principles about *meaning* connections'. And the whole point of the verification principle is to provide a criterion for assessment of claims about *meaning*. If the application of the principle is to rely on judgments about connections of meaning between observation statements and nonobservation statements, then it seems doubtful that any non-question-begging critique of metaphysics will ensue.

analyticity, it seems highly implausible to claim that the verification principle is true by definition or by meaning. Certainly, even quite detailed examination of the meaning of the principle seems not to have revealed its truth either to me or to many other philosophers. Yet, on the other hand, the claim that there are analytic principles that connect the verification principle to observation statements does not have the ring of truth.

Third, even if we could find a plausible formulation of the verification principle that is not unjustifiable on its own terms, there is still a question about the reasons that one might have for accepting it. Plantinga (1967:167ff.) makes the point well:

Suppose that the criterion could be stated in a way that satisfied the verificationist. . . . Why should anyone accept it? Why should the theist not retort as follows: "Your criterion is obviously mistaken; for many theological statements are not empirically verifiable; but theological statements are meaningful; hence it is false that all and only verifiable statements are meaningful"? What could the verificationist reply? What sort of argument could he bring forward to show the theologian that he ought to accept the verifiability criterion and stop proclaiming these meaningless pseudo-statements? About all he could say here would be that his criterion does fit scientific and commonsense statements and does not fit theological statements. And to this the theologian could agree with equanimity; there are, no doubt, many properties which distinguish scientific and commonsense statements from theological statements. But, of course, that does not suffice to show that theological statements are meaningless or logically out of order or anything of the sort.

What goes for theologians goes for metaphysicians in general. Given that there are people who rationally accept some religious or metaphysical principles – and this seems a small concession – then it would seem to follow that there are people who can reasonably reject a successfully formulated, non-self-defeating version of the verification principle. So the dialectical effectiveness of appeal to such verification principles, even among fully rational disputants, should reasonably be expected to be minimal.[42]

Fourth, the key concepts that are used in the formulation of the verification principle are not unproblematic. In particular, there are serious questions that can be raised about the use of the terms 'obser-

42 One might reasonably think that consideration of the claims of religion and metaphysics is *pointless*. Moreover, one might think this on the basis of something like the following 'principle of significance': The only statements that are worth at-

vation statement' and 'analytic statement'. The recent history of philosophy suggests that (i) there may be no uncontroversial way of drawing the line between the observational and the nonobservational, and (ii) there may be no uncontroversial way of dividing statements into those that are analytic and those that are not. Since it would require a large digression to take up these issues, I shall not pursue this point further.

Finally, it should be noted that – at least prior to the publication of Carnap's *Meaning and Necessity* – the logical positivists uniformly eschewed, or otherwise overlooked, the use of modal idioms, that is, talk of 'necessity', 'possibility', 'conceivability', and so on. One consequence of this fact appears in Hempel's account of observation statements – for, if the "objects" referred to in that account can be merely possible, then it is not clear that very much will eventually be excluded by the verification principle: If God is a logically possible object, then even statements about God would be meaningful on this construal of the account. Moreover, there seems to be some plausibility in the thought that a criterion of meaningfulness might be linked to a criterion of possibility, namely, that a statement is meaningful if – though surely not only if – the state of affairs that it describes is possible. And, even if conceivability is an inadequate criterion for logical possibility – for example, can I conceive of a disproof of the four-color map theorem? – it seems very plausible to suggest that conceivability is a criterion for meaningfulness. It is surely reasonable to claim that the resources for constructing more plausible criteria for meaningfulness lie closer to hand if one is allowed to avail oneself of the resources of modal and other intensional idioms.

In sum, although there was a time when the logical positivist critique of the meaning of religious claims seemed to carry some force, I think that it is now quite clear that that critique need not perturb theists at all. It is not really at all plausible to think that there is a generally acceptable criterion of meaningfulness that shows immediately and, finally, that no religious or metaphysical claims are meaningful.[43]

tending to are those that are either (i) analytic, or (ii) verifiable, or (iii) consequences of this very principle. However, it would be unwarrantedly parochial to think that everyone else ought to have the same views about which statements are worth attending to.

43 Nielsen (1971) mounts a sustained attack on the meaningfulness of religious language; much of his attack is given qualified support by Martin (1990: ch. 2). More needs to be said to show that this attack fails; but such discussion must be deferred to another occasion.

(8) CONCLUDING REMARKS

That completes my initial survey of some of the main turns in the history of ontological arguments. Of course, this survey is far from complete; there are many kinds of ontological arguments that have as yet received no consideration. However, those other arguments – and the important historical figures who have defended or attacked them – will be treated in the remainder of this work.

What follows is a discussion of the main kinds of ontological arguments that have been put forward, of the main responses that have been made to them, and of the deficiencies from which, in my opinion, these arguments genuinely suffer. The discussion is organized on conceptual, rather than historical, lines. Moreover, it is intended to suggest that there is good reason to think that there is no argument that (i) proceeds from premises all of which are such that a reasonable agnostic or atheist who attends to them sufficiently ought to be able to accept them on *a priori* grounds and (ii) reaches the conclusion that God exists by a valid sequence of reasoning from the premises mentioned in (i).

As I mentioned at the beginning, there are six kinds of ontological arguments that I distinguish. The next six chapters treat these different kinds of ontological arguments in turn. Where applicable, the analyses developed are applied to the arguments outlined earlier; and they are also applied to arguments that have not yet been discussed.

Chapter 2

Definitional arguments

CONSIDER the following arguments, which I take to be paradigmatic cases of definitional ontological arguments:

1. God is a being which has every perfection. (Definition)
2. Existence is a perfection. (Premise)
3. (Hence) God exists. (From 1, 2)

1. God is an existent supremely perfect being. (Definition)
2. (Hence) God exists. (From 1)

It seems clear that there is no good reason for an agnostic to be persuaded by these arguments. Why not?

First, it should be noted that these arguments can be paralleled to their detriment. Corresponding to the first argument, there are many arguments of the following form:

1. God* is a being that has all perfections except for moral perfections – and the moral attributes of God* are as follows: . . . . (Definition)
2. Existence is a perfection. (Premise).
3. (Hence) God* exists. (From 1, 2)

And corresponding to the second argument, there are many arguments of the following form:

1. m is an existent F. (Definition)
2. (Hence) m exists. (From 1)

Thus, parallel to the second argument, there are arguments that purport to establish the existence of existent unicorns, existent round squares, and so on. And parallel to the first argument, there are arguments that purport to establish the existence of a vast range of distinct all-but-perfect beings. The existence of these parallels strongly suggests that there is something wrong with the thought that these arguments ought to be recognized by agnostics as sound proofs of the existence of God.

What has gone wrong? One traditional objection to the first argument is that existence is not a perfection. However, since the second argument does not involve the premise that existence is a perfection, this objection will not touch the second argument. Since it seems plausible to suggest that the two arguments go wrong in the same way, there must be something else that is wrong with the first argument.[1]

Another traditional suggestion is that because existence is not a real predicate, existence cannot be either a defining property or a perfection. It is, I think, hard to accept the contention that existence cannot be a defining property. Suppose that, following Mackie (1982), I define 'Remartian' to mean 'existent intelligent creature native to the planet Mars'. Then surely it is quite clear what is required for a being to satisfy the definition: It must be an intelligent creature native to the planet Mars, and it must actually exist; an intelligent creature native to the planet Mars in another possible world is not a Remartian. Perhaps there is something to be made of the doctrine that existence is not a real predicate; nonetheless, it seems very unlikely that any correct version of that doctrine will have the consequence that there is something improper about definitions that involve the word 'exists.'

Mackie suggests that even if we grant that existence can be a defining property, we can still object to the second form of argument on the following grounds: Suppose that no two Martians are ever the same height. Then, it would be contradictory to say, 'The tallest Remartian does not exist', since this would be to attribute both existence and nonexistence to the tallest Remartian. But, at the same time, we are quite sure that there are no Martians, and hence that there are no Remartians either. That is, it cannot be contradictory to say, 'There are no Remartians'. So the solution to our worry is to draw a distinction between sentences of the form 'X does not exist' – which are self-contradictory if existence is a defining property of X – and sentences of the form 'There is no X' – which is not self-contradictory even if existence is a defining property of X.

However, this suggestion can hardly be satisfactory. The problem

---

1 Perhaps existence is not a perfection. See Chapter 10 for some relevant considerations.

is that 'X does not exist' and 'There is no X' seem to be two different ways of saying the same thing. Surely there is no more difficulty in denying that the tallest Remartian exists than there is in denying that there is a tallest Remartian. It must be admitted that it does sound odd to say, 'The tallest existent intelligent creature native to the planet Mars does not exist'. But, as we shall see, this oddness can be explained without adopting Mackie's suggested distinction.

So what has gone wrong in the original arguments? Well, in one sense, the answer is nothing. Consider the second argument. We begin with the claim that *according to the relevant definition,* God is an existent supremely perfect being. And the conclusion that we can draw from this claim is that, *according to that definition,* God exists. We only go wrong if we suppose that the conclusion, that God exists, can be detached from the scope of the original act of definition. More perspicuously, the correct version of the second argument might be represented as follows:

1. By definition, God is an existent supremely perfect being. (Definition)
2. (Hence) According to the preceding definition, God exists. (From 1)

If we adopt this representation, then – of course – we will insist that the inference from 'According to that definition, X exists' to 'X exists' is simply invalid.[2] Hence, even though the argument is sound, it gives no support at all to the contention that God exists.

Perhaps it will be objected that it is unnecessarily cumbersome to have explicit "by definition" operators to represent acts of definition formally. This is a fair objection: There are no explicit by definition operators in the original piece of reasoning. However, it is important to recognize that in the context of the presentation of the argument, there is an *implicit* by definition operator that is operative. The whole argument occurs within the scope of the definition of 'God' as "an existent supremely perfect being" – and so it is a mistake to suppose that the conclusion of the argument is established outside the scope of that implicit operator.

There are many similar implicit operators that create analogous difficulties – for example, 'according to that story', 'according to that theory'. Consider the claim that Santa Claus lives at the North Pole. Strictly speaking, this is not true – for there is no one who lives at the

2 The inference from 'According to Mackie's definition, the tallest Remartian exists' to 'The tallest Remartian exists' is obviously invalid.

North Pole. But what is true is that according to the well-known fiction, Santa Claus lives at the North Pole. Moreover, because we usually have no difficulty in keeping track of the implicit operators that govern contexts of discourse, we shall usually find no difficulty in assenting to the simple sentence 'Santa Claus lives at the North Pole', precisely because we see that assent as implicitly governed by the qualification 'according to the well-known fiction'.

Another useful case is provided by Euclidean geometry. Consider a proof, in Euclidean geometry, of the claim that the internal angles of a triangle sum to 180 degrees. The proof – if it is fully explicit – will begin with certain postulates and will end with the conclusion that the internal angles of a triangle sum to 180 degrees. But, of course, we will only be able to detach the conclusion from the proof – that is, draw the conclusion that the internal angles of a triangle sum to 180 degrees – if we accept the postulates of Euclidean geometry. If we do not accept those postulates, then all that we can conclude from the proof is that, according to Euclidean geometry, the internal angles of a triangle sum to 180 degrees.

Perhaps it might be said that this case is not parallel to the original arguments – for those arguments involve explicit definitions, and the case of Euclidean geometry involves postulates. However, there is a genuine parallel, for, in each case, one must satisfy oneself that the theoretical constructions – definitions or postulates – involved are true of things in the world before one can detach the conclusions from the scope of those theoretical constructions.

Given that there can be implicit operators that govern contexts of discourse, one might expect that there are sentential constructions that draw attention to these implicit operators. And indeed there are. Sentences like 'There really are Xs' and 'Xs really exist' can be used to cancel the suggestion that there are any implicit operators governing one's discourse about Xs. If I say, 'There really are bunyips', then, other things being equal, what I intend to do, is to combat the suggestion that I see my discourse about bunyips as governed by an implicit operator: 'according to the well-known bush legends', 'according to the story that I am in the process of telling', and so on. Of course, there can be degrees of embedding of implicit operators, as when one story is embedded within another. And, in such cases, sentences like 'There really are Xs' and 'Xs really exist' may only function to bump the discourse up one or more levels. The utterance 'There really are dragons' might mean 'There are dragons in the world of the story within the story, and moreover, there are dragons in the world of the story'.

Given this complexity, it is possible to use sentences of the form 'There are Xs' and 'Xs exist' to play different roles. For example, one might use sentences of the forms 'Xs exist' and 'Xs don't exist' for utterances that are governed by implicit operators, while reserving sentences of the forms 'There are Xs' and 'There are no Xs' for utterances that are not governed by implicit operators. This is what Mackie does when he discusses the case of the tallest Remartian. When he says, 'Remartians exist', he sees this utterance as governed by the implicit operator 'according to the definition'; but when he says, 'There are no Remartians', he does not take this utterance to be governed by any implicit operators. However, *contra* Mackie, there is nothing that determines that this use has to be constant across different contexts – that is, there is nothing to prevent someone else, in different circumstances, from using 'There are Remartians' to express the claim that is governed by the implicit operator 'according to the definition'; and using 'Remartians do not exist' to express the claim that is not governed by any implicit operators.

There does seem to be one constraint on the interchangeability of 'Xs do not exist' and 'There are no Xs' – namely, those cases in which 'X' explicitly involves the word 'exists'. As we noted earlier, the claim 'The tallest existent intelligent creature native to the planet Mars does not exist' sounds odd. It might be suggested that the difficulty in this case is due to the definite description rather than to the presence of the word 'existent'. However, it seems that it would be no less odd to say, 'Existent unicorns do not exist'. Given that the use of 'exists' is uniform, this sentence can only be construed as a contradiction. Of course, it is clear enough what one who used this sentence would be trying to say – for it can be rendered quite clearly as 'There are no existent unicorns'. And this seems to suggest that there is a fundamental difference between the construction 'There are Xs' and 'Xs exist'.

But this appearance is illusory. Consider locutions of the form 'Those Xs that there are do not exist' and 'There aren't any of those Xs that there are'. The second of these is contradictory; and the first can be construed along the same lines as 'There are no existent unicorns'. A definition of 'Remartian' of the form 'intelligent creature native to the planet Mars, of which there is at least one' is awkward – but the difficulty is due to the fact that the existential quantifier is not a grammatical predicate, rather than to a relevant difference in the function of the existential quantifier and the predicate 'exists'.

In sum, then, the arguments that were introduced at the beginning of this section go wrong in their use of definitions. If one introduces a singular term 'X' using a definition, and if one – either implicitly or explicitly – builds the notion of existence into the definition, then one cannot conclude outright that X exists. Rather, all that one can conclude is that, according to one's definition, X exists. Similarly, if one introduces a plural term 'X' using a definition, and if one – either implicitly or explicitly – builds the notion of existence into the definition, then one cannot conclude outright that Xs exist. Rather, all that one can conclude is that, according to one's definition, Xs exist.

Of course, this is not to deny that one can legitimately introduce terms by definition into arguments without supposing that one's conclusions are governed by ontologically neutralizing operators. If I have proved that an equation has a unique solution – though I don't yet know what the solution is – and if I call that solution 'q', then I am quite entitled to claim that my proof shows that q exists. It would be absurd to insist that, strictly speaking, all my proof shows is that, according to my definition of 'q', q exists. In this case, the sole function of my definition is to establish an uncontroversial use for the expression 'q'; and other things being equal, I am perfectly entitled to do this.[3] However, in the cases considered earlier, the function of the definition was to provide materials from which conclusions could be drawn – and in those cases, any conclusions that I draw must be seen to fall within the scope of the definition.[4]

Perhaps a theist might seek to defend these arguments as follows: It is true that these arguments involve definitions. However, it is a mistake to think that there is a parallel between, say, the definition of 'God' as 'the existent supremely perfect being' and the definition of 'Rod' as 'the existent tallest intelligent creature native to the planet Mars'. The sentence 'God is the existent supremely perfect being' is

---

3   Of course, I will do well to have distinct names for distinct things, and so forth.
4   A different kind of case – suggested to me by Frank Jackson – that might be thought to make difficulties for my account is provided by the following argument:

1. The leader of the House is the prime minister. (Definition)
2. Paul Keating is the leader of the House. (Premise)
3. (Hence) Paul Keating is the prime minister. (From 1, 2)

Here, of course, there is no temptation to include a qualifying operator in the detached conclusion. The absence of this temptation is explained by the fact that the ontically committing singular term – 'Paul Keating' – is not introduced in the definitional premise; this contrasts with the cases discussed in the main text in which the ontically committing term – 'God', etc. – is introduced *only* by way of the definitional premise.

true; and hence the first definition is what we might call a 'true definition'. But the sentence 'Rod is the existent tallest intelligent creature native to the planet Mars' is false, because there is no tallest intelligent creature native to the planet Mars; and hence the second definition is what we might call a 'false definition'. That is, the arguments about God have true premises, involving true definitions; and the parallel arguments about other creatures very often have false premises, involving false definitions. Moreover, the argument form is valid. So the arguments do prove that God exists and do not prove that any other beings – which do not exist – exist.

In effect, what this amounts to is the observation that a theist will see no difficulty in 'discharging' the definitional operator in the case of God but will see the same difficulty as the agnostic or atheist in the case of many other beings. Surely this observation is correct. However, it provides not the slightest reason for an agnostic to discharge the definitional operator in the case of God. What the agnostic is unsure about is precisely whether the definitional operator can be discharged in the case of God. Of course, the agnostic is well aware that the theist believes that it can: But the theist's insistence on this point gives the agnostic no further reason to believe that the theist is right.

(1) BEGGING THE QUESTION

It is often objected against various forms of ontological argument that they 'beg the question'. This complaint has a reasonable foundation – illustrated in the preceding paragraph – but is often poorly explained. The point is a dialectical, or dialogical, one, namely, that what an agnostic or atheist requires in an argument for the existence of God is a compelling reason to believe that God exists, but that what the theist very often supplies is an argument whose alleged soundness can only be recognized by someone who already believes that God exists. It is not arguments – in the sense of sets of premises and conclusions – that can be question begging; rather, it is the dialectical, or dialogical, use to which arguments can be put that can beg questions.

Rowe (1976a:431) objects to a version of St. Anselm's argument as follows:

Given (1) Anselm's concept of God, (2) his principle that existence is a great-making quality [of God], and (3) the premise that God, as conceived by Anselm, is a possible thing, it really does follow that Anselm's God actually exists. But . . . we can now see that in granting Anselm the premise that God is a possible thing we have granted far more than we intended to grant. . . .

53

[This premise] amounts to the assertion that some existing being is supremely great. And since this is, in part, the point the argument endeavours to prove, the argument begs the question, it assumes the point it is supposed to prove.

There are two important questions that can be asked about this objection: (i) How does the premise that God is a possible thing 'amount to' the assertion that some existing thing is supremely great? (ii) How does this purported fact – that is, that the premise 'amounts to' an assertion of part of the conclusion – establish that the argument begs the question?

A natural interpretation of (i) is that the conjunction of the premises of the argument entails the conclusion of the argument – and hence (?) a natural interpretation of (ii) is that in a non-question-begging argument, the conjunction of the premises of the argument should not entail the conclusion of the argument. But that can't be right. If there is any use at all for the label 'begs the question', it cannot be the case that all valid arguments beg the question. Yet there seems to be no other plausible interpretation of the claim that the premise to which Rowe adverts amounts to the assertion of part of the conclusion of the argument.

Davis (1976a: 437) accepts the following as an account of begging the question:

An argument begs the question iff either (1) the conclusion or a proposition logically equivalent to the conclusion appears as a premise or as a conjunct of a premise, or (2) the truth of a premise depends upon the truth of the conclusion (i.e. there is no reason to accept the premise unless the conclusion is already accepted).

But, since any argument can be represented as a single-premise argument, this characterization entails that all valid arguments beg the question. Davis goes on to note that one might conclude from Rowe's account that all valid arguments beg the question – but fails to note that exactly the same is true of his own characterization.

Rowe (1976b:443) distinguishes between three different ways in which an argument may beg the question:

An argument begs the question against someone when it employs a premise that is unacceptable to that person. . . . An argument begs the question in itself in a logical way when a premise in an argument, or a main conjunct of a premise, is identical to the conclusion. . . . An argument begs the question in itself in an epistemological way when its premise cannot be known independently of its conclusion.

He goes on to suggest that the ontological argument begs the question against itself in the epistemological way. Moreover, he claims that begging the question against someone is a "relatively harmless" feature that is possessed by many arguments and that does not prevent an argument from being a good proof of its conclusion.

Against Rowe, I would suggest that neither the logical nor the epistemological way of begging the question merits any attention. Given that any argument is equivalent to a single-premise argument, it follows (i) that every valid argument begs the question in the logical way and (ii) that, for a logical competent target, every valid argument begs the question in the epistemological way. Moreover, I would suggest that begging the question against someone is not harmless: Rather, it undermines the dialectical effectiveness of an argument. Of course, it can be true that a dialectically ineffective argument is still sound – but, in the dialectic of argumentation, it is not enough to have logic and truth on one's side.

It might be suggested – compare Davis (1976b) – that an argument begs the question in the epistemological way when its premise cannot be reasonably believed or accepted independently of the conclusion. But this doesn't help. Given logical competence, one cannot reasonably believe the premises of a valid argument without also believing the conclusion. So, even with this amendment, it is still true that for a logically competent target, every valid argument begs the question. Surely it would be wrong to suggest that valid arguments fail to beg the question only insofar as their targets are less than logically competent.

Walton (1978:213) suggests that whether a given form of argument begs the question depends upon "factors of the epistemic context of the argument" – that is, on whether, in an epistemic sense, there is "enough distance" between the premises and the conclusion of the argument. Even if we grant that the metaphor of distance can be explained,[5] this still seems to be on the wrong track. In particular, it entails that any valid argument with a sufficiently simple logical form begs the question. But that isn't right. Even a simple argument by *modus ponens* – that is, an argument in which there is "minimal distance" between premises and conclusion – can fail to beg the question.

Gale (1991:213) recognizes that the concept of begging the question

---

5 Perhaps in terms of the complexity of the urn models needed to validate the argument – cf. Rantala (1975) and Hintikka (1975).

is dialectical. He suggests that it concerns "what propositions the opponent of the argument is willing to concede prior to the presentation of the argument." According to Gale, "It will not be fair for the opponent of the argument, after it has been given and discovered to be valid, to charge that it begged the question, for at that time he was willing to grant its premises."

This still isn't quite right. Whether an argument begs the question against a view to which I am strongly committed shouldn't depend upon such factors as my logical acumen. Consider the case of the modal argument that Gale discusses. Suppose I am strongly committed to the view that God does not exist, but concede that it is possible that God exists solely on the grounds that I can see no harm in this concession. If I am later convinced that the modal argument in question is valid, then, no doubt, I shall wish to retract my concession that it is possible that God exists. In these circumstances, it seems to me that it will then be correct for me to say that the argument begged the question against me – for, in fact, I was all along implicitly committed to the view that it is not possible that God exists – though it will also be correct to say that the argument did not beg the question against the view to which I *professed* allegiance.

I suggest that something like the following is an adequate partial characterization of the "fallacy" of begging the question:[6] Suppose that I am committed to a claim that p as part of my perhaps tacit reasonable commitment to a broader consistent set of claims C. Suppose further that an opponent produces an argument of the form 'Q_1, ..., Q_n; therefore not p', where the negations of one or more of the Q_i are claims that belong to C. Then that argument begs the question against me. Moreover, this is true even if I cannot provide a clear characterization of the set of claims C. Of course, if one is to object to an opponent that he is begging the question, then one needs to have a firmer grip on the nature of the set of claims C. But it is one thing to recognize that a question is being begged, and another for the begging of a question to take place.

Note that this characterization does not entail that all ontological arguments beg the question. Suppose we grant that an atheist is

---

6 The condition that I provide is sufficient, but clearly not necessary: Consider, for example, the case of *reductio* arguments against opponents who hold inconsistent views. Since I claim that, on the relevant readings, ontological arguments satisfy this sufficient condition, I needn't concern myself here with a search for conditions that are both necessary and sufficient.

reasonably committed to a broader theory N that entails that God does not exist, or that an agnostic is reasonably committed to a broader theory N that does not relevantly entail that God exists. It might still be the case (i) that N is logically inconsistent, or (ii) that $N \cup \{p\}$ is inconsistent, where p is some proposition that any reasonable person – or perhaps any reasonable agnostic or atheist – must accept on *a priori* grounds. In either of these cases, there can be a non-question-begging ontological argument.[7]

I conclude that given an adequate characterization of the fallacy of begging the question, it is clear that definitional ontological arguments do beg the question against many reasonable atheists and agnostics. There are certain claims about the permissibility of discharging sentential operators that are at least tacitly rejected by atheists and agnostics, but upon which the success of definitional ontological arguments depend.

7 Here, I take for granted that one can be reasonably committed to an inconsistent theory. This seems correct, especially if the commitment in question is largely tacit. Further discussion of the issues that arise here must be deferred.

Chapter 3

Conceptual arguments

HERE is a simple example of a conceptual ontological argument:

1. I conceive of an existent God. (Premise)
2. (Hence) God exists. (From 1)

This argument can, it seems, be paralleled to its discredit:

1. I conceive of a nonexistent God. (Premise)
2. (Hence) God does not exist. (From 1)

However, it might be objected that the two arguments are not really parallel. In order to decide whether they are, we need to decide on the sense that we are to give to the expression 'conceive of'.

There are a number of different sense that can be given to the expression 'conceive of'. Suppose that I am asked to conceive of – think about, form an idea of – the current president of the United States. There seem to be at least four different ways in which I can respond to this request: (i) I can consider the description 'the current president of the United States', but without making any commitment to the existence of anyone who conforms to that description; (ii) I can consider the description 'the current president of the United States', while being committed to the view that there is no one who conforms to that description; (iii) I can consider the description 'the current president of the United States' and take it that the description provides a correct characterization of a unique person who conforms to it, even if there is no independent characterization that I could give of that person; and (iv) I can consider the description 'the current president of the United States' and take it that the description provides a correct characterization of a person whom I can also characterize independently.

Given this distinction among senses that can be given to the expression 'conceive of', there are a number of different assessments that can be made of the truth of the sentence 'I conceive of X'. If 'conceive of' is taken in either the third or the fourth sense just described, then it can only be true that I conceive of X if there is an X that is the object of my conception. But if 'conceive of' is taken in either the first or the second sense just described, then it can be true that I conceive of X even if there is no actual X that is the object of my conception. In the third and fourth senses, I cannot conceive of the greatest prime number; but in the first and second senses, I can. Note that there is a further sense in which 'I conceive of X' can be true – namely, one in which I somehow or other have a conception of X but in such a way that the expression 'X' plays no part. Or, to put it slightly differently there is a sense in which it can be true that X exists, that I conceive of X, but that I do not conceive of X *as* X.

The distinctions just drawn can be applied to the premises of the arguments given. Is there a sense in which an agnostic will concede that she does, or can, conceive of an existent God? Certainly. The agnostic is in no doubt that she can consider the expression 'an existent God'. But what she is unsure about is whether there is any being that is correctly described by this expression. And, so, of course, an agnostic will not allow that it follows from the fact, that in this sense she conceives of an existent God, that God exists.

Of course, the situation is different for a theist. A theist will hold, not only that he consider the expression 'an existent God', but also that this expression picks out a unique individual that he could characterize in other ways. But, if this is what is meant by the claim that one conceives of an existent God, then of course it follows from that claim that God exists. In this form, the theist will take the argument to be sound – but, of course, it is also apparent that the argument is dialectically useless. Similar considerations apply to the second of the arguments given. In this case, on the appropriate construal, an atheist will hold that the argument is sound – but there will be not the slightest reason for a theist to be perturbed by this fact.

There are more complicated arguments – versions of St. Anselm's arguments – to which similar considerations apply. Consider the following argument:

1. I conceive of a being than which no greater can be conceived.
2. If a being than which no greater can be conceived does not exist, then I can conceive of a being greater than a being than which no

greater can be conceived – namely, a being than which no greater
can be conceived that exists.

3. I cannot conceive of a being greater than a being than which no
greater can be conceived.

4. (Hence) A being than which no greater can be conceived exists.

One question that arises immediately concerns premise 3. If all that is
required for conceiving is consideration of a description, then surely I
can entertain the description 'a being greater than a being than which
no greater can be conceived'. Yes; but I cannot suppose that what I am
then doing can be coherently described as conceiving of a being
greater than a being than which no greater can be conceived. The
argument will still go through provided that 'conceive' is read as
'coherently conceive' throughout.

But trouble resurfaces at another point. In the sense of 'coherence'
in question, is it true that I can coherently conceive of a being than
which no greater can be coherently conceived? This seems to depend
upon the assumptions that I am prepared to make about the 'greater
than' relation. If it merely imposes a partial ordering on the domain
to which it is applied, and if that domain is infinite, then there are
three possibilities: (i) There is a unique being that is greater than any
other in the domain; (ii) there is an infinite chain of beings, each of
which is greater than some others and less than some others, but there
is no single being that is greater than any other in the domain; and
(iii) there is more than one being that is such that there is no being
that is greater than it, but there is no single being that is greater than
any other in the domain. If I suppose that either (ii) or (iii) obtains,
then one might want to say that I cannot coherently conceive of a
being than which no greater can be coherently conceived. On the other
hand, one might want to say that alternative (i) shows that it is
possible for me to form a coherent conception of a being than which
no greater can be coherently conceived – though, because of my
commitment to (ii) or (iii), I will take this coherent conception to be
unexemplified.

In any case, the argument runs afoul of the same objection as the
simpler argument given earlier. In what sense will an agnostic grant
that premise 1 is true? Only in the sense that she can consider the – let
us grant coherent – description 'a being than which no greater can
be conceived.' Moreover, what makes her consideration count as a
conception of a being than which no greater can be conceived is
precisely the fact that the token that she considers is equiform with

any other token of the form 'a being than which no greater can be conceived'.[1]

Given that an agnostic will only grant that premise 1 is true if it is shorn of any referential or denotational implications, it is easy to see that she will not be persuaded that 2 is true. Whether or not there is a being than which no greater can be conceived, it is simply not true that I can coherently conceive of a being that is greater than a being than which no greater can be conceived. So, if we interpret 2 as a material conditional, 2 will only be true if it has a false antecedent – that is, only if it is true that there is a being than which no greater can be conceived. But since the agnostic is undecided about the truth of the claim that there is a being than which no greater can be conceived, she will equally be undecided about the truth of 2. On the other hand, a theist will naturally think that 2 is true; and an atheist will naturally think that it is false.

It might be suggested that the argument can be repaired by insisting that premise 1 be interpreted in a stronger sense, which requires that one can only conceive of a being than which none greater can be conceived if there is a being than which none greater can be conceived for one's conception to be about. But, of course, no agnostic will grant 1 under this interpretation.

It might also be suggested that the argument can be repaired by appeal to a suitable bridging principle that connects concepts and the entities that fall under them. In particular, one might follow Stephen Makin (1988) in appealing to the following principle:

M. If 'F' is a selective and intrinsically exemplified concept, and 'G' is not, then, *ceteris paribus*, Fs are greater than Gs.

The argument runs as follows: Suppose that the selective concept 'being than which no greater can be conceived' is not intrinsically exemplified. Then, by (M), any existent thing is greater than a being than which no greater can be conceived. But that is absurd. So the concept 'being than which no greater can be conceived' is exemplified – and hence there is an existent being than which no greater can be conceived.[2]

---

1 Talk of 'tokens' and 'equiformity' here is perhaps controversial. The point is that considerations about the denotation or reference of the conception are completely irrelevant to the question whether it counts as a conception of a being than which no greater can be conceived.

2 Makin himself rejects (M) in favor of a modalized version that refers to necessarily exemplified concepts. This change is irrelevant to the kind of criticism that I am about to make.

It is a delicate matter to say why this argument fails, even though it is quite clear that it is specious. A good place to start is with the consequent of principle (M), that is, the sentence '*F*s are greater than *G*s'. Under what circumstances are sentences of this form true? More particularly, what are the truth-conditions for sentences of this form when one or both of the predicates is unexemplified? Should an atheist or agnostic hold that it is false that any existent thing is greater than a being than which no greater can be conceived, simply on the grounds that there is no being than which no greater can be conceived – compare the claim that it is false that anyone is taller than Santa Claus? If so, then principle (M) should simply be rejected.

Suppose, instead, that an atheist or agnostic wishes to agree with the claim that any existent thing is greater than a being than which no greater can be conceived.[3] In this case, the atheist or agnostic could be supposing that the 'greater-than' relation depends upon the nonnuclear or noncharacterizing properties of the Meinongian objects that it relates; and she could further be supposing that the Meinongian object picked out by the expression 'being than which no greater can be conceived' does not possess the nonnuclear property of existence. Whether or not existence is a great-making property that outweighs all other properties taken *in toto*, the idea here is clear: The object denoted by the expression 'being than which no greater can be conceived' fails to be greater than existing objects because existing objects have nonnuclear properties that it fails to have. Understood in this way, principle (M) is correct – but no absurd consequences follow from its conjunction with the denial of the instantiation of the description 'being than which no greater can be conceived'.

Suppose, finally, that an atheist or agnostic wants to save a little more of the intuitions that motivate Makin's argument, without buying into a Meinongian ontology. Then she might say that the claim that any existent thing is greater than a being than which no greater can be conceived can be read in a way that sounds absurd, namely, that the properties attributed *via* the description of any existent thing are greater than the properties attributed *via* the description 'being than which no greater can be conceived'. But now we must be careful. What do we mean by 'the properties attributed *via* the description'? Suppose we grant that properties can be attributed implicitly, so that

3 In this paragraph, I make use of terminology that is explained in Chapter 5. Those unfamiliar with Meinongian theories might wish to come back to it after they have read Chapter 5.

'being than which no greater can be conceived' attributes the property of existence. Then it will certainly be true that the properties attributed *via* the description 'being than which no greater can be conceived' will be greater than the properties attributed *via* any other description – but it need not be true that there is anything to which those properties are attributed; that is, it need not be true that there is anything that possesses those properties. Indeed – tying this point to the distinction between the neutral and committing senses of 'conceive of' – we see here a need to attend to the expression 'intrinsically exemplified concept'. An atheist or agnostic can agree that 'being than which no greater can be conceived' is intrinsically exemplified in a neutral sense: The concept says of itself that it is exemplified; but she will deny that it is intrinsically exemplified in a committing sense: There is nothing that falls under the concept. So, this time, principle (M) is disambiguated: On the committing reading of 'concept of', even if the properties ascribed by the concept F are greater than those ascribed by the concept G, it needn't follow that Fs are greater than Gs, since there might be no Fs or Gs – that is, there might be nothing to which the properties are ascribed – and principle (M) will be false; while on the neutral reading of 'concept of', if the properties ascribed by the concept F are greater than those ascribed by the concept G – so that, in this neutral sense, Fs are greater than Gs, and principle (M) is true – nothing at all absurd follows from the claim that the description 'being than which no greater can be conceived' is uninstantiated.

I conclude that this version of the argument fares no better than the others discussed earlier.[4] Moreover, I suggest that it is quite clear that no conceptual ontological argument will be capable of convincing an agnostic. Aquinas and Hume were right: There is no argument of the form 'I conceive of X, so X exists' that establishes the existence of X for one who is initially agnostic about the existence of X.

---

4 There is one more move that a proponent of Makin's argument might make, namely, to suggest that there are some concepts of which it is true that the properties that they intrinsically attribute depend upon their relational referential properties. So, for example, it might be said that in order to be the concept 'being than which no greater can be conceived', the concept must be instantiated: The attributed properties and the referential properties cannot be separated in this instance. But, of course, this move just shifts the focus of the debate: What atheists and agnostics will now be concerned to deny or to doubt is that there is any such concept. Moreover, the question whether there is such a concept just reduces to the question whether there is a being than which no greater can be conceived. Cf. the subsequent discussion of experiential arguments.

Perhaps you might be inclined to object that there are areas in which it is possible to build *a priori* bridges between the conceptual and the real. For example, isn't it possible to show *a priori* that there is a prime number between 24 and 30? But, if there is a prime number between 24 and 30, then there are prime numbers, and hence numbers. So the existence of some things can be demonstrated *a priori.*

This is too quick. Suppose I am agnostic about the existence of numbers – that is, suppose I am in the grip of nominalistic scruples. I will agree that according to the principles of number theory, it is correct to say that there is a prime number between 24 and 30. However, I will not agree that the 'according to the principles of number theory' operator can be discharged. The quantification over numbers occurs within the scope of an appropriate operator; consequently, it is not ontologically committing. Given my nominalistic scruples, it seems most unlikely that there is an *a priori* argument that is available to me and that will lead me to the conclusion that there really are numbers. But it also seems doubtful to claim that my nominalistic scruples must be irrational.

The point here is perfectly general. What is denied by the person who denies that it is possible to build *a priori* bridges between the conceptual and the real is that there are *a priori* considerations that will lead anyone who is antecedently, and reasonably, agnostic about the existence of nonmental entities of a certain kind to the conclusion that there really are entities of that sort. There might be some sense to the claim that one who is antecedently convinced of the existence of nonmental entities of a certain kind can construct *a priori* arguments whose conclusion is that there really are entities of that kind, and that the person in question can reasonably regard as sound – but that is an entirely different question.

Chapter 4

Modal arguments

THERE are four kinds of modal arguments that I shall consider in this section. The first kind turns on the use that can be made of the 'actually' operator; the second kind turns on the use that can be made of the 'necessity' operator; the third kind turns on a weak version of the principle of sufficient reason; and the fourth kind turns on the properties of incomprehensible beings.

(1) MODAL ARGUMENTS INVOLVING ACTUALITY

A simple version of a modal ontological argument that involves the 'actually' operator is the following:

1. It is possible that it actually is the case that God exists. (Premise)
2. (Hence) God exists. (From 1)

There are modal logics in which this is a valid argument. In particular, if a "nonshifty" actually operator – that is, an actually operator that is such that even when it is embedded in the scope of other operators, it always refers back to the world of its utterance – is added to the modal logic S5, then the argument is valid.

However, if the actually operator is given a nonshifty reading, then there is no reason for an agnostic to assent to the premise. After all, on this reading, the possibility judgment in question just amounts to a judgment that God exists. Any reasonable agnostic will see equal merit in the following argument:

1. It is possible that it is actually the case that God does not exist. (Premise)
2. (Hence) God does not exist. (From 1)

Consequently, these arguments advance one no further if one is initially undecided about the question of God's existence.[1]

Of course, it is also possible to give the actually operator a "shifty" reading in these arguments. In this case, though, while the premises might then reasonably be thought to be true – depending upon the conception of God in question – the arguments are both patently invalid. For, in this case, the premises amount simply to the claims that it is possible that God exists and that it is possible that God does not exist.[2]

A closely related argument can be obtained by making use of world-indexed properties. In particular, consider the world-indexed properties *exists-in a* and *does-not-exist-in-a*, where *a* is a name for the actual world. Making use of the idiom of possible worlds discourse, we can construct the following argument:

1. There is a possible world in which God has the property *exists in a*. (Premise)
2. (Hence) God exists. (From 1)

Once again, this is a valid argument. But, again, it is not an argument that gives an agnostic the slightest reason to think that God exists. For, again, there is a parallel valid argument that leads to the conclusion that God does not exist:

1. There is a possible world in which God has the property *does not exist in a*. (Premise)
2. (Hence) God does not exist. (From 1)

A more complex modal argument that involves the actually operator is discussed by David Lewis (1970). This argument is derived from St. Anselm's argument by interpreting St. Anselm's talk of 'conceivability' in terms of talk about 'conceivable worlds'. The argument, for which there are four alternative formulations of the third premise, goes as follows:

---

1 Throughout this section, I rely upon Lewis's indexical analysis of actuality. This analysis is controversial. The principal objections to it may be found in Adams (1974) and van Inwagen (1980). I think that these objections are adequately met by Salmon (1987:73–90); consequently, I shall not pursue them here.
2 Perhaps there are further premises that can be added to the premise that it is possible that God exists from which it follows that God exists. We shall consider this possibility in the next section.

1. For any understandable being x, there is a world w such that x exists in w.

2. For any understandable being x, and for any worlds w and v, if x exists in w but x does not exist in v, then the greatness of x in w exceeds the greatness of x in v.

3a. There is an understandable being x, such that for no world w and being y does the greatness of y in w exceed the greatness of x in the actual world.

3b. There are an understandable being x and a world v, such that for no world w and being y does the greatness of y in w exceed the greatness of x in v.

3c. There is an understandable being x such that for no worlds v and w and being y does the greatness of y in w exceed the greatness of x in v.

3d. There is an understandable being x such that for no world w and being y does the greatness of y in w exceed the greatness of x in w.

4. The actual world is a world.

5. (Hence) There is a being x existing in the actual world such that for no world w and being y does the greatness of y in w exceed the greatness of x in the actual world.

Lewis notes that the argument is invalid with premise 3b or 3d, that the argument is valid with premise 3a or 3c, and that 3c implies 3a. So the crucial question is about the acceptability of the premises 1, 2, 3a, and 3c.

The status of premise 1 is curious. In his original paper, Lewis allows that conceivable worlds can be logically or metaphysically impossible. However, in a subsequent appendix to the paper, Lewis contends that this is a mistake: All worlds are logically possible worlds. But if we modify the argument by interpreting 'conceivable' to mean "logically possible," then it becomes less clear that it has anything much to do with St. Anselm's argument. On the other hand, premise 1 is then obviously true: For any logically possible being x, there is a logically possible world w, such that x exists in w.

Premise 2 is controversial. On the one hand, it is doubtful that St. Anselm would have accepted it. What St. Anselm seems to have held – making allowance for the translation of his argument into the idiom of logical possibility – is that it is true of the greatest possible being that *it* is greater in a world in which it exists than in a world in which it does not. This is quite compatible with the claim that it is true of other beings that they need be no greater in worlds in which they exist than in worlds in which they do not exist. Moreover, and on the other hand, it is not clear that we should not agree with St. Anselm. Consider a speck of mud *m* that exists in *w*, but does not exist in *v*. Does it seem right to say that *m* is greater in *w* than in *v*? I have no clear intuitions about this.

Premise 3c amounts to the claim that it is possible that there is a being that has maximal greatness in every world. Since this is a version of modal arguments involving necessity, I shall defer discussion of it to the next section. It is very plausible to claim that it can be perfectly reasonable for an agnostic to reject this premise.

The interesting premise is 3a. As Lewis notes, there are two different ways in which one might seek to defend it. First, one might seek to infer it from a more general claim. One candidate for such a claim is 3c – but we have deferred discussion of that claim to the next section. Another candidate is the following:

G: For any world *v*, there is an understandable being *x* such that for no world *w* and being *y* does the greatness of *y* in *w* exceed the greatness of *x* in *v*.

As Lewis notes, this claim is one that an agnostic will reasonably reject – for surely one could reasonably hold that there is variation in the maximum amount of greatness instantiated in different worlds. It certainly seems to me that one could reasonably hold that there are dismally mediocre possible worlds that contain nothing but dismally mediocre possible beings.

The other option is to defend 3a directly. Premise 3a claims that it is possible that there is a being whose greatness in the actual world exceeds (i) the greatness of any other being in any world and (ii) the greatness of itself in any other world. If we read the expression 'the actual world' in a nonshifty way, then it seems that an agnostic can reasonably reject this premise. After all, it is hard to see that there is any non-question-begging consideration that tells in favor of this premise, as well as against the claim that it is possible that there is no being whose greatness in the actual world exceeds (i) the greatness of any other being in any world and (ii) the greatness of itself in any other world.

Lewis (1970:184) considers the possibility that 'being actual' is a great-making property: "It may well seem plausible that the actual world, being special by its unique actuality, might also be special by

being a place of greatest greatness." But this is a very weak suggestion. If 'being actual' is a great-making property that outweighs all
other great-making properties – that is, if any actual object is thereby
greater than a merely possible object – then it will be true that if there
is a greatest actual object, it satisfies 3a. However, even if there is a
greatest actual object, this is nothing that an agnostic need reject. After
all, the greatest actual object could turn out to be, say, the physical
universe; and then the religious implications of the proof would be
nil – the point being that, on this reading, a merely possible God is
not as great as an actual gnat. On the other hand, if 'being actual' is
merely one among many great-making properties, then the agnostic
has been given no reason to believe that the greatest possible object is
actual.[3]

Lewis claims that it would be a mistake for a defender of the
ontological argument to appeal to the consideration that 'being actual'
is a great-making property, on the grounds that this overlooks the fact
that 'actually' is indexical. However, this seems doubtful. One can
hold the semantic theory that 'actually' is an indexical while also
holding the metaphysical view that 'being actual' – as those words are
used by us – picks out a great-making property. Of course, there may
be compelling reasons to reject modal actualism in favor of modal
realism. But that is surely an independent issue.

To sum up, the modal arguments involving 'actually' that have
been discussed in this section can be reasonably rejected by an agnostic. Moreover, it seems most unlikely that there is a modal argument
involving 'actually' that cannot be reasonably rejected by an agnostic.
For, in the end, the judgments that one makes about what is possibly
actual – in the nonshifty sense – are simply constrained by the judgments that one makes about what is the case. If I am reasonable, then
I will judge that it is possible that actually *p* iff I judge that *p*. Thus,
while other judgments about what is possible may be based on intuitive considerations, principles of recombination, principles of imagi-
nability, and so on, reasonable judgments of the form 'It is possible
that actually *p*' will be based on precisely the same considerations that
form the foundation of nonmodal judgments. And, of course, the
judgments that one makes about what is possibly actual in the shifty

---

3 Here, we recapitulate the arguments discussed at the beginning of this section. The
   defender of the argument will reasonably insist that it is possible that the greatest
   possible object is actual; and the opponent of the argument will reasonably insist
   that it is not possible that the greatest possible object is actual.

sense will simply amount to judgments about what is possible. In this sense, if I am reasonable, I will judge that it is possible that actually p iff I judge that it is possible that p.

(2) MODAL ARGUMENTS INVOLVING NECESSITY

The following is a simple version of a modal ontological argument that involves a 'necessity' operator:

1. It is possible that it is necessarily the case that God exists. (Premise)
2. (Hence) God exists. (From 1)

There are various propositional modal systems in which this is a valid argument. In particular, it is a valid argument in B and S5.

A very similar argument has been defended, at least after a fashion, by Alvin Plantinga. Say that an entity possesses *maximal excellence* iff it is omnipotent, omniscient, and morally perfect, and that an entity possesses *maximal greatness* iff it possesses maximal excellence in every possible world – that is, iff it is necessarily existent and necessarily maximally excellent. Then consider the following argument:

1. There is a possible world in which there is an entity that possesses maximal greatness. (Premise)
2. (Hence) There is an entity that possesses maximal greatness. (From 1)

Under suitable assumptions about the nature of the accessibility relations between possible worlds – namely, that such relations are those of the propositional modal systems discussed in connection with the preceding argument, for example, B and S5 – this too is a valid argument.

A natural first objection for an agnostic to make is that these arguments can be paralleled by equally plausible arguments that lead to contradictory conclusions. Thus, parallel to the first argument we have:

1. It is possible that it is necessarily the case that God does not exist. (Premise)
2. (Hence) God does not exist. (From 1)

Moreover, if we say that an entity possesses *no maximality* iff it exists in a world in which there is no maximally great being, then we can provide the following parallel to the second argument:

1. There is a possible world in which there is an entity that possesses no maximality. (Premise)
2. (Hence) There is no entity that possesses maximal greatness. (From 1)

Given the assumption that there is no reason for an agnostic to prefer the premises of the earlier arguments to those of the later arguments, it seems that an agnostic is perfectly justified in rejecting both. Of course, the agnostic will allow that either maximal greatness or no maximality is exemplified in all worlds – but he holds that the arguments provided give him no help in deciding which. Similarly, if he grants that either it is necessary that God exists or else it is necessary that God does not exist, the agnostic will allow that one of the relevant arguments has a true premise – but, again, he will hold that the arguments give him no help in deciding which. However, the agnostic need not grant that either it is necessary that God exists or else it is necessary that God does not exist. In particular, he may hold that whether this is so depends upon the conception of God that is operative. If logical or metaphysical necessity is taken to be a property of God, then, on this conception, either it is necessary that God exists or else it is necessary that God does not exist. But if it is held that God is neither logically nor metaphysically necessary, then, on that conception, it is not true that either it is necessary that God exists or else it is necessary that God does not exist.

It might occur to you to wonder whether it should be granted, as it standardly is, that the logic of logical and metaphysical possibility is S5. In particular, you might be persuaded by the argument of Salmon (1989) that, in fact, the correct logic for logical and metaphysical possibility is T. This is an interesting question, but I doubt that we need to investigate it here.[4] For suppose that it is true that the correct logic for logical or metaphysical possibility is T. We define the property of ancestral maximal excellence as follows: x has *ancestral maximal excellence* in w iff x has maximal excellence in every world that lies on

---

4 The issue has been much discussed in recent times. For an argument that S5 is the correct logic for logical and metaphysical possibility, see Plantinga (1974a). Quinn (1982) gives some reasons for thinking that Plantinga's case is unconvincing – and, as mentioned in the main text, Salmon (1989) provides some interesting arguments for the conclusion that Plantinga's contention is incorrect. Chandler (1993) provides a useful exploration of the use of weaker modal logics in the formulation and discussion of ontological arguments.

an accessibility chain that leads to or from w. We can then construct the following argument:

1. There is a world in which there is an entity that possesses ancestral maximal excellence.
2. (Hence) There is an entity that possesses ancestral maximal excellence.

By construction, this argument is truth preserving in every model for T – that is, it is a valid argument according to T. Of course, it might be hard to write down this argument using the standard modal operators. In particular, it is not easy to see how to formulate an attribution of the property of ancestral maximal excellence. But that is no objection.

I think that it should be quite clear that there is a valid ontological argument – involving a suitably cooked up modification of the property of maximal excellence – based on any propositional modal logic. All that is required is that one has some way of defining the property of possessing maximal excellence in all worlds and of stating that this property is instantiated in a world.[5]

Perhaps it will be objected that there is no reason to think that existence in all worlds – as opposed to existence in all accessible worlds – is a great-making property. But I don't share this intuition. It seems to me to be controversial to suppose that existence in all accessible worlds is a great-making property. But, if it is granted that existence in all accessible worlds is a great-making property, then it seems to me to be no more controversial to suppose that existence in all worlds is a great-making property.[6]

Is there anything further that can be said in defense of the claim that it is possible that it is necessary that God exists? There are a number of suggestions that have been made in the literature.

The most popular strategy is to equivocate – that is, to claim that it is possible that God is "necessary" is some sense other than logical or

---

5 Note that I talk here about 'worlds', not 'possible worlds'. I take it that a possible world is one that is accessible from the world of utterance. Moreover, I take it that Plantinga's argument was intended to be about possible worlds, and not about worlds in general.

6 What about the suggestion that there are impossible worlds? No problem. Logical or metaphysical possibility is certainly restricted to the possible worlds; so we needn't concern ourselves with worries about what, if anything, lies outside that realm.

metaphysical necessity. Thus, for example, Malcolm (1960) tries to defend the claim that it is possible that God is sempiternal. But, as many people pointed out, even if true, this claim is irrelevant to the argument. A similar point can be made for reinterpretations in terms of (i) eternal existence, (ii) immutable existence, (iii) uncaused existence, (iv) self-caused existence, (v) aseity, (vi) unconditional existence, (vii) indestructible existence, (viii) incorruptible existence, (ix) incorporeal existence, (x) simple existence, (xi) immaterial existence, (xii) nondispositional existence, (xiii) factually necessary existence, and (xiv) independent existence, insofar as these are taken not to entail logically necessary existence.

Carl Kordig (1981:207) tries a slightly different tack: "Define God as a most perfect being. What is most perfect is, in particular, deontically perfect. What is deontically perfect ought to exist. Thus, God ought to exist. . . . But what ought to exist can exist. Hence God can exist."

This argument can be paralleled to its discredit: "Define Rod as a most perfect island. What is most perfect is, in particular, deontically perfect. What is deontically perfect ought to exist. Thus, Rod ought to exist. . . . But what ought to exist can exist. Hence Rod can exist." Perhaps it will be objected that it is absurd to suppose that a most perfect island – even if there could be such a thing – is deontically perfect. Fair enough; but similar examples can be constructed involving entities to which the notion of deontic perfection does apply, for example, most perfect prime ministers, most perfect doctors.[7]

There is a more pressing objection. Suppose I grant that there ought to be a deontically perfect being. Suppose I also accept that 'ought' implies 'can'. Then what follows is that there is a possible world in which there is a deontically perfect being. Does it follow that there is

---

7 Kordig's argument is criticized by Grim (1982b) and Martin (1990). Note that the use of a definition as the first premise of the argument is not harmful in this case – i.e., the argument is untouched by my previous criticism of definitional arguments. Clearly, the definitional move could be delayed until after it has been established that a most perfect being exists.

   For more on the notion of deontic perfection, see, e.g., Purtill (1973). I take it that a deontically perfect being is such that (i) The being fails to have no property that it ought to have and (ii) the being has no property for which it is not the case that the being ought to have it. Perhaps (ii) is too strong, and all that is required is (iii) the being has no property that it ought not to have ((ii) entails (iii), but not vice versa). If existence and necessary existence are perfections, then nontheists should dispute the claim that there ought to be a perfect being that is deontically perfect.

such a being in the actual world? Not at all. Suppose I also grant that there is a possible world in which there is a deontically perfect being that is omnipotent, omniscient, and perfectly good. Does it now follow that there is such a being in the actual world? No, of course not. In order to get out the conclusion that such a being exists in the actual world, we need the further suppositions that the being in question is necessarily existent and that it possesses the previously mentioned properties necessarily. But no agnostic is going to say that there is a possible world in which there is a necessarily deontically perfect being that is necessarily omnipotent, necessarily omniscient, necessarily perfectly good, and necessarily existent.

So much for the defense of the claim that it is possible that it is necessary that God exists. It is hard to believe that there is a defense of this claim that will convince an agnostic. What of the opposing view, namely, that it is possible that it is necessary that God does not exist?

Here, I think that the answer depends upon the conception of God in question. If God is taken to be 'the greatest possible being', then it may be necessary that God does not exist.[8] If God is taken to be necessarily omnipotent, necessarily omniscient, and necessarily morally good, then it may be necessary that God does not exist.[9] But, for a less demanding conception of God, it may be clear that the only difficulty involves the notion of necessary existence. And, in that case, it seems that an agnostic can reasonably have no opinion about whether the existence of such a being is possible or not.

The modal intuitions of theists and atheists differ. Is there any independent reason to prefer those of one to those of the other? Michael Tooley (1981:426ff.) suggests that there is a reason to prefer those of the atheist, essentially on grounds of simplicity: "A natural line of thought is . . . that what sets of nonmodal sentences are true in some world cannot be dependent upon the truth values of modal sentences. . . . The only way of showing that there is no possible world in which [a nonmodal sentence] is true is by showing that it entails a

---

8 Perhaps there is an unending sequence of possible beings, each one greater than the one before. Or perhaps there are a number of possible beings that are equally great, and than which no other is greater. In either case, it will be necessarily true that there is no greatest possible being.

9 Perhaps at least one of the notions of omnipotence, omniscience, and perfect goodness is inconsistent, or necessarily unexemplified. Perhaps at least one of the notions of necessary omnipotence, necessary omniscience, and necessary perfect goodness is inconsistent, or necessarily unexemplified.

contradiction." Tooley then applies this line of reasoning to Plantinga's modal ontological argument:

The statement 'There is no maximally excellent being' is a non-modal sentence, so unless it can be shown to entail a contradiction, one is justified in concluding that there is a possible world in which it is true. And it will then follow that the property of maximal greatness is not capable of being exemplified.

Mathematical statements seem to pose a problem for Tooley's criterion. Consider the sentence 'Goldbach's conjecture is true'. This is a nonmodal sentence. Moreover, neither I nor anyone else can show that it entails a contradiction. So, by Tooley's criterion, I am justified in concluding that there is a world in which it is true. Similarly, the sentence 'Goldbach's conjecture is false' is a nonmodal sentence. Again, neither I nor anyone else can show that it entails a contradiction. So, by Tooley's criterion, I am justified in concluding that there is a world in which it is true. But, if mathematical statements are either necessarily true or else necessarily false, then it cannot be true both that there is a world in which Goldbach's conjecture is true and that there is a world in which Goldbach's conjecture is false.

Note that, following Tooley, I said that neither I nor anyone else *can* show that the sentence in question entails a contradiction. But what sort of modality is expressed by 'can'? Not logical or metaphysical possibility – for it seems likely that one of the sentences 'It is logically possible for me to show that Goldbach's conjecture is true' and 'It is logically possible for me to show that Goldbach's conjecture is false' is true. I suggest that, in fact, Tooley's use of a modal operator here is hyperbolic: All he means to say is that unless one thinks that a sentence *has been shown to*, or more generally *does*, entail a contradiction, one is justified in concluding that there is a possible world in which it is true.

Perhaps Tooley can reasonably reply to this criticism by exempting mathematical statements from the scope of his claim. After all, given a mathematical statement S, there is at least *prima facie* reason to suppose that either S is necessarily true and not-S is necessarily false, or else S is necessarily false, and not-S is necessarily true. But there are other statements that pose similar problems. Suppose that we agree with Kripke that there are (i) necessities of identity, (ii) necessities of origin, and (iii) necessities of constitution. Consider the claim that there is a world in which I originated from a sperm–ovum pair other than that from which I in fact originated. It seems implausible to suggest that it can be shown that this claim entails a contradiction – but that does not seem to show that it is implausible to say that the claim is metaphysically necessarily false. Perhaps there is some plausibility in the idea that noncontradiction is a criterion for narrowly logical possibility – but it is much less plausible that noncontradiction is a criterion for broadly logical or metaphysical possibility. Of course, Tooley might deny that there is any alethic modality other than narrowly logical possibility: But it is not clear that a theist could not reasonably dissent from this judgment.

Even if a theist were to concede that it is true that there is no alethic modality other than narrowly logical possibility, it seems that such a person could reasonably object to the notion that Tooley can reasonably exempt *only* mathematical statements from the scope of his claim. The reason for the exemption, according to Tooley (1981:427) is that, in this case, it is plainly wrong to hold that "what sets of sentences of modal order less than n are logically consistent must not be dependent upon the truth values of sentences of modal order equal to or greater than n." Given that Tooley must make *one* exception, why shouldn't a theist make *two*? In restricting the scope of the exemption to mathematical statements, Tooley would simply be begging the question against the theist.

Robert Adams (1988:26) has a different objection to the idea that the consistency and inconsistency of sets of purely nonmodal propositions should be viewed as the basic modal facts from which all other modal facts are derived:

I suspect that there are not enough purely non-modal propositions to do the jobs the argument requires them to do. Many, probably most of our ordinary (and our scientific) concepts have modal aspects. To say of an individual that it is a dog or an oak tree, that it is composed of water or of steel, that it has a positive electrical charge, that it is red or blue, or that it is understanding the conversation it is hearing, is to say a lot about what is causally (and hence logically) possible for that individual. If possible worlds are given by propositions containing such concepts as these, they are not given by purely nonmodal propositions.

This argument contains a logical error. Anything that is causally possible is logically possible. But it may not be true that to say much about what is causally possible for an individual is to say much about what is logically possible for an individual. If logical possibility far outruns causal possibility, then to say what is causally possible for an individual will be to say very little about what is logically possible for that individual. But there is considerable plausibility in the claim that logical possibility far outruns causal possibility.[10]

The argument also trades on an ambiguity in the notion of a purely nonmodal description. On the one hand, a description can be explicitly or implicitly purely nonmodal if it does not explicitly or implicitly involve modal expressions. Thus, for example, 'necessarily existent being' is explicitly modal; and, if 'God' is a descriptional name, equivalent to the rigidified description 'the actual necessarily existent creator of the world', then 'God' is implicitly modal. Of course, the notion of 'involvement' invoked here is in need of further explication; but perhaps we can get by on the preceding characterization. On the other hand, a description can be purely nonmodal if it does not have an extension that varies across possible worlds. Thus, for example, ordinary proper names – at least if Kripke is right that these are rigid designators – and mathematical expressions are purely nonmodal on this conception. Of course, there are no interesting scientific concepts that are purely nonmodal in this sense – and that suggests that this latter does not provide an interesting sense in which descriptions can be purely nonmodal.

Consider Adams's claim that 'dog' is not a purely nonmodal term. By this, he does not mean that it is not purely nonmodal in the first of the senses given in the preceding paragraph. Rather, what he means is that the term somehow carries information about what is causally, and logically, possible for objects that fall under it. I suggest that, in effect, this just amounts to the claim that the term is not purely nonmodal in the second of the senses given earlier. Given information about the way that the extension of a term varies across possible worlds, we can use causal laws to obtain information about the causal possibilities of objects that lie in the extension of the term. But the modal aspect belongs to the causal laws, not just to the variable extension of the term.

Other cases that Adams discusses are more difficult. Should we say that the term 'knows' is purely nonmodal, in the first of the senses that I have discriminated? Since it seems plausible to suggest that an analysis of this term will involve modal vocabulary – consider, for example, Nozick's account in terms of 'tracking' – it seems that good sense could be given to the contention that this term is not purely nonmodal. On the other hand, however, it might be doubted that the term has an analysis – and hence (?), it might be held that there is no

10 For a related criticism of Adams, see Bricker (1991:618n9).

genuine sense in which talk of knowledge involves a commitment to talk of possibility.

I conclude that there is nothing in Adams's argument to deter someone from holding the view that facts about the consistency and inconsistency of sets of purely nonmodal propositions *are* the basic modal facts from which all other modal facts are derived.[11] But, on the other hand, there is nothing but considerations of simplicity to prevent someone from holding that the view in question, while being close to the truth, admits of a few exceptions.

Tooley's atheist can provide a very simple theory about the nature of modal facts. This theory will include a principle of recombination that admits of no exceptions: If p and q are purely nonmodal, and 'p and q' is not contradictory, then it is possible that p and q. Adams's theist will have a slightly less simple theory about the nature of modal facts. In particular, the theory will include a more complex version of the principle of recombination: If p and q are purely nonmodal, and 'p and q and God exists' is not contradictory, then it is possible that p and q. There are numerous possibilities that the atheist recognizes but the theist does not – even though these possibilities are generated by the simplest version of the principle of recombination.

Does this extra complexity in the theist's account weigh against that account? Yes; but, of course, the theist will contend that the extra complexity is offset by gains elsewhere. And so – of course – the decision between the two different accounts of the nature of logical space must be settled by nonmodal considerations.

In sum, modal ontological arguments involving necessity do not give an agnostic the slightest reason to believe that God exists. In the end, the question whether such arguments are sound reduces to a question about the nature of logical space that, to the extent that it is taken to be genuinely open, can only be decided by nonmodal considerations.[12]

Of course, this leaves open the question whether there is some other value that modal ontological proofs involving necessity have for theists – and, by parity, that modal ontological disproofs involving necessity have for atheists. However, I shall defer discussion of this question to Chapter 12.

11 Here, 'consistency' and 'inconsistency' are to be construed in terms of contradiction – i.e., they are not themselves to be given a modal construal.

12 For further assertions about which modal intuitions should be preferred, see – among others – Forgie (1991), Morris (1985), Sennett (1991), and Strasser (1985).

(3) MODAL ARGUMENTS INVOLVING EXPLICABILITY

The paradigmatic example of a modal argument involving explicability is to be found in Ross (1969a,b). The formulation to be discussed here is that of Gale (1991):

1. It is impossible that anything prevent the existence of God. (Premise)
2. For every individual x, if it is a fact that x exists or it is a fact that x does not exist, it is possible that there is an explanation for the fact that x exists or the fact that x does not exist. (Premise)
3. God does not exist. (Assumption for *reductio*)
4. It is possible that there is an explanation of the fact that God does not exist. (From 2, 3)
5. It is not possible that there is an explanation of the fact that God does not exist. (From 1)
6. It is false that God does not exist (From 3, 5, 6 by *reductio*)

Gale claims that premise 1 is a conceptual truth about God and that 2 – a weak version of the principle of sufficient reason – is unexceptionable. He goes on to suggest that the major problem that confronts a proponent of the proof is the dubious inference of premise 5 from 1. However, I think that 1 and 2 are open to doubt, while the inference of 5 from 1 is probably acceptable. I shall consider these claims in turn.

The problem with premise 1 is that it contains an occurrence of the name 'God'. I have already noted – in the discussion of definitional arguments and conceptual arguments – that an argument that begins with a premise of this form is bound to be dialectically inefficacious. No agnostic or atheist will concede that God *is* such that nothing can prevent God's existence. Rather, they will hold that according to the relevant concept – or definition, or theory, or whatever – God is such that nothing can prevent God's existence. But then, the rest of the reasoning of the proof falls within the scope of the relevant 'according to' operator, and is thus deprived of dialectical force.

The problem with premise 2 is that it is not clear what it means to say that, for any existent x, it is possible that there is an explanation of the fact that x exists. Suppose that there is no explanation of the fact that the actual universe exists. Suppose also that there are other possible universes – perhaps even universes that are *extremely* similar to the actual universe – that are such that there is an explanation of their existence. Do these suppositions involve a case in which there is a possible explanation of the fact that the universe actually exists, even though there is actually no explanation of the fact that the universe exists? I don't think so. If the actual world has no explanation, then it is necessarily the case that the actual world has no explanation – that is, this is a world-indexed fact about the actual world. Of course, what is true is that it might have been the case that we lived in a world in which there is an explanation of the existence of that world. But that is not at all the same as the claim that it might have been the case that there is an explanation of the fact that the world in which we actually live exists.[13]

Gale (1991:204) claims that even waiving any problems that confront premises 1 and 2, the inference from 1 to 5 is dubious. He suggests that "it implicitly assumes that the only possible explanation for the fact that some individual does not exist is a causal one in terms of something that (causally) prevents the existence of this individual. But this is plainly not the case." However, this does not seem right. The proper construal of the claim that nothing could prevent the existence of God is that no state of affairs could obtain that is incompatible with the existence of God.[14] Given the correct construal of the notion that nothing could prevent the existence of God, it clearly follows that there is no possible explanation of the fact that God does not exist – for there can be no such thing as the fact that God does not exist. Note, in particular, that the state of affairs that God does not exist is incompatible with the existence of God – so it is ruled out by the correct construal of premise 1.[15]

13 One might also wonder whether there could be facts that are *essentially* inexplicable. Define *x* to be an object that exists in a world *w* only if the existence of *x* in *w* is inexplicable. Could there be such an object? I don't see why not. But, if so, then it would seem that it is not the case that the fact that *x* exists has an explanation in any world in which *x* exists – and hence that the fact that *x* exists does not even have a possible explanation in any world in which *x* exists.

14 In order to be totally unlimited and invulnerable to outside force, it is not sufficient that God be immune to the causal influence of other beings, contrary to the supposition made by Gale. Rather, God must, e.g., be such as to make it impossible that there are any morally unjustified evils.

15 Perhaps the claim that nothing could prevent the existence of God is better construed as the claim that no *suitably independent* state of affairs could be incompatible with the existence of God. Even so, it seems that Gale's objection would be incorrect, for why should this suitable independence be construed in causal terms?

Of course, this way of construing the argument means that it is really a disguised version of a much simpler argument, namely:

1. It is necessary that God exists. (Premise)
2. (Hence) God exists. (From 1)

This is a fine argument, except for dialectical purposes.

(4) MODAL ARGUMENTS INVOLVING INCOMPREHENSIBILITY

Joel Friedman (1979) defends a modal ontological argument that he calls "the mystic's ontological argument." He claims that this argument avoids the three major problems that confront traditional ontological arguments, namely, (i) the temptation to use 'existence' as a predicate, (ii) the temptation to misuse names and definite descriptions, and (iii) the temptation to commit modal fallacies. In short, the argument runs as follows:

1. Necessarily, something is incomprehensible. (Premise)
2. (Hence) Necessarily, there is a maximally incomprehensible being. (From 1)
3. By definition, God is the maximally incomprehensible being. (Definition, from 2)
4. (Hence) God necessarily exists. (From 2, 3)

In this form, the argument does seem to involve an error. There is nothing in premise 2 that guarantees that it is the same being that is maximally incomprehensible in each world – so the definition at line 3 can only be well formed if it is taken to mean: 'By definition, God is the *actual* maximally incomprehensible being'. But then, of course, it does not follow that God necessarily exists, that is, that God exists in all possible worlds; rather, all that follows is that it is necessarily true that God actually exists. So, in fact, Friedman's short argument does involve a misuse of definite descriptions that leads to a modal error.

Friedman also presents a more detailed, two-stage presentation of his argument, as follows. At the *first* stage, he presents an argument in a nonmodal language with first-order quantification, in which names and definite descriptions are supposed to be free of existence suppositions:[16]

16   I include Friedman's own annotation.

1. God is the maximally incomprehensible being. (Mystic's definition of God)
2. Something is incomprehensible. (Plausible premise)
3. There is exactly one whole having as parts all and only the incomprehensible things. (Instance of the principle of whole formation)
4. A whole is nonempty iff it has at least one part. (Definition)
5. There is exactly one nonempty whole having as parts all and only the incomprehensible things. (From 2, 3, 4)
6. If all the parts of a nonempty whole are incomprehensible, then that whole is also incomprehensible. (Plausible premise)
7. The nonempty whole having as parts all and only the incomprehensible things is itself incomprehensible. (From 5, 6)
8. A whole is maximally incomprehensible iff it is incomprehensible and everything that is incomprehensible is part of that whole.
9. There is a maximally incomprehensible being. (From 5, 7, 8)
10. There is at most one maximally incomprehensible being. (Plausible premise, justified by identity of indiscernibles)
11. There is exactly one maximally incomprehensible thing. (From 9, 10)
12. (Hence) God exists. (From 1, 11)

Then, at the *second* stage of the argument, it is observed that it is plausible to assert the necessitation of each of the premises in the argument – that is, the necessitations of 1, 2, 3, 4, 6, 8, and 10 – and it is then noted that the necessitation of the conclusion follows, by the uncontroversial rule of modal distribution. It should be clear that this more extended argument contains exactly the same error as the short argument; and, moreover, it should also be clear that Friedman's decision to give a two-stage presentation of his argument helps to obscure the fact that there is a problem in the justification of the necessitation of the definitional premise.

Suppose, however, that we focus just on the first stage of Friedman's argument – that is, on the first-order argument that purports to prove that God exists. As Friedman asserts, this argument does not face any of the "major problems" that he claims confront other ontological arguments. Moreover, there is no doubt that the argument is logically valid. So the only remaining questions concern (i) the truth of the premises and (ii) the intuitive acceptability of the definition of God.

One important class of questions concerns the notion of incomprehensibility. Friedman (1979:75) offers a definition: x is *incomprehensible* iff x is first-order indefinable and unperceivable, and x also has no examples or instances, or perhaps good analogies, that are either definable or perceivable. The restriction to first-order definability is included because of the consideration that "any given incomprehensible thing can always be comprehended in a higher-order way" – e.g., as the first-order incomprehensible thing I am now thinking about. It might be thought that this restriction indicates that Friedman has only defined *first-order incomprehensibility* – and that this reflection in turn suggests the further consideration that the mystic's God might be more properly thought of as a being that is n^{th}-order incomprehensible, for all n. On the other hand, this thought seems to be incoherent – for at what level is it supposed to be comprehended? – so perhaps we will do better to stick with Friedman's characterization.

Friedman (1979:74) claims that it is plausible to think that there is an incomprehensible being. Why? He offers a number of arguments, which turn on (i) Cantorian considerations about the cardinality of space-time points and the set-theoretic hierarchy, and (ii) Russellian and Tarskian considerations about the semantic paradoxes. Thus, for example, he claims that "given Cantor's proof of non-denumerably infinite sets, we cannot comprehend every set, since there are only a denumerably infinite number of names and definitions." However, this argument does not show that there are incomprehensible beings; rather, what it shows is that, necessarily, there are beings that are not comprehended. There is nothing in this argument – nor in any of the other arguments that Friedman gives – that shows that there are particular beings that *cannot* be comprehended. For all that Friedman's argument shows, it may be that, for any being, there is a language in which that being is first-order definable – even though, necessarily, there is no language in which all beings are first-order definable. So, while we should grant that there are beings that are not comprehended, we have not yet found any reason to grant that there are beings that are incomprehensible.

I think that one can reasonably be agnostic on the question whether there are incomprehensible beings. For example, one could reasonably think that for all that one knows, there may be epiphenomenal beings – that is, beings which have no effects on us. Such beings would clearly be incomprehensible in Friedman's sense. However, I suspect that one could also reasonably believe that there are no incomprehensible beings. Of course, this is just to emphasize a point that has come up many times before in connection with other ontological arguments, namely, that Friedman's ontological argument, when treated as a demonstration of the existence of a maximally incomprehensible being, is not dialectically effective.

Suppose that the preceding objection is correct. Could we nevertheless hold that Friedman's argument does establish the existence of a *maximal uncomprehended being* – namely, that being that has, as its parts, all of those beings that are not comprehended? There is an obvious question about relativity that arises at this point – for different beings are comprehended by different persons at different times. So, let us suppose that we fix a time, *t*. Can we say that Friedman's argument shows that, at *t*, there is a maximal uncomprehended being? Perhaps. Suppose that we think that mereology provides an ontological free lunch – that is, there is nothing ontologically controversial about constructing mereological sums. Then, given that we accept that there are uncomprehended beings, we shall suppose that there is a being that is the sum of all the uncomprehended beings – and hence we can allow that there is a sense in which there is a maximal uncomprehended being.[17]

Of course – even waiving any questions about mereology – there is an obvious comment to be made here, namely, that the religious significance of the watered-down version of Friedman's proof is plainly *nil*. There is no reason at all to think that the mereological sum of uncomprehended beings is an object that is worthy of worship. Moreover, it seems that it would be fatuous – if not incoherent – to suppose that it is the creator and sustainer of all things. One point worth noting is that for any instantiated predicate '*F*', there will be a being that is the mereological sum of all those things that instantiate the predicate '*F*' – that is, there will be a maximal *F* being – though, as I mentioned earlier, it may not be the case that this being itself instantiates the predicate '*F*'. So why pick 'uncomprehended' as the predicate that is used to define God: Why not opt instead for 'red', or 'happy', or 'weighs more than one kilogram'?

I conclude that Friedman's mystical ontological argument is no better than any other ontological arguments: For, on the only reading on which it might plausibly be thought, by atheists and agnostics, to be sound, it has a conclusion that is entirely devoid of religious significance.

---

17 In general, one cannot infer from the fact that a being is a sum of things that are *F*, that the being in question is *F*. However, let us suppose – as seems plausible – that a sum of uncomprehended being will be itself uncomprehended.

Chapter 5

Meinongian arguments

THERE is no easily stated version of the type of ontological argument that I call 'Meinongian'. What these arguments have in common is that they rely upon, or assume, a theory of objects that, in relevant respects, is similar to the theory of objects defended by Meinong. Hence, these arguments cannot be understood in isolation from the theory of objects – and so I begin with a sketch of the relevant features of that kind of theory.

The theory begins with the assumption that there are properties. This assumption is intended to be understood in a way that does not exclude the possibility of nominalism – that is, it leaves open the possibility that talk of properties ought to be reconstrued as talk of predicates. The theory also assumes that predicate expressions in natural language uniquely express properties – so that, for example, each of the following expresses a different property: '   is round', '   is round and square', '   is square and round', '   is taller than Dudley Moore', '   prefers the squalid life of a stockbroker to the noble life of a politician'.

Against this background, *objects* are specified by, or perhaps identified with, unordered collections of properties. Any distinct collection of properties specifies a distinct object. Thus, for example, the property '   is round and square' specifies a distinct object from the property '   is square and round'.[1]

The general class of objects is perhaps not very interesting. But, given certain plausible assumptions, there are subclasses of this gen-

---

1 No doubt, there are questions about the level at which syntactic differences become irrelevant. Perhaps '__ is not round and square' and '__ isn't round and square' express the same property; but perhaps they do not. We needn't settle this question for present purposes.

eral class that are more interesting. Let us suppose that there is a primitive relation of *compatibility* that is defined for any collection of two or more properties. Let us further suppose that there is a distinguished subclass of *simple* properties, from which complex properties are generated by – here unspecified – principles of construction. We do not suppose that all simple properties are compatible; for example, ' is round' and ' is square' will be incompatible simple properties *if* they are simple properties. Nor do we suppose that the relation of compatibility can be analyzed in terms of purely logical consistency – as the example just mentioned shows, we may need "meaning postulates" in order to make judgments of compatibility. Finally, we leave open the question whether unstructured predicates in natural language express simple properties; and we leave open the question whether there are complex predicates in natural language that also express simple properties.

The class of *complete* objects is specified to be the class of objects that is comprised of, or that is determined by, collections of compatible properties with which no further properties – that is, no properties that do not already belong to the collections in question – are compatible. We suppose that complete objects are identified by their simple properties – distinct complete objects must differ in their simple properties; complete objects that agree in their simple properties must be identified.

Given this much, we have the materials to formulate an ontological argument. We suppose that ' exists' expresses a simple property. Furthermore, we suppose that *real* objects – that is, the objects that populate the world in which we live – either correspond to, or else may be identified with, certain complete objects. In particular, we suppose that real objects correspond to, or perhaps are identical with, those complete objects that include the simple property of existence. Finally, we also suppose that *collections* of (real) objects correspond to certain incomplete objects, namely, those that consist of compatible properties all of which belong to the (real) objects in question. Thus, for example, corresponding to the object that consists of the single property of being red is the collection of all the (real) objects that are red. We then argue as follows:

1. The predicate ' is a being than which no greater can be conceived' picks out an object, the properties of which are all compatible. (Premise)
2. A complete object that falls under the predicate ' is a being

than which no greater can be conceived' will either possess the property of existence or it will not. (Premise)

3. No complete object that falls under the predicate '   is a being than which no greater can be conceived' fails to possess the property of existence. (Premise)

4. If there is a complete object that falls under the predicate '   is a being than which no greater can be conceived' that possesses the property of existence, then there is exactly one complete object that falls under the predicate '   is a being than which no greater can be conceived' that possesses the property of existence. (Premise)

5. (Hence) The unique object that falls under the predicate '   is a being than which no greater can be conceived' possesses the property of existence. (From 1, 2, 3, 4)

6. (Hence) There is a real object that falls under the predicate '   is a being than which no greater can be conceived'. (From 5)

Of the four premises in this argument, 1 and 4 could both be reasonably disputed. It is not clear that the predicate '   is a being than which no greater can be conceived' does pick out a compatible collection of simple properties. Nor is it clear that if the predicate '   is a being than which no greater can be conceived' does pick out at least one compatible collection of simple properties, then the predicate '   is a being than which no greater can be conceived' does not pick out compatible collections of simple properties that are mutually incompatible. So there is certainly room for an atheist or agnostic to reject the argument on these grounds.

The third premise requires further justification. The point is that, if *per impossible* an object that did not have the property of existence fell under the predicate '   is a being than which no greater can be conceived,' then there would be a greater object that fell under the predicate, namely, one that had exactly the same properties except for possessing existence instead of nonexistence. Here, we need not be assuming that existence is, in general, a great-making property. But what we must assume is that existence is a great-making property of a being than which no greater can be conceived. Again, this premise could be reasonably disputed by an atheist or agnostic.

There are further difficulties that face the argument. In particular, it seems that it can be paralleled to its discredit, for consider:

1. The predicate '   is a being than which no greater can be conceived, except that it has moral properties X' picks out an object, the properties of which are all compatible. (Premise)

2. A complete object that falls under the predicate '   is a being than which no greater can be conceived, except that it has moral properties X' will either possess the property of existence or it will not. (Premise)

3. No complete object that falls under the predicate '   is a being than which no greater can be conceived, except that it has moral properties X' fails to possess the property of existence. (Premise)

4. If there is a complete object that falls under the predicate '   is a being than which no greater can be conceived, except that it has moral properties X' that possesses the property of existence, then there is exactly one complete object that falls under the predicate '   is a being than which no greater can be conceived, except that it has moral properties X' that possesses the property of existence. (Premise)

5. (Hence) The unique object that falls under the predicate '   is a being than which no greater can be conceived, except that it has moral properties X' possesses the property of existence. (From 1, 2, 3, 4)

6. (Hence) There is a real object that falls under the predicate '   is a being than which no greater can be conceived, except that it has moral properties X'. (From 5)

It seems that, if the original argument is acceptable, then this form of argument can be used to establish the real existence of implausibly many, distinct, all-but-perfect beings. Perhaps it will be objected that the first premise is not plausible in this case. This seems unlikely. Why isn't the greatest power, intelligence, knowledge – at least of nonmoral matters – and so on compatible with any complete collection of moral characteristics?

Where, then, does the original argument go wrong? Consider, again, the inference from 5 to 6. How does it follow, from the claim that the unique object that falls under the predicate '   is a being than which no greater can be conceived' possesses the property of existence, that there is a real object that falls under the predicate '   is a being than which no greater can be conceived'? In outlining the theory of objects, we suggested that it is plausible to suppose that real objects correspond to, or perhaps are identical with, those complete objects that include the simple property of existence. However, we need to be careful how we interpret this suggestion.

On the one hand, this suggestion might merely be taken to draw a distinction between two different kinds of complete objects that include the simple property of existence. On the one hand, there are the objects of this kind that really exist; and, on the other hand, there are the objects of this kind that don't really exist. Of course, on this construal, the inference from 5 to 6 is simply invalid: For all the premises of the argument tell us, it may be the case that the unique object that falls under the predicate '   is a being than which no greater can be conceived' does not really exist.

On the other hand, this suggestion might be taken as a principle of plenitude: Every complete object that includes the simple property of existence is a real object. But, on its most natural interpretation, this suggestion is completely implausible: There are many complete objects that include the simple property of existence but that do not really exist – for example, all of the denizens of other possible worlds. On a less natural interpretation, in which the simple property of existence is understood as the simple property of real existence, this suggestion *sounds* much more plausible. However, even though it sounds plausible to say that every complete object that includes the simple property of real existence is a real object, there is not the slightest reason for an agnostic to accept this claim either. Earlier, in order to give the argument a run for its money, I was deliberately vague about whether we should suppose that real objects (i) merely correspond to those complete objects which include the simple property of existence or else (ii) are identical with those complete objects that include the simple property of existence. But the details of this supposition are important.

Suppose, first, that real objects merely correspond to those complete objects that include the property of existence. Then, as intimated earlier, there are two possibilities: (i) There is a one–one correspondence between real objects and complete objects that include the property of existence; and (ii) there are complete objects that include the property of existence that do not correspond to any real objects. Possibility (ii) is obviously fatal to the Meinongian ontological argument. So let us consider (i). If there is a one–one correspondence between real objects and complete objects that include the property of existence, then it follows that the replacement of the complement of the simple property of existence by the property of existence in a complete object will lead always to an incomplete object. That is, replacement of nonexistence with existence in any complete object – for example, in any merely possible object – must lead to an incomplete object.

Similarly, the addition of existence to an object that would be complete if nonexistence were added to it instead must also give rise to an incomplete object. But then, even if the properties determined by the predicate ' is a being than which no greater can be conceived' are compatible, it does not follow that the properties determined by the predicate ' is a being than which no greater can be conceived and that exists' are compatible. On this reading, the third premise has no support from the theory of objects – and hence an agnostic who accepts this version of the theory of objects can reasonably reject the conclusion of the argument.

Suppose, on the other hand, that real objects are identical to those complete objects that include the property of existence. Then we can make exactly the same objection as we made to (i) in the preceding paragraph. Unless one is antecedently convinced that there really is a being than which no greater can be conceived, and even if one grants that there is a completable object that corresponds to the predicate ' is a being than which none greater can be conceived', one need not concede that there is a complete object that corresponds to the predicate ' is a being than which none greater can be conceived, and that exists'.[2]

In sum, then, the Meinongian ontological argument discussed here suffers from the same problem as conceptual ontological arguments and modal ontological arguments involving 'actually'. On one reading, the argument is simply invalid; and, on another reading, the argument is valid but it has a premise that no agnostic or atheist has any reason to accept. That there is such a convergence is gratifying, though perhaps to be expected. After all, each of these kinds of argument is plausibly seen as a way of reading St. Anselm's ontological argument.

My assessment of Meinongian ontological arguments differs from that of Peter King (1984). He provides a careful formulation of a Meinongian version of St. Anselm's argument and suggests that its sole flaw lies in the debatable assumption that the predicate ' is a being than which no greater can be conceived' picks out a compatible collection of simple properties. However, I think that his assessment is mistaken.

The crux of his formal version of the argument runs as follows:[3]

2 A *completable* object is an incomplete object, all of whose properties are compatible.
3 I have renumbered the premises and made other consequent changes.

1. For any intentional object x that includes neither existence nor nonexistence, the intentional object x-as-existing is distinct from x. (Premise)
2. g is the greatest intentional object – that is, g is such that for all intentional objects x, if x and g are distinct, then g is greater than x. (Definition)
3. g does not exist in reality. (Assumption for *reduction*)
4. g-as-existing is greater than g. (Premise)
5. g is greater than g-as-existing. (From 2)
6. (Hence) g exists in reality. (From 3, 4, 5 by *reductio*)

The main problem with this argument is that the definition and the premises – that is, 1, 2, and 4 – contradict one another. From these definitions and premises, using classical logic, one can draw any conclusion one wishes. Hence, it is unsurprising that one can use them to "establish" that God exists.

Despite the flaw in this formalization, King (1984:154) presents an intuitive argument that is similar to the one that I developed earlier. I think that the principal flaw in that intuitive argument occurs when he says:

Note that we may speak of an item as both existing in reality and in the understanding when there is an intentional object which corresponds to some real item. This is a handy abbreviation. Moreover, we might be tempted to identify the two, as Anselm does: there is nothing inherently absurd in saying that real objects are also intentional objects.

As I argued earlier, it is vitally important for Meinongians to pay more attention to the nature of the relationship between general – intentional – objects and real objects.

Chapter 6

Experiential arguments

A SIMPLE version of an experiential ontological argument is the following:[1]

1. The word 'God' is not susceptible of an explicit definition but is a term whose meaning can only be had on the basis of religious experience. (Premise)
2. A body of experience adequate as a basis for an understanding of this term must also be adequate as an evidential basis for assent to the proposition that God exists. (Premise)
3. (Hence) A denial of God's existence is indicative of a failure to grasp the meaning of the word 'God'. (From 1, 2)

Rescher (1959a) notes that there seem to be words of which it is plausible to claim that their meaning can only be grasped on the basis of experience. In particular, this seems true of words that designate experiences or aspects of experience – words for perceptual contents (colors, odors), words for sensational contents (aches, pains), words for feelings (alacrity, lethargy), and words for emotions (anger, delight). But, given that there are some words of which it is true to say that their meaning can only be grasped on the basis of experience, why should it be thought unreasonable to hold that the meaning of the word 'God' can only be had on the basis of religious experience?

There are a number of observations that need to be made.

As things stand, we don't really have here an *a priori* argument for the existence of God. At the very least, we need to add the further premise that there is at least one person who grasps the meaning of the word 'God', in order to reach the conclusion that God exists. In the light of this observation, we can reconstruct the core of the argument as follows:

---

1 From Nicholas Rescher (1960:144).

1. The word 'God' has a meaning that is revealed in religious experience. (Premise)
2. The word 'God' has a meaning only if God exists. (Premise)
3. (Hence) God exists. (From 1, 2)

It can still reasonably be objected that 1 is not a premise that anyone could claim to know *a priori*. Rescher seems to claim that since experience of God is necessary for the acquisition of the concept of God, an appeal to *that* experience in an argument for the existence of God does not render the argument *a posteriori*. But this is confused. We can grant that a claim can be known *a priori* only if it can be known through reflection on its constituent concepts, while allowing that experience may be required to obtain those concepts. But we should not grant that a claim can be known *a priori* if it can be known through reflection on both (i) its constituent concepts and (ii) whatever was required for the acquisition of those concepts. I do not know *a priori* that there are red things, even if it is true that I could only have grasped the meaning of the word 'red' on the basis of exposure to red things – for I do not know *a priori* that the word 'red' has a meaning. If experience plays a crucial role in the *justification* of a knowledge claim, not merely in the *acquisition* of the concepts required for the formulation of the claim, then that claim is not *a priori*.

In our assessment of our reformulation of the argument, we need to be careful in our use of the word 'meaning'. In one sense, it means 'semantic content'. In another sense, it means something like '(experienced) significance': 'The birth of my son was an event of great meaning for me'. No doubt, there are further meanings of 'meaning' – but we shan't need to consider them here.[2]

Suppose that we understand the use of the word 'meaning' in the argument to mean 'semantic content'. Moreover, let us suppose that the semantic contents of predicates are properties. Then there is some plausibility to the claim that, for example, the semantic content of the word 'red' – that is, the property of being red – can only be grasped by creatures like us on the basis of experiences that involve that property – that is, experiences in which there are presentations of the property of being red.[3] But there seems to be little plausibility in the corresponding claim about the word 'God'. Suppose we grant that the

---

2 In one further sense, it means 'content', where this includes nonsemantic propositional content due to pragmatic factors.
3 This claim is controversial; however, for present purposes, we do not need to decide whether it is true.

word 'God' has an existent object – God – as its semantic content. It is hard to see how one could hope to defend the claim that one can only grasp this content if one has experiences that directly involve that object. After all, one can grasp the content of other proper names in ways that do not require one to have experiences that directly involve their contents – for example, by participating in conversations in which others use those names to refer to the objects in question. Why should we suppose that the word 'God' is special in this regard?

'Object-involving' and 'externalist' accounts of content have recently enjoyed some popularity. On these accounts, the contents of sentences and thoughts that involve objects *essentially* involve those objects. Suppose, for example, that I have the thought that George Bush is untrustworthy. On a not implausible, but also not uncontroversial, account of the nature of content, the content of this thought involves a particular individual, the person George Bush. But, if that person had not existed, I would not have been able to have a thought with this content – that is, I would not have been able to have the thought that George Bush is untrustworthy. Of course, the words 'George Bush is untrustworthy' could have appeared before my mind – and in circumstances in which I took it that 'George Bush' referred to an existent person – but that would not have been a case in which I had the same thought that I actually have when I think that George Bush is untrustworthy.

Suppose that we apply this kind of analysis to the claim that God exists. A theist – that is, someone who holds that God exists – will maintain that the content of the claim that God exists involves a particular individual, the entity God. Moreover, the theist will claim that thoughts about God would be unavailable if God did not exist. But none of this will furnish materials for an argument for God's existence that an agnostic or atheist ought to find convincing – for, of course, what an agnostic doubts, and what an atheist disputes, is that the content of the claim that God exists involves a particular individual. Object-involving and externalist accounts of content have at least *prima facie* problems in accounting for empty singular terms. But, to be even remotely plausible, any such theory will agree that the contents of some sentences involving ostensibly directly referential singular terms do not involve actually existing individuals – for example, the sentence 'Santa Claus has a white beard' does not have, as part of its content, an actually existing individual who lives at the North Pole. An atheist can maintain, and an agnostic can be uncertain whether to agree, that 'God' is like 'Santa Claus'.

94

In sum, if 'meaning' is understood as 'semantic content' in the reconstructed version of Rescher's argument, then there may be reason to say that premise 2 is true – since there are theories of semantic content according to which ostensibly directly referential singular terms have semantic content only if they uniquely refer to existing objects – but there will not be the slightest reason for an agnostic or atheist to grant that 1 is true. No doubt some religious experience *purports* to be of an existing individual – but what reason is there to suppose that it actually *is* of such an individual?

What if 'meaning' is understood as 'experienced significance'? Then, premise 1 seems more plausible: Religion, including discourse about God, certainly seems to have an experienced significance for those who subscribe to it. But no atheist or agnostic will grant that the word 'God' only has an experienced significance if God exists – that is, no agnostic or atheist will grant 2. Moreover, it is not clear that a theist should concede it either. For it certainly seems that there actually are significant experiencings of incompatible deities – but there cannot actually be incompatible deities.[4]

It might be felt that the preceding discussion does not do justice to the position of the theist. What the theist contends is that, somehow, the atheist or agnostic does not properly understand the claims that she fails to accept. Surely there *is* something correct in this. From the standpoint of the theist – at least when that standpoint is narrowly construed – the claim that God does not exist *can* appear to betray a failure of understanding. Perhaps there is a useful comparison to be drawn with the following case: You are standing in the middle of a field, looking at a tree. You are not drugged, dreaming, or demented. You are as justifiably confident as you ever can be that epistemic conditions are normal. You say, 'What a lovely tree!' Your companion – who is also not drugged, dreaming, and so forth – says, 'What tree? There is no tree there'. Won't your natural response, if you take this utterance seriously, be that – somehow – your companion does not really understand what she is saying?

But, of course, there is at least one other possibility: Perhaps you do not understand what your companion is saying. Suppose it turns out that she has good reason to believe that the object at which you are looking is a holographic image, or that she has good reason to

4 Some theists – e.g., John Hick – have tried to defend the view that there is no incompatibility in the claims of rival religions. I find this very implausible, but I do not propose to take up the issue here.

believe that the object at which you are looking is made from plastic, and so forth. From a narrow perspective, which takes a very large number of one's own presuppositions for granted, the claims of others will often seem to betray a failure of understanding. But, from a broader perspective, in which less of one's own presuppositions are assumed, what previously appeared as a failure of understanding now appears as a straightforward disagreement about the facts.

This distinction – between narrower and broader perspectives – casts light on experiential ontological arguments. Proponents of these arguments correctly record how things appear from their own perspective, suitably narrowly construed. But they do not correctly record how things appear from a wider perspective – and yet it is this wider perspective that must be considered when one assesses the dialectical or dialogical strength of those arguments.[5]

5   It should be noted that Rescher himself is well aware of the dialectical inefficacy of his argument. Discussion of the question whether there is any other use that his argument could have is taken up in Chapter 12.

Chapter 7

"Hegelian" arguments

I AM NOT confident that what I have to say in this section is an accurate representation of the thought of Hegel, or of any subsequent Hegelians. However, what I provide is a characterization of certain kinds of *a priori* arguments for the existence of God that might perhaps be arrived at on the basis of a reading of some of the work of, say, R. G. Collingwood or E. E. Harris. There are three kinds of arguments: (i) an argument that, albeit tendentiously, can be traced back to Kant's *Critique of Pure Reason*; (ii) an argument that can be traced back to some ideas in Plato; and (iii) an argument that can be traced back to some ideas in Husserl and other continental phenomenologists.

(1) THE NEO-KANTIAN ARGUMENT

In this section, I discuss an argument that can be traced back to Kant. This argument is a kind of transcendental deduction of the existence of God. In presenting this argument, I draw on Harris (1972)(1977), though I doubt that he would approve of the use that I have made of his work.

In *The Critique of Pure Reason*, Kant provides the materials for an *a priori* proof of the necessity of belief in the existence of God. Very roughly, this argument goes as follows:

1. Perception of objects is possible only as a result of an *a priori* synthesis under the categories and the pure forms of intuition. (Premise)
2. An *a priori* synthesis under the categories and the pure forms of intuition is possible only if reason utilizes an idea of the sum of all possibilities: the Ideal of Pure Reason. (Premise)
3. Perception of objects is possible. (Premise)

4. (Hence) Reason utilizes an idea of the sum of all possibilities: the Ideal of Pure Reason.

Kant himself did not think that this demonstration of the fact that Reason uses the concept of God – the Ideal of Pure Reason – amounted to a demonstration of the existence of God. In his view, it would be wrong for us to make an inference from the necessity of our employment of a certain concept to the existence of an object that falls under that concept. Even though it is true that there can be no coherent use of the understanding and no adequate criterion of empirical truth unless one presupposes the systematic unity of nature as guaranteed by the Ideal of Pure Reason, nonetheless it would be a baseless hypostatization to conclude that there is an object that conforms to the Ideal of Pure Reason.

Drawing upon resources from recent philosophical discussions, we might try to defend a distant relative of the Kantian point as follows:[1] The 'presupposition' of the systematic unity of nature is merely an epistemological preference for theories that are simple, coherent, fruitful, explanatorily powerful, and so on. This presupposition, though unavoidable – and, indeed, constitutive of rational thought – is strictly heuristic; that is, it is not underwritten by any metaphysical assumptions that guarantee the systematic unity of nature. Moreover, the 'adequate criterion of empirical truth' to which this view gives rise is a deflationary account of truth: Those claims that one takes to belong to the simplest, most coherent, most fruitful, most explanatorily powerful theory are precisely those claims that one takes to be true.

However, this defense of the Kantian point would not really be available to Kant. The problem is that Kant claims that the presupposition involves the Ideal of Pure Reason – that is, the concept of God. But if one accepts that the presupposition of the systematic unity of nature is merely an epistemological preference for theories of a certain kind, then one needs some further account of the connection between this epistemology and ontology. Moreover, there seems to be only one plausible candidate: The ontology that one accepts is identified with

---

1 Since Kant himself thought of the Ideal of Pure Reason as a unifying principle in a quite different sense, I do not pretend that this defense bears any close connection to Kant's thought. My reason for proceeding in this way is that Kant's own conception of the Ideal of Pure Reason – namely, as an object that possesses all positive properties – is either (i) clearly incoherent, in case contrary properties can be positive, or (ii) only dubiously well defined, in case some other understanding of the notion of positive properties is required.

the ontological commitments of the theory that one accepts. But, if Kant is right that our theory commits us to the Ideal of Pure Reason then – on this picture – there can be no subsequent disavowal of that commitment: We are committed to the claim that God exists.[2]

The 'Hegelian' response to Kant picks up on this point. It agrees with Kant that we have an epistemological commitment to the Ideal of Pure Reason – the *a priori* precondition of all empirical knowledge – but correctly rejects the subsequent disavowal of the ontological commitment that this epistemological commitment requires. Now, of course, this is a highly tendentious reconstrual of Hegel's rejection of subjective idealism – so tendentious, indeed, that I am prepared to make no claim for its correctness when considered *as* an interpretation. In particular, the anachronistic projection of a pragmatic perspective is surely a distortion. However, it yields one of the few interpretations of Hegelian treatments of the ontological argument that I find intelligible.

There is an obvious response to the argument just given. It is one thing to prefer theories that are simple, coherent, fruitful, explanatorily powerful, and so on; it is quite another to adopt a theory that postulates the existence of the Ideal of Pure Reason in order to *account for* the systematic unity of nature. Of course, a preferred theory will provide some account of the systematic unity of nature – that is, it won't merely say that according to any theory that one can reasonably adopt, it will turn out that nature is systematically unified. But the account given needn't be one that postulates the existence of the Ideal of Pure Reason; instead, it could be just the observation that nature is governed by such-and-such laws, which happen to be simple and small in number.

In sum, then, the Kantian argument – and its Hegelian descend-

---

2 Kant's actual view seems vulnerable to a related objection that arises from G. E. Moore's observation that claims of the form 'not p, but I believe that p' are paradoxical. If I hold that I am obliged to believe that p, then – on pain of falling into a related Moorean paradox – I am committed to the claim that p. If I am obliged to presuppose, i.e., believe in, the existence of the Ideal of Pure Reason in order to believe that I perceive objects, then I am committed to the claim that the Ideal of Pure Reason exists *if* I do believe that I perceive objects. On the other hand, if Kant supposes that one can be an instrumentalist about the Ideal of Pure Reason – i.e., one can treat it, say, as a useful fictional device that facilitates *a priori* synthesis – then it is quite unclear how one could hope to defend the claim that this is the only possible such instrument; and it is also unclear whether one could then consistently believe that the result of that *a priori* synthesis is perception of objects.

ents – rely upon a conflation of two distinct ideas under the description 'the Ideal of Pure Reason'. According to the first of these ideas, a preference for simple, coherent, fruitful, explanatorily powerful theories is constitutive of rationality. Using this idea, premise 2 of the argument is plausible – at least leaving aside the commitment to the Kantian categories and forms of intuition – but the conclusion of the argument is too weak to be of an interest to a theist. According to the second of these ideas, a belief in the existence of a being that ensures the systematic unity of nature is constitutive of rationality. Using this idea, the conclusion of the argument is certainly of theological interest – but the problem is that an agnostic or atheist will reasonably reject premise 2.

It is perhaps also worth noting that there is a tempting *ad hominem* response to Kant's rejection of the argument outlined earlier. In *The Critique of Practical Reason*, Kant explicitly endorses a corresponding "proof" of the existence of God as a postulate of pure practical reason:

1. It ought to be the case that the best possible state of affairs – in which moral dessert and happiness are in harmony with one another – actually obtains. (Premise)
2. It is possible for the best possible state of affairs to actually obtain. (From 1, since 'ought' implies 'can')
3. It is not within our power to actually bring about the best possible state of affairs. (Premise)
4. (Hence) There must be a rational and moral being that has the power to bring moral desert and happiness into harmony with one another.

There are various difficulties that this argument faces, but that I do not wish to take up here. The one point I wish to make is that granted the assumption that Kant takes premise 1 to be a 'postulate of practical reason' – that is, something that we must believe if we are to be able to act with practical reason – it follows that Kant holds that the conclusion is a 'theorem of practical reason'. But then the conclusion of this argument seems to be on all fours – epistemologically speaking – with the conclusion of the previous argument. If we can use the Idea of Pure Reason while at the same time disavowing any commitment to the existence of an object that corresponds to that idea, why shouldn't we use the idea of the possibility of the *summum bonum* while at the same time disavowing any commitment to the possibility of its existence? No doubt, it will be objected that it is incoherent to suppose that one could act on a use of the idea of the possibility of the *summum bonum* that disavows commitment to the possibility of its existence. But, of course, if that is correct, exactly the same point can be made about the supposition that one could adopt a theory that uses the Idea of Pure Reason while at the same time disavowing commitment to its existence.

(2) THE NEO-PLATONIC ARGUMENT

In this section, I discuss an idea that some commentators allege can be traced back to Plato, or to Greek neo-Platonists – for example, Plotinus – or to subsequent neo-Platonists – for example, St Augustine. This idea seems to me to be substantially similar to one of the leading ideas in Hegel's justification of "the ontological argument" – hence its inclusion in the present chapter.

Beckaert (1967:114, 115, 112) defends a neo-Platonic interpretation of "the ontological argument" in the following words:

We recognise here the Platonic procedure which, moving in the "intelligible order," means to remain in touch with the objective when it is raised to the absolute – which is the mind's proper orientation. The In-Itself, which is induced or rather (according to Plotinus) perceived in its radiance, is also the By-itself, since it exists neither through an efficient cause, nor through a material cause, nor through an instrumental cause, nor again, since it is not derived *ex nihilo* through an efficient cause or through itself.

We here reach the conclusion of the Augustinian method of "degrees," or of the Plotinian perception of Being, where there is imposed on the one hand the necessity of the absolute Source, and on the other hand the disclosure that the intuition of this absolute would be impossible if it were not objective.

The idea of God (which is in fact imposed) is in itself absurd without an internal necessity of existence; the intuition of God (which is in fact given) would be impossible (as an act of thought) if it were not objective; and God is "unthinkable" in abstraction from (and *a fortiori*, with the negation of) his existence.

Although the meaning of these paragraphs is hardly clear, I think that Beckaert's position can be reasonably described as follows: The neo-Platonic interpretation of "the ontological argument" reduces the argument to two intuitions, namely, (i) the intuition that there must be an ontological ground – an Absolute Source, God; and (ii) the intuition that the source of the intuition mentioned in (i) must be the ontological ground – the Absolute Source, God. All that the proponent of "the ontological argument" aims to do is to draw attention to these two intuitions – for, clearly, anyone who shares these intuitions – and, indeed, anyone who shares merely the first of these intuitions – will agree that it must be the case that there is an ontological ground – an Absolute Source, God. Of course, a proponent of "the ontological argument" may protest that it is unfair to suggest that the argument reduces to 'mere intuitions' – that is, he may prefer to claim that the argument embodies "profound insights" or "elemental intuitions" or whatever; but he will agree that a proper grasp of "the ontological argument" requires an acceptance of the view that there *must be* an ontological ground, on which all other existence depends.

The effect of this interpretation of "the ontological argument" is to undermine its status as an *argument*. It is common knowledge that what the defender of the argument believes is that there is an ontological ground – and, moreover, that the defender of the argument believes that he has direct and immediate knowledge that there is such a ground. However, a genuine *debate* about the content of those beliefs – that is, a debate about the alleged existence of an ontological ground – requires a framework in which the existence of the ontological ground is not taken for granted, that is, a framework in which the claim that there is an ontological ground can be "suspended." If the defender of "the ontological argument" insists that no such framework can be established – that is, it is unintelligible to suppose that there could be a 'suspension' of the claim that there is an ontological ground – then there is no possibility of debate, or argument, or proof. And, in that case, the dialectic simply reaches an *impasse*. Perhaps the defender of "the ontological argument" might suppose that the fact that the dialectic reaches an *impasse* shows that his position is unassailable; however, the cost of that unassailability is that the views of otherwise ostensibly reasonable persons are rendered absolutely unintelligible. Moreover, the production of "the ontological argument" seems to be an evidently profitless performance, for it is absurd to suppose that reiteration – or stating one's position more vehemently – can somehow overcome the *impasse*.

There is a genuine philosophical problem that arises at this point. It would not be fair simply to characterize the position of the defender of "the ontological argument" as one in which he gratuitously claims, 'I don't understand what you are saying' whenever someone denies that there is an ontological ground. For his position is (i) that it is a necessary truth that there is an ontological ground and (ii) that he knows *a priori* that there is an ontological ground. Consequently, it seems that he must hold (iii) that no matter what theory *T* is held by his opponents, *T* entails that there is an ontological ground and (iv) that no matter what theory *T* is held by his opponents, there are *a priori* grounds on which they can recognize that there is an ontological ground. But, in that case, how can he make sense of the position of his opponents except by supposing that some intellectual – or perhaps moral – failing prevents their recognition of the necessary *a priori* status of the claim that there is an ontological ground?

Perhaps as follows. If our theist supposes that there is absolutely *no* chance that his position might be wrong, then it might be that it is impossible for him to make any sense of the idea that there can be reasoned acceptance of competing positions. After all, he supposes that there is not the slightest room for doubt that he knows *a priori* that there is an ontological ground – and hence, surely, anyone else who was not intellectually or morally deficient would know this too. However, if our theist recognizes that his beliefs are fallible, then presumably he will be able to acknowledge the possibility that someone else might be right on the question of the existence of an ontological ground even though, given his present beliefs, he cannot form any positive conception of the content of alternative views. So it seems that a defender of "the ontological argument" needn't take the strong view that the position of his opponents is unintelligible; he might settle for the weaker view that he is unable to understand what they are about.

However, if a defender of "the ontological argument" takes the weaker view that he is unable to understand the position of opponents of the argument, then any dialectical point in his insisting on the argument is surely lost. The argument might provide an effective diagnosis of why it is that he is unable to understand his opponents; but it is hard to see how he could suppose that the argument would provide his opponents with some reason to agree with him.[3] So I conclude that a reasonable proponent of "the ontological argument" will agree that, in the end, his 'argument' is mere exposition: The content of his position is given in the content of the argument; but

---

3 Note that there seems to be no difficulty in the supposition that her opponents understand her position perfectly well. Of course, they don't agree with her – but agreement is clearly not a necessary condition for understanding.

whether there is anything in that content that *ought* to persuade others with whom he initially disagrees is not something on which he is competent to judge.

The considerations that have arisen in our discussion of Beckaert's views are relevant to other defenses of "the ontological argument." Compare Hegel:[4]

Being in its immediacy is contingent; we have seen that its truth is necessity. In addition, the concept necessarily includes being. Being is simple relation to self, the absence of mediation. The concept, if we consider it, is that in which all distinction has been absorbed, or in which all categorical determinations are present only in an ideal way. This ideality is sublated mediation, sublated differentiatedness, perfect clarity, pure transparency and being-present-to-self. The freedom of the concept is itself absolute self-relatedness, the identity that is also immediacy, unity devoid of mediation. Thus the concept contains being implicitly; it consists precisely in the sublating of its own one-sidedness. *When we believe that we have separated being from the concept, this is only our opinion.* When Kant says that reality cannot be "plucked out" of the concept, then the concept is there being grasped as finite. But the finite is what sublates itself, and when we were supposed to be treating the concept as separate from being, what we had was the self-relatedness that is implicit in being itself.

However, the concept does not only have being within itself implicitly – it is not merely that we have this insight but that the concept is also being on its own account. It sublates its subjectivity itself and objectifies itself. Human beings realise their purposes, i.e. what was at first only ideal is stripped of its one-sidedness and thereby made into a subsisting being. The concept is always this positing of being as identical with itself. In intuiting, feeling, etc. we are confronted with external objects; but we take them up within us, so that they become ideal in us. What the concept does is to sublate its differentiation. *When we look closely at the nature of the concept, we see that its identity with being is no longer a presupposition but the result.*

What Hegel asserts, in this passage, is that any denial of the claim that God exists is the expression of a mere mistaken opinion. However, it would be absurd to suppose that there is anything in this passage that counts as an *argument* calculated to persuade those who deny that God exists that they are wrong. Rather, Hegel takes for granted his own theistic theory of the world, and his further contention that this theory is both necessary and known *a priori*, and then merely ex-

4 Hegel (1985/1831:355), my italics.

pounds the theory. Of course, such exposition might be an aid to clarification or understanding – but it seems clear that it cannot be hoped to play a justificatory or dialectical role.[5]

(3) HAIGHT'S ARGUMENT

In this section, I examine another kind of argument that appeals to considerations about presuppositions, due to David Haight (1981:184). This argument is as follows:[6]

Using the analogy of a movie screen brings into focus a way of symbolising the ontological argument in phenomenological terms. God would be the movie projector operator who sets up the screen and who thereby is behind both the transcendental Ego and the screen out of which thought objects are constituted by the Ego. This makes God the Ground of the unity between thinking and the thought-about, noesis and the noema, that which is beyond the division between concept and object of concept, because in God concept and "object" are the same, which is what proponents of the ontological argument have always argued. If so, then every statement and hence every thought presuppose the background of God, making every statement not only ontological, but implicitly theological, therefore accounting for Anselm's contention that the atheist's denial of God is self-contradictory.

The point on which I wish to focus is Haight's contention that given the claim that God is the Ground of the unity between thinking and that which is thought about, "every statement and hence every thought presuppose the background of God."

The analogy of the movie screen suggests the following construal of this claim: If God did not exist, then there would be no statements and no thoughts; hence, every statement or thought is about God. But this is absurd. For, by parity, one could argue as follows: If there were no oxygen, then there would be no statements and no thoughts; hence, every statement or thought is about oxygen. But the conclusion of this argument is one that even Haight should recognize to be evidently absurd. That something is a necessary condition for the existence of

---

5   No doubt, some readers will think that I have been most unfair to Hegel et al. in this
    section. Such readers will, I hope, regard these remarks as a challenge, namely, to
    produce a clear and concise statement of their favorite ontological argument, com-
    plete with readily scrutinizable premises. If there is an ontological *argument* in
    Hegel's work, I have been unable to find it.
6   I have rewritten the first sentence, but without altering Haight's meaning.

statements or thoughts does not entail that that thing is part of the content of those statements or thoughts.

Perhaps, though, the analogy of the movie screen should be ignored. Instead, perhaps, Haight should be taken to be mounting an argument along the following lines: It is a necessary truth that God exists; consequently, every statement or thought entails that God exists; hence, it is part of the content of every statement or thought that God exists. Again, this seems absurd. For, by parity, one could argue as follows: It is a necessary truth that arithmetic is undecidable; consequently, every statement or thought entails that arithmetic is undecidable; hence, it is part of the content of every statement or thought that arithmetic is undecidable. But the conclusion of this argument is one that most people would take to be absurd.[7]

Perhaps the claim about the *content* of statements and thoughts should also be ignored. Instead, perhaps, Haight's claim should be taken to involve the propositional commitments of theorists. Given that it is a necessary truth that God exists, it follows that every theorist is implicitly committed to the claim that God exists, since any set of propositions entails every necessary proposition. Again, this seems wrong. First, it will follow from this line of thought that every inconsistent theorist – and that probably includes all of us – is committed to every claim; and, second, it will follow that even consistent theorists are implicitly committed to claims that they do not understand. Given a conception of propositions on which everyone is committed to the necessary proposition, it is plain that attention should be turned to *sentential* commitments – and then it becomes clear that theorists can fail to have any implicit commitment to the sentence 'God exists' even if it is true that that sentence expresses a necessarily true proposition. And, in any case, it may well be more plausible to adopt some other conception of propositions, according to which there are many different, and not necessarily mutually entailing, necessary propositions.

Despite its failings, the argument to which Haight gives expression remains a permanent temptation. Many philosophers have fallen into the trap of supposing that their opponents are implicitly committed to

7 The exception is those theorists – e.g., possible worlds theorists – who hold that all necessary statements and thoughts have the same content – e.g., the set of all possible worlds. However, such theorists are unlikely to hold, e.g., that the claim that grass is actually green is *about* the undecidability of arithmetic – i.e., they are unlikely to use their notion of propositional content in the explanation of what it is for a statement or a thought to be about a particular subject matter.

claims that those philosophers themselves take to be necessary. However, (i) this supposition can clearly be mistaken, namely, in those cases in which those philosophers mistakenly take the claims in question to be necessary; and (ii) even when the claims in question genuinely are necessary, it seems clear that one could reasonably hold a theory that did not entail the truth of those claims – for example, the ancient Babylonians could reasonably have held a theory that failed to entail that Hesperus is identical to Phosphorus; and, indeed, the ancient Babylonians could reasonably have held a theory that entailed that Hesperus is distinct from Phosphorus.

Chapter 8

Application to historical arguments

GIVEN THE preceding system of classifying ontological arguments, and given the further assumption that there are no ontological argu ments that do not belong to at least one of the categories in the system, we can provide a critique of the historically important ontological arguments that does not depend upon controversial points of interpre- tation of those arguments. The point of the present chapter is to show how this can be done. Some people will find the application of the foregoing absolutely straightforward; nonetheless, it may be worth- while to provide a detailed summary of the preceding results.

(1) THE ARGUMENT FROM *PROSLOGION 2*

There are a number of somewhat plausible interpretations of the argument in *Proslogion 2*. If we represent the argument in a logically inperspicacious way, then it has just two premises and a conclusion:

1. A being than which no greater can be conceived exists in the understanding. (Premise)
2. If a being than which no greater can be conceived does exist in the understanding but does not exist in reality, then a being than which no greater can be conceived that does exist both in the understanding and in reality is greater than a being than which no greater can be conceived. (Premise)
3. (Hence) A being than which no greater can be conceived does exist in reality. (From 1, 2)

We can interpret this argument in three different ways: (i) as a concep- tual argument, (ii) as a modal argument involving actuality, and (iii) as a Meinongian argument. As I have already argued, on each of these interpretations, the argument has two different readings. On one of the readings, the argument is valid, but premise 1 is a claim that an atheist or agnostic can reasonably reject; and, on the other reading, the argument is simply invalid.

On the *conceptual interpretation,* the argument may be represented as follows:

1. One can conceive of a being than which no greater can be conceived. (Premise)
2. If a being than which no greater can be conceived does not exist, then one can conceive of a being greater than a being than which no greater can be conceived, namely, a being than which no greater can be conceived and that exists. (Premise)
3. (Hence) A being than which no greater can be conceived exists. (From 1, 2)

In premise 1, 'conceive of' can be understood either to be ontologically committing or to be ontologically neutral. If it is understood to be ontologically committing – so that one can only conceive of something that exists – then the argument is valid, though the second premise is redundant. However, no agnostic or atheist will be prepared to accept 1, understood in this way. On the other hand, if 1 is understood to be ontologically neutral, then the argument is simply invalid. At most, what follows from 1 and 2 is that in the ontologically neutral sense, one can conceive of an existent being than which no greater can be conceived – that is, one can form the mental description 'an existent being than which no greater can be conceived'. But one's ability to form this kind of description simply has no implications for the existence of a being than which no greater can be conceived. Another way of putting the same point is this: Given 1 and 2, it follows that according to the conception of a being than which no greater can be conceived, a being than which no greater can be conceived actually exists. However, this whole claim is governed by the scope of the 'according to the conception' operator: It would simply be a logical error to detach the conclusion that a being than which no greater can be conceived actually exists.

On the *modal interpretation,* the argument may be represented as follows:

1. There is a possible being x, such that for no world w and being y does the greatness of y in w exceed the greatness of x in the actual world. (Premise)

2. For the possible being x described in 1, and for any worlds w and v, if x exists in w but x does not exist in v, then the greatness of x in w exceeds the greatness of x in v. (Premise)
3. (Hence) There is a being x that exists in the actual world and that is such that for no world w and being y does the greatness of y in w exceed the greatness of x in the actual world. (From 1, 2)

In premise 1, 'actual' can be understood in either a shifty or a non-shifty way. If it is understood to be nonshifty – so that 'the actual world' always refers to *our* world, that is, the world of utterance, even when it is embedded in the scope of modal operators – then the argument is valid. But, of course, on this interpretation, no agnostic or atheist will accept 1. On the other hand, if 'actual' is understood in a shifty way – so that the reference of 'the actual world' can shift to the world of evaluation when the expression is embedded in the scope of modal operators – then the argument is simply invalid.[1]

On the *Meinongian interpretation*, the argument may be represented as follows:

1. The predicate '   is a being than which no greater can be conceived' picks out a unique object, the properties of which are all compatible. (Premise)
2. No complete object that falls under the predicate '   is a being than which no greater can be conceived' fails to possess the property of existence. (Premise)
3. (Hence) There is an existent object that falls under the predicate '   is a being than which no greater can be conceived'. (From 1, 2)

In evaluating this argument, we must decide how we are going to treat the claim that a complete object possesses the property of existence. On the one hand, we might decide that only existent complete objects can possess the property of existence. In that case, the argument is clearly valid: But no agnostic or atheist will concede premise 2, since no atheist or agnostic will concede that there is a complete object that possesses the property of existence and that falls under the predicate '   is a being than which no greater can be conceived'.[2]

---

1 Note that 'the actual world' occurs within the scope of a modal operator in premise 1, but not in 3.
2 As I explained in the earlier discussion, an agnostic or atheist can reasonably dispute whether there is a complete object that corresponds to the predicate '__ is a being than which no greater can be conceived and that exists', even if she concedes that

On the other hand, we might decide that nonexistent complete objects can possess the property of existence. In that case, the argument is simply invalid.

Although I cannot prove this, I think that it is clear that there is no other way of interpreting *Proslogion* 2 that gives rise to a plausible argument. Consequently, we can see that the argument can be reasonably rejected by atheists and agnostics even without discussion of the controversial claims that relate greatness and existence. Of course, for some atheists and agnostics, there may be further reasons to reject the argument. However, the virtue of the preceding analysis is that it requires no assumptions about controversial questions. Even if existence is both a predicate and a perfection, and if the notion of a unique being than which no greater can be conceived is coherent, the argument of *Proslogion* 2 fails – at least when considered as a dialectical tool in the debate between theists and their opponents.

A somewhat harder question is whether one could reasonably believe (i) that existence is both a predicate and a perfection and (ii) that the notion of a being than which no greater can be conceived is coherent. Since I think that the answer to this question is yes, I think that some theists could reasonably think that the argument of *Proslogion* 2 is sound, that is, validly proceeds from true premises. However – despite the claims of some commentators – I do not think that this is much of a recommendation of the argument. I shall return to this topic in Chapter 12.[3]

(2) THE ARGUMENT FROM *PROSLOGION 3*

There are various interpretations of the allegedly independent argument in *Proslogion 3*. If we represent the argument in a logically inperspicuous way, then it has just one premise and a conclusion:

1. There is in the understanding a being than which no greater can be conceived and that cannot even be conceived not to exist. (Premise)
2. (Hence) There really exists a being than which no greater can be conceived and that cannot even be conceived not to exist. (From 1)

there is a complete object that corresponds to the predicate ' __ is a being than which no greater can be conceived'.

3   It should be noted that some commentators have interpreted the argument of *Proslogion* 2 as a definitional argument – see, e.g., Ferguson (1992). Textually, this is quite implausible. Moreover, as we have already seen, definitional arguments are easily refuted.

We can interpret this argument in three different ways: (i) as a conceptual argument, (ii) as a modal argument involving necessity, and (iii) as a Meinongian argument. On each of these interpretations, there are two different readings. On one of those readings, the argument is valid, but the premise in one that can be reasonably rejected by atheists and agnostics; and, on the other reading, the argument is simply invalid.

On the *conceptual interpretation*, we can represent the argument as follows:

1. One can conceive of a being than which no greater can be conceived and that cannot even be conceived not to exist. (Premise)
2. (Hence) There really exists a being than which no greater can be conceived and that cannot even be conceived not to exist. (From 1)

In premise 1 'conceive of' can be taken to be either ontologically committing or ontologically neutral. If it is taken to be ontologically neutral, then the argument is simply invalid. On the other hand, if it is taken to be ontologically committing, then no atheist or agnostic will accept the premise.[4] Note that I have assumed that the expression 'one can conceive of' governs the whole of the sentence. If we suppose that 'that cannot even be conceived not to exist' does not lie in the scope of 'one can conceive of', then it may be harder to make the ontologically neutral reading.

On the *modal interpretation*, we can represent the argument as follows:

1. It is possible that there is a being than which no greater can be conceived and that necessarily exists. (Premise)
2. (Hence) There is a being than which no greater can be conceived and that necessarily exists. (From 1)

In this argument, we need to make some assumptions about the nature of logical space. If we suppose that the S5 axiom is correct, then an agnostic or atheist will grant that the argument is valid, but will deny that the premise is true. On the other hand, if we suppose that the S5 axiom is incorrect, than an agnostic or atheist may allow that the premise is true, but the argument will be invalid. This is like the earlier analyses: The question is how to interpret the notion of possibility that is invoked in the premise.

4 This just parallels the earlier analysis of the argument in *Proslogion 2*.

On the *Meinongian interpretation*, we can represent the argument as follows:

1. The predicate '   is a being than which no greater can be conceived and that cannot even be conceived not to exist' picks out an object, the properties of which are all compatible.
2. (Hence) There is a real object that falls under the predicate '   is a being than which no greater can be conceived and that cannot even be conceived not to exist'.

The analysis of this argument is just as for the Meinongian interpretation of the argument in *Proslogion* 2. If a Meinongian object that includes the property of necessary existence must exist, then no agnostic or atheist will grant the premise. But if a Meinongian object that includes necessary existence need not exist, then the argument is invalid.

As in the preceding case, I do not think that there is any other plausible interpretation of the argument in *Proslogion* 3. So, once again, the argument can be rejected by agnostics and atheists even before any controversial questions are investigated. Moreover, it is evident that exactly the same considerations extend to the arguments of *Proslogion* 15 and the *Responsio*. Consequently, these arguments will not be discussed here.

(3) THE CARTESIAN ARGUMENT

The Cartesian version of the ontological argument can be encapsulated as follows – once again, the encapsulation is not meant to be logically perspicuous:

1. The idea of a supremely perfect being includes the idea of existence – that is, the idea that a supremely perfect being exists. (Premise)
2. The idea of a supremely perfect being is the idea of a being with a true and immutable nature. (Premise)
3. Whatever belongs to the true and immutable nature of a being may be truly affirmed of it. (Premise)
4. (Hence) a supremely perfect being exists. (From 1, 2, 3)

This argument is most plausibly interpreted as a conceptual argument, though perhaps one that is based on an underlying Meinongian ontology. The main problem with the argument is that, at some point, it purports to discharge an operator. There are several plausible candidates for the point at which this discharge occurs.

In premise 2, the claim that the idea of a supremely perfect being is the idea of a being with a true and immutable nature could be taken to assert that, in fact, *there is* a being with a true and immutable nature that falls under the idea of a supremely perfect being. Understood this way, 2 is a claim that agnostics and atheists will reasonably reject.

Suppose, instead, that 2 is just taken to mean that there is no suggestion of gerrymander in the idea of a 'supremely perfect being', and suppose that we waive any worries that we might have about the significance and plausibility of this claim. Then 3 just amounts to the bald suggestion that from the claim that one has the nongerrymandered idea supremely perfect being, one can discharge the operator and conclude that there is a supremely perfect being. But, of course, no agnostics or atheists will accept this step. While they will grant that whatever belongs to the true and immutable nature of a being can be truly asserted of that being *within the scope of relevant intensional operators*, they will not concede that whatever belongs to the true and immutable nature of a being can be truly asserted of that being *outright*.

Finally, if 3 is construed in the more restrictive way, then the conclusion of the argument simply does not follow from the premises. On this construal, the discharge of the operator occurs in the move from the premises to the conclusion.

In sum, the Cartesian argument is subject to precisely the same criticism as the argument of St. Anselm. No matter how it is interpreted, either (i) it is invalid, or (ii) it has at least one premise that atheists and agnostics will reasonably reject. Moreover, this can be seen before any of the controversial premises of the argument are investigated.

(4) GENERAL REMARKS: THE GENERAL OBJECTION

I have argued that the famous historical versions of the ontological argument – that is, arguments of St. Anselm and Descartes – can all be seen to have the following status: No matter how they are interpreted, these arguments have one reading on which every reasonable person will agree that they are invalid, and another reading on which those who are not antecedently convinced of the truth of the conclusion of the argument can reasonably reject one of the premises.

Does it follow that I think that there is a general objection, which can be seen to apply in advance to all possible reformulations of these historical arguments? Yes. Here it is: In any version of one of the historical arguments, it will be the case that the singular terms and quantifiers – names, definite descriptions, indefinite descriptions, and so forth – used in the statement of the argument – to refer to, or to denote, or to range over a collection that is supposed to include, that divine object whose existence is to be established by the argument – either occur embedded in the scope of further sentential operators or do not occur thus embedded. If they do not occur thus embedded, then an opponent of the argument can reasonably object that the question has been begged. On the other hand, if they do thus occur, then there is a question about the detachment of the conclusion of the argument from the scope of the operators. If the operators are extensional – and hence permit the inference of the desired conclusion – then, as in the case of the modal arguments, an opponent of the argument can again reasonably insist that the question has been begged. But, if the operators are intensional, then they won't permit the inference of the desired conclusion. So, no matter how the argument is formulated, an opponent can always either (i) reasonably claim that the question has been begged or else (ii) object that the inference is simply invalid.[5]

Lest it be thought that this general objection is itself question begging, note should be made of the following point: An agnostic or atheist who utters the words 'God is a being than which no greater can be conceived' is engaged in a bit of role playing, or storytelling – compare an adult who says, 'Santa Claus lives at the North Pole'. In each case, there is a sense in which strict speech requires the insertion of an 'according to the well-known story (myth, legend)' operator; in

---

5   In the statement of the general objection, I rely on a distinction between *extensional* and *intensional* operators. My terminology may be unfortunate, for nothing in the objection hinges on the effect of substitution of co-referring terms within the scope of the operators in question. Rather, the point at issue, at least for the case of singular terms, concerns the amenability of singular term positions within the scope of the operators to *purely* objectual quantification. More generally, the point at issue is whether vocabulary that occurs within the scope of the operators must be regarded as carrying ontological commitment. Examples of intensional operators in this sense are 'according to such-and-such story (theory, myth)' and '*a* believes that', on the noncommittal reading of 'believes'. Examples of extensional operators in this sense are '*a* knows that' and 'necessarily', at least on the Kripkean understanding of this operator.

neither case is there any commitment to a referent for the proper names used. Since an atheist or agnostic who is speaking strictly won't accept any claims in which the essentially theistic vocabulary falls outside the scope of such intensional operators, there is no way that any ontological argument can make headway against an alert opponent. It is only by the lights of some theists that it is possible that there is a maximally great being and so on.

This general argument applies to experiential and what I am calling 'Hegelian' ontological arguments just as much as to the other kinds of ontological arguments. What it shows is that it can be seen in advance that no ontological arguments of the kinds that I have considered will be dialectically effective. Moreover, this general objection also suggests a stronger conclusion, namely, that there cannot be a dialectically effective ontological argument. Given that there are reasonable agnostics and atheists, there can be no ontological argument that provides them with a reason to change their views. Of course, there might be other reasons for them to change their views – for example, it might be demonstrable that the simplest, most powerful, most explanatory, and so on theory of the universe is one that includes the claim that there is a God. But those reasons cannot be the burden of an *a priori* argument.[6]

One qualification to this argument: Most ontological arguments can be recast in a form in which, at least on the surface, they involve no singular terms or quantifiers – for they can be recast in a form that refers only to the instantiation of properties: 'It is possible that maximal greatness is instantiated. Hence, maximal greatness is actually instantiated'. However, this argument still applies to the canonical reformulation of those arguments in the language of first-order quantification – and that suffices to show that the arguments are no good; talk of the instantiation of properties is just an alternative way of making existential quantifications.

A second qualification to this argument: Some Meinongians and free logicians hold that it is possible to make 'naked' use of the referential apparatus of a language – singular terms, quantifiers, and

---

6 I have hedged my bets a little here: All I have claimed is that my general objection *strongly suggests* that there cannot be a successful ontological argument. However, it is only a general endorsement of fallibilism that prevents me from making a bolder claim. As things stand, I cannot even *imagine* what form a successful ontological argument could take.

so on – without incurring actual ontic commitments. On such views, however, a distinction *must* be drawn between characterizing and noncharacterizing – or nuclear and nonnuclear – predicates; and the naked use of noncharacterizing predicates will then be taken to import ontic commitments *via* the associated referential apparatus. So, for example, on these views, the claim 'God is perfect' will import ontic commitments that arise through the naked use of the – let us suppose – noncharacterizing predicate 'is perfect', even though the use of the singular term 'God' in other constructions – for example, 'God is omnipotent' – need not impute such ontic commitment. Instances of the schema 'The *F* is *F*' are known *a priori*, on the theoretical basis of the views in question, *only* in those cases in which the substituting instances are characterizing predicates.

A final qualification to the preceding argument: It is important that the scope of the general objection is limited to positive ontological arguments for the existence of deities, and negative ontological arguments against the existence of deities *that run parallel to the positive arguments.* It is no part of the general objection to deny that there can be successful negative ontological arguments against some conceptions of deities – for example, those that are logically inconsistent. More generally, it is no part of the general objection to deny that there can be successful negative ontological arguments in other areas – for example, against the existence of *certain* numbers, or *certain* sets, and so on. Furthermore, it is no part of the general objection to deny that there are some ontological categories whose actual instantiation can be known *a priori* – for example, the general category of existents – and neither is it part of the general objection to deny that there can be dialectically effective *a priori* arguments for the existence of particular beings *given* background agreement about the instantiation of an ontological category. However, the success of the general objection depends upon the claim that there is no ontological category about whose instantiation theists and their opponents must agree on *a priori* grounds, and that can serve as the basis for an ontological argument for the existence of a deity. While reasonable theists and their reasonable opponents may be obliged to agree that there are causally related objects, or temporally related objects, any such agreement depends upon *a posteriori* – or at least synthetic *a priori* – considerations and gives rise to kinds of *cosmological* arguments that are not defeated, nor intended to be defeated, by the general objection. Moreover – the claims of defenders of Neoplatonic ontological arguments notwithstanding – if there is an ontological category that *can* serve as the foundation for a valid ontological argument for the existence of a deity, then reasonable atheists and agnostics will simply deny that the category is instantiated.[7]

7 My general objection to ontological arguments is independent of Mill's well-known arguments against the utility of deductive arguments. *Contra* Mill, I hold that deductive arguments *can* serve dialectically useful functions, particularly when there are numerous premises and many steps of argumentation. However, there *are* circumstances in which deductive arguments for positive existential conclusions cannot be dialectically effective, namely, those in which there is sufficient disagreement about background ontology.

Chapter 9

Are there (other) global objections to ontological arguments?

At the end of the preceding chapter, I concluded that there is a global objection to ontological arguments – that is, an objection that suggests in advance that no ontological argument can be dialectically effective. It is important to emphasize that it is not part of this objection to claim that no ontological argument can be sound. For all that I have said, it may be that there are sound versions of all ontological arguments.

Other philosophers have thought that it is possible to show in a single stroke, once and for all, either (i) that no ontological arguments can be *sound* or else (ii) that no ontological arguments can be thought to be sound on *a priori* grounds. In this chapter, I shall consider several such attempts. Of course, I have already argued that the Humean, Kantian, and logical positivist attempts to carry out this project fail. I shall not repeat those arguments in this chapter. Moreover, I shall hold over discussion of the claim that existence is not a predicate until the following chapter.

(1) THE MISSING EXPLANATION ARGUMENT

The following line of argument is adapted from a more general argument in Johnston (1992). It is intended to establish that there could not be an ontological argument that provides anyone with a good reason to believe that God exists – that is, there could not be an ontological argument that could reasonably be taken to be sound on *a priori* grounds.

Suppose that there is a sound ontological argument and that this argument establishes not only that God exists, but also that God is omniscient, omnipotent, and so forth. Suppose further – as many theists believe – that God's knowledge of the free actions of human agents is based upon, or derives from, those free actions.[1] Given these suppositions, we are committed to the following pair of claims:

1. It is *a priori* that for any proposition that *S*, God judges that *S* iff it is the case that *S*.
2. For some proposition that *S*, God judges that *S* because it is the case that *S*.

Moreover, in premise 2 the sense of the word 'because' involves the suggestion of a responsiveness, on the part of God's judgment that *S*, to how things are in the world – that is, to the state of affairs that *S*.

However, as Johnston suggests, there is considerable initial plausibility to the thought that given a claim of the form 'It is *a priori* that *T* iff *T**' and a sentence of the form '*S* because *T**', one ought to be able to make use of an obvious principle of substitution to obtain a sentence of the form '*S* because *T*' that is 'possibly explanatory' in just the same sense as the initial claim, that is, the claim of the form '*S* because *T**'. Yet, in the case in question, the sentence

3. For some proposition that *S*, God judges that *S* because God judges that *S*

is an explanatory solecism – that is, it is not possibly explanatory: One can see *a priori* that the 'because' in 3 cannot involve a suggestion of 'responsiveness' if the sentence is to be true. Thus, given the plausible principle of substitution, we must reject at least one of premises 1 and 2. But 2 is not something that many theists will regard as negotiable – and so the only option is to reject 1. And, hence, there can be no reasonable acceptance of an ontological argument.

As noted inter alia by Menzies and Pettit (1993), there is really only one question about Johnston's argument, namely, Is the principle of substitution correct? It certainly seems plausible, but I suspect that there are independent reasons why it would be reasonable for some theists to reject it. In particular, it seems to lead to very counterintuitive conclusions when applied to other cases. Consider, for example, the following pair of claims:

1 There are theists who deny that there is any proposition *S* for which it is true that God judges that *S* *in response to* the fact that *S*. Such theists will not be moved by the argument under consideration. Whether their position is defensible is not a question that I can pursue here; *prima facie*, appeals to middle knowledge and/or divine compatibilism do not seem hopeless.

1. It is *a priori* that the sentence 'Snow is white' – as uttered in the present context – is true iff snow is white.
2. The sentence 'Snow is white' – as uttered in the present context – is true because snow is white.

The first of these claims seems incontestable – how could one reasonably fail to accept the *T*-schema on *a priori* grounds? But the second claim is a truism – except for those who accept a strongly deflationary account of truth and hence maintain that 2 is ill formed.[2] So the upshot of the application of Johnston's argument is that the apparent truism, 2, must be rejected because it has no intelligible construal under the only acceptable account of truth, namely, the strongly deflationary account. But, if it comes down to a choice between the rejection of the substitution principle and the acceptance of a strongly deflationary account of truth, why shouldn't one reasonably opt for the former? After all, this move has the obvious benefit of preserving ordinary intuitions about the acceptability of claims – such as 1 and 2 – that involve the truth predicate.

Another pair of claims that can be used to make the same point is the following:

1. It is *a priori* that the ball is red iff the ball falls in the extension of the predicate 'is red' – as that predicate is used in the present context.
2. The ball falls in the extension of the predicate 'is red' – as that predicate is used in the present context – because it is red.

Once again, the first claim seems incontestable: All instances of the schema *a* is *F* iff *a* falls in the extension of the predicate 'is *F*' as that predicate is used in the present context can be known *a priori* to be true. And the second claim seems inescapably explanatory: We would naturally say that the reason why the ball falls in the extension of the predicate 'is red' is because the ball is red. So it seems that the substitution principle that forms the foundation for the missing explanation argument is mistaken: It can happen that substitution of *a priori* equivalents transforms a sentence with genuine explanatory potential into an explanatory solecism.

I conclude that the missing explanation argument does not provide a decisive objection to the acceptability of theistic belief on the basis

2   Cf. Field (1986).

of an ontological argument – for all that the argument shows, one could reasonably believe that one knows *a priori* that God exists and is omniscient.[3]

(2) THE THOMISTIC OBJECTIONS

As noted earlier, St. Thomas Aquinas (1920:21) rejected St. Anselm's ontological argument. He provides two different objections, each of which can be construed as a general objection to ontological arguments.

His first objection – in the reply to the argument in the *Summa Theologica* – is this:

Granted that everyone understands that by this word 'God' is signified something than which nothing greater can be conceived, nevertheless, it does not therefore, follow that he understands that what the word signifies actually exists, but only that it exists mentally. Nor can it be argued that it actually exists, unless it be admitted that there actually exists something than which nothing greater can be thought; and this precisely is not admitted by those who hold that God does not exist.

Claims about the content of this objection are inconclusive. It can be interpreted simply as the bald assertion that there are no true *a priori* existence claims.[4] Understood this way, it seems to be merely question begging. It can also – though perhaps with considerable charity – be interpreted as a precursor of the objection that I pressed at the end of the preceding chapter. The claim that Aquinas makes is that the argument is either invalid or question begging – and with this I agree. However, it is not clear what are supposed to be the grounds that support his contention. What we can say is that to the extent that there is anything that supports the assertions made by Aquinas, his general objection agrees with the one proposed at the end of the preceding chapter.

The second objection that St. Thomas makes – in the further com-

---

3 Of course, if one makes the nonstandard assumption that one's ontological argument demonstrates the existence of a nonomniscient God, then one will hold that the missing explanation argument doesn't even constitute a *prima facie* objection to that ontological argument. If, for example, it is logically impossible for there to be an omniscient being – i.e., a being that for any proposition that S, judges that S iff S – then it will not be true that, e.g., a being than which no greater can be conceived is omniscient.

4 Cf. Copleston (1957).

ment in the *Summa Theologica* – is, very roughly, to claim that the proposition that God exists is necessary *a posteriori;* that is, we can only know that God exists on the basis of experience. This objection seems straightforwardly question begging: Proponents of ontological arguments insist that the proposition that God exists is necessary *a priori,* and that the ontological argument itself shows that we can know that God exists independently of experience.[5]

(3) THE USE OF SINGULAR TERMS

Barnes (1972:81) provides a general objection to ontological arguments based on "a close scrutiny of the logical role played by the term 'God' in [the] premises and [the] conclusion [of those arguments]." According to Barnes, ontological arguments fail because of the use that they make of singular terms, that is, names and definite descriptions. In particular, arguments that use definite descriptions – for example, 'the being than which no greater can be conceived' – are question begging because they presuppose that there is exactly one thing that satisfies the relevant definite description. And arguments that use other singular terms – in particular, names – fall to the same problem, for all uses of singular terms must be underwritten by identifying uses of definite descriptions.

It seems to me that this objection is partly correct. What is correct is the claim that the use of singular terms in ontological arguments should arouse suspicion. Whenever a singular term appears in the conclusion of an ontological argument, one should ask, How is the use of this singular term in that conclusion justified? The argument began with certain premises that belong to a particular theory – the theistic theory of the proponent of the argument. In that theory, the singular terms used in the statement of the conclusion of the argument are taken to refer. But what justifies the move – and what step in the argument effects the move – from the claim that, according to the theory, the terms refer, to the claim that the terms actually do refer? Does the argument offer someone who does not initially subscribe to the theory a reason for supposing that the singular terms in question actually do refer?

However, although Barnes's suspicions about the use of singular terms in ontological arguments are well founded, there are a number

---

5 This second Thomistic objection is essentially that of Hume. Earlier, I rejected the Humean argument on the same kind of grounds.

of reasons why his overall diagnosis is unsatisfactory. First, and most important, there are ontological arguments that do not involve any singular terms, or at least none that deserve to attract any suspicion – for example, those discussed in Adams (1971) and Lewis (1970). These arguments are completely untouched by Barnes's analysis. Second, it is not clear that it is the mere use of singular terms that undermines those ontological arguments in which singular terms are used. In, say, conceptual ontological arguments, the use of singular terms in the premises of those arguments seems to be unproblematic, at least on some readings. But what is problematic is the way that the singular terms in question are supposed to interact with certain sentential operators – for example, 'according to the definition', 'according to the concept', 'according to the theory'. As I have argued, one needs to attend to the use of all quantifiers, singular terms, and these sentential operators in order to obtain a correct perspective on the status of ontological arguments. Finally, it is doubtful that, in general, the use of other singular terms should be tied to the use of related identifying descriptions. As Kripke (1980) argues, it seems wrong to say that the *meaning* of proper names is given by associated definite descriptions – for, often, there seems to be no suitable definite description to be found. On the other hand, there is some plausibility to the view that 'God' should be treated as a descriptive name, that is, as an abbreviation for a rigidified definite description – so perhaps this last criticism is not very significant.

Purtill (1975:110) defends a similar analysis of ontological arguments:

The ontological argument fails to "adequately establish the existence of a being which is properly called 'God'." Furthermore, we can see that any argument of this general form is open to the same fatal objection: no matter how much we pack into the definition of our terms, it is always possible to simply raise the possibility that these terms fail to refer.

But, as we have seen, this isn't strictly correct. Suppose that I have constructed a proof in which no singular terms are used and that has an existential conclusion – for example, a nonconstructive proof that establishes that a particular equation has a unique solution. Suppose I then introduce a name that, by definition, refers to the being whose unique existence is established by the proof. Then it will not be open for anyone who accepts the proof to reasonably object that it is still possible that the name fails to refer. Thus, while Purtill's objection does overthrow some ontological arguments – namely, those that make substantial uses of the word 'God' – there are many ontological arguments that it does not touch. In order to overthrow those further arguments, account must be taken of the use of quantifiers and so on.

(4) FURTHER ATTEMPTS

There are a number of purported general objections to ontological arguments that remain to be discussed. These arguments form a motley bunch. Some of them are discussed only in the literature notes to this section.

(a) *Paulsen's argument*

David Paulsen (1984) claims that all ontological arguments take for granted some version of the following assumption: If a proposition p is logically possible, then the state of affairs s affirmed by p really could obtain. What this amounts to is (roughly) the suggestion that ontological arguments all conflate logical possibility with metaphysical possibility. Even if we restrict our attention to modal ontological arguments, we might have reason to reject the thought that this suggestion provides an analysis of the crucial error involved in those arguments. The notions of logical possibility and metaphysical possibility are not so clear that we can reject out of hand the claim that theistic intuitions about the possibility that God exists are intuitions about the metaphysical possibility of God's existence. Moreover, it is not really clear whether Paulsen's conception of ontological possibility involves some kind of conflation with the notion of compatibility with the ontology of the actual world. And, finally, in any case, it may well be what theists really want to lay claim to is intuitions about the logical possibility of God's existence.

Paulsen constructs a "model" in which everything that exists or "ontologically" can exist is compounded from self-existing, self-accounting, unproducible, unpreventable, indestructible, independent quanta of mass-energy. He claims that, in this model, a perfect being is logically possible but metaphysically impossible. But what does he mean by the expression 'ontologically can exist'? Since a reasonable metaphysics will surely allow that it is metaphysically possible for there to be kinds of things – for example, entelechies, spirits – that do not actually exist, it seems that what he must mean is that the things in question belong to the ontological categories of the actual world. But, in that case, Paulsen hasn't really produced a model in which a perfect being is metaphysically impossible; rather, he has produced a model in which perfect beings are excluded from the ontological categories of the actual world. Consequently, it is clear that his alleged model simply begs the question against his theistic opponent.

Paulsen's argument for the claim that ontological arguments are implicitly committed to the principle that he identifies is puzzling. He writes:

> Just as no argument can prove that God exists-in-reality if God's real existence is logically impossible, no argument can prove that God exists-in-reality if God's existence is ontologically impossible. Thus, for [an] argument to be a proof that God exists in reality, the following conditions must be met: (i) the argument must affirm that God's existence-in-reality is ontologically possible (OPP); (ii) OPP must be true; (iii) the person for whom the argument is a proof must have good reason to believe OPP to be true; and (iv) the person's reasons for affirming that OPP is true must be logically and epistemically independent of the conclusion that God exists-in-reality. (1984:45)

But surely a proponent of ontological arguments can reply that (i) is a consequence of the conclusion of ontological arguments. Given that an ontological argument establishes that God actually exists, it follows that God's existence in reality is ontologically possible. Moreover, given that the argument – which does not rely on the assumption that OPP is true – establishes that God exists, premise (ii) is also established by the argument, and (iii) and (iv) are satisfied. So, proponents of ontological arguments do not have an implicit prior commitment to the principle that Paulsen identifies; rather, the conclusion of the ontological argument forces them to incur that commitment. Of course, one may well share Paulsen's skepticism that there could be a probative argument from a premise about mere logical possibility to a conclusion about actual existence – but it does not seem that that skepticism is well expressed in the claim that ontological arguments are implicitly committed *in advance* to the principle that Paulsen identifies.

(b) *Read's argument*

Stephen Read (1981) suggests that St. Anselm's argument is undermined by its use of the phrase 'to exist only in the understanding'. For in answer to the question, What could it mean to say that something that exists is greater than something that does not, that is, than something that exists only in the understanding? Read can only suggest that if the thing that does not exist were to exist, then it would not be greater than the thing that exists. And that cannot be what St. Anselm requires, for then it would follow that a being that exists only in the understanding is just as great as an otherwise identical being that also exists in reality.

Read's problem can be answered by the observation that, in St. Anselm's proof, there is really only *one thing* about which two contrary hypotheses are considered, namely, (i) that *it* exists only in the understanding and (ii) that *it* exists both in the understanding and in reality. The claim is that *it* is a greater being – on the absolute scale of greatness of objects – if *it* exists in reality than if *it* merely exists in the understanding, because existence in reality is a great-making attribute. Read's comparative evaluation misrepresents the nature of St. Anselm's argument. Read considers this response, and suggests that the subject has been changed: Instead of discussing a relation between objects, we are now discussing a relation between states of affairs. But, in fact, the argument was never about *relations*; rather, it concerned the *properties* of a single being – or, if one prefers, the properties of a singular term that purports to refer to a single being.[6]

(c) *Richman's argument*

Robert Richman (1976:88) objects to a version of St. Anselm's argument in the following terms: "For the argument to go through, God's existing *in re* as well as *in intellectu* must be a logically distinct state from God's existing merely *in intellectu*; but for the argument to be valid, God's existing merely *in intellectu* must be logically equivalent to God's existing *in re* as well as *in intellectu*." This argument seems to generalize: In most, if not all, ontological arguments, a distinction is drawn between God's existing in some qualified way – for example, in another possible world, as an object of thought – and his existing in the actual world; but, for the argument to be valid, there must be a logical equivalence between the qualified form of existence and existence in the actual world.

Of course, as soon as the generalization of the argument is stated, it is obvious that the argument fails. All that ontological arguments require is a one-way entailment – from God's existence in a qualified way to God's existence in the actual world – and this does not require

---

6 Note that, if it were correct, Read's criticism would extend to almost all ontological arguments – though not perhaps to the experiential arguments.

the further assumption that God's existence in the qualified way is identical to God's existence in the actual world. So Richman's argument fails.[7]

(d) *Robinson's argument*

William Robinson (1984) distinguishes between three different senses – which he calls *strong, weak,* and *trivial* – of the expression 'to have the idea of x'. He then suggests (i) that it is a necessary condition for the success of ontological arguments that we have the idea of God in the *strong* sense, but (ii) that, in fact, we only have the idea of God in either the *weak* sense or the *trivial* sense. Clearly, the success of Robinson's argument depends upon his explanation of the different senses of the expression 'to have the idea of x' – but, unfortunately, Robinson only offers some examples that are intended to illustrate the different senses. Thus, he says, that to have the idea of a mechanical apple peeler in the weak sense is just to understand a description – 'device into which you could put an apple, turn a crank, and after a while get a peeled apple' – that one could recognize to apply to something, but that to have the idea of a mechanical apple peeler in the strong sense, one must possess an understanding of how to construct such a device, or of how such a device could work. Furthermore, he says that to have the idea of a solid planar figure whose number of edges equals twelve times the number of shapes used in its construction in the weak sense is just to understand the description, to have the ability to identify the figure described, to distinguish the figure from others – for example, those with a higher or lower ratio of shapes to edges – and to draw logical consequences from the description; but to have the idea of a solid planar figure whose number of edges equals twelve times the number of shapes used in its construction in the strong sense, one must be able to draw such a figure, know how many shapes will enable the construction of such a figure, identify the figure as a cube, and so on.

These examples run together various different criteria for having an idea in the strong sense: for example, (i) knowledge of essences, (ii) practical knowledge – such as knowledge of how to construct the

---

7 Wainwright (1978b) and Rabinowicz (1978) both make the observation that it is one thing to say that two states are logically equivalent, and another to say that those states are identical; this observation is correct and suffices to defeat Richman's argument.

thing in question – (iii) possession of relevant alternative identificatory information, and (iv) possession of substantial theoretical information. Moreover, the suggested criteria seem not to be relevant to the case of the idea of God, about which Robinson (1984:53) writes:

> Since I have the idea in the weak sense, I am in a position to know many things. I understand that anything that is entitled to be called "God" has to be a being such that the very content of the idea of that being entails that that being exists. So I know that if I were to have this idea, in the strong sense, I would be in a position to know that it is necessary for what this idea is of to exist, and therefore that what this idea is of exists. However, since I do not have the idea of God in the strong sense, I am not in a position to actually know these things.

Consequently, it seems to me that Robinson's promising critique is ultimately unsuccessful.

In my view, Robinson's point is better formulated as a distinction between different attitudes that one can take toward a theory. Corresponding to the possession of an idea in the strong sense is the attitude of accepting the theory – that is, taking it that the terms of the theory refer and that the claims made by the theory are true. Corresponding to the possession of an idea in the weak sense is the attitude of understanding but failing to accept a theory – that is, not taking it that the terms of the theory refer or not accepting that the claims made by the theory are true. And corresponding to the possession of an idea in the trivial sense is the attitude of recognizing that one is in a position in which one does not understand a theory – that is, recognizing nothing more than that the theory is couched in syntactically well-formed sentences. The atheist or agnostic recognizes that if she accepted the theistic theory, then she would judge that the ontological argument is sound; but, because she does not accept the theistic theory, she is not in a position to make that judgment. And there is nothing in the ontological argument that compels her to change her attitude toward the theistic theory.

Chapter 10

Is existence a predicate?

T H E best-known – most often cited – objection to ontological arguments is encapsulated in the Kantian slogan 'Existence is not a predicate'. I have already argued that Kant himself did not provide an adequate explanation – justification – of the critique that he supposed to be embodied in this claim. In this chapter, I propose to argue that the many subsequent attempts to explain the content of the claim have fared no better.[1] I shall also suggest, albeit tentatively, that there is a straightforward sense in which existence is a predicate – and that this sense is all that defenders of ontological arguments need to invoke in order to defend themselves against the neo-Kantian onslaught.

(1) REAL PREDICATES

As Barnes (1972) notes, the point of the slogan 'Existence is not a predicate' is not to claim that finite parts of the verb 'to exist' do not function as grammatical predicates in sentences that are in subject-predicate form. After all, that claim would seem to be falsified immediately by the existence of sentences of the form '*a* exists,' where *a* belongs to the category of singular terms, namely, proper names, definite descriptions, demonstratives, indexicals, pronominal compound expressions. Barnes suggests that this argument should be treated with care, since grammarians have no agreed canons for the division of sentences into subject and predicate. But this seems unnecessarily cautious: If there is any viable division of sentences into subject terms and predicate expressions, then '*a*' will be a subject term

---

1 My task here is made easier by the excellent discussions in Plantinga (1967), Barnes (1972), and Salmon (1987). In each of these works, it is contended that no one has ever produced a defensible elucidation of the claim that existence is not a predicate.

and 'exists' a predicate expression in sentences of the form '*a* exists', at least in those cases in which *a* is a canonical singular term.

What, then, is the point of the slogan 'existence is not a predicate'? The traditional answer, noted by Barnes, is to claim that existence is not a *logical* predicate – that is, the *deep logical structure* of sentences whose *surface* form contains finite parts of the verb 'to exist' do not contain any predicates that correspond to those surface features. The *locus classicus* for the kind of suggestion is the analysis of definite descriptions in Russell (1905). Superficially, it appears that definite descriptions are singular terms – for example, 'the man in the corner' is a subject term in the sentence 'The man in the corner is drinking a martini'. However, according to Russell, analysis reveals that the deep logical form of this sentence is quantificational – 'There is one and only one man in the corner, and he is drinking a martini'. In the deep structure, revealed by the Russellian analysis, there is no subject term that corresponds to the surface subject term 'the man in the corner'.

This suggestion faces various difficulties. First, it is possible to be skeptical about the existence of deep logical structure.[2] Second, even if one accepts that sentences do have deep logical structures, one might doubt that those structures are massively different from surface structures.[3] Finally, even if one is prepared to countenance deep structures that depart significantly in form from surface structures, one might doubt that the deep structure of a sentence of the form '*a* exists' could fail to include a predicate expression that corresponds to the surface predicate expression 'exists'. At the very least, it seems that some impressive argument will be required.

There is no shortage of candidate arguments. I shall briefly review some of the best known.[4] The central contentions of the arguments that I shall discuss are (i) that all genuine propositions are about their subjects, (ii) that all genuine singular terms refer, (iii) that all genuine singular terms purport to refer, (iv) that there are no genuine singular terms, (v) that existence is a second-order predicate, (vi) that existence

---

2 Cf. Stich (1975).
3 Thus, for example, one might object to the Russellian analysis of definite descriptions that it involves a gratuitous mutilation of surface form. In its place, one might opt for an analysis of the particle 'the' as a kind of functor – cf. Evans (1982). On this kind of analysis, definite descriptions would still be counted as singular terms – subject expressions – albeit with significant internal structure.
4 These arguments are well discussed by Plantinga (1967) and Barnes (1971), so I can afford to be brief.

is a quantifier, (vii) that existence does not admit of qualifications, (viii) that existence is not a property.

(2) ATTEMPTED DEFENSES 1: PROPOSITIONS AND SINGULAR TERMS

These attempted defenses divide into two categories – those that focus on the properties of propositions and singular terms and those that focus on the properties of the finite parts of the verb 'to exist'. I shall look first at those arguments that focus, at least in part, on general properties of propositions and singular terms.

(a) *All genuine propositions are about their subjects*

Broad (1953) provides several arguments that can be construed as support for the contention that all genuine propositions are about their subjects. First, in connection with negative propositions – that is, propositions of the form '*As* are not *F*' – he observes that negative existentials cannot be paraphrased by sentences of the form 'There are *As* and none of them exist' or by sentences of the form 'If there were any *As*, none of them would exist', even though (all) other negative propositions can be paraphrased by sentences of the form 'There are *As*, and none of them is *F*', or else by sentences of the form 'If there were any *As*, none of them would be *F*'. Indeed, according to Broad (1953:182), the paraphrases for the negative existentials are "self-contradictory and meaningless." Second, in connection with positive propositions – that is, propositions of the form *As* are *F* – Broad observes that affirmative existentials cannot be paraphrased by sentences of the form 'There are *As* and none of them fail to exist' or by sentences of the form 'If there were *As*, none of them would fail to exist', even though (all) other positive propositions can be paraphrased by sentences of the form 'There are *As* and none of them fails to be *F*', or else by sentences of the form 'If there were any *As*, none of them would fail to be *F*'. Indeed, according to Broad (1953:183), the paraphrases for the positive existentials are "mere platitudes." The conclusion that Broad draws from these arguments is that positive and negative existential propositions cannot be given an analysis in which they are about their subjects – for, if they could be given such an analysis, then the paraphrases that he considers would be perfectly in order.

Numerous objections can be raised. The most obvious is that

Broad's proposed paraphrases obviously do not preserve either meaning or truth. The sentence 'Cats do not bark' seems to be properly analyzed by the following disjunctive sentence: 'Either there are cats, and none of them barks; or there are no cats'. The suggestion that Broad makes either overlooks the second disjunct or else supposes that the negation in the original sentence is internal. Perhaps Broad's claim might be reconstrued as the observation that in simple subject-predicate sentences, 'exists' does not admit of internal negation; however, even if this is true, it is hardly reason to affirm the slogan that existence is not a predicate. Or, if this is what is meant by the slogan that existence is not a predicate, then it seems that it is unlikely to provide an obstacle to ontological arguers. Broad might object that he does offer a disjunctive analysis: "Either there are cats, and none of them barks; or there are no cats, but if there were, none of them would bark'. But there is nothing subjunctive about the original sentence – so this analysis also does not preserve either meaning or truth.

There are further objections that can be tabled. First, as Plantinga (1967:41) notes, there are many general propositions that are resistant to Broad's proposed paraphrases for positive and negative propositions, and yet that are plainly about their subjects. Consider 'Buffalo once abounded on the Great Plains'. As Plantinga says, this does not mean either that there are some buffalo and all of them once abounded on the Great Plains; nor does it mean that if there were some buffalo, all of them would once have abounded on the Great Plains. Nonetheless, it seems quite clear that this proposition is about buffalo. Given this fact, why does it matter that existential propositions are resistant to Broad's general strategy of paraphrase? Broad is not without means of reply here. Quantifiers admit of different temporal qualifications. In particular, there are quantifiers that quantify over objects that once existed, but that no longer exist. We can use one of these quantifiers to paraphrase the problem sentence: 'There once were some buffalo, and they all abounded on the Great Plains'; or 'If there were once some buffalo, they would then have abounded on the Great Plains'. These paraphrases seem all right, at least if we waive the previous objection, but the corresponding paraphrases for existential sentences would not have been acceptable to Broad. We shall return to this line of thought later.

Second, Broad's discussion says nothing directly about singular propositions. Presumably, it is meant to be adapted as follows: Negative singular propositions – that is, propositions of the form '*a* does not *F*' – can be paraphrased by sentences of the form 'There is something that is identical to *a* but it does not *F*' or by sentences of the form 'If there were something that is identical to *a* it would *F*', except in the case of negative existential singular propositions, in which case the paraphrases obtained are self-contradictory and meaningless. Similarly, positive singular propositions – that is, sentences of the form '*aFs*' – can be paraphrased by sentences of the form 'There is something that is identical to *a*, and it *Fs*', or by sentences of the form 'If there were something that is identical to *a*, then it would *F*', except in the case of positive existential singular propositions, in which case the paraphrases obtained are mere platitudes. Plantinga (1967:41) claims that there are singular propositions that are resistant to this line of analysis.

Consider: *Cerberus is my favourite beast of fable.* This is true – let us suppose – and about Cerberus; but surely it is false that Cerberus exists and has the property of being my favourite beast of fable. It is also false that if Cerberus existed, he would have the property of being my favourite beast of fable – if Cerberus existed I would be much less favourably inclined towards him.

Plantinga's suggestion that we should reject the paraphrases is correct – that is, we should grant that the paraphrases are false even though the original is true. However, it is not clear that we should agree with him that the proposition is *about* Cerberus – and hence it is not clear that we should agree with him that this argument provides a refutation of Broad's central claim. Broad's intuition is that a proposition cannot be *about* a nonexistent subject – and so Plantinga's claim that his proposition is about Cerberus is just a denial of Broad's main intuition. But what reason do we have to agree with Plantinga? Plantinga (1967:40) does provide a rhetorical flourish:

One can hope for what does not exist, and search for it, as Ponce de Lion demonstrated. One can even draw pictures of it. Why, then, cannot one talk about or refer to what does not exist? The fact, of course, is that one can; it is not at all difficult, for example, to tell stories about ghosts – indeed, I have seen it done. And when one tells a story about ghosts, then what one says is presumably about ghosts.

But this hardly constitutes a compelling argument.

Plantinga's point is one about ordinary language. We all use the word 'about' in a way that strongly suggests that we *can* speak with perfect propriety when we say that we talk about dragons, ghosts, Cerberus, and so on. However, this does not show that Broad is wrong to insist that in the context of a philosophical discussion of the properties of propositions, one should hold that no proposition can be about a subject that does not exist. Indeed, it seems that Broad can claim his own support from ordinary language – for the use that many people make of the word 'about' strongly suggests that one *can* speak with perfect propriety when one says that we do not talk *about* dragons, ghosts, Cerberus, and so on since *there are no* dragons and ghosts, and *there is no* Cerberus, for us to talk *about*. I venture to suggest that most people would agree that there is nothing improper about the use of 'about' in either of the ways now mentioned *in the appropriate circumstances.* Of course, the important question then becomes, When is it appropriate to talk in each of these ways?

The obvious answer is that it all depends upon the information that is to be conveyed by the utterance. Since 'about' has both an existentially committing and an existentially neutral use, the question of the appropriateness of its use depends upon the question whether that use will be existentially committing or existentially neutral. If the use is existentially committing, then it is simply a mistake to say that the claim that Cerberus is my favorite beast of fable is *about* Cerberus; but if the use is existentially neutral, then that claim is, at least in the relevant respect, perfectly in order. So it seems that we can agree both with Plantinga and with Broad: In the existentially committing sense, only genuine propositions – that is, propositions about existing subjects – are about their subjects; but in the existentially neutral sense, all propositions are about their subjects.

Does this mean that there is something to Broad's objection after all? No. Apart from the putative point about internal negation, there is no relevant difference between 'Dragons do not have fur' and 'Dragons do not exist'. However we construe the notion of aboutness, it is clear that either both of these sentences are about dragons, or else neither of them is. Similarly considerations apply to the sentences 'Cerberus is my favorite beast of fable' and 'Cerberus exists' – either both are about Cerberus or else neither is. So even an examination of the intuitive underpinnings of Broad's arguments does nothing toward showing that existential claims require a different kind of analysis from nonexistential claims.

Although Broad's argument is a failure, there may be something more that can be said for the suggestion that only genuine propositions are about their subjects. Suppose that we grant that sentences express propositions – and, in particular, suppose that we grant that simple subject-predicate sentences have singular propositions for their contents. That is, suppose that a true sentence of the form '*Fa*' has a singular proposition of the form $\langle a,F \rangle$ for its content, where a' is the referent of $'a,'$ and F' is the content of $'F'$. Then it seems that true negative existential sentences will not have complete propositions for their contents, since the singular terms that appear in these sentences do not have referents. An obvious suggestion is that the contents of these sentences will be gappy – for example, a sentence of the form not$E!a$ will express a proposition of the form $\langle \text{not} \langle \, , E! \rangle \rangle$. It seems not unreasonable to say that these gappy propositions have no subjects – and hence that no true negative existential proposition is about its subject. However, this does not mean that we should go on to say that these gappy propositions are not genuine propositions. After all, any sentence that contains a nonreferring name expresses a gappy proposition; and any simple sentence that contains only referring names expresses a nongappy proposition. So the contrast here is not between existential propositions and nonexistential propositions, even though all true negative existentials and all false existentials are gappy; rather, the existence of components of the propositions serves as a ground for the distinction between those that have gaps and those that do not.

In what sense could we say that positive and negative existential sentences are special? Not on syntactic grounds, for the distinction between gappy and nongappy contents cannot be drawn on these grounds. Not on narrowly semantic grounds, either, for the distinction between gappy and nongappy propositions does not coincide with the distinction between existential and nonexistential sentences. Perhaps on broadly semantic grounds: For, as we have seen, it is clear *a priori* that all true negative existential sentences and all false positive existential sentences will have gappy propositions for their contents. However, it seems doubtful that this provides us with a reason to say that existence is not a genuine predicate. For one thing, exactly parallel considerations would lead us to say that empty singular terms are not genuine singular terms. And, for another thing, the considerations adduced do not provide any reason for rejecting sentences – definitions, descriptions – in which 'exists' is used as a predicate. While we know *a priori* that all true negative existential sentences and all false positive existential sentences will have gappy propositions for their contents, we do not know *a priori* which are the true negative existentials or the false positive existentials. So, while it can be conceded that existential sentences and propositions have special properties, this concession seems to have no untoward consequences for the defender of ontological arguments.

Broad's discussion is usefully compared with Moore (1936). Moore suggests that the sentence 'Tame tigers growl' is ambiguous between 'All tame tigers growl', 'Most tame tigers growl', and 'Some tame tigers growl'; but that the sentence 'Tame tigers exist' is not ambiguous between 'All tame tigers exist', 'Most tame tigers exist', and 'Some tame tigers exist'. Moreover, he claims that, whereas 'Tame tigers do not growl' is a sentence that makes perfect sense, 'Some tame tigers do not exist' is simply nonsense. Moore goes on to suggest that these differences between 'growl' and 'exist' indicate one true thing that might be meant by the claim that existence is not a predicate.

It is tempting to reply that Moore's argument is based on a confusion between semantic and pragmatic notions of meaning. Typically, in uttering a sentence of the form '*F*s *G*' – in circumstances where one means to be speaking the literal truth – one will presuppose that there are *F*s. But if this presupposition is taken to be the presupposition that all *F*s exist, then there will clearly be problems with utterances of sentences of the form 'Some *F*s exist', 'Most *F*s exist', and 'All *F*s exist', since these will violate Gricean conversational maxims. Similar considerations apply to the negated sentences as well. Moore's argument shows that there are pragmatic oddities that can readily arise in connection with 'exists' and its cognates – but this does nothing at all toward showing that 'exists' is semantically unusual, fails to express a property, and so on.

Of course, there are related predicates – 'actually exists', 'actually presently exists', and so on – for which there is not even pragmatic oddity in Moore's sentences. Since 'exists' sometimes does duty for these related predicates, it is possible to read Moore's sentences in ways in which there is not even a *prima facie* appearance of semantic failure.

(b) *All genuine singular terms refer*

Closely related to the preceding arguments, there is a line of thought that defends the view that all genuine singular terms must refer. Barnes (1972:41) represents the argument as follows:

Take the sentence 'Theatetus exists'; suppose that it is in subject-predicate form (as, say, 'Theatetus flies' is), and that 'exists' is a logical predicate. Then, in the proposition the term 'exists' is (in Strawson's phrase) "applied to" Theatetus. Now, it is in general true that if a predicate *P* is applied to *a*, *a* must exist: for otherwise there would be nothing for *P* to be applied to. But then the proposition that Theatetus exists cannot be false: for if it is in subject-predicate form, what its subject stands for, Theatetus, exists – and hence it is true. Its form guarantees its truth.

This argument stands in need of supplementation. Barnes (1972:40) presents the necessary background in a discussion of Strawson's analysis of referring expressions:

Although there is controversy, there is also a certain general congruency of opinion about the characteristic function of a subject: the subject of a subject-predicate proposition is said to stand for or refer to or single out or identify that which the proposition is about.

It certainly seems to me to be correct to say that the proper function of singular terms in atomic sentences is to enact singular reference. However, a thing can have a proper function that it fails to fulfill – compare, blunt knives, clogged arteries, and so on. So it is simply a mistake to infer, from the fact that the proper function of singular terms in atomic sentences is to effect singular reference, that all genuine singular terms in atomic sentences must refer. What is true is that all *successful* singular terms – that is, all singular terms in atomic sentences that fulfill their proper function – do refer; but this fact is quite compatible with the further, obvious point, that many singular terms in atomic sentences fail to fulfill their proper function.[5]

The discussion from the preceding section may help here. If the singular term 'Theatetus' fulfills its proper function, then the sentence 'Theatetus exists' expresses the proposition ⟨Theatetus, exists⟩; and, from the form of this proposition, we can recognize that it is true – though, of course, from the form of the sentence, we cannot recognize that it expresses a true proposition. On the other hand, if the singular term 'Theatetus' fails to fulfill its proper function, then the sentence 'Theatetus exists' expresses the gappy proposition ⟨, exists⟩; and from the form of this proposition, we can recognize that it is false – though, again, of course, the form of the sentence does not tell us that it expresses a false proposition.

Barnes's presentation of the argument also relies on a conflation of linguistic expressions with their contents, exemplified in his use of the word 'proposition' to refer to sentences. In the sentence 'Theatetus exists', the word 'exists' is concatenated with the word 'Theatetus'. If the word 'Theatetus' refers, and the word 'exists' expresses a property,

---

5   Hereafter, I shall suppress my use of the qualification 'in atomic sentences'; however, this qualification is intended throughout. The reason for the qualification is to allow for views on which embedded singular terms have more than one proper function.

then the sentence will effect the attribution of a property to an object. But if either 'Theatetus' fails to refer or 'exists' fails to express a property, then the sentence will not effect the attribution of a property to an object. Once the elementary distinction between linguistic expressions and their content is recognized, it is immediately apparent that there is no plausible formulation of the argument.

Barnes himself makes a different objection to the argument. He suggests that it relies on the Parmenidean dogma that whatever can be spoken about exists, or, more explicitly, the following range of theses that clarify that dogma:

(1) If a predicate is applied to *a*, then *a* exists.
(2) If *a* is identified, then *a* exists.
(3) If *a* is referred to, then *a* exists.
(4) If a proposition is about *a*, then *a* exists.

Barnes offers three arguments that purport to show that none of (1)–(–4) is true.

First, he notes that it is possible to apply predicates to, to identify, to refer to, and to talk about persons and things that no longer exist. Second, he notes that there are characters in fiction that do not exist. And third, he notes that there is a range of ontologically controversial entities – numbers, propositions, properties, states of affairs – to which we apply predicates, and so on and yet whose ontological status remains controversial.

The first objection shows that (1)–(–4) need to be interpreted with some care if they are to be held to be true. If 'exists' is read as 'actually presently exists', then (1)–(–4) are obviously false. However, 'exists' can be given a wider reading – according to which anything that was, is, or will be 'exists'. On that reading, the first objection fails.

It might be objected that the example can be amended: Consider instead the case of merely possible, or even impossible, objects. But the same response can be made. If we want to say that there are objects that might have actually existed, or that there are objects that could not have actually existed, then we can give 'exists' a reading on which those things also exist. And, again, the objection will fail. On the other hand, if we do not want to say that there are objects that might have actually existed, or that there are objects that could not have actually existed, then we shall say that, in fact, we cannot identify, or refer to, or talk about, or apply predicates to such objects. Instead, we shall be fictionalists: We shall say that, according to certain stories – theories, games of make believe, and so on, – there are certain objects. However, since there actually are no such objects – all there really are are the stories, and so on – there are no objects to identify, or refer to, or talk about, or apply predicates to. Of course, according to the stories, and so on there are objects to identify, refer to, talk about, and apply predicates to. But the 'according to the stories, and so on' operator is not eliminable here.[6]

The other objections can be treated in the same way. For each of the controversial entities – fictional objects, properties, propositions, states of affairs, numbers, and so on – we have two options. On the one hand, we can say that these things exist, while perhaps denying that some of them actually presently exist; and, on the other hand, we can be fictionalists and deny that there are any such objects. Either way, we shall find no obvious difficulty in maintaining that all of (1)–(–4) are true.

I conclude that we can meet the objection that all singular terms refer without accepting Barnes's claim that there are existentially intensional relations – that is, relations that relate nonexistent objects.[7]

(c) *All genuine singular terms purport to refer*

A possible response to the objections raised in the preceding section is to make a slight alteration to the thesis about singular terms. Rather than claim that all genuine singular terms refer, say instead that all genuine singular terms purport to refer. As Barnes (1972:44) puts the point, "Surely the utterer of a typical subject-predicate proposition purports to refer to the subject of that proposition; but the utterer of a [negative] existential proposition does not, typically, purport to refer to anything."

Following Cartwright (1960), Barnes claims that in typical utterances of negative existential sentences – for example, typical utterances of 'Dragons do not exist', 'Fafner does not exist' – one does purport to refer – for example, to dragons and to Fafner, respectively. However, he disputes Cartwright's claim that there are some typical utterances of negative existential sentences – for example, typical utterances of 'Carnivorous cows do not exist' and 'The man who can beat Tal does not exist' – in which one does not purport to refer,

---

6 Presentists will take a similar line about the initial example – i.e., they will be fictionalists about the past and future.

7 I leave discussion of some difficulties that fictionalists encounter to the Literature Notes.

and hence disputes Cartwright's claim that there are some negative existential sentences that are not in subject-predicate form.

Barnes is surely right to dispute Cartwright's examples. In 'The man who can beat Tal does not exist', the definite article functions as a universal quantifier – that is, there is not even a *prima facie* case for the claim that this sentence is a negative existential. Similarly, the most plausible reading of 'Carnivorous cows do not exist' – namely, 'There are no carnivorous cows' – treats 'carnivorous cow' as a predicate; again, there is not even a *prima facie* case for the claim that this sentence is a negative existential.

However, it is far from obvious that it is correct to claim that in typical utterances of sentences of the form *'a* does not exist', one purports to refer to an object *a*. Indeed, one might reasonably claim that since one is asserting the sentence *'a* does not exist', one holds that there is no object for the name *'a'* to refer to. And in that case, one will certainly deny that in uttering a sentence of the form *'a* does not exist', one purported to refer to an object *a*. The case of sentences of the form '*Fs* do not exist' is more complicated. In these sentences, '*F*' is best regarded as a predicate. The import of an utterance of the sentence '*Fs* do not exist' is that the extension of the predicate 'F' is empty. But, unlike the case of singular terms, it is not clear that it follows from this that the predicate should be taken to have no semantic content. Indeed, on some theories of properties, most – perhaps all – predicates that have null extension nonetheless express properties. Henceforth, we shall ignore the case of general terms.

Of course, it is possible to hold a theory on which all – or virtually all – singular terms refer, and on which all typical uses of singular terms purport to refer. Salmon (1987) holds that names can refer to actually existent entities, merely possible entities, fictional characters, impossible entities, and so on. He then suggests that there may be genuinely nonreferring names – that is, names that do not refer to an entity that belongs to any of these categories. However, given the ontological commitments that he is prepared to accept, it is hard to see how there could be a name that failed to refer to anything at all.

Does this mean that there is still a way of maintaining the thesis that existence is not a predicate by adopting the view that all genuine singular terms refer and purport to refer? No. One who adopts the kind of ontology that Salmon proposes will insist on a firm distinction between the predicates 'actually exists', 'actually presently exists', 'merely possibly exists', 'merely impossibly exists', 'exists', and so on. All – or perhaps nearly all – of these predicates will be genuine predicates; moreover, it will not be true – except perhaps in one special case – that all genuine singular terms purport to refer to refer to entities that lie in the extension of any one of these predicates. The exceptional case, if there is one, would be the most general predicate that applies to all the objects in one's ontology. In order to facilitate discussion, let us introduce the term 'subsists' to be this most general predicate.[8]

If we suppose that there are no genuinely nonreferring terms, then every term refers, and purports to refer, to a subsistent entity. Moreover, there can be no true sentences of the form '*a* does not subsist' and no false sentences of the form '*a* subsists'. Furthermore, on the assumption that there are no genuinely empty predicates – that is, no predicates that do not at least pick out some impossible objects – all sentences of the form 'Some *F*s subsist' and 'Most *F*s subsist' will be true but unassertable; and all sentences of the form 'All *F*s subsist' will be trivially true. Two questions can then be asked: (i) Do these considerations show that 'subsists' is not a predicate? (ii) Do these considerations show that there is something wrong with ontological arguments?

Clearly, these considerations do show that 'subsists' is a trivial predicate. However, it is one thing to be trivial and another to fail to be genuine. For all that has been said, the triviality of 'subsists' seems not to offer the slightest reason for saying that it fails to express a property. Of course, as we noted earlier, 'subsists' will not be open to internal negation. So, if that is taken as a criterion for expressing a property, then 'subsists' does not express a property. But what reason would there be to adopt this criterion?

Furthermore, it is clear that these considerations do nothing toward showing that there is something wrong with ontological arguments. The most important point is that no ontological argument makes use of the predicate 'subsists'. Given that one accepts that 'subsists' is a grammatical predicate, it seems that one will also accept that 'actually exists', and so on are logical predicates. But ontological arguments are all couched in terms of 'actually exists', and so on. So even if one eschews the fictionalist approach in favor of an abundance of ontological commitments, one is not committed to theses about singular terms that entail that 'exists' is not a real predicate.[9]

8 Of course, Meinong has a quite different use for this term.
9 Could there be an ontological argument from subsistence to existence? No, clearly not: Analogues of this kind of ontological argument would establish the existence of

(d) *There are no genuine singular terms*

A quite different formulation of a neo-Kantian objection to ontological arguments – though perhaps not one that can be counted as a different construal of the notion that existence is not a predicate – is obtained if we suppose that the essential point of the objection is the claim that there are no genuine singular terms. There are at least two different ways of elaborating this point.

The first, Quinean suggestion is that in the canonical classical first-order formulation of our theories, singular terms are all eliminated in favor of predicates. So, for example, instead of the name 'Socrates', one has the predicate 'Socratizes': The sentence 'Socrates loves dialec-tic' is rendered in canonical notation as 'The unique thing that Socrat-izes loves dialectic'.

If one adopts this suggestion about the canonical formulation of theories, then it becomes very difficult to formulate ontological argu-ments – at least, given only the resources of classical first-order logic. However, if one were to eschew Quinean strictures against free logics and modal logics – and, in particular, if one allowed oneself the use of predicates such as 'actually exists' in a free quantified modal logic – then one would still be able to formulate ontological arguments even if all singular terms were reparsed according to the Quinean direc-tive.[10]

Even if one were to accept Quine's strictures against free logics and modal logics, one might wonder why his suggestion about the reparsing of singular terms ought to be adopted. Perhaps the point is that, in classical logic, it is taken for granted that all of the proper names have referents – but that there is no guarantee that singular terms in our best theories will have referents. Unfortunately, this is surely an argument in favor of the adoption of free logic rather than in favor of the Quinean reparsing. Although I cannot give a conclusive argument, it seems to me that there is no good reason to think that there is anything wrong with either free logic or the use of singular terms in ordinary language; and hence, there is no good reason to support the Quinean reparsing program. At the very least, this seems

an unbelievable range of necessarily existent beings – cf., the discussion of the uses of parody in the next chapter.

10   The formulations of the argument of *Proslogion* 2 in Adams (1971) and Lewis (1970), as well as the argument given in Plantinga (1974), do not involve any singular terms.

to be a very weak platform on which to launch an attack on ontological arguments.

The second, quasi-Russellian suggestion is that in the canonical reformulation of our language, singular terms are given a two-step analysis: First, those that are not definite descriptions are treated as abbreviations for definite descriptions; and, second, definite descriptions are given a quantificational analysis. I have already noted – in the earlier discussion of Kant's discussion of ontological arguments – that the first step of this analysis is not very plausible. There is one line of thought that is not evidently hopeless – namely, the thought that '*a*' should be analyzed as 'the one who is actually called '*a*', as that name is used in the present context'. The problem with this analysis is that it does not actually eliminate the singular term '*a*'; if the analysis is to succeed, then there must be a practice of using that singular term. Since there is no other plausible descriptional analysis of singular terms, I conclude that this suggestion poses no threat to ontological arguments.

This second suggestion is only *quasi*-Russellian because Russell thinks that there are some genuine singular terms that are not amenable to the two-step process, namely, the demonstratives – 'logically proper names' – 'this' and 'that'. According to Russell, sentences of the form '*a* exists' are completely meaningless if '*a*' is a genuine singular term – so that, for example, a sentence of the form 'This exists' is completely meaningless. This seems clearly wrong. Of course, if we can rule out the possibility of reference failure – which is what Russell thought must be done in the case of genuine singular terms – then we can be quite sure that a sentence of the form '*a* exists' will be true. But that something is guaranteed to be true does not show that it is meaningless, even though it may show that it is pragmatically unassertable. As Moore (1936) pointed out, considerations about compositionality – for example, that the evident meaningfulness of the sentence 'This might not have existed' depends upon the meaningfulness of 'This exists' – suggest that it would be a serious error to claim that sentences of the form '*a* exists' are meaningless. Again, the evident conclusion is that this proposal poses no threat to ontological arguments.

In sum, even though there may well be reason to be suspicious of the use that is made of singular terms in ontological arguments – and, in particular, that there may well be reason to suspect that presuppositions about the successful reference of singular terms lead some ontological arguments to beg the question – it seems clear that their suspicions are not well captured in views that deny that there are any genuine singular terms.

(3) ATTEMPTED DEFENSES 2: EXISTENCE

I turn now to a consideration of accounts of the view that existence is not a predicate that focus more explicitly on the analysis of the finite parts of the natural language verb 'exists'.

(a) *Existence is a second-order predicate*

One of the best-known accounts of the claim that existence is not a predicate is encapsulated in Frege's, and Russell's, contention that existence is a second-order predicate. According to Frege, we must distinguish between properties of objects, which are expressed by first-order predicates, and properties of concepts, which are expressed by second-order predicates. In *The Foundations of Arithmetic*, he argues as follows:

> The content of a statement of number is an assertion about a concept. This is perhaps clearest with the number o. If I say 'Venus has o moons', there simply does not exist any moon or agglomeration of moons for anything to be asserted of; but what happens is that a property is assigned to the concept 'moon of Venus', namely that of including nothing under it. If I say 'the Kaiser's carriage is drawn by four horses', then I assign the number four to the concept 'horse that draws the Kaiser's carriage'.[11]

Moreover, according to Frege, existence is analogous to number:

> "Affirmation of existence is in fact nothing but denial of the number nought." ... The proposition that horses exist is a perfectly respectable subject-predicate proposition; but it does not predicate existence, or anything else, of horses. It says nothing of Bucephalus, Barbary, White Surrey and the rest; it is about the *concept* 'horse', and it says of the concept that it is instantiated – that it does *not* "include nothing under it."[12]

Finally, Frege claims that it is not possible to use 'there is' as a first-order predicate:

---

11 Translated by J. L. Austin, second edition, Oxford: Blackwell, 1953, p. 59e; cited by Barnes (1971:51).
12 Barnes (1971:51–2). The sentence from Frege's *Foundations of Arithmetic* is from p. 65e.

I do not want to say it is false to assert about an object what is here asserted about a concept; I want to say it is impossible, senseless, to do so. The sentence 'There is Julius Caesar' is neither true, nor false, but senseless.[13]

As Barnes (1972:54) notes, the considerations adduced thus far do not carry any weight against ontological arguments. For, even if Frege is right that general statements about existence must be given a second-order analysis, there are many ontological arguments that involve singular terms – and nothing that has been said thus far bears on the question of the analysis of sentences of the form '*a* exists'. And, in fact, Frege allows that sentences of the form '*a* exists' are not senseless. So, in fact, it seems that Frege's arguments do not even make a *prima facie* case against ontological arguments – despite the fact that he claims that "because existence is a property of concepts, the Ontological Argument for the existence of God breaks down."

Moreover, even if Frege's view were amended to impose a second-level analysis on singular existential sentences – and even if this amendment went unquestioned – it seems that ontological arguments could still emerge unscathed. For, as William Forgie (1972:263) points out, defenders of ontological arguments could agree with Frege that all existence sentences subsume a first-level concept under a second-level concept, and yet maintain that there is a first-level property of existence in terms of which that second-level concept can be explicated. That is, defenders of ontological arguments could *agree* with Frege that affirmation of existence is denial of the number nought; and they could agree that the proposition that horses exist is about the concept 'horse', saying of that concept that it is instantiated. But defenders of ontological arguments would *deny* that there is *nothing more* to the affirmation of existence than denial of the number nought; and they would *deny* that the proposition that horses exist says *nothing* about Bucephalus, Barbary, White Surrey, and the rest.

In sum, even if we agree with Frege that 'exists' should be analyzed as a second-order predicate, it is unclear why we cannot also claim that existence is a first-order property; and, more importantly, it is hard to see why we should agree with Frege that 'exists' should always be analyzed as a second-order predicate.

---

13 "Concept and Object," in *Translations from the Philosophical Writings of Gottlob Frege*, second edition, edited by P. Geach and M. Black. Oxford: Blackwell, 1960, p. 50, cited by Barnes (1971:52).

(b) *Existence is a quantifier*

Perhaps the most natural reply to the claim that 'exists' might be analyzed as something other than a second-order property is to invoke the authority of Quine (1953). It may seem plausible to say that quantification involves the expression of second-order properties; and it is well-known that Quine holds that there is a very close connection between existence and quantification, conveniently summarized in the slogan 'To be is to be a value of a bound variable'.

In fact, Quine's views on existence and quantification are not easy to encapsulate. First, it should be noted that Quine's principal concern is with the ontological commitments of theories: What he claims is, roughly, that a theory is committed to the existence of an object iff that object must be counted among the values of the variables in a suitable first-order reformulation of the theory. Second, as Salmon (1987:51ff.) emphasizes, it should not be supposed that it is the values of the variables for any old quantifiers that reveal one's ontological commitments; rather, it is the values of the variables for, say, the presentist and actualist quantifiers, or – perhaps – for the most broad-ranging quantifiers, in your theory.

I suspect that Quine himself thought that there is only one genuine kind of objectual quantifier; but this seems wrong. Even if one follows Quine in rejecting modalities, there are still tenses to consider. As Salmon points out, a literal construal of the Quinean dictum seems to be refuted by the observation that while dinosaurs are the values of some of today's variable, no dinosaurs exist. However, Quine would no doubt reply that, in fact, dinosaurs do tenselessly exist. Alternatively, the Quinean dictum could be amended as Salmon suggests: 'to-be-or-to-have-been-or-to-be-going-to-be is to be the value of a bound variable'. If modal considerations are allowed, we can go further along this line: 'to-be-or-to-have-been-or-to-be-going-to-be-or-to-possibly-be-or-to-possibly-have-been-or-to-possibly-be-going-to-be'. And no doubt many theorists – for example, Meinong – would want further extensions.

Quine also says that to be is to be one of everything. This seems truistic, at least on those readings on which 'to be' and 'everything' are given the same scope. Clearly, if 'to be' is read as 'to have been, or to be, or to later be, or to possibly have been, or to possibly be, or to possibly come to be', and 'everything' is read as 'everything that presently, actually is', then it won't be true that to be is to be one of everything – but this fact should occasion no surprise. The natural

147

interpretations of the claim that to be is to be one of everything are (i) that each thing that actually presently exists is one of all the things that actually presently exists, (ii) that each thing that tenselessly exists is one of all the things that tenselessly exist, (iii) that each thing that possibly exists is one of all the things that possibly exists, and (iv) that each thing that subsists is one of all the things that subsists. Which interpretation one favors will presumably depend upon what one takes to be the most expansive quantifier in one's global theory.[14]

So far, the Quinean claim seems uncontroversial. However, as Barnes notes, if it is true (i) that everything exists and (ii) that everything has some predicate that is true of it, then it seems to follow that, for any predicate '*F*', a thing is *F* iff it is both *F* and exists:

For any property F and any object x, x is F iff x is an existent F.

This principle seems to have important consequences for some ontological arguments, if it is true. For, if being *F* and being an existent *F* are the same thing – which is what the principle seems to say – then it is hard to see how it can make sense to claim that it is greater, or better, or more perfect to exist than not to exist. Since nothing that fails to exist has any properties at all – that is, since there isn't any *thing* that fails to exist – it is hard to see how existence can be counted as an attribute that makes something better. In particular, one is tempted to ask, "Better than what?" The answer can't be better than similar things that do not exist – for there aren't any of *those*.

But, of course, we need to be careful how we interpret this principle. If 'existent' is read as 'subsistent' in our statement of the principle, then there is still room for the view that, for example, it is greater, or better, or more perfect to actually, presently exist than to subsist but not to actually, presently exist. Moreover – as Salmon (1987:97) emphasizes – there is also room for the view that there are things that do not actually, presently exist, but that nonetheless actually, presently have properties. Consider the dinosaurs: None of them actually, presently exists – but they all actually, presently have the property of being extinct. As Salmon puts the point: Predication precedes existence.

It should be noted that there may be no obligation to accept Salm-

---

14 As I explained earlier, it seems that one must opt for some package of quantifiers and fictionalist analysis: one who opts for a presentist, actualist quantifier will need the most extensive fictionalist analyses; while one who opts for a subsistent quantifier may need no fictionalist analyses at all.

on's dictum. It appears that it is still open for a Quinean to hold that the most broad ranging quantifier is tenseless but actual, and that the only things that tenselessly have properties are actual. For, even if one eschews Quine's view about the desirability of reparsing singular terms, it may still be possible to account for the many apparent attributions of properties to nonactual entities to which we appear to be committed, via the invocation of suitable fictionalist analyses. Consider, for example, the case of fictional characters. Barnes (1971:48ff.) and Plantinga (1967:39ff.) mention the following sentences, which they suggest provide counterexamples to the Quinean claim that to be is to be one of everything:[15]

(i)   Mr. Slope was one of Trollope's most felicitous creations.
(ii)   Mr. Slope was modeled on a well-known bishop's chaplain.
(iii)   Mr. Slope is emulated by a host of college chaplains.
(iv)   Very many of the heroes revered by the Greeks never existed.
(v)   Some of the creatures in Ovid's *Metamorphoses* do not exist.
(vi)   Cerberus is my favorite beast of fable.
(vii)   Dragons do not have fur.
(viii) More books have been written about Hamlet than about Lyndon Johnson.

However, I suggest that these sentences can be given paraphrases along the following lines:[16]

(i)   In the novel, various characteristics are attributed to Mr. Slope. The attribution of that combination of characteristics is particularly felicitous.
(ii)   In the novel, various characteristics are attributed to Mr. Slope. A relevantly similar combination of characteristics was possessed by a well-known bishop's chaplain.
(iii)   In the novel, various characteristics are attributed to Mr. Slope. That combination of characteristics has served as a paradigm for a host of college chaplains.
(iv)   According to the legends of the Greeks, there are various heroes

15 The enumeration is mine.
16 In some cases, these paraphrases are schematic, in the sense that talk of 'various characteristics' needs to be replaced by some more definite account of the relevant characteristics; however, I cannot see that there is any in principle difficulty for the kinds of paraphrases that are suggested. In all cases, the scope of a sentential operator – e.g., 'in the novel' – is restricted to the sentence in which the operator occurs.

with various sets of characteristics; and, in virtue of what the legends say about those heroes, certain feelings of reverence were produced in the Greeks; but actually there are no such heroes, that is, there are no heroes who possess those sets of characteristics.

(v)   According to Ovid's *Metamorphoses*, there are various creatures with various properties. In some cases, there are no such creatures, that is, there are no creatures that possess those properties.

(vi)   (a) According to certain stories, Cerberus exists and has certain properties.
       (b) According to certain – not necessarily other – stories, other fabulous beasts exist, and have certain properties.
       Considered solely with respect to the information mentioned in (a) and (b), I prefer the stories referred to in (a) to the stories referred to in (b).

(vii) According to the relevant stories, dragons do not have fur.

(viii) (a) According to the Shakespearean play – and subsequent films, plays, and so on, – Hamlet is a character with certain attributes.
       More books have been written about the aspect of the Shakespearean play, and so on, referred to in (a) than about any aspect of Lyndon Johnson.

In these examples, we get suitable translations by (i) paraphrasing in terms of properties and – if one is beset by nominalistic scruples – (ii) construing properties in terms of predicates. We suppose that intensional operators are open to quantifying in – anaphoric reference, and so on – to predicate position, even though they are not similarly open in singular term positions.

I suggest that one might reasonably hold that similar paraphrases can be used to explain away other unwanted apparent ontological commitments. If one adopts fictionalist analyses of, for example, mathematical and modal sentences, then one can continue to use sentences in which one appears to attribute properties to possibilia and numbers without supposing that there are any possibilia or numbers, and without violating the thesis that only the things that are can have properties.

Barnes (1972:55, 48) also offers some examples involving tenses as counterexamples to Quine:[17]

---

17   The enumeration is mine.

(ix) Only a few copies of the first Shakespeare folios exist.
(x) Socrates is a celebrated philosopher.
(xi) Socrates is a model for all aspiring philosophers.

These examples seem to be best treated by allowing that things that do not presently exist can nonetheless possess properties now:

(ix) Only a few copies of the first Shakespeare folios still exist. At time T_1, there were N copies of the first Shakespeare folios. Now, only x percent of those folios continue to exist.
(x) Although Socrates does not presently exist, there was a time at which Socrates did exist; and, moreover, it is true now that Socrates has the property of being a celebrated philosopher.
(xi) Although Socrates does not presently exist, there was a time at which Socrates did exist; and, moreover, it is true now that Socrates has the property of being a model for all aspiring philosophers.

Does this mean that we must modify the Quinean claim that only things that exist can have properties? Not at all. In order to cope with these examples, all we need say is that anything that tenselessly exists can presently possess properties, even if it does not presently exist. And that is still a way of maintaining the view that only things that exist possess properties. Of course, it is not a way of maintaining the view that only things that presently exist can presently possess properties. But why should anyone wish to maintain that view?

In sum, there is a range of positions that one might take on questions about the connections between quantification, predication, and existence. At one end of the range, there is the actualist view that everything tenselessly exists, and that things that do not presently exist can presently possess properties. On this view, other apparent ontological commitments are explained away using fictionalist analyses. At the other end of the range, there is the quasi-Meinongian view that everything subsists, and that anything that subsists can actually, presently possess properties even if it does not presently exist, or actually exist, or even possibly exist. On this view, there may be no apparent ontological commitments that need to be paraphrased away using fictionalist analyses.

Moreover, no matter which position one takes in this range, it seems that (i) one will be able to endorse the Quinean claim that one's ontological commitments are revealed by the values of the "largest" quantifiers to whose literal use one is at least tacitly committed; (ii) one will be able to endorse the Quinean claim that everything exists; (iii) one will be able to endorse the consequent claim that only things that exist – in the "largest" sense – presently, actually have properties; and (iv) there will be nothing in any of this that gives one the slightest reason to say that existence is not a predicate in any sense that threatens the soundness of ontological arguments.[18]

(c) *Existence does not admit of analysis*

Another doctrine that is associated with the work of Quine is that the finite parts of the verb 'to exist' are primitive, unanalyzable, and univocal. This doctrine can be understood to have several different components, which we shall examine in turn.

First, this doctrine can be taken to embrace the claim that existence does not admit of qualifications – that is, there are not different *modes* of existence. This doctrine itself admits of at least two different interpretations. On the first interpretation, what is denied is that it makes sense to say that there are *degrees of reality*; while, on the second interpretation, what is denied is that there are different *kinds* of existence – for example, possible existence, past existence, fictional existence.

The doctrine that there are degrees of reality is very hard to understand. Suppose we fix our attention on present, actual existence. What could it possibly mean to say that some things presently, actually exist to a greater or lesser degree than others? Since it seems completely evident to me that present, actual existence is a nondegreed property, I shall not – because I cannot – attempt to pursue this line of enquiry.[19]

18 None of what I say here is incompatible with the Meinongian position that there are things that do not exist, and to which Meinongians have no ontological commitment – for these Meinongian claims require that 'exist' and 'ontology' are not given "large" readings. In the largest sense, the Meinongian agrees that everything exists, but she holds that some of those things that exist do not *really* exist. Of course, divergent uses of terminology are a fertile source of groundless controversy in this area.

19 Daniel Nolan has suggested one way to make sense of the idea that existence is a degreed property, namely, that it might sometimes be a *vague* matter whether something exists. Consider, for example, the erosion of a mountain. Between the times at which the mountain definitely exists, and those times at which it no longer definitely exists, there are times where it is indefinite or vague whether the

The doctrine that there are different modes of existence seems to be straightforwardly true. Almost everyone will agree that there are different acceptable quantifiers – for example, 'there once was but no longer is', 'there never has been and isn't but there will be'. Corresponding to these different quantifiers, there are different modes of existence – past existence, present existence, future existence. Of course, there is disagreement about which quantifiers are acceptable: Some will accept the quantifiers 'there possibly is' and 'there fictionally is'; but others will insist that possible existence and fictional existence are unacceptable modifications of existence. However, this is disagreement about which modes of existence to countenance, not disagreement about whether there are modes of existence.

Could the doctrine that there are degrees of reality now be resurrected in the claim that modes of existence form a hierarchy? It isn't easy to see how.

Descartes – following his Scholastic teachers – held that there is an ontological hierarchy: modes, attributes, finite substances, infinite substances. But this hierarchy bears no plausible relation to our discussion of modes of existence. Finite substances and infinite substances can both have present existence, or past existence, or future existence, or – if one's theory permits – possible existence, and so on. And modes and attributes may not have any place in our ontology.

Perhaps one might hold that actual existence outranks merely possible existence. However, it is quite unclear how the other modes of existence should be included in this hierarchy. How, for example, should present existence compare with past existence? This does not seem to be a very promising line of enquiry.

Second, the doctrine can be taken to embrace the claim that it is not possible to provide a materially adequate analysis of existence in terms of, say, self-identity. Thus, for example, Barnes (1971:63) claims (i) that any such analysis has the false consequence that anything we

---

mountain still exists. Moreover, it seems that one could say that it is indefinite or vague *to a greater or lesser degree* whether the mountain still exists. However, that existence can be a degreed property in this sense is irrelevant to my present concerns: What matters is whether existence can be a degreed property in those cases in which such vagueness is ruled out – i.e., whether two things that both definitely exist can nonetheless differ in degree of existence. In case higher-order vagueness threatens, we can be even more precise: What matters is whether things can differ in degree of existence when both definitely exist, definitely definitely exist, definitely definitely definitely exist, and so on. I am unable to see how this could be the case.

talk about exists, and (ii) that '*a* exists' and '*a* is self-identical' have different senses.

These objections can be met. I have already argued that there is no difficulty in accepting the view that anything that we talk about exists; and there is no reason why we should expect a materially adequate analysis to preserve sense. If we did insist this, then we should have no means of escaping from Moore's paradox of analysis – for no analysis that preserves sense could possibly be illuminating.

Moreover, an adequate analysis does not seem hard to find. As Salmon (1987:63) notes, it is quite well-known that

the term 'exists' is fully and completely definable in formal logic as a first-order predicate of individuals, using standard, actualist, Frege–Russell existential quantification. Its definition (which also employs the logical notions of identity and abstraction but nothing more) is the following: $(\lambda x)(\exists y)(x = y)$. Less formally, the English word 'exists' may be regarded as being defined by the phrase 'is identical with something', or more simply 'is something'. This yields an alternative way to give substance to the idea that to be is to be one of everything: To be one of everything is to be something.

As I noted in the earlier discussion of the Kantian critique of ontological arguments, it seems that there is a straightforward sense in which existence is a predicate even in classical first-order logic. Of course, in that stystem, for any name '*a*', the sentence '$[(\lambda x)(\exists y)(x = y)]a$' will be true, so the predicate will be trivial. But in, say, free logic, this predicate will be highly nontrivial. Curiously, Barnes (1971:57) says that while free logics are doubtless of formal interest, "advocacy of them appears to be an excessive reaction to the alleged deficiencies of standard logic, at least so far as the interests of the ontological argument are concerned." But, on the contrary, free logics provide a clear demonstration of the possibility of having nontrivial predicates that express some modes of existence.

Barnes, after rejecting an analysis in terms of self-identity, himself suggests that in its primary sense, 'to exist' should be analyzed as 'to be somewhere'. This might seem promising as an analysis of 'actual existence', at least if one ignores tricky cases like numbers, mental states, and so on. However, it seems quite unsuitable as an analysis of 'subsistence' or 'possible existence'. The only answer to the question of where are possible worlds located is in logical space. But I doubt that it should be supposed that logical space is anywhere. And it sounds quite peculiar to say that impossible objects are located in illogical space.

Third, the doctrine can be taken to embrace the claim that it is not possible to paraphrase all sentences that involve the predicate 'exists' with sentences that use only the existential quantifier 'there is'. Barnes (1972:61) provides some examples that he claims demonstrate the truth of this thesis:[20]

(i)   The agents he named under torture were later found not to exist.
(ii) There are times when I feel like screaming.
(iii) There are solecisms in every speech he makes.

These examples can be given paraphrases along the following lines:

(i)   For any x, if x is a name he produced under torture, then it is not the case that there is some y such that x refers to y.
(ii) Times that I feel like screaming occur.
(iii) In every speech that he makes, solecisms occur.

There are two points to note. First, it is true that there are a number of ontological categories for which the quantifier 'there is' seems appropriate, and yet the predicate 'exists' does not: Whereas, it is true that individuals *exist*, events *happen*, times *occur*, states of affairs *obtain*, and properties *have instances*. Since all of these ontological categories can be represented by existential quantifiers in canonical notation, 'exists' in ordinary language must be supplemented with various cognates if one is to claim a natural equivalence with 'there is'. However, this supplementation does not undermine the basic claim about the equivalence of 'there is' and 'exists' when we restrict our attention to individuals.

Second, the paraphrases for the natural language sentences may be quite involved and may involve quantification over entities – for example, names – that do not seem to be referred to in the original sentences. However, this does not undermine their utility as paraphrases. The point of the paraphrases is to say everything that one who wanted to assert the original sentence could want to say, but using an existence predicate instead of a quantifier. This point can be satisfied even if the resulting sentence is not extensionally equivalent to the original.

There are other examples that raise difficulties – especially in the form of sentences that already mix quantifiers and predicates:

1. There are no existent unicorns.

---

20 The enumeration is mine.

Here are three sentences that could be considered to be paraphrases:

1a. No unicorns there (possibly) are (actually) exist.
1b. There aren't (actually) any unicorns that there (possibly) are.
1c. No (possibly) existent unicorns (actually) exist.

Even without the parenthetical inclusions – which help to indicate how these sentences should be read – it is possible to make correct sense of these paraphrases. The point is that these sentences require the invocation of two different modes of existence: And these different modes can be represented either by predicates or by quantifiers.[21] Once the possibility of modifying quantifiers and predicates is recognized, it seems clear that these kinds of examples do not present any difficulty either.

Since none of the doctrines mentioned in this section is true, none of them can be considered a satisfactory explication of the claim that existence is not a predicate. Consequently, none of them provides a stick with which to beat defenders of ontological arguments. Moreover, even if these claims were true, it is hard to see how they would bear on ontological arguments. Even if 'exists' is unanalyzable, univocal, and primitive, it seems that one could still use it in framing definitions, and so on. Perhaps the doctrine that existence is a perfection might be hard to hold onto under these circumstances – but not all ontological arguments rely on this kind of assumption.

(d) *Existence is not a property*

The last sort of objection that I wish to consider is less traditional. The guiding idea is that 'exists' should be given an analysis that is somehow analogous to the analysis that redundancy theorists give to the "truth"-predicate or to the analysis that deflationary theorists give to the word 'refers'. Since there are a number of different ways of giving deflationary analyses of truth and reference, there are a number of different potential ways of understanding the suggested analogy.

A first thought is that the deflationary position is a consequence of nominalism: There are no properties and hence, *a fortiori*, the predicates 'is true' and 'refers' do not express properties. This is not a promising suggestion for opponents of ontological arguments – for, of

21 If, according to syntactic criteria, one uses only one kind of predicate or quantifier throughout, then one will have to rely on contextual factors – e.g., stress – in order to convey one's meaning.

course, what opponents of the arguments want is a sense in which 'exists' is distinguished from other predicates because it fails to express a property. Moreover, nominalism is a controversial doctrine: It would be disappointing for opponents of ontological arguments if that opposition had to be tied to acceptance of nominalism.

A second thought is that the deflationary position should be construed as a doctrine about the *eliminability* of the predicates 'is true' and 'refers' from a canonical statement of one's global theory. This thought can be spelled out as a claim about the *analytic definability* of those predicates, the *contextual definability* of those predicates, or the *utility* of those predicates. If deflationism is a claim about the analytic definability of predicates, then it is hard to see why it counts as an eliminativist doctrine – for a predicate that can be analytically defined in terms of substantial predicates is surely thereby itself substantial. So this is not a promising analogy for opponents of ontological arguments. If deflationism is a claim about the contextual definability of predicates, then it is more plausible to claim that it is an eliminativist doctrine; however, the problem is that it is dubious that any such strategy can be made to work. The obvious suggestion, in the case of 'exists', is that the sentences in question should be paraphrased by sentences that contain existential quantifiers – but, as I have already argued, it is hard to see how this could be taken to show that existence is not a predicate. If deflationism is a claim about the utility of certain predicates in the statement of global theory – say, that the predicates 'is true' and 'refers' will not figure in the vocabulary that is used to state that theory, and will not be definable in terms of the vocabulary that is used to state that theory – then the most important question concerns the plausibility of that claim. It seems obvious that there are true sentences of the form '*a* exists': So a global theory that does not entail these sentences – perhaps after the invocation of suitable definitions – would seem thereby to be shown to be incomplete. Again, this does not seem to be a very promising strategy for opponents of ontological arguments.

A third thought is that the deflationary position should be construed as a doctrine about the function of the predicates 'is true' and 'refers' in ordinary language. For example, on the Brandom (1984) version of this view, the expression 'refers' is *nothing but* a complex anaphoric pronoun-forming operator; and, on the Field (1986) version of this view, the expression 'is true' is *nothing but* a device of infinitary conjunction. These views face problems in the form of recalcitrant sentences that seem not to fit the analyses – for example, 'Some terms do not refer', 'Sentences divide into two classes: those that are definitely true, and those that are not definitely true'; however, we shan't focus on this apparent problem here. A more pressing concern is that it is unclear why it cannot be the case that, for example, 'is true' is a device of infinitary conjunction, and also the truth-predicate expresses a property. Perhaps any device of infinitary conjunction is bound to express a substantial property; at any rate, the deflationary theorist needs to provide some justification for the "nothing buttery" that is present in his view. Even if the opponent of ontological arguments can give a description of a linguistic function that is served by the finite parts of the verb 'to exist', it is quite unclear how those opponents could go on to argue that there is nothing more to those parts of the verb than that linguistic function.

Perhaps there is some other way of deflating the claim that existence is a property; however, I have not been able to find it. I conclude that it is reasonable to think that there is no suitable parallel to deflationary treatments of truth and reference that can be successfully applied to existence.[22]

(4) (MAYBE) EXISTENCE IS A PREDICATE

So far, I have provided some reasons for thinking that arguments in favor of the view that existence is not a predicate fail. I now turn to some considerations that are intended to support the view that existence is, after all, a predicate. Some of these considerations were foreshadowed in the preceding discussion.

First, it should be noted that existential sentences can be given metalinguistic truth-conditions, along the following lines:

(1) '*a* exists' is true iff '*a*' refers.
(2) '*a* does not exist' is true iff '*a*' does not refer.

This only helps if we can explain what we mean by 'refers' – that is, 'refers to one of the things that there is'. Here, we look to the Quinean conception of the objects in the domain of quantification for assistance. Which names refer depends upon the relations between names and objects in the domain of quantification. Of course, existence is not

---

22 In effect, I am contending that deflationary treatments of truth and reference do not succeed either – i.e., do not succeed in showing that neither truth nor reference is a real predicate. My discussion is too cursory to establish this conclusion; however, I hope that it indicates the direction that a more detailed argument would take.

construed as a relation; rather, reference is. But the notion of reference can be used in the explication of the use of the predicate 'exists'. We can see that the predicate has a use, even though it is satisfied by everything. Compare the Tractarian complaints about the identity predicate. Here, too, we can find a use for the predicate if we look to the metalinguistic analysis. But, again, the claims expressed using the predicate are not themselves metalinguistic. When I say, truly, '*a* exists' or '*a* = *b*', I am making a claim about *a* because I am referring to *a*. When I say, truly, '*a* does not exist', I am not making a claim about any particular object, because '*a*' does not refer.

Second, it is useful to compare the following two schemas:

A. '*a* is red' is true iff '*a*' refers to one of the things that there is, and that thing is red.
B. '*a* exists' is true iff '*a*' refers to one of the things that there is (and that thing is one of the things that there is).

There is a redundancy in (B), but this does not show that there is an important disanalogy between (A) and (B); rather, it just shows that (B) reduces to our earlier metalinguistic analysis, (1). Since (1) is composed of two potentially informative parts – we take for granted that the right-hand sentence is potentially informative, and then note that the left-hand sentence must be too, given the material equivalence – we conclude that '*a* exists' is potentially informative. This suffices to show that 'exists' is a genuine predicate, in a fairly robust sense.

Third, it should be noted that what one supposes that there is is what one's favored theory tells one that there is: for many of us, roughly, the world as described by science. Part of what there is is a lot of storytelling, make-believe, imagining, and so on. Although we use such locutions as 'The story is about *X*', we suppose that '*X*' here is not amenable to existential quantification – that is, it is not ontologically committing. In a suitable redescription of our practice, this claim would be eliminated – and that redescription is the one that reveals our genuine ontic commitments. Nonetheless, locutions like 'The story is about *X*' are useful shorthand, especially since the suitable redescriptions are likely to be very complicated – compare the earlier discussion of the examples from Barnes and Plantinga. Moreover, the fact that there are stories, make-believe, imaginings, and so on provides the grounds for the explanation of the function of the finite parts of the verb 'to exist'. The metalinguistic analysis of existence relies on the thought that there can be nonreferring terms; and those nonreferring terms get used, with perfect propriety, in the telling of stories, the acting out of make-believe, the exposition of radically false theories, and so on. The function of the finite parts of the verb 'to exist' is to draw our attention to the nonreferring uses of singular terms: But in fulfilling this function, it acts as a genuine predicate that is true of everything – compare our earlier discussion.

Fourth, as I have noted several times, there is one feature of the predicate 'exists' – on its "largest" reading – that distinguishes it from other predicates: Unlike other predicates, 'exists' seems not to admit of internal negation.[23] As I have already stressed, this apparent fact does not show that existence is not a genuine predicate – for there is no non-question-begging reason to insist that genuine predicates must admit of internal negation. Perhaps a useful comparison is with 'is either red or not red': No sentence in which the internal negation of this predicate is predicated of a singular term can be true; but this does not show that the predicate is not genuine, fails to express a property, and so on.

Fifth, it should be noted that there are some ontological positions that entail that there are further senses in which 'exists' differs from other predicates – for example, on the standard Meinongian view, 'exists' does not belong in the class of nuclear or characterizing predicates. However, there is nothing in any of these positions that suggests, for example, that no identifying description can include the word 'existent'; rather, these positions entail restrictions on the conclusions that can be drawn from the use of those descriptions. Moreover, while the Meinongian insistence that existence is extranuclear does serve to undermine Meinongian ontological arguments, it leaves some other ontological arguments – for example, the modal ontological arguments – untouched. And, in any case, a thoroughly general treatment of ontological arguments should, if possible, remain neutral between the various ontological positions, – that is, it should not take a stance on the question whether Meinongianism is correct.

Last, it should be stressed that it is not really important to my purposes that it turn out that existence *is* a predicate; it will suffice if I have managed to show that it is very difficult to decide whether or

23 Of course, this is not true of the restricted uses of 'exists': 'actually exists' and 'actually presently exists' do admit of internal negation. Moreover, we deliberately ignore the behavior of the predicate in the neighborhood of intensional operators – 'according to the story', 'according to the definition', etc. – since the effect of these operators is partly to pretend to enlarge the extension of the term 'exists'.

not existence is a predicate – or, even more minimally, that it is very difficult to mount a decisive argument in favor of the view that there is a sense in which existence is not a predicate that poses a serious threat to ontological arguments. What I really want to defend is the idea that it is sensible to try to provide compelling reasons for refusing to pay any more attention to ontological arguments without so much as taking up the question whether existence is a predicate – and hence to justify the trouble that I have taken in trying to show how ontological arguments fail.

Chapter 11

The uses of parody

THROUGHOUT these chapters, I have often adverted to arguments that parody the ontological arguments under consideration. In this section, I wish to collect together the different sorts of parodies that might be made of ontological arguments and to consider the uses to which they might be put. I shall divide the initial discussion according to the different conceptions of God that are invoked in the arguments.

(1) BEINGS OF KIND *K* THAN WHICH NO GREATER BEINGS OF KIND *K* CAN BE CONCEIVED

We have already seen that Gaunilo maintained that St. Anselm's argument could be paralleled with an argument that purports to establish the existence of an island than which no greater island can be conceived. Moreover, there seems to be nothing special about Gaunilo's choice of 'island' in this example: If he is right, it seems that St. Anselm's argument can be paralleled by an argument that purports to establish the existence of a being of kind *K* than which no greater being of kind *K* can be conceived, for any kind of object *K*.

Some kinds *K* of objects make for more plausible parallels to St. Anselm's ontological arguments than do others. In particular, given that it is a premise of the argument that a being of kind *K* than which no greater being of kind *K* can be conceived and that actually exists is greater than a being of kind *K* than which no greater being of kind *K* can be conceived but that does not actually exist, there are kinds that make for *prima facie* implausible parallels. Most obviously, there are kinds that don't seem to admit of greatness in any intelligible sense – for example, numbers, propositions, handshakes, fingernails.

The last example may be controversial. Why couldn't there be a fingernail than which no greater fingernail can be conceived? Of course, the same question arises for traditional responses to Gaunilo's example of an island than which no greater island can be conceived. A number of suggestions can be considered.

One suggestion that might be made is that nothing with spatiotemporal parts admits of greatness in the relevant sense.[1] On the assumption that God does not have spatiotemporal parts, this suggestion appears to point to a relevant distinction between God and many other beings. But is it plausible to claim that nothing with spatiotemporal parts admits of greatness in the relevant sense? Why can't there be an X than which no greater X can be conceived, even though X has spatiotemporal parts? Perhaps there is an implicit assumption that something with spatiotemporal parts is subject to dissolution.[2] But this assumption need not be granted: If an X than which no greater X can be conceived is not subject to dissolution, then perhaps some things with spatiotemporal parts are not subject to dissolution. Another assumption that might be made is that anything with spatiotemporal parts is contingent.[3] But, again, this assumption need not be granted: If an X than which no greater X can be conceived exists necessarily, then perhaps some things with spatiotemporal parts exist necessarily. Some theists hold that God does have spatiotemporal parts, since they hold that God has temporal parts. Such theists would certainly reject the assumptions mentioned in this paragraph.

Another suggestion that might be made is that the expression 'X than which no greater X can be conceived' only applies coherently in the case of properties that have a relevant *limit*. Plantinga (1974b:91ff.) expresses the idea as follows:

The idea of an island than which it is not possible that there be a greater is like the idea of a natural number than which it is not possible that there be a greater, or the idea of a line than which none more crooked is possible. There neither is nor could be a greatest possible number, indeed, there isn't a greatest actual number, let alone a greatest possible. And the same goes for islands. No matter how great an island is, no matter how many Nubian

---

1 For the claim that nothing with spatiotemporal parts admits of greatness, see Losoncy (1982:211) and Mann (1976:419).
2 For the claim that nothing that is susceptible to dissolution or change admits of greatness, see Devine (1975b). For the claim that anything with spatiotemporal parts admits of dissolution, see Henry (1955) – where the ancestry of this view is traced to Boethius and Gerbert.
3 For the claim that anything with spatiotemporal parts is contingent, see Mann (1976:419ff.). See Back (1983:199ff.) for a discussion of the view that the notion of 'part' with which St. Anselm operates is the notion of a 'subjective part', i.e., a constituent of a Platonic form.

maidens and dancing girls adorn it, there could always be a greater – one with twice as many, for example. The qualities that make for greatness in islands – number of palm trees, amount and quality of coconuts, for example – have no intrinsic maximum. That is, there is no degree of productivity or number of palm trees (or of dancing girls) such that it is impossible that an island display more of that quality. So the idea of a greatest possible island is an inconsistent or incoherent idea; it's not possible that there is such a being.

One line of response to this argument is suggested by Grim (1982a). He claims that it is not obvious that the greatest possible island must have the greatest possible size – that is, the greatest possible island must have an infinite surface area. In particular, an island with an infinite surface area would be the wrong size for all sorts of activities – for example, circumnavigations. But, if the greatest possible island has a finite surface area, then – given certain plausible assumptions about, for example, the geometry of space-time and the nature of the physical world in which the greatest possible island exists – there will certainly be a limit to the number of palm trees and coconuts that it can sustain. Moreover, it is then not immediately obvious that other features of the island cannot determine a unique answer to the question of the number of palm trees and coconuts on the greatest possible island. More generally, Grim suggests that Plantinga's argument is the product of two "elementary fallacies," namely, (i) the thought that if something that is the best F possesses the attribute G, then it is the best G – "The physique of our best novelist must be the best physique; the hairs of our most respected statesman must be our most respected hairs; the number of dancing girls on the greatest island must be the greatest number of dancing girls"; and (ii) the thought that 'greatest', in the present context, means 'largest', and not 'grandest' or 'most perfect'.

This response seems weak. Even if we were to grant that the greatest possible island need not have an infinite surface area, it seems pretty clear that there won't be a unique answer to the question of the number of palm trees and coconuts on the greatest possible island. Palm trees and coconuts will be weighed against such things as banana trees, mango trees, golf courses, swimming pools, reefs, beaches, and cocktail bars.[4] But it seems incredible to suppose that there is some sense in which there is a unique answer to the question of the best possible balance among these things. Are we falling victim to Grim's first "fallacy"? No. If G is one of the attributes in terms of

---

4 Strictly, it seems that the subject has changed from "islands" to "holiday resorts"; the change is irrelevant from the overall standpoint of St. Anselm's argument.

which the greatness of F is to be assessed, then the magnitude of G is relevant. The physique of a novelist is irrelevant to her goodness as a novelist; but the presence of a sufficient number of golf courses, say, is not irrelevant to the goodness of a holiday resort.

Perhaps, then, we should instead accept the idea that the greatest possible island will have an infinite surface area – and, moreover, that it will have an infinite supply of banana trees, mango trees, golf courses, swimming pools, reefs, beaches, and cocktail bars. Given that the greatest possible island has an infinite supply of each of these things, it will *not* be the case that it *could* have a greater supply of these things.

What about the problem that one could not circumnavigate an island with infinite surface area? Well, it seems doubtful that the ability to be circumnavigated is really a great-making property of islands; indeed, why shouldn't it be contended that an island would be greater if it couldn't be circumnavigated? But, in any case, surely an island with infinite surface area can be circumnavigated provided either (i) that one has an infinite amount of time, or (ii) that one can travel infinitely quickly. Perhaps, then, one ought to hold that a greatest possible island will confer eternal life and infinite attributes upon its inhabitants – for example, as a result of the substitution of an elixir of life for drinking water. For some theists, these suppositions ought not to be evidently absurd, for heaven might well be taken to be an island than which no greater can be conceived.

Philip Devine (1975b:256) writes:

Even if we judge the perfection of an island not by its state at any one time but by its whole career, a perfect island is impossible. For it is not possible to accommodate everything we might desire of an island – including adequate room – within the limited spatio-temporal scope being an island involves. If it is suggested that a perfect island – somewhat like a magic penny – might have the property of producing whatever one wanted as soon as one wished for it, the reply is that in this case the goodness of the island will depend on the wisdom of the person on it. And since no human being will be perfectly wise in his use of the powers of the island (the stories about magic pennies and the like emphasise that this is so), the island will partake of the imperfection of its inhabitants.

It seems that a traditional theist ought not to suggest that a perfect island would grant all of the wishes of its inhabitants as soon as they made them. For it will then follow immediately that God is not perfect, since he does not grant all of our wishes as soon as we make them. If we consider, instead, the suggestion that the island has God-like powers of providing for its inhabitants, then it is not obvious both that (i) God can be perfect and (ii) the island cannot be perfect. In order to respond to this suggestion, it seems that Devine needs to be able to rule out the possibility of limited – localized – pantheism. This may not be an easy task.

I conclude that Plantinga's case against the island than which no greater can be conceived is inconclusive. Moreover, following Grim, I note that Plantinga's argument can be readily adapted to make a case against the being than which no greater being can be conceived, since one of the properties of a being than which no greater can be conceived is that this being will have made a world than which no greater can be conceived. For suppose that we can conceive of a world W^* greater than the world made by a being than which no greater can be conceived. Then, *per impossibile*, we can conceive of a being greater than a being than which no greater can be conceived, namely, a being that is exactly similar to a being than which no greater can be conceived except that it makes W^* instead. But, presumably, what goes for islands also goes for worlds: No matter how great a world, no matter how many admirable beings adorn it, there could always be a greater – that is, one with an even greater number of admirable beings. So, if Plantinga's argument against an island than which no greater island can be conceived goes through, it also shows that there is no being than which no greater being can be conceived.

Should we accept that there are coherent expressions of the form 'being of kind K than which no greater being of kind K can be conceived'? I am not sure. One problem is that it is not clear what are the constraints on the relevant notion of conceivability. What is required for a *conception of* a being? A mere form of words? An attribution of an extensive range of attributes? An existent being that is – somehow – the content of the conception, even though it is not characterized by the conception? An existent being that is correctly characterized by a range of attributed properties? A closely related problem is that it is very tempting to suppose that judgments about great-making properties are properly irreducibly subjective – that is, people can reasonably and irreconcilably disagree about the attributes of, for example, an island than which no greater island can be conceived. For some people, an island than which no greater island can be conceived will be deserted; for others, it will be populated by their relatives and friends; for yet others, it will be populated solely by Eskimoes, and so on. This is not just a question about the possibility of disagreement about the nature of an island whose identity is antecedently fixed by the expression 'island than which no greater island can be conceived': Rather, it is an expression of the thought that the expression 'island than which no greater island can be conceived' fails to fix the identity of any entity at all. Conceiving is always conceiving *by* someone. What is conceivable is always what is conceivable *for* someone. It is a big step to suppose that there is a – greatly idealized – limit in which the conceivings – and judgments about conceivability – of all reasonable persons converge.

Given these reservations, could one reasonably hold that there is only one coherent expression of the form 'being of kind K than which no greater being of kind K can be conceived'? I expect so. If one is a certain kind of theist, one can hold that God is the greatest conceivable being and reject the coherence of other expressions of the form 'being of kind K than which no greater being of kind K can be conceived' on the grounds that the existence of God renders such expressions unintelligible.[5] For this kind of theist, it seems knowable *a priori* that expressions of the form 'being of kind K than which no greater being of kind K can be conceived' fail to refer, except in the case of God. It does not seem to be too inaccurate to express this view in the claim that it is incoherent – unintelligible – to claim that there is a being of kind K than which no greater being of kind K can be conceived.

What is *my* attitude toward expressions of the form 'being of kind K than which no greater being of kind K can be conceived'? Complete indifference. If there is no logical problem involved in this kind of linguistic construction – that is, if these expressions do not lead to paradoxes – then I am prepared to allow that they have some *prima facie* intelligibility in some cases.[6] However, this concession of intelligibility is not coupled with any commitment to the existence of objects that are characterized by the expressions in question. For all that I can

5 How could there be an island than which no greater island can be conceived – i.e., an island that cannot even be conceived not to exist – given that God has the power to annihilate everything, except perhaps for God? Surely the acknowledgment that God would have the power to annihilate an island than which no greater island can be conceived is an acknowledgment that it is inconceivable that there is an island than which no greater island can be conceived.

6 Not in all. I can make some sense of the notion of an island than which no greater island can be conceived; but I can do nothing with the idea of a detached fingernail than which no greater detached fingernail can be conceived. If X is such that I can make little sense of the notion of a good X – a better X, a worse X – then I struggle to make sense of the notion of an X than which no greater can be conceived.

see, there is no good reason for me to allow that any expression of the form 'being of kind K than which no greater being of kind K can be conceived' refers to a unique possible object. Moreover, I see no point in pursuing this question, since I see no way in which I am likely to find out that there are such possible objects.

(2) MOST PERFECT BEINGS OF KIND K

Another favored formula in ontological arguments is 'the most perfect being'. Many of the considerations that apply to formulas of the form 'most perfect being of kind K' are similar to those that apply to formulas of the form 'being of kind K than which no greater being of kind K can be conceived'. However, there are some new considerations that arise.

In particular, there is a question about how we should construe the notion of a most perfect being. In the preceding section, I took it that the notion of greatness that is invoked in the notion of being than which no greater being can be conceived is a notion drawn from value theory – that is, a notion of being unsurpassably good, or unsurpassably valuable. This would suggest that exactly the same construal should be given to the notion of a most perfect being – and, in that case, we should reach the same conclusions as we did in the preceding section. However, there are some proponents of the relevant ontological arguments – that is, arguments that make use of the expressions 'being than which no greater being can be conceived' and 'most perfect being' – who would object that it is a misunderstanding to suppose that greatness and perfection have anything to do with goodness or value. Rather, they contend that these are terms that have application in the context of a Neoplatonic metaphysics that makes essential use of the notion of degrees of existence.[7]

For example, Brecher (1974:103) claims:

'Greater' [and 'more perfect' are] to be understood in a Platonic sense; not as 'better' . . . but as 'ontologically greater', although for Anselm, as for Plato, that which is higher in the ontological scale is also what is more excellent. It is God's greatness, not his excellence, however, which is the basis of Anselm's argument for his existence.

7   Cf. Barnes (1972), Brecher (1974) (1985), Crocker (1972), Mason (1978:5), Tartarkiewicz (1981).

Brecher goes on to claim that a suitable criterion for ontological greatness – one that was probably developed by Plato, and then taken over
by Anselm – is the following: *A* is ontologically greater than *B* iff (i) *A*
is more cognitively reliable than *B*; and (ii) *A* is more valuable than *B*.
Of course, the second clause in this criterion undercuts the claim that
ontological greatness is independent of goodness and value; but the
first clause is intended to add a further constraint that prevents the
possibility of Gaunilo-type counterexamples to ontological arguments.

It is not clear how we are to understand the notion of greater
cognitive reliability. Brecher – echoing Bonaventure – tells us that it
would be nonsense to suppose that there could be an island that was
more cognitively reliable than any other. But this doesn't help: For,
until we understand what is required for something to have great
cognitive reliability, we have no way of assessing the claim that an
island cannot do so.

I suspect that the only way to understand this claim is as follows.
We assume that there is a hierarchy of kinds of beings, ordered
according to their 'degree of existence' or their 'ontological grounds'.
The details of the hierarchy are unimportant, except for the following:
(i) There is – and can be – only one being in the hierarchy that is not
dependent on anything else, and this being is God; and (ii) consequently, all finite substances, for example, islands, are – and, indeed,
must be – ontologically dependent on that infinite substance – God –
that serves as the ontological ground for all of the finite substances.
Given this conception of the hierarchy of kinds of beings, and given
that 'being than which no greater can be conceived' and 'most perfect
being' are simply intended to characterize the infinite substance –
God – that stands at the apex of the hierarchy, it is a little easier to
understand why the claim, that there might be an island than which
no greater can be conceived, might be thought to be simply absurd.

However, the price of intelligibility is the renunciation of any
thought that the relevant ontological argument ought to convince
any reasonable person. The most obvious problem is that one can
reasonably doubt that there is any such hierarchy; in particular, if
there is no infinite substance, then it is not true that all finite substances are ontologically dependent on an infinite substance. Moreover, even if one concedes that beings can be ranked according to
their ontological greatness, one could hold (i) that there is no greatest
being – that is, the hierarchy is not bounded above, (ii) that there are
a number of beings that are equal in ontological greatness, but not

surpassed by any other beings, or (iii) that the hierarchy is actually topped by a finite being, for example, the physical universe. If the argument is taken to rely on Neoplatonic metaphysics, then it is completely lacking in probative force; there are very few nonbelievers who are committed to such a metaphysics.

In sum, there is a genuine question about whether there are certain kinds of parodies of the arguments given by St. Anselm and Descartes, since there is a question about the metaphysical assumptions that are implicitly built into their arguments. It may be possible to rule out almost all formulas of the form 'being of kind K than which no greater being of kind K can be conceived' and 'most perfect being of kind K' on the ground that beings of kind K cannot occupy a suitable position in the Neoplatonic hierarchy. However, the point of introducing the formulas in question is still served – for the invocation of the Neoplatonic hierarchy undermines the dialectical effectiveness of the original arguments. Of course, this is not to say that a believer in the hierarchy shouldn't judge that the arguments are sound. On the contrary. But it is to say that such a believer ought not to judge that those who reject the argument are, in virtue of that fact alone, necessarily subject to failings of rationality.

(3) NECESSARILY EXISTENT BEINGS OF KIND K

At the end of the preceding section, I left it open that there might be a few parodies that survive the acceptance of the Neoplatonic hierarchy. The parodies that I have in mind are similar to an important class of parodies that can be directed at modal ontological arguments that involve the notion of necessity. These parodies were first suggested – at least as far as I have been able to discover – by Paul Henle (1961), in his critique of Malcolm's version of Anselm's argument.

Henle writes:

Let us designate by 'Nec' a certain being who has necessary existence but who is otherwise less remarkable. He has a certain amount of knowledge, though nothing extraordinary, and certain power, though he is unable to cause motion. . . . Nec has a big brother, NEc, who also exists necessarily but who can cause uniform rectilinear motion and is a little wiser than Nec. There is another brother, NEC, who can cause acceleration, and only typographic inadequacies prevent my enumerating a spate of others.

As Henle notes, these beings seem to create some perplexity for defenders of modal ontological arguments. For, at least to anyone who is not antecedently committed to the existence of God, it is hard to see any reason why the existence of these beings is any less plausible than the existence of God. And yet, if there is a *valid* ontological argument for the existence of God, then there are *valid* ontological arguments for these beings too.

Henle claims that a theist can object that the existence of God is not compatible with the existence of these further beings – for God is supposed to be omnipotent, and yet he won't be able to destroy any of these necessarily existing beings. This seems wrong, for it is no part of the claim, that God is omnipotent, that God should be able to do the logically impossible – and yet it will be logically impossible for God to destroy Nec et al.

Henle also claims that Nec and his family could be readily dismissed by those who believe in the Neoplatonic hierarchy discussed in the preceding section. Given the assumption that the apex of the hierarchy must be completely perfect – omniscient, omnipotent, and so on – and given the further assumption that only the unique being at the apex of the hierarchy can be necessary – that is, ontologically independent – existence it follows that Nec et al. do not exist. However, it can reasonably be asked why only a completely perfect being can be necessarily existent. There are relatively minor modifications of the Neoplatonic picture that make room for Nec et al. Why aren't these modifications worthy of serious consideration?

Henle's discussion can be generalized in various ways. The most interesting generalization is that of Kane (1984), who introduces the notion of a less than perfect, necessarily existing being (LPN) – that is, a being that necessarily exists, but that (just) falls short of the possession of one or more perfections – for example, it is just less than omniscient, or just less than omnipotent, or less than omnibenevolent. For example, consider a being that is perfect except that it knows nothing about transfinite arithmetic, a being that is perfect except that it feels slightly irritated whenever anyone takes its name in vain, and so on.

It seems that we can generate infinite numbers of LPNs. For convenience, the following discussion will presuppose that omniscience, omnipotence, and omnibenevolence are the only relevant attributes of God. It seems to me that this presupposition is harmless in the present context.

First, suppose that we can quantify benevolence using real number percentages. If we make the assumption that moral properties are not necessarily linked to knowledge and power – that is, any kind of moral property is compatible with omniscience and omnipotence – then, for each $0 < r < 100$, there is an LPN that is omniscient, omnipotent, and possesses benevolence to degree r. Of course, God possesses benevolence to degree 100 – that is, in the form of omnibenevolence. And if we deny the assumption that moral properties are not necessarily linked to knowledge and power – on, say, the grounds (i) that there is, properly speaking, moral knowledge, and (ii) that moral knowledge is intrinsically (or internally, or necessarily) linked to moral motivation – we can still maintain that there is an LPN that is all but omniscient, all but omnipotent, and that possesses benevolence to degree r.

Second, we can suppose that there is a hierarchy O_i of omniscient, or all but omniscient (and omnibenevolent, or all but omnibenevolent) LPNs that are also all but omnipotent in the following way: For each i, O_i is limited only by O_j, for all $j > i$. Thus, for example, O_2 can do things that O_1 cannot do, but not *vice versa*. When it comes to a competition between O_1 and O_2 in which there is a winner, the winner is always O_2. This hierarchy can extend into the transfinite, if we wish.

Third, we can suppose that there is a hierarchy of all but omnipotent (and omnibenevolent, or all but omnibenevolent) LPNs that are also all but omniscient in the following way: For each i, O_i knows everything about things outside the hierarchy and also everything about beings below it in the hierarchy – that is, about O_j, for all $j < i$ – but does not know some things about itself and beings above it in the hierarchy – that is, about O_j, for all $j \geq i$. That is, these beings are omniscient about worldly matters of fact, but ignorant about some things to do with themselves. In this discussion, I have supposed that omniscience is a consequence of omnipotence. This might be denied; but, since an omnipotent being ought to be able to answer every question correctly, it does seem that only an omniscient being can be omnipotent.

And so on. It is easy for an atheist or agnostic to think that LPNs make a decisive case against ontological arguments – that is, they show why it is reasonable for atheists and agnostics to reject those arguments. For, from the perspective of the agnostic or atheist, there is no more reason to believe in God than there is to believe in any LPN, since ontological arguments for one or the other are precisely parallel. But no one should want to believe in all of the LPNs. So the reasonable response is to reject both ontological arguments for God and ontological arguments for all of the LPNs.

Of course, things look different from the perspective of the theist –

that is, someone who already believes in God. If the existence of LPNs is incompatible with the existence of God, then that is a reason to reject the claim that it is possible that there are LPNs. Moreover, it can then still be contended that only ontological arguments for the existence of God are sound. However, this contention must be tempered by the recognition that the arguments in question are bound to be dialectically inefficacious.

(4) ACTUALLY EXISTENT BEINGS OF KIND *K*

In a reply to the *Meditations,* Caterus objected that Descartes argument could be adapted to prove the existence of 'an existent lion' – that is, it could be used to give an *a priori* proof of the existence of a member of a class that is only contingently instantiated. This argument seems completely general. If Descartes' argument is an instance of the form '*x* is an existent *F*; therefore *x* exists', then it seems that it can be adapted to prove the existence of anything at all – for example, the existent round square, the existent prime number that is divisible by four, and so on.

Descartes' reply to this objection is to insist on a distinction between *true and immutable essences* on the one hand and *fictitious essences* on the other. What he claims is that 'God' expresses a true and immutable essence, whereas 'existent lion' expresses a merely fictitious essence.

It is very unclear what the principle behind this distinction is supposed to be. Kenny (1968b) describes it as follows: Let *E* be an essence that can be defined by the predicates '*F*' and '*G*', so that a thing has *E* iff it has both *F* and *G*. If *E* is a true and immutable essence, then it will be impossible for us to conceive of a *G* that is not *F*. But if we can conceive of a *G* that is not *F*, then *E* will merely be a fictitious essence.

Kenny's reconstruction is beset by numerous difficulties. One important difficulty is that it requires that no property that belongs to the divine essence belongs to any other essence. Thus, (i) since necessary existence belongs to the divine essence, there is no other true and immutable essence to which necessary existence belongs, that is, numbers (propositions, properties, and so on) are not essentially necessary existents; (ii) since incorporeality belongs to the divine essence, there is no other true and immutable essence to which incorporeality belongs, that is, Cartesian minds and angels are not essentially incorporeal; (iii) since indivisibility belongs to the divine essence, there is no other true and immutable essence to which indivisibility belongs, that is, points of space-time are not essentially indivisible; (iv) since eternity belongs to the divine essence, there is no other true and immutable essence to which eternity belongs, that is, numbers ('eternal propositions', properties, etc.) are not essentially eternal; and so on. Some of these claims make Descartes' own philosophy inconsistent – for example, the claim that Cartesian minds are not essentially incorporeal; others are merely independently implausible – for example, the claim that numbers are not necessary existents. Together, they suggest that Kenny's understanding of the distinction is not one that anyone ought to want to adopt.

There are further difficulties, too. In particular, one might wonder how the distinction between fictitious essences and true and immutable essences can be used to support the claim that it is the argument about existent lions that should be rejected. All that follows from the distinction is that there is at most one essence that involves existence – but this claim is perfectly compatible with the further claim that existence does not form part of the divine essence. Now, of course, it would not be very plausible to insist that existence is part of the true and immutable essence of the existent lion – for, why the existent lion rather than, say, the existent tiger? But the discussion from the preceding section suggests a stronger way in which to make this point: There are incompatible essences that could suitably be called "divine," but which is the one that is true and immutable? Why couldn't it turn out, say, that the true and immutable divine essence – the one that contains necessary existence – is one that contains the property of being slightly less than omniscient in *these* (specified) respects?

At this point, it seems clear that Descartes won't have a non-question-begging reply. Of course, that is not to say that it won't seem to him that he has a satisfactory reply. On the contrary, it seems to him that the divine essence really does possess the property of necessary existence, and that no other essences possess this property. Moreover, I am prepared to grant that it may be perfectly reasonable for him to believe this. However, I also want to insist that he should be able to see that he does not have a dialectically effective reply – that is, one that a reasonable agnostic or atheist ought to find persuasive. Given that one reasonably doubts that the divine essence is true and immutable, Descartes does not provide the slightest reason for one to give up this doubt.

Slightly different considerations arise in connection with a more recent discussion of a similar kind of objection. Rowe (1976) introduces the concept of a *magican*, that is, an actual magician. Generalizing, Rowe invites us to consider terms of the form 'an actual F', where F is any predicate at all. It certainly seems that one can form the concept of an actual F, for any F; and the parody of ontological arguments involving actuality then seems to follow.[8]

A number of objections have been raised against this argument.[9] William Wainwright (1978c:30) says, "Although the concept of [magican] ostensibly picks out a unique set of Meinongian pure objects, it does not in fact succeed in so doing and is, therefore, ill-formed." This is confused on two counts. First, 'magican' does pick out a unique set of pure objects, namely, the null set. Second, that 'magican' picks out the null set of pure objects does not show that it is ill formed. Compare it with 'actuperson', which picks out the unique set of actually existing persons. There is no reason to say that this predicate is ill formed. Note, too, that we do not say that names are 'ill formed' if they fail to refer, either in the actual world or in any world. Parity suggests that predicates deserve similar consideration even when their extension is empty in every world. The important point is that, *a priori*, one cannot tell which @-predicates pick out the null set.

Wainwright presents an argument that is intended to defend his conclusion. In effect, this argument goes as follows:

0. The concept 'magican' is well-formed. (Assumption for *reductio*)
1. Magicians exist iff magicans exist. (Premise, relying on 0)
2. It is contingent whether magicians exist. (Premise)
3. (Hence) It is contingent whether magicans exist. (From 1, 2)
4. It cannot be contingent whether magicans exist. (Premise)
5. The concept 'magican' is not well formed. (From 0, 3, 4 by *reductio*)

In this argument, premise 1 is knowable *a priori* and 2 is true. Nonetheless, 3 is false. What this shows is that the substitution principle that is used to obtain 3 from 1 and 2 is incorrect. Given that 1 is contingent *a priori*, the failure of this substitution principle should not seem surprising.

---

8   In this discussion, we take for granted that 'actual' is to be given a nonshifty interpretation. On a shifty interpretation, the relevant ontological argument simply fails to establish its conclusion. Kennedy (1989) takes Rowe to task for failing to distinguish between the two interpretations; this criticism seems justified but irrelevant to the main point that Rowe wants to make.

9   Other aspects of Rowe's argument have also been much discussed: Recall the earlier discussion of begging the question.

Bruce Russell (1985:40) says:

Since the concept of a magican is coherent, it is false that a magican is an impossible being. Since a magican is by definition an existing magician, it is false that a magican is a thing which does not exist, but which might have existed. So a magican is neither a possible nor an impossible being.

This is also confused. Given that there are no magicians, it is simply impossible that there are any magicans. However, as we noted in the preceding paragraph, the necessary and the *a priori* have clearly parted company in the present kind of context – so there is no reason to think that the failure to detect an *a priori* problem with the concept of a magican shows that it is possible that there are magicans.

Stone (1989:80) has yet another objection to Rowe. He suggests that Rowe is committed to the implicit claim that a magican is a possible being just in case there is a possible being that is a magican; and he then suggests that this claim is false. Furthermore, he proposes to replace the suspect claim with the claim that a magican is a possible being just in case there is a possible being that is a magican if it is actual. This also seems confused, at least given the way in which I use the word 'actual'. The point to which Stone is adverting is that in other worlds in which there are magicians, it will be true to say, 'It is possible – and indeed, actual – that there are magicans'. However, this does not mean that it is correct for us to say that there are possible beings that would be magicans if they were actual. After all, a magican must be something that exists in *our* world; and anything that exists in another world does not exist in our world. So, even if 'actual' is used in a shifty sense, this claim is not correct. What if 'magican' is also used in a shifty sense? Well, then, there will be no difference between the expressions 'magican' and 'magician' when they embed in the scope of modal operators – and hence there will be no force to the original ontological arguments.

Philip Devine (1975b:259ff.) takes a different tack. He suggests that there is no suitable parallel between concepts of the form 'an actual *F*' and those concepts that are typically used in ontological arguments: 'being than which no greater can be conceived', 'most perfect being', and so on. For there is obviously something "cooked up" about concepts of the form 'an actual *F*'; but – at least according to Devine – there is nothing cooked up about the concepts that are typically used in ontological arguments. Devine cites Schopenhauer's critique of ontological arguments with qualified approval:

On some occasion or other someone excogitates a conception, composed out of all sorts of predicates, among which however he takes care to include the predicate actuality or existence, either openly stated, or else wrapped up for decency's sake in some other predicate, such as perfection, immensity, something of the kind. ... The predicate reality or existence is now extracted from this arbitrary thought conception, and an object corresponding to it is presumed to have real existence independently of the conception.

In Devine's view, this is partly right: Typically, parodies of ontological arguments are produced by "wrapping up" existence in a predicate. However, he suggests that the same cannot be said of the ontological arguments themselves:

[To] say that existence is comprised in the nature of God is not necessarily to say that God's nature can be resolved into omniscience and omnipotence and perfect goodness and ... existence. ... There need be no independently specifiable concept "conditionally perfect" such that it is just like that of God, except that what is conditionally perfect need not exist.

This sounds incredible, but Devine does provide an argument. Consider the claim that whatever is red is colored. This claim is necessarily true: But it is not the case that to be red is to be colored and to possess some further, independent, differentiation – that is, there is no way of "factoring" the claim that something is red into (i) the claim that something is colored and (ii) a claim that is just like the claim that something is red except that it reserves judgment about whether or not that thing is colored.[10]

This argument seems suspect. 'Red' and 'colored' are related as determination and determinable – to be red just is one of the ways of being colored. Hence, it is unsurprising that "factorization" is impossible. But is it credible to say that 'existent' and 'perfect' are related as determination and determinable – that is, to exist is one of the ways (or perhaps the only way) of being perfect? Surely not. After all, it seems equally correct to say that to exist is one of the ways – indeed, the only way – of being colored. But this doesn't show that 'existent' and 'coloured' are related as determination and determinable. This is not to say that the position that Devine defends has been shown to

10 Devine notes that we could construct a suitable second claim – e.g., we could say that the thing is conditionally red – that is, such that if it is colored at all, then it is red. However, he goes on to observe that it would be "eccentric" to claim that our analysis then shows that 'red' is really an abbreviation for 'conditionally red and colored'.

177

fail; rather, it is to say that his argument does not establish that the position is correct.

Other people have also defended the view that there is an important difference between "natural" conceptions of God – 'a being than which no greater can be conceived', 'a most perfect being' – and "cooked up" conceptions that can be used in parodies of ontological arguments.

For example, Stone (1989:84) notes that some concepts are just "pasted together out of various features" and suggests that what needs to be considered is whether the property of being the greatest conceivable being is an *essential* property. His characterization of essential properties relies upon his – by my lights – peculiar construal of 'actual'; and its effect is to bar all cooked up concepts of the form 'an actual *F*'. However, quite apart from the details of this characterization of essential properties, we can ask, Why should we think that *essential* properties can form a suitable basis for ontological arguments? Why shouldn't we invoke some other criterion that shows that the concepts used in ontological arguments are merely cooked up? In particular, why shouldn't we object that, if 'a being than which no greater can be conceived' is taken to 'include' the property of actual existence, then it is cooked up, but if it is not taken to 'include' the property of actual existence, then it is not cooked up? These considerations about what is natural surely cut both ways, for what theists find "natural" is likely to be quite different from what atheists and agnostics find "natural."

The crucial point cannot be that the word 'actual' does not occur in the expression 'being than which no greater can be conceived'. For it is not uncontroversial that it is true that anything that fits the description 'being than which no greater can be conceived' exists in the actual world, and not merely in some other possible world. An atheist or an agnostic can object that the theistic *construal* of this description involves an inappropriate gerrymander.

I conclude that the debate about 'magicans' results in deadlock. To some theists, 'magican' does not seem relevantly like 'being than which no greater can be conceived'; but, to some atheists and agnostics, 'magican' does seem relevantly like 'being than which no greater can be conceived'. Moreover, from the atheistic or agnostic viewpoint, it can seem that the theist has a fetishistic attachment to certain forms of expression. It can certainly be disputed that there is something special about the form of words 'being than which no greater can be conceived' that naturally requires that these words entail the further words 'actually exists'.

(5) MAXIMAL BEINGS OF KIND *K*

Perhaps the easiest major ontological argument to parody is the one due to Plantinga.[11] Since Plantinga's argument is cast in terms of properties, and since there can be properties that are necessarily empty, there is no problem in constructing arguments that share the form of his ontological argument. Earlier, I mentioned the property of *no maximality*, which is possessed by any entity that exists in a world in which there is no maximally great being. We might also consider the property of *near maximality*, which is possessed by a being iff it does not exist in every world, but has a degree of greatness not exceeded by that of any being in any world.

As Tooley (1981:424) suggests, we can clearly generalize: For any predicate '*P*', we shall say that *x* is *maximally P* iff *x* exists in all possible worlds, and is *P* in every world; *x* is *no maximally P* iff *x* exists in a world in which there is no maximally *P* being; and *x* is *near maximally P* iff *x* does not exist in every world, but possesses *P* to a degree that is not exceeded by that of any being in any world. For each of these cases, we can construct an argument with the same form as Plantinga's ontological argument.

Furthermore, as Tooley also notes, we can construct arguments with explicitly contradictory conclusions. Suppose (i) that *x* is a *maximal universal solvent* iff *x* exists in every world and is a universal solvent in every world, that is, is capable of dissolving anything in that world; and (ii) that *x* is *maximally insoluble* iff *x* exists in every world and is insoluble in anything in every world. The construction of ontological arguments for these two concepts leads to a contradictory result.

Also, as Tooley notes, we can construct an argument for the existence of the devil. Suppose that it is analytically true that *x* is the devil iff *x* is omnipotent, omniscient, and perfectly evil, and that *x* is *maximally evil* iff *x* exists in every possible world, and is omnipotent, omniscient, and perfectly evil in every world. Clearly, we can parallel Plantinga's ontological argument with an argument that the devil

---

11 Interestingly, Plantinga is quite unconcerned by this possibility. This is an indication that his conception of the point of ontological arguments differs from that of his predecessors.

exists. Moreover, this argument can be generalized. Suppose that we can quantify positions on a spectrum between perfect good and perfect evil – that is, we can say that a being is evil to degree r iff it lies r percent of the distance between perfect evil and perfect good. Then we shall say that x is maximally evil to degree r iff x exists in every possible world and is omnipotent, omniscient, and evil to degree r in every world.[12]

Finally, as Tooley (1981:426) notes, we can construct arguments with conclusions that are known to be empirically false. Suppose that x has the *relative maximal* property $Q(P)$ iff x has property P is every world that contains all of the individuals involved in the property P.[13] Then, for example, we can adapt Plantinga's proof to show that

there is an entity which possesses the relative-maximal property Q which is based upon the relational property of being an omnipotent, omniscient and morally perfect wombat doing the twist on the top of this page. And since every individual which is involved in this property – namely, this page – exists in this world, it follows [by an argument parallel to Plantinga's ontological proof, that] this world contains an omnipotent, omniscient, and morally perfect wombat doing the twist on the top of this page.

Perhaps some of these alleged parallels can be rejected. In particular, the argument for the existence of an omnipotent, omniscient, and morally perfect wombat doing the twist on the top of this page seems to have a premise that is known to be false – namely, that it is possible that there is an entity that possesses the relative maximal property Q that is based upon the relational property of being an omnipotent, omniscient, and morally perfect wombat doing the twist on the top of this page. For, since we know that there is no omnipotent, omniscient, and morally perfect wombat doing the twist on the top of this page, we know that it is not possible that there is an entity that possesses the relative maximal property Q that is based upon the relational property of being an omnipotent, omniscient, and morally perfect wombat doing the twist on the top of this page.

The point here is that although the argument that Tooley gives

---

12 There are questions about the compatibility of omnipotence, omniscience, and evil that could be raised against these constructions. I shall not bother to pursue these questions here.

13 If R is a relational property, then R involves the individual a iff it is necessarily the case that for any x, x's having R entails the existence of the individual a. For instance, if anything possesses the property of being five miles from the Eiffel Tower, then the Eiffel Tower must exist.

shares the *form* of Plantinga's ontological argument, there is probably no one who would accept the relevant possibility premise. Thus, the argument might not be thought to really pose a threat to the theistic argument. Similar remarks might be made about the generalized argument involving the property of being relatively maximal with respect to $Q(P)$ and the generalized argument involving the property of being maximally P. In very many cases, the relevant possibility premise can be rejected on grounds that are shared by all parties to the debate about theism. Moreover, the same point applies, I think, to the case of the maximal solvent and the maximal insoluble substance: It is – or at least should be – common ground that it is not physically possible that there is a universal solvent; nor is it physically possible that there is a universally insoluble substance. Consequently, the relevant possibility premises do not hold in this case either.

However, as Plantinga himself concedes, there are plenty of genuine parallels to his original argument – for example, the arguments involving no maximality and near maximality. Furthermore, it seems that the arguments that lead to the conclusion that there are maximally evil beings to degree r pose a genuine problem. Perhaps this could be disputed. A theist could argue that since there is a maximally evil being of degree zero, it is not possible that there is a maximally evil being of any other degree. But to argue thus would be to miss the point. Given that a maximally evil being of any degree exists, then it is not possible that there is a maximally evil being of any other degree. But, from an uncommitted standpoint, it seems that no maximally evil being of a given degree is more likely to exist than any other. So all of the ontological arguments involving maximally evil beings of degree r seem equally good, since the crucial premise from which they start seems equally good in each case. I shall discuss this issue further in the concluding section of this chapter.

(6) DEVILS, AND SO ON

One particularly interesting genre of parodies of ontological arguments is provided by arguments that purport to establish the existence of different kinds of devils. I shall consider some examples of this genre that are based on the Anselmian formula: 'a being than which none greater can be conceived'.

First, consider the formula 'a being than which no worse can be conceived'. It seems that it would be worse if a very bad being existed both in the understanding and in reality than if it merely existed in the understanding. Consequently, it seems that – if the Anselmian formula is understood as 'a being than which no better can be conceived' – then the Anselmian argument can be successfully parodied using this formula.[14]

Second, consider the formula 'a being than which no less can be conceived'. It seems that it could be contended that even an insignificant being would be greater if it existed than if it did not exist – and, if so, then the Anselmian argument can be parodied to show that a being than which no less can be conceived does not exist.[15]

It has been suggested that these arguments admit of a generalization. Consider any degreed relational predicate '*F*'. Construct the description 'a being than which none which is more *F* can be conceived'. Then construct an argument along the following lines: Suppose that a being than which none which is more *F* can be conceived. Then we can conceive of a being that is more *F* – namely, one than which none which is more *F* can be conceived and that actually exists. But this is absurd: (Hence) a being than which none which is more *F* can be conceived exists. The main assumption behind this argument is that only something that exists can possess properties. It is not obvious that this assumption should be rejected.[16]

If we interpret the Anselmian formula as 'a being than which no better can be conceived', then the first line of parody seems cogent. However, there are some lines of objection.

First, as Devine (1975b) notes, a defender of ontological arguments might object that the notion 'a being than which no worse can be conceived' is incoherent. That is, whereas it is possible to have all good qualities – perfections – to an unlimited degree, it is not possible to have all bad qualities – imperfections? – to an unlimited degree. Even the devil must possess intelligence, and so on – that is, some qualities that are intrinsically good.

---

14 Richman (1958)(1976), Haight and Haight (1970), Haight (1974) present arguments of this sort and defend their use as parodies. Gale (1991) calls a similar being whom he introduces GCAD – for "greatest conceivable abstract demon" and "greatest cad."

15 Grant (1957) claims that this argument is an ontological proof that the Devil does not exist. Dauenhauer (1971:58) claims that it commits St. Anselm to the existence of "a thinkable, indeterminate, temporal, contrary-to-fact state of affairs."

16 Many modal metaphysics include the assumption that only objects that exist in a world possess properties in that world. If we suppose that there *is* only one world, then we end up with the conclusion that only actually existent objects possess properties.

Even if it is granted that the devil must possess some qualities that are intrinsically good – why should it be conceded that intelligence is intrinsically good? – this response seems dangerous. The obvious difficulty is that an opponent of ontological arguments will very likely doubt that the notion 'a being than which no greater can be conceived' is coherent. Thus, this response draws attention to the likely dialectical ineffectiveness of the argument.

Second, as I have already noted, a defender of ontological arguments will very likely not grant that we should interpret the Anselmian formula as 'a being than which no better can be conceived' – though, of course, this leads to difficulties of its own.

If we interpret the Anselmian argument to mean 'the highest being in the ontological hierarchy', then the second line of parody seems cogent. However, it is not clear that a defender of ontological arguments has any reason to be disturbed by it. St. Anselm himself seems to have noted that a being than which no lesser can be conceived does not exist; indeed, he says that it is, strictly speaking, nothing. This seems preferable to Dauenhauer's rather bizarre ontological speculation about the "backwash" of being. Note, too, that there is no good reason to identify 'a being than which no less can be conceived' with the devil of traditional theology. Equally, of course, there is no good reason to identify 'a being than which no worse can be conceived' with the devil of traditional theology. The traditional conception of the devil is of a being with many positive attributes and an overweaning pride.

The assumption that lies behind the generalization of the preceding arguments can be questioned. In particular, it will be disputed by modal realists and Meinongians. I don't propose to take a stand on this issue here; however, it should be noted that there are some people who – it seems reasonably – will be persuaded by the generalized parodies that ontological arguments fail.

(7) WHAT DOES PARODY SHOW?

Time to take stock. There are many different ways in which people have sought to parody ontological arguments. As we have seen, it is possible to argue about the details of these parodies. However, there are more fundamental questions that need to be asked. In particular, there is a large question about the point of the production of parodies that requires some attention.

Tooley (1981:427) claims that the production of parodies reveals that modal ontological arguments involving necessity instantiate a form of argumentation that if applied to structurally identical and equally justified premises, leads to contradictory conclusions. This seems too strong: It is not true that everyone ought to concede that the premises involved in the parodies are equally acceptable, even in the case of maximally evil beings of degree *r*. It seems that one could perfectly reasonably accept that the premise of the genuine modal ontological argument involving necessity is true, and hence that the premises of the competing arguments are necessarily false. In particular, it seems that anyone with an antecedent commitment to the truth of the claim that there is a maximally great being is bound to say this.

Perhaps this is to misunderstand Tooley; perhaps his point is that on the basis of purely *a priori* considerations, there is no reason to accept the premise of the genuine modal ontological argument involving necessity rather than the premise of one of the parodies. But this seems dubious on two counts. First, one might think that there are *a priori* considerations – to do with the simplicity of hypotheses, say – that favor the premise of the genuine modal ontological argument over all of its competitors. Of course, the adequacy of this suggestion can be debated. However, it is not clear that one would be necessarily unreasonable if one were to accept it. I myself think that it is a mistake to suppose that considerations of simplicity serve as a guide to the truth of *a priori* claims; however, I doubt that I could offer decisive arguments in favor of this position. Second, it is not clear that one might not reasonably accept certain claims *a priori*, even though one is unable to *justify* – or provide arguments in support of – one's acceptance of those claims. This possibility should not be dismissed out of hand: Many appeals to "intuition" in philosophy seem to be appeals to claims that have just this kind of status. So, it is not obvious that one might have a reasonable *a priori* intuition that only the premise of the genuine modal ontological argument is acceptable. Perhaps this is wrong. But until it is shown to be wrong, Tooley's argument is clearly incomplete.

Grim (1982a:39ff.) draws a slightly different conclusion:

What parody shows is that the 'possibility' premise of the ontological argument is not to be granted lightly, since similar 'possibility' premises in the parodies would force us to accept any number of odd and unlikely things. Thus parody shows that the argument is clearly insufficient as a 'proof'; the necessary 'possibility' premise is one for which additional justification is required as much as it would be for the bald claim that the God of the definition actually exists. . . . Successful parody . . . puts the onus squarely on the defender of the ontological argument to show why his 'possibility' premise is any more worthy of acceptance than the similar premises of the parodies; why the acceptance of his premise over its rivals amounts to anything more than an entirely arbitrary adoption of a favorite mythology.

This also seems too strong. If a defender of an ontological argument is only concerned to defend the view that the argument can reasonably be thought to be sound – that is, thought to proceed validly from true premises – then he need not be concerned with the task of "justifying" the acceptance of its premise over the rival premises of the parodies. Perhaps there is nothing that would be recognized as a "justification" of the relevant premise that the defender of the argument has to offer, and yet it is still the case that he is acting perfectly reasonably in accepting it.

However, what is true is that if the defender of an ontological argument is concerned to defend the view that the argument can reasonably be thought to be potentially dialectically effective against agnostics and atheists, then the existence of certain kinds of parodies should make him think again. From the point of view of certain kinds of atheists and agnostics, there is no more reason to accept the premise of ontological arguments than there is to accept the premises of certain parodies. Consequently, the ontological argument offers them no more reason to believe in God than the parodies offer reasons to believe in a host of other incompatible entities. Now, perhaps one reasonable response, when confronted with such a situation, is to make an arbitrary leap. And perhaps another reasonable response is to leap to the rejection of all the entities involved. However, it is *certainly* clear that yet another reasonable response is to withhold judgment – that is, to refuse to accept the conclusions of any of the arguments, at least on the basis of those arguments. The point of the parodies is to illustrate the *dialectical impotence* of the original arguments.

Many recent defenders of ontological arguments – for example, Plantinga (1974a) – have conceded that these arguments are dialectically impotent. However, they often also contend that there is some other purpose that these arguments serve. We shall turn to an examination of these other alleged uses of the arguments in the next chapter.

Chapter 12

Are ontological arguments of any use to theists and/or atheists?

Despite the negative conclusions that can be drawn about the utility of ontological arguments as instruments of persuasion, some theists and atheists continue to see value in some types of ontological arguments. In particular, some theists hold that ontological arguments can be used to demonstrate certain facts about the rationality of their beliefs: namely, either (i) that theism is rational, (ii) that nontheism is unintelligible, or (iii) that theism is absolutely epistemically secure. Similar positions can be occupied by atheists. In this chapter, I shall concentrate on defenses that have been offered for the theistic views (i)–(iii); exactly parallel considerations will apply to the atheistic counterparts, but will go unmentioned.

There is one unproblematic possible use for ontological arguments that can be conceded from the outset. It *might* be that some ontological arguments – for example, ontological arguments involving necessity – can have a use in the systematic exposition of theistic positions. There can be no objection to the use of dialectically inefficacious proofs in the exposition of a view – for the aims of exposition and dialectic are very different. However, once this has been conceded, it should be noted that it seems very implausible to think that it is actually the case that the arguments discussed in the earlier part of this book are suitable candidates for such roles. A straightforward exposition of theism surely ought to begin with the assertion that God exists – rather than, for example, the assertion that it is possible that God exists – since this provides a more immediate picture of the commitments of the view.[1] Henceforth, I shall disregard the possible use for ontological arguments that has been canvassed in this paragraph.

---

1 In any case, the Spinozistic model for expounding philosophical doctrine is one that has found few adherents.

(1) THE RATIONALITY OF THEISTIC BELIEF

The best-known example of a view that holds that ontological arguments are dialectically impotent and yet have important positive consequences for theists is that of Plantinga (1974a:221). He makes the following claim: "Our verdict on these reformulated versions of St. Anselm's argument must be as follows. They cannot, perhaps, be said to *prove* or *establish* their conclusion. But since it is rational to accept their central premise, they do show that it is rational to *accept* that conclusion."

What does a proof of a conclusion C from premises $P_1, \ldots, P_n$ show? In general, all it shows is that the set of sentences $\{P_1, \ldots, P_n,$ not-$C\}$ is inconsistent. Note that, in general, it does not show that the set of sentences $\{P_1, \ldots, P_n, C\}$ is consistent – for, in the general case, there is no guarantee that the set of sentences $\{P_1, \ldots, P_n\}$ is consistent. So, in general, the only consequence that a proof has for rational belief is this: If I accept that there is a proof of the conclusion C from the premises $P_1, \ldots, P_n$, then I will be irrational if I believe all of $P_1, \ldots, P_n$, and not-C. In general, from the fact that I accept that there is a proof of the conclusion C from the premises $P_1, \ldots, P_n$, it does not follow that I am rational if I believe all of $P_1, \ldots, P_n$ and C

Suppose that the set of sentences $\{P_1, \ldots, P_n\}$ is consistent. Then a proof of the conclusion C from the premises $P_1, \ldots, P_n$ shows that the set of sentences $\{P_1, \ldots, P_n, C\}$ is consistent. Does it now follow that if I accept that there is a proof of the conclusion C from the premises $P_1, \ldots, P_n$, then I am rational in believing $\{P_1, \ldots, P_n, C\}$? Of course not. For all that has been said, the set of sentences $\{P_1, \ldots, P_n\}$ might be consistent and yet such that I would not be rational if I were to believe them. For one thing, some of the members of this set might contradict other things that I believe. Moreover, this set of sentences might violate other canons of reasonable belief – for example, (perhaps) simplicity, explanatory adequacy.[2]

Suppose that the set of sentences $\{P_1, \ldots, P_n\}$ is such that I reasonably believe all of the members of this set. Suppose further that I accept that there is a proof of the conclusion C from the premises $P_1, \ldots, P_n$. Then it follows that if I come to believe C on the basis of the proof, I reasonably believe all of the members of the set $\{P_1, \ldots, P_n,$

---

2 I make no firm commitment to any account of the content of the canons of reasonable belief. However, I do suppose that there are such canons; and moreover, I think it likely that simplicity and explanatory adequacy are among those canons.

C}. Does it follow that the proof shows that it is reasonable for me to accept C? Yes and no. What the proof shows is that it is reasonable for me to accept C given that it is reasonable for me to accept $P_1, \ldots, P_n$. But, of course, the proof, by itself, does not show that it is reasonable for me to accept $P_1, \ldots, P_n$. So the proof, by itself, does not show, outright, that it is reasonable for me to accept C.

Consider the ontological argument that Plantinga claims can be used by theists to show that it is reasonable for them to believe that God exists:

1. There is a possible world in which there is an entity that possesses maximal greatness. (Premise)
2. (Hence) There is an entity that possesses maximal greatness. (From 1)

There are two questions that need to be answered before we can claim that there is any sense in which this argument shows that it is reasonable for a theist to accept its conclusion: namely, (i) Can it be reasonable for a theist to accept the premise of the argument? (ii) Can it be reasonable for a theist to accept the premise of the argument independently of her acceptance of the conclusion of the argument?

One plausible way to answer (i) is the following: It can be reasonable for a theist to believe that there is an entity that possesses maximal greatness. But if there is an entity that possesses maximal greatness, then it is possible that there is an entity that possesses maximal greatness. So it can be reasonable for a theist to believe that there is a possible world in which there is an entity that possesses maximal greatness. But, of course, this justification of the reasonableness of the theistic belief that it is possible that there is an entity that possesses maximal greatness undermines the claim that Plantinga's argument shows that it is reasonable for a theist to believe that there is an entity that possesses maximal greatness. For now, the justification offered by the argument is circular: In the end, we must presuppose that it is reasonable for a theist to believe that there is an entity that possesses maximal greatness in order to reach the conclusion that it is reasonable for a theist to believe that there is an entity that possesses maximal greatness.

Hence, the natural response to (i) forces us to look for an answer to (ii): Is there some suitably independent guarantee of the reasonableness of the theistic belief that it is possible that there is an entity that possesses maximal greatness – that is, is there some guarantee that does not presuppose the reasonableness of the theistic belief that there is an entity that possesses maximal greatness?

Plantinga (1974b:220–1, italics added) compares the claim that it is possible that there is an entity that possesses maximal greatness to Leibniz's Law (LL): For any objects x and y, and property P, if $x = y$, then x has P iff y has P:

Some philosophers reject [(LL)]; various counterexamples have been alleged; various restrictions have been proposed. None of these "counterexamples" are genuine in my view; but there seems to be no compelling argument for [(LL)] that does not at some point invoke that very principle. Must we conclude that it is improper to accept it, or to employ it as a premise? No, indeed. The same goes for any number of philosophical claims and ideas. Indeed, philosophy contains little else. Were we to believe only [that] for which there are incontestable arguments from uncontested premises, we should find ourselves with a pretty slim and pretty dull philosophy. . . . So if we carefully ponder Leibniz's Law and the alleged objections, *if we consider its connections with other propositions we accept or reject and still find it compelling,* we are within our rights in accepting it – and this whether or not we can convince others. But then the same goes for the proposition it is possible that there is an entity which possesses maximal greatness.

To this argument, van Inwagen (1977:392) objects (i) that Leibniz's Law is a bad example of the sort of proposition that Plantinga needs to make his case, and (ii) that there are other propositions that seem not to be relevantly different from the claim that it is possible that there is an entity that possesses maximal greatness, but for which Plantinga's line of reasoning seems incorrect. I shan't discuss (i) further; but it is interesting to consider the case that van Inwagen offers in defense of (ii).

Suppose that we call a real number *septiquaternary* if '7777' occurs in its decimal expansion, and that we call a real number *perimetric* if it measures the circumference of a circle whose diameter measures 1. Consider the claim that it is possible that something is both septiquaternary and perimetric. According to van Inwagen, "One may not rationally accept [this claim]. Perhaps there are propositions such that it would be rational to accept them or to accept their denials in the absence of any evidence or argument; if so, [this claim] is not one of them." But, if van Inwagen is right, then we do need some further argument to show that the theist has reason to suppose that the claim that it is possible that there is an entity that possesses maximal greatness is relevantly different from the claim that it is possible that something is both septiquaternary and perimetric.

It could be argued that van Inwagen is wrong. Certainly, it seems that one could rationally believe that something is both septiquaternary and perimetric – perhaps because one has been told this by a trusted authority – and hence that one could rationally believe that it is possible that something is both septiquaternary and perimetric: Mathematical knowledge, beyond that of a most rudimentary kind, is not a prerequisite for rationality. Similarly, it does not seem to be plausible to claim that one could not accept either this claim or its denial in the absence of any evidence or argument. It could happen that one rationally believes that something is both septiquaternary and perimetric even though one no longer possesses any evidence or argument that one could give in support of this belief. In that case, too, one could rationally believe that it is possible that something is both septiquaternary and perimetric: Rationality does not require that one keep track of the grounds of one's beliefs.

Moreover, even if van Inwagen is right, it could be held that there is a relevant difference between the case that he describes, and the case that Plantinga discusses, namely, that van Inwagen's example is drawn from mathematics. The most important feature of mathematical propositions is that they are susceptible of demonstration, at least in the form of informal proof. If there is something that is both septiquaternary and perimetric, then – it might be said – there must be a demonstration that this is so; and if it is not the case that there is something that is both septiquaternary and perimetric, then, too – it might be said – there must be a demonstration that this is so. Of course, it will be added, we may never discover the relevant demonstration; and, moreover, it may even be impossible for us to discover that demonstration. But the reason we are tempted to say that one cannot rationally believe that it is possible that something is both septiquaternary and perimetric is that (i), so far, no relevant demonstration has been discovered, and (ii) when (if) a relevant demonstration is discovered, then the claim that something is both septiquaternary and perimetric will either be shown to be necessarily true or it will be shown to be necessarily false. If one believes both (i) and (ii), then it seems that one cannot also reasonably believe that it is possible that something is both septiquaternary and perimetric. But, since there is nothing that corresponds to (i) in the case of theistic beliefs, there is nothing in van Inwagen's argument to undermine the view that one can reasonably believe that it is possible that there is an entity that possesses maximal greatness.[3]

It seems, then, that van Inwagen's objection is unsuccessful. However, there is a more important objection to Plantinga's position, suggested by the italicized part of the preceding quotation. We have seen that Plantinga's argument requires a suitably independent justification of the reasonableness of belief in the claim that it is possible that there is an entity that possesses maximal greatness. But the procedure that Plantinga specifies – namely, consideration of the connections of this claim with other propositions that the theist accepts or rejects – seems bound to undermine the independence of the justification. Surely, one of the crucial claims that needs to be considered when one wishes to know whether one can reasonably believe that it is possible that there is an entity that possesses maximal greatness is the claim that there is an entity that possesses maximal greatness. But if *that* claim is considered, then the final endorsement of Plantinga's ontological argument will not *show* that one is rational in one's acceptance of the conclusion of that argument.

The considerations that I have advanced here do not depend upon the observation that it is very unlikely that there actually has been, is, or will be anyone who reasonably accepts the claim that it is possible that there is an entity that possesses maximal greatness but who does not accept the claim that there is an entity that possesses maximal greatness, and who is then brought to an acceptance of the latter claim *via* consideration of Plantinga's ontological argument. However, if it is accepted that the argument cannot be used to show that one is rational in one's acceptance of the conclusion of the argument unless it can be shown that one's acceptance of the premise of the argument is suitably independent of one's acceptance of the conclusion, then it seems plausible to suggest that the argument can only be used to *show* that one is rational in one's acceptance of the conclusion in the unusual circumstances just described. Could there be such a case? Perhaps. *Prima facie*, it seems that there could be someone who reasonably accepts the claim that it is possible that there is an entity that possesses maximal greatness on the basis of testimony, who understands the claim, but who has not yet seen that it entails that there is an entity

3   I make no commitment to the account of mathematics sketched in this paragraph. It does seem to me that it is an account that could be reasonably accepted – and, in the present context, that would be enough.

that possesses maximal greatness. But then, when that person uses Plantinga's argument to reach the conclusion that there is an entity that possesses maximal greatness, it seems that the argument does show that it is reasonable for them to accept the conclusion.

But even here, appearances are deceptive. Questions about the reasonableness of holding certain beliefs are either (i) *global* questions, that is, questions of overall consistency, coherence, simplicity, and explanatory power, or else (ii) *local* questions about relative reason-ableness, that is, questions about what it is reasonable to believe given other beliefs. In this latter sense, what Plantinga's argument shows is that the *inference* of the conclusion that there is an entity that possesses maximal greatness is reasonable, given the prior beliefs of the person in question. But, as I have already explained, this does not show that continued *belief* in that conclusion is reasonable, in the global sense. Even for someone who comes to the new conclusion that there is an entity that possesses maximal greatness *via* an application of Plantinga's argument, the fact that that person used Plantinga's argument does not show that the belief in question is rational.

In sum, Plantinga is wrong: There is no interesting sense in which his argument shows that it is rational for a theist to believe that there is an entity that possesses maximal greatness. Of course, this might not be construed as a bad result by some theists. Given that Plantinga's argument can be paralleled by one that has the conclusion that there is no God, it would seem that an atheist could adopt Plantinga's argument to show that it is rational for an atheist to believe that there is no entity that possesses maximal greatness. Any theists who wish to claim that atheism and agnosticism are irrational ought not to be dismayed by the failure of Plantinga's argument.

(2) THE IRRATIONALITY OF NONTHEISTIC BELIEF

A number of theorists have contended that ontological arguments can be used to show that there can be no coherent expression of nontheis-tic belief. Of course, these theorists do not deny that there could be reasonable people who never turn their attention to religious ques-tions, and hence who fail to be theists because they do not possess the concepts that are required to entertain theistic beliefs. However, what these theists do deny is that there could be *reasonable* people who do possess the relevant theistic concepts, but who fail to accept the rele-vant theistic beliefs.

The view that I am discussing doesn't follow simply from the fact that the theorists in question believe that some ontological arguments are sound – that is, it isn't true that everyone who accepts ontological arguments must hold that these arguments show that nontheists are incoherent. Compare the case of someone who has a grasp of elementary logic and number theory, but who mistakenly believes that number theory is decidable. Such a person has implicitly inconsistent beliefs – for some of his beliefs entail the negation of something else which he believes – but it seems wrong to say that his beliefs are incoherent. We can make perfect sense of the idea that someone might have this set of beliefs; and we can see clearly how it might seem to someone that those beliefs are consistent.[1]

Barnette (1975) provides a reconstruction of St. Anselm's defense of the view that atheists are fools. On this reconstruction, the question, Does the being than which no greater can be conceived exist? turns out to be: (i) *well-formed* that is, it presupposes the truth of none but true sentences; (ii) *closed*, that is, it has only one possibly correct answer; and (iii) answerable only by a 'yes'. Given all of these considerations, Barnette suggests that it is reasonable for St. Anselm to hold that anyone who thinks that the answer to the question is 'no' is a fool. Moreover, Barnette suggests that it remains to be shown that St. Anselm is wrong about this – that is, he suggests that he might be prepared to agree with St. Anselm.

The main point to note is that it could be disputed that the considerations that are advanced will suffice to establish that the atheist is a fool. Even if the question is well formed, closed, and correctly answerable only by 'yes', it is unclear why it would be foolish – irrational – to give the answer 'no'. Of course, one would be making an error in giving that answer: But the contention of St. Anselm and Barnette is that the atheist doesn't merely make a factual mistake. But why? Consider the case of someone who believes that there is a general solution to quintic equations – compare the well-known formula for quadratic equations. The question, Is there a general solution to quintic equations? is (i) well formed, (ii) closed, and (iii) answerable only by a 'no', as Galois established. Nonetheless, it seems that there need be nothing foolish in my acceptance of a 'yes' answer – for example, because I believe that there is a general solution to quintics

4 A better comparison might be with the case of someone who makes a mistaken identification – e.g., she wrongly believes that Joan is *that* person whom she saw at the beach. In this case, her belief is necessarily false – but we can make perfect sense of the idea that she has that belief.

on the authority of a trusted but misinformed mathematics teacher; or because I have constructed what I mistakenly, but quite reasonably, take to be a proof; and so on. It is one thing to reject a necessary truth that is knowable *a priori;* it is another thing to be irrational in doing this. Russell and Whitehead were not irrational when they set out to write *Principia Mathematica,* even though, necessarily, the project was doomed.

It should also be noted that the position for which Barnette argues relies on the assumption that there is a valid reconstruction of St. Anselm's argument. The reconstruction that he actually gives is invalid, since it relies on an equivocation of the notion 'understanding'. Barnette rejects the suggestion that there is an intelligible claim expressed by the sentence 'There is something understood to be the greatest conceivable being and that is understood not to exist'. But, of course, an atheist can perfectly well understand the description 'greatest conceivable being' and yet hold that there is nothing that falls under this description. Moreover, as I have already argued, any valid ontological argument is bound to be question begging. So Barnette can only reach the conclusion that the atheist is a fool by begging the question against the atheist in the construction of his ontological argument.

It seems to me that it could be reasonable for some theists to hold that there are sound ontological arguments; however, the same cannot be said for arguments that purport to show that atheists and agnostics are, in virtue of their refusal to be persuaded of the truth of theism by ontological arguments alone, irrational. *Prima facie,* this view is absurd; and closer examination does nothing to make it appear more plausible.

(3) THE ABSOLUTE SECURITY OF THEISTIC BELIEF

Closely related to the idea that ontological arguments can be used to show the incoherence of nontheistic belief is the idea that ontological arguments can be used to demonstrate the absolute security of theistic belief – that is, to show that theists can rationally dismiss any doubts about the truth of their beliefs without giving them even the slightest consideration. I think that it may be true that a theist can rationally dismiss doubts about the truth of her beliefs without giving those doubts serious consideration – but, as I now propose to argue, I do not think that ontological arguments can be used to establish the point. I begin with a discussion of a view of the type in question.

Kielkopf (1984:26) provides a clear example of a view in which an ontological argument is used to try to establish the absolute security of theistic belief. His argument is encapsulated in the following "line of reflection," which bears obvious affinities to the experiential onto-logical argument defended by Rescher:

1. To take seriously doubts about God's existence requires having a thought of God along with suspension of judgment over whether or not the thought is of anything. (Premise)
2. To have a thought of God is to have a thought of a most holy being. (Premise)
3. To have a thought of a most holy being requires one to be engaging in the process of thinking of a most holy being. (Premise)
4. Thinking of a most holy being is, among other things, accepting the reality of what is being thought about. (Premise)
5. So, to take seriously doubts about God's existence requires among other things, accepting the reality of what is thought about while allegedly suspending judgment about the reality of what is thought about. (From 1, 2, 3, 4)
6. (Hence) The believer is not irrational in dismissing doubts about God's existence as ill-considered remarks of fools. (From 5)

No doubt, the line of response is clear: No agnostic or atheist will accept both 1 and 4, in the sense in which Kielkopf understands them. If 'thought of' is interpreted in an ontologically neutral way in 1, then an agnostic or atheist will concede 1 – but, of course, the agnostic or atheist will then deny 4: One can form the description 'most holy being' without supposing that anything conforms to that description. On the other hand, if 'thought of' is interpreted in an ontologically committing way, then an agnostic or atheist will not concede 1 – for what the atheist or agnostic wants to deny is that there is anything that lies in the extension of the name 'God'. So – unsurprisingly – Kielkopf's believer reaches the conclusion that agnos-tic or atheistic avowals are the "ill-considered remarks of fools" only by misrepresenting the content of those avowals. If the believer seri-ously tries to understand the position of agnostics and atheists, then she will not be able to reach the conclusion that they are fools – though she may need to engage in semantic ascent in order to represent their views.

Despite the failure of Kielkopf's argument, it seems to me that there might be something more to be said for the view that a theist could reasonably ignore the counterclaims of agnostics and atheists. The point is simply one about cognitive efficiency: One cannot spend all of one's time worrying about possible objections to the position that one holds. So, unless one thinks that there is positive reason to suspect that one's view is deficient, one is perfectly justified in supposing that there is no need to amend one's view. Moreover, the fact that there are alternative views that one might hold – which are, in some sense, no less adequate – does not provide one with a positive reason to change one's view. One would have cause to worry if one suspected that one's view was inconsistent at a particular point, or admitted of simplification at a particular point, or failed to be empirically adequate at a particular point, and so on – but the mere intelligibility of atheist and agnostic positions provides not the slightest reason for a theist to suppose that her view suffers from these defects. Of course, atheists and agnostics might claim that theism is inconsistent, or unnecessarily complex, or empirically inadequate, or explanatorily deficient, and so on – and those claims might be ones that a theist ought to take seriously. However, even a theist who acknowledges this point might hold that the shortness of life provides a reasonable excuse for her failure to take up those counterclaims – that is, even a theist who acknowledges that reasonable atheists and agnostics make such claims might still be justified in holding that those claims can be reasonably ignored. Of course, none of this is intended as a defense of the view that theistic belief has a special status in virtue of which it is "absolutely secure." Many other beliefs – for example, that there are other minds, that there is an external world, that the world was not created five minutes ago – can be defended in exactly the same way. Rather, the point is that if a theist wants a reasonable excuse for her failure to consider the arguments of atheists and agnostics, then appeal to considerations about cognitive efficiency seems to fit the bill.

The remarks that I have just made may seem outrageous. In particular, one might feel that theistic beliefs are so extraordinary that they cry out for more justification. Thus, for example, Salmon (1987:101n13) writes:

There is an epistemologically important point of disanalogy between belief in God and belief in other minds or the external world: The hypotheses of other minds and of the external world are extremely plausible (even with respect to the epistemic situation of someone who has not been philosophically indoctrinated since childhood concerning other minds or the external world), whereas the hypothesis of God's existence is fundamentally implausible (at least for those who are able to break free of their childhood religious indoctrination or who never had any), or, at most, not significantly more plausible that the hypothesis of the real existence of the mythological Olympian gods of old, or than other superstitious or occult hypotheses. . . . It is not the contestability or unprovability of the hypothesis of God's existence as much as its intrinsic implausibility that renders the hypothesis in need of evidence or proof for its justification.

But the important point is that judgments about intrinsic plausibility depend on background beliefs: For the believer, the atheistic hypothesis might be highly intrinsically implausible. So all that the believer need glean from remarks like Salmon's is that there are reasonable people who do not believe the theistic hypothesis. But why should this be cause for concern? Reasonable people disagree about ever so many things; and it would not be reasonable for one to suspend judgment, pending further investigation, every time one encountered reasonable disagreement.

Clearly, there is much more to be said about the epistemological issues that have surfaced in the last two paragraphs. However, I cannot pursue those issues here. Instead, I tentatively conclude that it may be reasonable for some theists to ignore the fact that there are reasonable agnostics and atheists – but I conclude more strongly that no ontological argument shows that this is so.

Conclusion

On the basis of the discussion in Chapters 2–7, I conclude that there are no ontological arguments that provide me with a good reason to believe that God – a being than which no greater can be conceived, a most perfect being – exists. Furthermore, though I have not emphasized this point, I also conclude that there are no ontological arguments that provide me with a good reason to believe that God – a being than which no greater can be conceived, a most perfect being – does not exist. The 'ontological disproofs' offered as parallels to the 'ontological proofs' are no more worthy of my acceptance, given that I start from a position of agnosticism.[1]

More generally, on the basis of the argument in Chapter 8, I conclude that there are perfectly general grounds on which I can dismiss the possibility of a dialectically effective ontological argument. Only those who make the relevant presuppositions will suppose that some ontological arguments are sound; but there is nothing in ontological arguments that establishes a case for those presuppositions from the standpoint of those who do not share them.

I also note that there may be various other grounds on which each ontological argument can be dismissed. Each of the following is a

---

1 A qualification is required here. There may be *a priori* arguments that show that certain deistic conceptions are inconsistent. Moreover, it may be that some of the traditional conceptions – e.g., 'most perfect being', 'being than which no greater can be conceived' – fall into this category. In that case, there will be *a priori* arguments that provide me with good reason to think that certain beings do not exist. However, (i) such arguments will not be the ontological disproofs that run parallel to the positive ontological arguments discussed in the text; and (ii) there is no reason to think that such arguments could be provided for all deistic conceptions. In my view, it is massively implausible to think that all deistic theories involve logical contradictions, or other debilitating *a priori* deficiencies; hence, in my view, it is massively implausible to think that there are successful *a priori* arguments against the existence of all deities.

claim that might be reasonably believed, though none is, I think, reasonably required:

(i) The formulas 'being than which no greater can be conceived', 'most perfect being', and 'maximally great being' are incoherent.[2]

(ii) The formulas 'being than which no greater can be conceived', 'most perfect being', and 'maximally great being' are coherent but necessarily empty.

(iii) Existence is not a perfection or great-making property – and neither are particular modes of existence, for example, necessary existence or actual existence.

Some ontological arguments might also reasonably be rejected on the grounds that they presuppose objectionable ontologies – for example, Meinongian ontological arguments might reasonably be rejected on the grounds that they presuppose an ontology of Meinongian objects.

Moreover, as the discussion of Chapter 11 revealed, all ontological arguments can be successfully parodied by spoof proofs that purport to establish the existence of uncountably many pseudodeities. Of course, by 'successful', I do not mean that everyone is obliged to grant that these spoofs are sound iff ontological arguments are sound; rather, I mean that one *could* reasonably regard the spoofs as providing arguments for the existence of uncountably many pseudodeities that are just as good as the cases that ontological arguments make for God.

Finally, on the basis of the discussion in Chapter 12, I conclude that there is no other use to which ontological arguments can be adapted by theists or atheists: Given their dialectical impotence, there is no other purpose that they can successfully achieve. Thus, I conclude that ontological arguments are completely worthless: While the history and analysis of ontological arguments makes for interesting reading, the critical verdict of that reading is entirely negative.

2   See Webb (1989) for a recent defense of this view.

Literature notes

I<small>N THESE</small> literature notes, I provide more detailed textual support for some of the contentions made in the main text. Moreover, I provide critical discussion of relevant works in the literature that are not discussed in the main text. Thus, these notes are part footnote and part literature survey. In order to facilitate use of these notes, I begin with a table of contents, which uses the same headings and order as the main text.

CONTENTS

PREFACE

Some writers have very dismissive attitudes toward ontological arguments. Consider, for example, Stace (1959:180):

[Broad] devotes a great deal of subtle logical analysis to showing that the ontological argument depends on the use of phrases like 'most perfect being' which are meaningless verbiage. So far as I know his treatment of this famous argument . . . is quite original. It certainly is most acute and ingenious. But I do not possess Broad's heroic patience and I simply cannot bear to discuss the dreary logomachy of the ontological argument. Probably Broad has completely demolished the argument. But I cannot bring myself to think that it needs demolishing.

Clearly, Stace would have wondered at the need for a large book devoted to the analysis of ontological arguments. Well, the proof of the pudding is in the eating; I hope that at least some readers won't complain of indigestion.

INTRODUCTION

Marion (1992) makes heavy work of the fact that Kant was the first to introduce the term 'ontological proof'. He suggests that because 'the absolutely perfect being' expresses an essence, but 'that than which no greater can be conceived' does not express an essence, it is a mistake to classify St. Anselm's argument as an ontological argument. But this terminological debate seems pointless; there are many other relevant respects – for example, that they proceed from premises all of which are alleged to be knowable *a priori* – in which the arguments of St. Anselm and Descartes are clearly very similar. Moreover, it is unclear why the expression 'that than which no greater can be conceived' fails to express an essence, and the same for 'a being greater than can be conceived'. No one thinks that ontological arguments reveal everything about the nature of God, though some proofs purport to demonstrate more than others. So why not just allow that St. Anselm's argument reveals less of the essence of God than does Descartes' argument?

Hartman (1961:675n85) suggests that St. Anselm's proof is not properly called "ontological"; but he also suggests that it could properly be called "metaphysical" or *"a priori"*. Similar qualms are expressed by Schofner (1971:117) – though perhaps only on behalf of Barth.

Losoncy (1990) suggests (i) that Gaunilo first formulated "the ontological argument;" (ii) that St. Anselm rejected Gaunilo's formulation of "the ontological argument;" and (iii) that the metaphysical argument of the *Proslogion* is not, in any sense, an ontological argument. This strikes me as mere playing with words. Of course, it must be conceded that Gaunilo misformulates St. Anselm's argument: But that is no reason to say that the original argument is not an ontological argument. Moreover, there is the matter of accepted linguistic usage: The paradigm cases of arguments that are denoted by the expression 'ontological argument' are those of St. Anselm and Descartes. To my ear, 'ontological argument' functions like a proper name: It carries no implications about the *nature* of the arguments that fall in its extension. Even if it turns out that the arguments of St. Anselm and Descartes have very little in common, that will not show that there is something inappropriate about the label 'ontological argument'; rather, it will suggest something interesting about the causal history of that label. For further discussion of Losoncy's claims, see Schufreider (1992) and Losoncy (1992).

1. SOME HISTORICAL CONSIDERATIONS

As far as I know, there has been no exhaustive *historical* study of ontological arguments, even for relatively narrow historical periods. In particular, I found the pre-Cartesian discussion of ontological arguments very hard to investigate. An accessible book of translations, commentary, and analysis would be very useful.

1.1. HISTORICAL SYNOPSIS

Gilson (1955) contains much information about the status of ontological arguments – versions of the arguments of St. Anselm – in the Middle Ages. Unfortunately, there is no subject index to this book, so the information is not easily accessed. As we have seen, Thomists rejected ontological arguments; but other philosophers of a more rationalistic bent – for example, Scotists – accepted them. Consequently, there were lively debates about ontological arguments during the golden age of Scholasticism. However, the victory of Occamist nominalism seems to have led to a widespread rejection of those arguments by the end of the fourteenth century. Among those who discussed St. Anselm's argument, there are the following: William of Auxerre, Richard Fishacre, Alexander of Hales, Matthew of Aquasparta, Johannes Peckham, Nicolaus of Cusa, Aegidius of Rome, William of Ware, Albertus Magnus, Peter of Tarentaise, Henry of Ghent, Gregory of Rimini, Robert Holcot, John of Beverley, John Wyclif, Richard Rufus of Cornwall, Pierre Oriole, and Richard Middleton.

For work on the views – about ontological arguments – of particular authors mentioned in the body of the text, I provide the following partial summary.

St. Anselm: Adams (1971), Allinson (1993), Anscombe (1993), Armour (1986), Back (1981) (1983), Barnes (1972), Barnette (1975), Beckaert (1967), Bouwsma (1984), Brecher (1974) (1985), Caird (1899), Campbell (1976) (1979) (1980), Charlesworth (1962) (1965), Cock (1918), Copleston (1950), Crawford (1966), Crocker (1972), Dauenhauer (1971), Dazeley and Gombocz (1979), Devine (1975b), Diamond (1974), Diamond (1977), Dore (1984b), Downey (1986), Dupre (1975), Ebersole (1978), Englebretsen (1984), Esmail (1992), Ferguson (1992), Feuer (1968), Gale (1991), Gilson (1955), Gracia (1974), Grant (1989), Grave (1952), Gregory (1984), Haight (1974), Harrison (1970), Hartman (1961), Hartshorne (1962) (1965), Hasker (1982), Henry (1955) (1967), Herrera (1972), Hick (1970), Hochberg (1959), Hoernle (1922), Hopkins (1972) (1976) (1978), Howe (1966) (1972), Hudson (1974), Huggett (1961), Hugly and Sayward (1990), Johnson (1965), Johnson (1973), King (1984), King-Farlow (1982), La Croix (1972a), Lewis (1970), Lochhead (1966), Losoncy (1982) (1990) (1992), MacGregor (1964), MacPherson (1965) (1974), Makin (1988), Mann (1967) (1972), Martin (1970), Martin (1990), Mascall (1949) (1966) (1971), Mason (1978), Matson (1965), Matthews (1961) (1963), McGill (1967), Miller (1961), Morreall (1984), O'Connor (1969), O'Loughlin (1989), O'Toole (1972), Oppenheimer and Zalta (1991), Pailin (1975) (1986), Patterson (1970), Penelhum (1971), Plantinga (1967) (1974a) (1974b) (1975), Platt (1973), Pottinger (1983), Power (1992), Read (1981), Reiss (1971), Robinson (1984), Rohatyn (1982), Ross (1969a), Rowe (1989), Sagal (1973), Schofner (1974), Schufreider (1977) (1978) (1981) (1983) (1992), Sen (1983), Shedd (1884), Smart (1949), Sontag (1967), Spade (1976), Stearns (1970), Stengren (1975), Stone (1989), Streveler (1976), Tichy (1979), Verweyen (1970), Webb (1896) (1915), Werner (1965), Williams (1993), Wolz (1951), Woods (1986).

St. Thomas Aquinas: Brown (1964), Copleston (1950) (1957), Duncan (1980), Freeman (1964), Gilson (1955), Hartshorne (1965), Mascall (1949) (1966) (1971), Matthews (1963), Miller (1961), Oakes (1972), Patterson (1970), Rousseau (1980), Webb (1896) (1915).

St. Bonaventure: Charlesworth (1965), Copleston (1950), Doyle (1974), Gilson (1955), Streveler (1976), Webb (1896).

Duns Scotus: Baumer (1966) (1980), Copleston (1950), Doyle (1979), Gilson (1955), Kielkopf (1978), Krull (1964), O'Brien (1964), Ross (1969a) (1969b), Wolter (1990).

Occam: Gilson (1955), Streveler (1976).

Descartes: Balz (1953), Broadie (1970), Caird (1899), Carnes (1964), Connelly (1969), Copleston (1958), Cottingham (1986), Crocker (1976), Curley (1978), Doney (1978) (1991), Dore (1984b), Dreisbach (1978), Forgie (1976), Goode and Wettersten (1982), Hartshorne (1965), Hick (1970), Hughes (1975), Humber (1970), Imlay (1969) (1971) (1986), Kemp-Smith (1952), Kenny (1968a) (1968b), Loewer (1978), MacGregor (1964), Mackie (1982), MacPherson (1965), Malcolm (1968), Mascall (1949), Miller (1955), Patterson (1970), Paullin (1906), Penelhum (1968), Plantinga (1974b), Sievert (1982), Webb (1989), Williams (1978), Wilson (1978).

Leibniz: Broad (1975), Brown (1984), Copleston (1958), Gotterbarn (1976), Hartshorne (1965), Howe (1966), Loewer (1978), Lomasky (1970), Mascall (1949), Paullin (1906), Russell (1900), Seeskin (1978), Strasser (1985), Webb (1989), Wilson (1979).

Spinoza: Caird (1899), Copleston (1958), Curley (1969), Earle (1951) (1979), Friedman (1974) (1978) (1982), Hallett (1957), Harris (1973), Hartshorne (1965), Jarrett (1976) (1978), Joachim (1901), McKeon (1928), Mascall (1949), Mijuskovic (1973), Munitz (1965), Parkinson (1954), Paullin (1906), Saw (1951), Scruton (1986), Webb (1989), Wienpahl (1979), Wolfson (1934), Young (1974).

Hume: Barnes (1972), Bradford (1983), Clarke (1971) (1980), Freeman (1964), Gaskin (1978), Harrison (1970), Hartshorne (1965), Hendel (1925), MacPherson (1965), Stove (1978), Tweyman (1992), Ward (1982), Williams (1981).

Kant: Abraham (1962), Ballard (1958), Barnes (1972), Baumer (1966), Bencivenga (1987), Bennett (1974), Braham (1932), Caird (1899), Campbell (1974) (1976), Cassirer (1954), Charlesworth (1965), Clarke (1971) (1980), Cock (1918), Copleston (1960), Diamond (1974), Dryer (1966), Engel (1963), England (1968), Ewing (1938), Ferreira (1983), Flimons (1923), Harris (1977), Hartshorne (1965), Hick (1970), Hintikka (1969) (1981), Hoernle (1922), Krull (1964), Laird (1941), MacGregor (1964), Mackie (1976), MacPherson (1965), Morscher (1986), Nelson (1993), Paullin (1906), Plantinga (1966) (1967) (1974b), Reardon (1988), Ross (1969a), Scruton (1982), Shaffer (1962), Smith (1968), Walker (1978), Ward (1982), Webb (1896), Williams (1981) (1986), Young (1974).

Hegel: Caird (1899), Dupre (1973), Ferrara (1975), Galloway (1950), Harris (1936) (1972), Hartshorne (1965), Laird (1941), Paullin (1906), Ryle (1935) (1937), Webb (1896).

Findlay: Campbell (1976), Clarke (1971), Diamond (1974), Franklin (1964), Hartshorne (1965), Hick (1961), (1967b), Hudson (1964) (1974), Hughes (1948), Hutchings (1964), Kellenberger (1970), Mascall (1971), Puccetti (1964), Rainer (1948), Schrader (1991), Sobel (1987), Zabeeh (1962).

Hartshorne: Baker (1980), Beard (1980), Brecher (1975a), Campbell (1976), Clarke (1971), Elton (1945), Ewing (1969), Goodwin (1983), Hick (1967b) (1970), Hubbeling (1991), Johnson (1977), Kapitan (1976), Keyworth (1969), Martin (1990), Mascall (1971), Nasser (1971), Nelson (1963), Pailin (1969a) (1969b), Purtill (1966) (1967), Robinson (1951), Ruf (1975), Vaught (1972), Wood (1973).

Literature notes

Malcolm: Abelson (1961), Abraham (1962), Allen (1961), Baier (1960), Baumer (1962), Beanblossom (1985), Bennett (1974), Brown (1961), Campbell (1976), Coburn (1963), Diamond (1974), Dryer (1966), Englebretsen (1984), Gale (1986) (1991), Hartshorne (1965), Henle (1961), Hick (1967) (1970), Huggett (1962), La Croix (1972b), Martin (1990), Mascall (1971), Matthews (1961), Oakes (1974), Penelhum (1961) (1971), Plantinga (1961) (1967), Scott (1966), Tomberlin (1972a), Yolton (1961), Zabeeh (1962).

Plantinga: Daher (1971), Gale (1988) (1991), Grim (1979a) (1979b) (1981), Hinchcliff (1989), Hughes (1970), Lucey (1986), Mackie (1982), Maloney (1980), Martin (1990), Mavrodes (1970), Oakes (1974), Purtill (1976), Sayward (1985), Sennett (1991), Tapscott (1971), Tooley (1981).

1.2. ST. ANSELM'S ARGUMENTS

Barth (1960) is the principal exponent of the view that St. Anselm did not intend to put forward any independent arguments for the existence of God in the *Proslogion;* other exponents of related views include Schufreider (1977)(1981)(1983), Smart (1949), Sontag (1967), and Verweyen (1970). According to Barth (1960:102), all that St. Anselm intended to do was to "expound and impart . . . the knowledge that is peculiar to faith, knowledge of what is believed from what is believed." Similarly, Sontag (1967:484) claims that "Anselm's 'arguments', then, are aimed at simply bringing about a grasp of the special difficulties involved in reasoning about God's nature at all." As Barnes notes (1972:6), there is overwhelming textual evidence against this kind of interpretation – for example, in the *Epistola de incarnatione verbi*, where Anselm announces that his intention in the *Proslogion* was to prove without the authority of Scripture that the fundamental Christian beliefs are true. Detailed refutations of Barth's view may be found in McGill (1967) and Charlesworth (1965). There is also some interesting criticism in Henry (1967). A defense of Barth's views may be found in Hartman (1961) and Potter (1965); a sympathetic – but in the end critical – discussion of Barth's views may be found in Schofner (1974).

Campbell (1976)(1979)(1980) also contends that St. Anselm did not intend to provide an independent argument for the existence of God. According to Campbell, what St. Anselm attempts to show is that the claim that God does not exist is, strictly speaking, unintelligible.

Moreover, he suggests that even if St. Anselm is successful in this task, he will not have established that one ought to say that God does exist – that is, the point is just that the speech act involved in the denial of God's existence is incoherent. I think that there is textual evidence that counts against this interpretation – in particular, I think that it anachronistically imports concepts that St. Anselm did not possess – but it is an interpretation that deserves further discussion – compare Chapter 12, Section 2, in the main body of the text.

McGill (1967:71ff.) distinguishes six different kinds of interpretations of the *Proslogion*, each of which turns on a different conception of St. Anselm's understanding of the idea 'a being than which no greater can be conceived'. McGill calls these interpretations (i) the realistic idea, (ii) the noetic datum, (iii) the limit to "conceiving," (iv) the reflexive discovery, (v) the revealed rule for thought, and (vi) the idea from the *Monologion*. McGill notes that there are textual difficulties for each of these kinds of interpretation – the interested reader is advised to consult McGill's text.

Another major controversy about the *Proslogion* concerns its structure – and, in particular, the question of when St. Anselm may be said to have established, at least to his own satisfaction, that God exists. There are three major views. The first view, defended – or at least assumed – by the vast majority of commentators – among them Adams (1971), Brecher (1985), Charlesworth (1965), Dore (1984b), Gale (1991), Henry (1955) (1967), Hopkins (1976), King (1984), Lewis (1970), Mann (1972), Pailin (1975), Stearns (1970) – is that the existence of God is established by the end of *Proslogion* 2. The second view, defended by Campbell (1976)(1979)(1980) and Schufreider (1977) (1978) (1992), is that the existence of God is not established until the end of *Proslogion* 3. The third view, defended by Herrera (1972), Hopkins (1978), La Croix (1972a), and Reiss (1971), is that the existence of God is not really established until the end of the entire work, or, at least, the end of *Proslogion* 23. On the first two views, most of the *Proslogion* is concerned with the attribution of properties to God; but on the third view, most of the *Proslogion* is concerned with the discovery of the properties of the being than which no greater can be conceived, in order that that being may be identified as God.

From my point of view, this debate is unimportant. For, whichever interpretation one chooses, one can only think that the overall argument succeeds if one thinks that the argument of *Proslogion* 2 establishes that there is a being than which no greater can be conceived. Since I contend that atheists and agnostics can reasonably reject this conclusion of *Proslogion* 2, I contend that atheists and agnostics need not concern themselves with questions about the internal logical structure of the remainder of the *Proslogion*. If the argument for the existence of a being than which no greater can be conceived fails, then – no matter how the rest of the argument proceeds – the *Proslogion* arguments fail to establish the existence of God.

It may also be worth noting that the debate seems unnecessarily heated – see, especially, Campbell (1980), Hopkins (1978), and Schufreider (1981). If the argument of *Proslogion* 2 establishes that there exists a unique being than which there is no greater, then the argument of *Proslogion* 2 does establish that God exists if God is the unique being than which there is none greater. But the defenders of the Anselmian argument all agree that God is the unique being than which there is no greater. So, they all agree that the argument of *Proslogion* 2 is a demonstration of the existence of God. However, what they disagree about is whether the argument of *Proslogion* 2 suffices for Anselm to draw the conclusion that God exists, rather than merely the conclusion that the unique being than which there is no greater exists. That is, the disagreement focuses on the question, What is required for the identification of the unique being than which there is none greater *as* God? And this seems to be a question that is not very profitable to debate.

Yet another topic that has often arisen in connection with the discussion of St. Anselm's argument is whether it presupposes the acceptability of some kind of causal principle – and, hence (?), the acceptability of a cosmological argument. Charlesworth (1962) claims that the notion of 'necessity' that is invoked in the argument must be a notion of 'causal necessity'. I think that it is quite clear that this contention is simply false – though it has taken many years for the point to be properly appreciated.

Various attempts have been made to formalize the argument of *Proslogion* 2–4. Perhaps the most ambitious attempt is that of Campbell (1976), who provides a seventy-four line demonstration. Campbell (1979:556) claims that his reconstruction shows that the *Proslogion* argument is formally valid, "a feat rarely accomplished by any philosopher." But even if it were true that his reconstruction did show that there is a formally valid formulation of the argument of the *Proslogion*, the further claim is absurd. Even without resorting to consideration of the work of Leibniz, Russell, and so on, it is plausible to claim that, most of the time, the arguments that philosophers give are valid – it is only the premises that they use that are controversial. Moreover, it is far from clear that the argument that Campbell gives is formally valid. In particular, it should be noted (i) that he provides only the sketchiest account of the rules of derivation in his natural deduction system; (ii) that he provides no semantics for the system that he uses; (iii) that he provides no clear account of the use of the subscripts that appear in his proof, for example, at lines (16) and (17); (iv) that he provides no clear account of the logical behavior of the "assertion sign" that prefixes some lines of the proof; and (v) that he does not satisfactorily explain how to understand the "ontologically neutral term forming indefinite description operator" that is used in the argument. Perhaps the most significant problem is that if, as he hints, the system is one due to Routley, then some account must be given of the characterization postulates, and so on that are involved. Routley (1980) stresses that existence – and existence-entailing attributes such as perfection – are not characterizing predicates. Moreover, it seems that any system that allows that existence – and existence-entailing attributes – are characterizing predicates is simply inconsistent. Yet the very first premise of Campbell's argument can only be justified in a non-question-begging way on the supposition that perfection is a characterizing predicate.

Perhaps the most convincing formalizations of arguments that are at least closely related to the arguments of *Proslogion* 2–3 are those of Adams (1971) and Lewis (1970). In each case, there are valid arguments on offer, and, moreover, valid arguments for which it is not incredible that intelligent people might believe them to be cogent.

1.2(a) *Chapter 2 of the* Proslogion

Gale (1991:221) claims that the principle 4a – 'For any individual x, if it is possible that x exists and x does not exist, then x could be greater' – is the weakest principle that is sufficient for the validity of St. Anselm's argument. However, as Mann (1972) emphasizes, there are weaker principles that St. Anselm could adopt – for example, 'If it is possible that a being than which no greater can be conceived exists, and a being than which no greater can be conceived does not exist, then a being than which no greater can be conceived could be greater'. It seems to me that defenders of versions of St. Anselm's argument tend to favor weaker formulations, such as the one that Mann gives; whereas opponents of versions of St. Anselm's argument often opt for stronger claims, such as the one that Gale proposes. In order to give the defenders of the argument a run for the money, it seems that a critic ought not to insist on the stronger formulations; but, at the same time, a critic can reasonably demand some justification for acceptance of the weaker formulations. No doubt, a proponent of one of the weaker formulations will *not* seek to justify that formulation by appealing to one of the stronger versions. But what other justification might be given? Why should I accept the weaker version if I do not also accept the stronger one? The cost of the insistence on the weaker formulation may be to ensure that the dialectical effectiveness of the proof is undermined.

Lochhead (1966:124) also defends the view that St. Anselm only meant to say that of nothing else but God is it true that real existence is greater than conceptual existence. This view seems to have the untoward consequence that it makes it unintelligible that God should have created the world – for, if the real existence of the world is no greater than its merely conceptual existence in God's mind, then what reason could God have for creation? Indeed, *pace* Lochhead, it suggests that St. Anselm would do better to subscribe to some version of the view that in a range of cases, real existence is "an intensifier of" – is greater than – merely conceptual existence. Alternatively, St. Anselm might follow Mann (1972) in supposing that the crucial claim is that for anything that exists solely in the understanding, there is something that exists in reality and that is greater – that is, perhaps, that the greatest being is not something that exists solely in the understanding. Again, the obvious problem is that this version of the premise seems clearly question begging, at least from a neutral, or uncommitted, standpoint.

O'Connor (1969:135) claims that St. Anselm's description of God should be 'being than which no greater can be' rather than 'being than which no greater can be thought' since, otherwise, "it builds into the definition relation to human thought as essential to God's nature." But this is a confusion. St. Anselm does not suppose that his description captures the essence or nature of God; indeed, he thinks that a complete grasp of that essence or nature necessarily eludes us. Rather, what St. Anselm supposes is that the description 'being than which no greater can be conceived' is true of God – that is, roughly that, as a matter of conditional necessity, God falls under this description. Consequently, there is nothing to be said in favor of O'Connor's further claim that "the unnecessary final word 'thought' in the formula for God is Anselm's *bete noire*."

Malcolm (1960) claims that whereas 'existence' is not a predicate, 'necessary existence' is a predicate. This seems obviously wrong: For surely *necessary existence* and *contingent existence* are nothing other than modes of *existence*. Oakes (1975a) tries to defend Malcolm's position with what is, in effect, the following argument: "God's existence is accounted for completely by his possession of the property of necessary existence. Surely it does not follow from God's possession of the property of necessary existence that existence-simpliciter – that is, the sort of existence that any existent being other than God possesses – is one of God's properties. In fact, it would seem clear that existence-simpliciter in not a property of God." But this argument confuses contingent existence with existence, that is, existence-simpliciter. Since necessary existence is a determination of existence, nothing can have necessary existence without having existence; but this is just to say that both existence and necessary existence are properties, or else that neither is. See Yolton (1961) and Baumer (1962) for an early discussion of this kind of objection to Malcolm. Penelhum (1971:369) makes a very clear case for the view defended in this paragraph.

McGill (1967:44n34) reports Barth's contention that "if God only had general existence, in the manner of all other beings, then not only would he not exist as God, but according to Anselm's own account ... he would not exist at all." Taken literally, this is absurd – compare the discussion of the preceding paragraph. However, a more charitable interpretation would take this to be an expression of the view that God's existence is not possibly contingent.

Plantinga (1967:67ff.) suggests that it is very hard to find a plausible interpretation of the claim that existence in reality is greater than existence in the understanding alone. After some discussion, he considers the following claim: "If A is distinct from B and has every property B has except for non-existence and any property A alone has, and A exists but B does not, then A is greater than B." But, for any apparently suitable A and B, the antecedent of this principle is contradictory: For consider the properties 'is identical with A or is F' and 'is identical with A or is not F', for some contingent property F. Both of these properties are possessed by A. Moreover, neither entails either nonexistence or identity with A. So it follows that B possesses both properties – and hence that B is identical to A. In view of this result, Plantinga gives up on this line of thought. However, as Tapscott (1971:605) notes, it seems that Plantinga's suggestion only requires slight modification in order to avoid the obvious counterexamples: "If A has every property B has except (1) non-existence, (2) any (nontautologous) property entailing or entailed by nonexistence, and (3) any (nontautologous) property entailing or entailed by identity with B, and A exists and B does not, then A is greater than B." Perhaps, then, the troublesome claim can be understood. However – as suggested by the list of theses in the main text – even if this is right, it is not clear that this claim is required by Anselm's arguments.

Brecher (1985:63ff.) claims that Plantinga's discussion of the principle that any existent being is greater than any nonexistent being is confused: The crucial point is that Anselm uses the word 'greater' to locate beings in the following scale: nonexistents, the material world, the forms (i.e., necessary existents), and God. Consequently, the other properties of things "have no bearing on their ontological greatness." Of course, this interpretation of Anselm's argument leaves a proponent of the argument with the task of justifying belief in the existence of the elements of the Platonic scale – for without that belief, there would be no reason to think that the argument establishes that God – that is, the element that tops the Platonic scale – exists. Note, too, that it would be an egregious error to suppose that terms that are used to locate beings in the scale can also be used to *characterize* objects – compare the subsequent discussion of Meinongian theories.

Miller (1955:37) suggests that St. Anselm held "a realism of essences accompanied by a Platonic–Augustinian notion of being as essence." Similar suggestions may be found in numerous other authors. Of course, any argument that relies on this realism is only as good as the defense that can be provided for the Platonic–Augustinian line.

Hick (1970:74) claims that principles connecting greatness and existence can be justified in the following way: "Neoplatonism apart, the premise that it is greater or more perfect to exist in reality than to exist only in thought would seem to represent a necessary presupposition or prejudice of consciously existing beings. For we should presumably not remain voluntarily in existence if we did not in practice accept this premise." This is pretty feeble. At best, the *alleged* necessary prejudice of consciously existing beings need only be that it is better for certain consciously existing beings – perhaps only themselves – to exist than not to exist; that is, there is no obvious way in which the principle can be extended to all beings. Moreover, it seems that consciously existing beings *could* think that it would have been best if they had only ever existed in thought but that, given that they do exist in fact as well as in thought, it is better to continue in existence than not to continue in existence. And so on.

1.2(b) *Chapter 3 of the* Proslogion

The question whether there are independent arguments in *Proslogion* 2 and *Proslogion* 3 has been much debated – compare Allinson (1993), Barnes (1972), Basham (1976), Campbell (1976) (1979) (1980), Englebretsen (1984), Hasker (1982), Henry (1967), Hopkins (1972) (1976) (1978), La Croix (1972a) (1972b), Losoncy (1990) (1992), Pailin (1975), Schufreider (1977) (1978) (1981) (1983) (1992), and Stearns (1970). Henry (1955) defends the view that there is no separate argument for the existence of God in *Proslogion* 3, but he also claims that the argument that is often thought to be found in *Proslogion* 3 is indeed found in the *Responsio*.

King (1984:155) claims to be able to show that St. Anselm's ontological argument cannot be adequately represented in modal logic. This claim may be correct if one limits oneself to restricted systems – for example, those with only the modal primitives 'necessary' and "possibly'. But if one avails oneself of further primitives – for example, 'actually' – and makes use of world-indexed properties, then there is more chance that one will succeed. Nonetheless, I think that King is partly right: One gets a better representation of St. Anselm's argument if one uses an explicitly hyperintensional idiom.

Englebretsen (1984:36) claims that the crucial question for the argument of *Proslogion* 3 is whether St. Anselm accepts the claim that something is conceivable iff it is logically possible. However, as many commentators have noted, it is doubtful that St. Anselm was working with any notion of logical possibility. And, on the other hand, if the argument is to be interpreted in terms of logical possibility, then it is obvious that the claim that Englebretsen mentions should be rejected.

Allinson (1993:18) claims that the correct argumentation of *Proslogion* 3 invalidates the argument of *Proslogion* 2; and, moreover, that the conclusion of *Proslogion* 2 is a "false but necessary premise in establishing the validity of *Proslogion* 3." In order to defend this bizarre claim, Allinson contends that 'is possible' should always be read as 'is contingent' – and then draws the conclusion that, for example, the S5-axiom – if it is possible that it is necessary that p, then it is necessary that p – is unintelligible. But possibility and contingency are distinct notions, and each has a perfectly respectable use: So the conflation that Allinson endorses should simply be resisted.

1.2(c) *Further chapters of the* Proslogion

The argument from *Proslogion* 15 is discussed in Rohatyn (1982). He suggests that the argument may be sound, and yet "give us no grounds for exuberance." However, he assumes that the notion 'greater than something greater than can be thought' is unintelligible; and yet, this seems clearly wrong. If there can be one being greater than can be thought, then why couldn't there be many such beings, a hierarchy of such beings, and so on?

Dazeley and Gombocz (1979) suggest that *Proslogion* 15 presupposes a distinction between levels of language – that is, between (i) the object-level claim that God is understandable and (ii) the metalinguistic claim that the expression 'that than which no greater can be conceived' is understandable. However, as they go on to note (1979:87), this interpretation immediately renders the central argument of the *Proslogion* invalid. Moreover, it more or less forces them to claim that "faced with the unpalatable alternatives of either accepting the difference of levels and so rendering the argument invalid, or of confusing them, Anselm opts for the 'validity' of his proof and in so doing obviously confuses the semantic levels." But this is absurd; if St. Anselm had recognized the distinction of levels, then he certainly would not have gone on to ignore it. The truth is, surely, that the attribution of a grasp of the twentieth-century distinction between object-language and metalanguage to St. Anselm is an unwarranted and anachronistic projection. This truth is somewhat ironic, since Dazeley and Gombocz go to some lengths to lambast Malcolm for providing an anachronistic interpretation of the *Proslogion*.

Distinctions between positive and negative conceptions of God has been proposed and discussed by many authors. Gracia (1974:374) suggests that the Anselmian formula 'being than which no greater can be conceived' should be given a negative interpretation: "What the Anselmian formula asserts . . . is that any creature conceived is somehow imperfect, since we can always conceive of a greater perfection than what it has, not positively, but only by removing whatever there is in it that limits its perfection." This claim is very hard to understand: Why shouldn't we say, rather, that we can always conceive of a greater perfection than that of a finite creature by *adding* perfection to it (cf. Gaunilo's response to St. Anselm's argument)?

1.2(d) *Gaunilo's objection and St. Anselm's reply*

Reiss (1971:522) appears to contain a particularly egregious misinterpretation of St. Anselm. In the *Responsio,* St. Anselm writes, "When [the fool] thinks of [a being than which no greater can be conceived], either he thinks of something than which a greater cannot be thought, or he does not think." Reiss takes this to be an expression of a surprising claim – namely, that "either one thinks about something than which no greater can be conceived, or else one does not think at all. . . . the alternatives for Anselm are either discourse [about God] or silence." But this is absurd; all that St. Anselm means to say is that there is no intelligible content to be assigned to the fool's claim that God does not exist; he makes no commitment to the further claim that no content can be assigned to all the other claims that are made by the fool.

Hartman (1961:653, 674) claims that Gaunilo misunderstood St. Anselm's project. In Hartman's view, St. Anselm presents a polemic or apology to which, "in last instance, [an infidel] must succumb" – even though that polemic "makes room for the God of Faith . . . who at last is demonstrated such that the thought of his non-existence is unthinkable in truth, though thinkable in foolishness." But one of Gaunilo's main points is that the polemic is ineffectual – that is, it presents nothing to which an infidel must succumb – precisely because all that the infidel requires is that the nonexistence of God is thinkable "in foolishness." The infidel can grant that if he were to believe in God, then he would think it "foolish" not to believe – that is, he would think that atheists failed to acknowledge that which grounds the very possibility of their thought, existence, and so on – but simply insist that since he does not believe, he can see nothing foolish in his unbelief. Moreover – and this is the important point – there is *nothing* in St. Anselm's "polemic" that gives the infidel the slightest reason to change his mind.

For discussions of Gaunilo's objection, see Adams (1971), Back (1981) (1983), Braham (1932), Brecher (1974), Caird (1899), Campbell (1976), Cock (1918), Cornman, Lehrer, and Pappas (1987), Crawford (1966), Crocker (1972), Devine (1975b), Downey (1986), Feuer (1968), Gregory (1984), Grim (1979a) (1979b) (1982a), Hartshorne (1965), Hopkins (1972) (1976), King (1984), Lochhead (1966), Losoncy (1982) (1990) (1992), Mann (1976), Miller (1961), New (1993), Paullin (1906), Plantinga (1967) (1974b), Power (1992), Read (1981), Schufreider (1978) (1992), Shedd (1884), Stearns (1970), Webb (1896), and Wolz (1951).

1.3. DESCARTES' ARGUMENTS

The connection between, and the status of, the arguments in *Meditation III* and *Meditation V* has been much discussed – for example, in the exchange between Imlay (1969) (1971), Humber (1970), and Hughes (1975). Imlay defends the – massively implausible – view that the argument of *Meditation V* is a causal argument; Humber and Hughes reasonably point out that there is no good reason to think that the argument of *Meditation V* presupposes, or requires, a causal principle. I shall discuss this dispute further when I turn to an examination of cosmological arguments.

Imlay (1986:111) discusses the interpretation of Descartes' claim that "that which we clearly and distinctly understood to belong to the true and immutable nature of anything, its essence, or form, can be truly affirmed of that thing." He suggests that the quantifier should be taken to refer to 'objects of thought' – and that, under this interpretation, the principle should be accepted by all except "extreme sceptics." However, it seems to me that this is mistaken. Given the admission of objects of thought, the acceptable principle is that whatever nuclear or characterizing properties belong to a true and immutable nature can be truly affirmed to belong to that nature – compare the discussion of Meinongian ontological arguments.

Kenny's suggestion that Descartes' ontological argument should be given a Meinongian interpretation was the subject of a symposium in 1968. Malcolm (1968:40) objected that Descartes' argument only required objects of thought, not Meinongian pure objects. However – as emphasized by Routley (1980) and others – it is a mistake to think that mere objects of thought are anything other than some of Meinong's pure objects. Penelhum (1968:46) makes the valuable point that Kenny misconstrues the nature of the objection that existence is not a predicate when that objection is located in the context of a theory of pure objects. For, of course, the point then becomes that existence is not a characterizing, or nuclear, property of objects – compare Routley (1980) and Parsons (1980). See the subsequent discussion of Meinongian ontological arguments in the main text and the related literature notes for more on this point.

As I hinted in the main text, interpretation of the argument of *Meditation V* is fraught with difficulty. Doney (1991) claims that there are two distinct arguments, which may be represented as follows:

1. If I can produce an idea of something from my thought, everything I perceive clearly and distinctly to belong to the nature of that thing really does belong to the thing. (Premise)
2. I find in me the idea of God, or a supremely perfect being. (Premise)
3. I perceive clearly and distinctly that actual and eternal existence pertains to this nature. (Premise)
4. (Therefore) Actual and eternal existence pertains to God. (From 1, 2, 3)

1. God is a (or the) first and supreme being. (Premise)
2. A first and supreme being has all perfections. (Premise)
3. Existence is a perfection. (Premise)
4. (Hence) God exists. (From 1, 2, 3)

The argument that I have discussed shares some of the features of each of these arguments; however, I do not think that it presents a weaker case for the conclusion that God exists than either of the separate arguments. Doney (1978) claims that the geometric argument of the *Second Replies* is also distinct from either of the arguments in *Meditation V*, and represents this argument as follows:

1. To say that something is contained in the nature or concept of some thing is the same as to say that it is true of that thing. (Premise)
2. Necessary existence is contained in the concept of God. (Premise)
3. (Therefore) It is true to say of God that necessary existence is in him, or that he exists. (From 1, 2)

This is a curious argument. One clear difficulty concerns (1), for, as it stands, it seems to have outlandish ontological consequences. At the very least, it seems that (1) should be restricted to nuclear or characterizing properties – compare the discussion of Meinongian ontological arguments. But, in that case, (3) won't follow from (1) and (2), since necessary existence is nonnuclear. Alternatively, one might follow Meinong and hold that while necessary existence is true of God, it does not follow that God necessarily exists.

Curley (1978:156) provides a careful, extended discussion of the argument of *Meditation V*. He suggests that the argument should be formulated as follows:

1. I have ideas of things that, whether or not they exist, and whether or not I think of them, have true and immutable natures or essences. (Premise)

2. Whatever property I perceive clearly and distinctly as belonging to the true and immutable nature of something I have an idea of really does belong to that thing. (Premise)
3. I have an idea of God as a supremely perfect being. (Premise)
4. I perceive clearly and distinctly that existence belongs to the true and immutable nature of a supremely perfect being. (Premise)
5. (Therefore) A supremely perfect being really does exist. (From 1, 2, 3, 4)
6. (Therefore) God exists. (From 5)

He then goes on to claim that (1) and (2), "although not without difficulty, are neither absurd nor inconsistent with other elements of [Descartes'] philosophy." But, without a distinction between nuclear and nonnuclear properties, (1) and (2) are absurd – compare the discussion of the preceding paragraph. Consequently, Curley is wrong to claim that the only serious difficulties for the Cartesian argument concern the coherence of the idea of a supremely perfect being. For similar reasons, Kenny (1968b:168) is wrong to think that the chief difficulty for Descartes is that it is impossible to provide a criterion of identity for Meinongian objects. Even if one thinks that there is a difficulty here, one ought not to think that it is the sole problem that undermines the Meinongian interpretation of the Cartesian ontological argument.

Gaskin (1978:73) notes that Samuel Clarke – who defended an argument that incorporated features of both traditional ontological and cosmological arguments – said of the Cartesian argument that it suffered from the following "Obscurity and Defect": "It seems to extend only to the Nominal Idea or mere Definition of a Self-Existent Being" and does not clearly refer that definition "to any Real particular Being actually existing without us."

1.4. LEIBNIZ'S CONTRIBUTION TO THE ARGUMENTS

As Copleston (1950:526) observes, Duns Scotus anticipated the Leibnizian attempt to show that the idea of God is the idea of a possible being. Scotus claimed (i) that we cannot observe any contradiction in the idea of a most perfect being, but (ii) that this does not amount to a demonstration that there is no contradiction involved. "We cannot show apodeictically and *a priori* that the most perfect being is possible, and that is why [Scotus] states elsewhere that the Anselmian argument belongs to the proofs which amount to no more than *persuasiones probabiles.*"

Many recent authors have agreed with Leibniz that the question of the consistency of the description 'most perfect being' – 'being than which no greater can be conceived', 'unique being which is omniscient, omnipotent, omnibenevolent, personal, eternal, and so on' – is one of the main difficulties that confronts ontological arguments. Indeed, Cargile (1975:69) goes so far as to say, "This question about the consistency of the concept of God is the fundamental question in the ontological argument." As the later chapters of this book demonstrate, Cargile's claim is wrong: There are more important questions for ontological arguments than the question about the consistency of the concept of God. Compare Downey (1986:49): "The fundamental issue in the ontological argument [is] the question whether the concept of God is consistent, as Leibniz recognized." Also, compare Brecher (1985:115): "The question of the existence of God is one and the same as the question of the intelligibility and coherence of 'God'."

Barnes (1972:84) suggests that a particularly pressing form of the question of the consistency of the concept of God arises if one asks, Under which generic sortal is it plausible to suppose that God falls? In Barnes's view, there is only one reasonable suggestion, namely, 'person' – but "it is . . . becoming clear that persons are essentially corporeal." This objection should cut no ice with proponents of ontological arguments – for it is part of their view that God is an incorporeal person. Of course, they can concede the *doxastic* possibility that they might be wrong – that is, they can concede that one need not be irrational if one were to believe that it is a necessary truth that persons are corporeal – but they will hold that, nonetheless, there is at least one incorporeal person.

Loewer (1978) argues that even if we could show that the formula $\exists x \Box \exists y (y = x)$ is consistent, this would not suffice to show that "the ontological argument" is sound. For, in quantified S5 without either the Barcan formula (BF) or the converse Barcan formula (CBF), there are models in which there are worlds in which this sentence is true, and yet there are also models in which there are worlds in which this sentence is false. So, even though the sentence is consistent, we cannot conclude that it is logically possible. Yet, according to Loewer, Leibniz clearly did suppose that once a sentence has been shown to be consistent, one can conclude that it is logically possible. Moreover, Loewer goes on to note that, in quantified S5 with both BF and CBF, the sentence in question is a theorem – so that under this interpretation of the argument, the putative proof of consistency is redundant. I think that Loewer is unfair to Leibniz. In particular, I do not think that Leibniz supposed that model-theoretic consistency entails possibility. Rather, Leibniz thought (roughly) (i) that proof-theoretic consistency entails coherent conceivability, and (ii) that coherent conceivability that is not otherwise contradicted entails logical possibility. But, in the case of God, there is nothing external that contradicts his existence; so the only question concerns the internal self-consistency of the notion of God. Of course, agnostics and atheists will object that there are plenty of coherently conceivable beings and states of affairs that do contradict the existence of God; but I can only suppose that Leibniz did not consider these beings and states of affairs seriously. One might try to use the notion of a 'canonical model' to fashion a response to Loewer's argument. The idea will be that any object that is internally consistent will exist in a world in the canonical model. Of course, the difficulty for Leibniz is that this will not be true of beings with modalized properties – for example, necessary existence. One might also try to use a weaker propositional logic as the base – for example, K or S4. In this case, there are other difficulties that arise – compare the discussion of modal ontological argument involving necessity, in Chapter 4.2 in the main text.

Lomasky (1970:262) discusses a number of objections to Leibniz's consistency proof. Apart from noting various difficulties for talk of simple, positive, unlimited qualities – for example, that it is not obvious that there are any simple qualities, and that it is not obvious that if there are any simple qualities, then those simple qualities that there are must all be compatible – he claims that Leibniz's argument fails because "mathematical induction is valid only if the conclusion applies to finite n's." This is a mistake. Since a simple induction *can* be used to extend Leibniz's argument about two properties to the case of transfinitely many properties, I ignored these considerations in my discussion in the main text.

Seeskin (1978:125ff.) provides a very confusing account of Leibniz's views. Among the claims that he makes are the following:

(i) 'Since the world is a collection of perceiving intelligences, the greater the amount of essence in the world, the more or clearer will be the perception which takes place'; (ii) 'existence is always preferable to non-existence . . . to exist is to contribute to the total amount of perfection attributed to the world as a whole'; (iii) 'existence adds nothing new to essence, but by creating this world God has insured that the things which do exist are the things whose essences already contain the greatest number of determinations'; (iv) . . .

'[there are] distinctions which have long been thought to contain built-in preferences – distinctions like prior and posterior, real and illusory, for its own sake and for the sake of another, essential and accidental, . . . active and passive'.

The main problem is how (i)–(iii) can be reconciled with the Leibnizian claim that this is the best of all possible worlds. For on what grounds could we hold that no more perceiving intelligences can be added to the world? Surely, for any world that God might have created, there will be another in which "more essence" is included. And there are other questions, for example: Why should more essence lead to clearer perception, rather than the reverse? Why should we suppose that the terms mentioned in (iv) are value laden?

Howe (1966:6ff.) suggests that Leibniz's consistency proof is otiose: "Anselm rightly proffered only a vivid description of actual discourse about God, for the conceivability of a concept is surely nothing but its use. . . . Affirmations about a necessary being made from within a theistic interest cannot be of the sort whose denial is intelligible; they must, by the very nature of their subject, be necessarily true, but within that sphere of discourse." People tried for centuries to square the circle: But this does not show that what they tried to do is logically possible. *Pace* Howe, it is insufficient for the logical possibility of instantiation of a concept that the concept be in use. I pass over the suggestion that claims can be "necessarily true within spheres of discourse," since this kind of discourse relativism is neither interesting nor plausible. An obvious danger for Howe's approach – exemplified in Crittenden (1969) – is that one might object that there is no everyday notion of a greatest conceivable being – that is, there is no use for the expression 'being than which no greater can be conceived'. Of course, this is a hopeless objection to St. Anselm – but it might be a very good objection to Howe.

Broad (1953:178ff.) has a careful discussion of the meaning of the expression 'most perfect being'. He distinguishes two interpretations, namely, (i) a *comparative* interpretation – "a being than which none greater is logically possible" – and (ii) a *positive* interpretation – "a being which possesses all positive powers and qualities to the highest possible degree" – but goes on to argue that nothing can answer to the former interpretation unless it answers to the latter. Moreover, in connection with (ii), he suggests that it is very doubtful (a) whether all positive properties are compatible with one another, and (b) whether there is an intrinsic minimum or upper limit to the possible intensity of every positive property that is capable of degrees. The main question to ask about this discussion is whether one ought to agree with Broad that the comparative interpretation requires the compatibility of all positive attributes. What are positive attributes, after all? The obvious answer – namely, those attributes that are possessed by God – is clearly no help to those who doubt that the concept of God is coherent. But any other answer is likely to be unsatisfactory.

Sen (1983:229) defends the Leibnizian consistency proof as follows: "Experience cannot testify to the incompatibility of the divine properties. Nor is a logical demonstration able to do so. . . . We are thus pushed to the inevitable conclusion that all the divine perfections are compatible with each other." This is a clear case of the fallacious inference from 'no incompatibility can be found or demonstrated' to 'compatibility obtains'.

Russell (1900:174) holds that the Leibnizian consistency proof is "certainly valid." However, he overlooks two problems, namely, (i) that there may not be any simple, absolute, positive, indefinable, and unlimited properties; and (ii) that even if there are simple, absolute, positive, indefinable, and unlimited properties, it is quite unclear why we should suppose that God possesses all (and only?) these properties. Of course, Russell thought that the Kantian objection, that existence is not a predicate, constituted a knockdown refutation of Leibniz's revised ontological argument. Broad (1975:152) presents a very similar discussion to that of Russell, except that he notes an epistemological difficulty for the view that there are simple, absolute, positive, indefinable, and unlimited properties, namely, that it is hard to identify the positive member of a pair of opposed properties. The examples that he gives are good/evil and red/green. However, as Brown (1984:62) notes, Leibniz would have claimed that the incompatibility of these pairs of properties shows that they are complex.

There is some evidence that Leibniz himself came to think that the ontological could not be made into a sound proof of God's existence. According to Brown (1984:112), "Later, [Leibniz] was inclined to think that [the ontological argument] presumed that God's existence was possible, and that, while this was a reasonable presumption, the ontological argument could provide no more that moral certainty of God's existence." Gotterbarn (1976:110ff.) provides an explanation of why this happened, namely, that Leibniz found it necessary to admit "disparates*" – that is, incompatible simples – into his metaphysics. For, of course, once this admission is made, the consistency proof cannot possibly succeed.

Gotterbarn (1976:106n6) also makes the interesting observation that there is some support for the view that Descartes argued for the possibility premise in the *Meditations*. Similarly, Russell (1900:173n1) claims that Descartes argues for the possibility premise in the response to the *Second Objections*. It seems to me that, at best, Descartes' argument consists in an appeal to the clarity, distinctness, and naturalness of the idea of God. Leibniz's attempted demonstration is surely an improvement on this.

There has been much recent discussion of Leibniz's conception of possibility. Following Adams, Margaret Wilson (1979) claims that Leibniz has two notions of impossibility, namely, (i) finitely demonstrable inconsistency and (ii) conceptual inconsistency. Moreover, she suggests that it is the former notion that should be used in interpreting Leibniz's use of modal vocabulary – for example, counterfactuals and modal *de re* discourse – but the latter that should be used in interpreting Leibniz's talk about possible worlds. While these distinctions would be relevant to a more extended discussion of Leibniz's defense of a modal ontological argument, they do not seem to bear on the discussion in the main text.

Godel developed an ontological argument that was inspired by the work of Leibniz. Godel's unpublished notes were reworked by Dana Scott, whose work in turn remains unpublished. However, Sobel (1987) and Anderson (1990) have made the argument available to the general public. I shall here present the argument in the form that Anderson gives to it:

Definition 1: x is God-like iff x has as essential properties those and only those properties which are positive.

Definition 2: A is an essence of x iff for every property B, x has B necessarily iff A entails B.

Definition 3: x necessarily exists iff every essence of x is necessarily exemplified.

Axiom 1: If a property is positive, then its negation is not positive.

Axiom 2: Any property entailed by (= strictly implied by) a positive property is positive.

Axiom 3: The property of being God-like is positive.

Axiom 4: If a property is positive, then it is necessarily positive.

Axiom 5: Necessary existence is positive.

Theorem 1: If a property is positive, then it is consistent (= possibly exemplified).

Corollary 1: The property of being God-like is consistent.

Theorem 2: If something is God-like, then the property of being God-like is an essence of that thing.

Theorem 3: Necessarily, the property of being God-like is exemplified.

Given Godel's generous conception of properties, and granted the acceptability of the underlying modal logic, the theorems listed do follow from the axioms. So the only remaining questions concern the interpretation of the undefined vocabulary and the truth of the axioms. There are worries on both counts. On the one hand, the notion of a positive property is simply taken to be primitive. Consequently, the proof will not persuade those who doubt that a suitable sense can be given to the notion of a positive property. Moreover, it may be possible to reinterpret the proof in a damaging way, though I have not been able to see how to do this. On the other hand, it seems that Axioms 3 and 5 are clearly controversial and that Axiom 2 is not above suspicion. In particular, acceptance of Axiom 3 is tantamount to the concession that it is possible that there is a necessarily existent being – a concession that no atheist or agnostic will be prepared to make. An atheist or agnostic might concede that, were there a God-like being, then the property of being God-like would be positive; but this is not enough for the purposes of the proof. Finally, it should be noted that one might well have doubts about both the generous conception of properties and the modal logic that are required for the proof.

1.5. HUME'S OBJECTIONS

Barnes (1972:32) claims that the following Humean counterargument is valid:

i.   Nothing is demonstrable unless the contrary implies a contradiction. (Premise)

ii. Nothing that is distinctly conceivable entails a contradiction. (Premise)

iii. Whatever we conceive as existent, we can also conceive as nonexistent. (Premise)

iv. (Therefore) There is no Being whose nonexistence implies a contradiction. (From 2,3)

v.   (Therefore) There is no Being whose existence is demonstrable. (From 1, 4)

He writes:

This argument is valid. . . . For suppose we conceive that *a* exists; then, by (iii), it is distinctly conceivable that *a* does not exist; hence, by (ii), that *a* does not exist does not imply a contradiction. This is Hume's (iv). Finally, by (i), that *a* exists is not demonstrable. Thus, if *a* is a being, that *a* exists is not demonstrable; and that is Hume's (v).

The problem with this argument is that it ignores the possibility that there might be beings of which we can form no conception. In order to make the Humean argument valid, we need to add the further claim that if the existence of a being is demonstrable, then we can conceive distinctly that it exists. Perhaps this claim might reasonably be taken to be analytic – in which case it might be conceded that the Humean argument is *informally* valid. Gaskin (1978:60) suggests that, by 'Being', Hume means 'thing we can distinctly conceive as existent.' Given this suggestion, the argument in question is valid – but there remains the question whether, by 'Being', Hume does mean 'thing we can distinctly conceive as existent'. At the very least, the meaning equivalence claim seems to be unduly psychologistic – though this is perhaps not a reason for refusing to attribute it to Hume.

Stove (1978) suggests that there is an inconsistency in Hume's treatment of *a priori* argument in Part IX of the *Dialogues*. It seems to me that Hume provides a two-stage objection, namely, (i) it is doubtful whether it is really possible to make sense of the notion of "necessary existence"; and (ii) even if we can make sense of that notion – and we shall now begin to talk as if we can – there are reasons to doubt that ontological arguments succeed: for example, why shouldn't we suppose, instead, that the physical world is a necessary existent? Consequently, I do not think that there is any inconsistency of the kind that Stove alleges. Stove fails to note, for example, the final comment that Hume (1948:60) makes: "So dangerous it is to introduce this idea of necessity into the present question!" This clearly counts against the view that Hume has merely *asserted* that the material universe probably exists necessarily. On the other hand, I agree with much else that Stove says against Hume – and, in particular, I agree with his judgment that the main Humean argument is simply question begging. Other authors who have observed that Hume's argument is question begging include Clarke (1971) (1980), Gaskin (1978), and Ward (1982).

Gaskin (1978:64ff.) suggests that Hume's argument suffers from a conflation of the psychological notion of inconceivability with the logical notion of self-contradiction. Moreover, he suggests that Hume's use of the term 'conceivable' is unstable: Sometimes it means 'understandable' – with the implication that contradictions cannot be understood – and sometimes it means 'imaginable' – with no implication that contradictions cannot be imagined. Consequently, Gaskin offers a reformulation of Hume's argument that eschews use of the notion of conceivability:

1. No assertion is demonstrable unless its negation is contradictory. (Premise)
2. No negation of a matter of fact is contradictory. (Premise)
3. All assertions about the existence of things are matters of fact. (Premise)
4. (Therefore) No negation of an assertion that some thing exists is contradictory. (From 2, 3)
5. (Therefore) There is no thing whose existence is demonstrable. (From 1, 4)

Gaskin suggests that this reformulated argument can only be questioned on two points, namely (i) whether (2) is true, and (ii) whether the existence of God is a matter of fact. However, there are further questions. In particular, (1) seems doubtful unless it is interpreted to mean that an assertion can only be demonstrated if it can be shown that a contradiction follows from its negation together with other assertions that we are prepared to make: *Reductio* proofs in mathematics usually draw upon axioms. But, even if we restrict ourselves to further assertions whose contents can be known *a priori,* it is not clear that there are no things whose existence is demonstrable. For example, if it is granted that I know *a priori* that I exist, then it seems that I can prove that a nonempty sum of all things exists – compare the discussion of this idea in the footnotes to Chapter 4, Section 4, in the main body of the text. So, given the plausible reading of (1), it seems that (2) may well be false.

Several authors – for example, Gaskin (1978:73), Passmore (1952), and Shaffer (1962:235ff.) – have noted that there is an inconsistency between the argument from the *Dialogues* and the following passage from Hume's *Treatise* (1978:66):

The idea of existence, then, is the very same with the idea of what we conceive to be existent. To reflect on any thing simply, and to reflect on it as existent, are nothing different from each other. That idea, when conjoined with the idea of any object, makes no addition to it. Whatever we conceive, we conceive to be existent. Any idea we please to form is the idea of a being; and the idea of a being is any idea we please to form.

The problem is that if it is true that whatever we conceive, we conceive as existent, then we cannot consistently conceive of anything as nonexistent. However, as Gaskin notes, it is probably best to treat this passage from the *Treatise* as a careless error. Tweyman (1993:141) defends the hypothesis that all that Hume meant to say in the *Treatise* was that anything that we can conceive is conceived as *possibly* existing.

Huggett (1961:201) provides a clear example of a recent author who has taken over Hume's dogmas:

The thought of X, like the thought of anything of any description, is necessarily the thought of a being that exists in reality. That is, we cannot think of X without thinking of it as existing in reality. If we go on to . . . suppose that X, which must be thought of as existing in reality, does not exist in reality, no self-contradiction is generated.

But surely, if X must be thought of as existing in reality, then we cannot suppose that X does not exist in reality – that is, surely Huggett contradicts himself in supposing (i) that we must always think of any thing that it exists in reality, yet (ii) that we can suppose of at least one thing – and perhaps of any thing – that it does not exist in reality. This same contradiction is of course present in Hume – compare Williams (1981:19) – though it is not relevant to the proof in the *Dialogues*.

Hendel (1925:348) makes the following interesting observation: "When Hume was a young man he was much impressed by the form of the ontological argument in Cartesian philosophy, the idea of a perfect being revealed to man in the consciousness of his own limitations in wisdom and goodness." Clearly, this admiration for the Cartesian argument was a passing phase.

1.6. KANT'S OBJECTIONS

Kant's objections to ontological arguments have been famously and vigorously criticized by Plantinga (1966) (1967). In particular, Plantinga goes to much trouble to find plausible interpretations of the claim that existence is not a real predicate. He suggests that there is no interpretation of the claim that is both plausible and threatening to all ontological arguments. This conclusion seems to me to be correct – compare the discussion in Chapter 1, Section (6)(b), and Chapter 10, both in the main text – even if the interpretations that Plantinga offers are not ones that can be plausibly ascribed to Kant (cf. Coburn 1966, 1971).

Engel (1963) also disputes the view that the Kantian objections to ontological arguments are decisive. Engel claims that while Kant's theory of predication enables him to give a "fairly plausible account of the three-fold function of the word 'is' . . . [that account] breaks down when confronted with the world of real things." However, it seems to me (i) that the theory of predication that Engel attributes to Kant is intrinsically implausible, precisely because of its treatment of the relationship between concepts and real objects; and (ii) that the attribution is itself implausible. Nonetheless, Engel does correctly perceive that much of the worry about whether existence is a real predicate is generated by the pragmatic oddity of utterances of certain kinds of sentences that involve the finite parts of the verb 'to exist'. Compare the discussion in Chapter 10 in the main text. There was a fairly fruitless subsequent quarrel about Engel's article – see Schwarz (1964) and Engel (1964).

Harris (1977:90) argues that Kant's objections to ontological arguments "run counter to the whole tenor of his own epistemological doctrine" and that "as if unwittingly, he provides the rebuttal of his own refutation." However, it seems to me that Kant's "epistemological doctrine" is not sufficiently well worked out – especially with respect to the claims that it makes about our knowledge of things in themselves – to justify this criticism. While there are strains in Kant's thought that suggest that he could endorse something like the Hegelian ontological argument, there are other currents that run against this view. Harris's claim is discussed further in Chapter 7, Section 1.

Ferreira (1983) suggests that the postulates of practical reason merely postulate the real possibility of God – that is, *contra* Harris, they do not postulate the actual existence of God. However, the recent construction of modal ontological arguments involving necessity, by Hartshorne, Malcolm, Plantinga, and others – compare Chapter 4, Section 2, in the main body of the text – suggests that a commitment to the real possibility of God requires a commitment to the actual existence of God. Thus, it seems to me that the "two contrasting strands" in the *Critique of Practical Reason* – that is, (i) the postulation of the existence of God and (ii) the postulation of the possibility of God – are actually one: In either case, one is committed to the actual existence of God. A better response to Harris is to deny that God's existence is a postulate of either pure or practical reason – that is, a statement of the content of the postulates in question need make no reference to God.

Baumer (1966:133) defends the claim that Kant decisively refuted ontological arguments. However, he makes it clear that a successful Kantian attack requires acceptance of (i) Kant's distinction between real and logical predicates, (ii) Kant's analysis of uses of the verb 'to be', (iii) Kant's account of concepts of actual and possible beings. I suspect that each of (i)–(iii) is too controversial to provide a firm foundation for an assault on ontological arguments. In particular, (iii) seems entirely misguided, since Kant takes the modalities to be only qualities of thoughts, not also qualities of things: "Kant argues that the sole distinction of possible and actual concepts is that possible ones are not while actual ones are related to something given in intuition."

Dryer (1966:18, 24) also defends the claim that Kant decisively refuted ontological arguments. Dryer claims (i) that Kant held that one can only secure knowledge that objects of a given kind exist by "employing the concept of existence as a predicate"; (ii) that Kant held that the existence predicate in existential judgments differs from other predicates in various respects, namely, (1) in not being a *determining* predicate – that is, in not imposing a restriction on the existing things to which the predicate could apply – (2) in not being a *real* predicate – that is, in not ascribing a determination to a thing (*res*) – and (3) in not being a predicate that *enlarges* the concept of a thing; (iii) that Kant held that, in its transitive use, 'are' does not express the existence predicate; and (iv) that Kant held that the actual existence of an object can only be verified if an object presents itself in observation, or if its existence can be inferred from the existence of other objects that present themselves in observation, or.... Leaving aside the thorny question of the correctness of Dryer's reading of Kant, there is an obvious difficulty for the contention that "there is more to the thought that a certain thing exists than there is to the conception of that thing, but by that thought we are not enlarging the conception of the thing" – namely, that the temptation to treat 'more to' and 'enlarge' as synonyms leads to a temptation to treat the contention as a contradiction. As Shaffer (1962) argues, it is hard to see how one could hold that there is a genuine disanalogy between 'exists' and 'red' – for why not say that, while there is more to the thought that a certain thing is red than there is to the conception of that thing, yet by that thought we are not enlarging the conception of the thing. But Dryer offers nothing more than the bald assertion that Shaffer fails to understand the Kantian claim.

1.6(a) *No existence claims are analytic*

Plantinga (1967:30) dismisses the first Kantian objection on the grounds that it is "simply irrelevant to Anselm's proof," since there is no reason why St. Anselm should hold that 'God exists' is analytic in Kant's sense. However, it seems to me that St. Anselm could equally well accept that 'God exists' is analytic in Kant's sense, but insist that Kant is simply begging the question against him in denying that there can be existence claims that are analytic.

As Oakes (1975b) notes, the Kantian analysis of analyticity in terms of concept containment is extremely problematic. Even if it is granted to Kant that no concept can contain existence, it simply does not follow that the claim that God exists cannot be analytically true unless one also accepts his account of analyticity. Moreover, since the metaphor of "containment" seems unsuited to the purposes of serious theorizing, it is not clear whether the concession that no concept can contain existence should be made, nor whether it matters if it is.

1.6(b) *Existence is not a predicate*

Morewedge (1970) claims that the doctrine that existence is not a predicate was first discussed extensively by ibn Sina. There is some debate about whether the doctrine – and the underlying distinction between essence and existence – is implicit in Aristotle. Schopenhauer (1897:16) – and see also Schopenhauer (1958:511) – clearly thought that it is

[though Aristotle] had never even heard of the Ontological Proof; yet as though he could detect this piece of scholastic jugglery through the shades of coming darkness and were anxious to bar the road to it, he carefully shows [in the *Posterior Analytics*] that defining a thing and proving its existence are two different matters, separate to all eternity; since by the one we learn *what* is meant, and by the other *that* such a thing exists.

On the other hand, Occam thought that no such doctrine is to be found in Aristotle – compare Morewedge (1970:235n6).

Morscher (1986:278–9) claims that the following passage – from *The One Possible Basis for a Demonstration of the Existence of God* – shows that Kant did in fact hold the view that existence is a higher-order predicate:

In those instances of ordinary speech where existence is encountered as a predicate it is not so much a predicate of the thing itself as it is of the thought one has of it. For example, existence belongs to a sea unicorn [i.e., a narwhal], but not to a land unicorn. This is to say nothing other than that the notion of a sea unicorn is a concept of experience, that is, a notion of an existent thing.

While this passage lends some support to the view that Kant might well have taken the view that existence is a second-order predicate if he had been acquainted with the modern logic of quantification, I do not think that it unequivocally supports the claim that Kant actually held that existence is a higher-order predicate. In particular, it is not clear how to construe the claim that "the notion of a sea unicorn is a concept of experience." Would a compelling hallucination as of a sea unicorn show that there are sea unicorns? Are there *really* unicorns in the world of a brain in a vat in which there are coherent unicorn experiences? At the very least, it is not clear to me that this passage isn't better interpreted as a statement of some kind of idealism, or internal realism – that is, as a claim about the metaphysics of statements of existence.

Cornman, Lehrer, and Pappas (1987:239ff.) provide an analysis of the Kantian argument for the view that existence is not a defining predicate – that is, not a predicate that can be used to define what something is. In their view, the suitably spruced up Kantian argument goes like this:

1. If a term is a real (defining) predicate, then it can be added to the meaning of a term to change its meaning. (Premise)
2. If a term is a descriptive predicate, then it is a defining predicate. (Premise)
3. If a term is a descriptive predicate, then it can be added to the meaning of a term to change its meaning. (From 1, 2)
4. The term 'exists' cannot be added to the meaning of a term to change its meaning. (Premise)
5. The term 'exists' is not a descriptive predicate. (From 3, 4)
6. Existence is a property only if 'exists' is a descriptive predicate. (Premise)
7. (Hence) Existence is not a property. (From 5, 6)

Cornman et al. object to this argument on the grounds that premise (6) is unacceptable: "The fact that the term 'exists' is conceded not to

232

be a real defining predicate, gives us no reason to think that the adjective 'existent' cannot be used in definitions." However, this seems bizarre – surely *'a exists'* and *a 'is existent'* are just two different ways of saying exactly the same thing. If there is a good argument in Kant, it should apply to all of the finite parts of the verb 'to exist', to all of the related expressions in other grammatical categories. Cornman et al. "grant (4) for the sake of the argument on the grounds that verbs are not used to refer to properties of things, and therefore are not real or defining predicates." But it is standard practice to suppose that verbs are used to express properties – for example, in *'John walks'*, the verb is used to attribute the property of presently walking to John. So we should not agree that the analysis of Cornman et al. shows that the Kantian objection fails.

Campbell (1974:98) claims (i) that the Kantian claim that existence is not a predicate is properly interpreted as the claim that existence is a *purely relational* predicate "whose function is to locate the thing thought of in the context of experience as a whole"; and (ii) that it is correct to claim that existence is a purely relational predicate. However, it just seems wrong to suppose that existence has an essential tie to "location in the context of experience"; after all, it might have been the case that no sentient beings ever arose in the universe, but it would still have been true that the universe, together with all of its nonsentient denizens, existed. Relatedly, one might have doubts that, for example, galaxies forever beyond our light cone belong to the context of experience, since it is physically impossible for us to have experiences of them; at the very least, one is led to wonder what the context of experience could be if such galaxies do belong to it. Finally, there is at least a hint of absurdity in the suggestion that the claim that the context of experience exists locates the context of experience in itself.

Sorenson (1959:126) writes: "To say that what is expressed by 'exist' is not a property . . . is to say that what is expressed by 'exist' is not a nonrelational property. It follows that it is a relational property, or simply: a relation." However, Sorenson's view is quite different from the view that Campbell attributes to Kant; for what Sorenson wants to claim is that existence is a property of signs: 'To be is to denote'. In my view, this simply confuses the content of attributions of existence with the circumstances that determine their truth or falsity.

Mackie (1976:261) claims that while the Kantian claim that existence is not a predicate fails, the substance of the Kantian critique of ontological arguments nevertheless prevails: "Kant's principle is that whatever a definition or concept includes, it is always a further question whether something exists to satisfy the definition, to instantiate the concept." But everyone should concede that, in some sense, the question of satisfaction is a further question; the important point, for defenders of ontological arguments, is whether that further question can be answered *a priori*. So the Kantian principle is question begging. Note that the revised principle applies equally well if existence is taken to be a first-order or a second-order attribute – that is, it does not presuppose any view about the status of existence.

1.6(c) *No negative existentials are self-contradictory*

Cargile (1975:73) objects to Kant's claim that "if [the triangle's existence] is rejected, we reject the thing in itself with all its predicates; and no question of contradiction can then arise" in the following words:

Consider, for example, 'A method for a ruler and compass construction of a perpendicular to a given line necessarily exists'. This is equivalent to 'If a method for a ruler and compass construction of a perpendicular to given line exists, then it necessarily exists'. The form of Kant's point, applied to this case, would require him to say that one can reject a method for such a construction, "and no question of contradiction can then arise." And if we ignore the irrelevant point that in Kant's philosophy, mathematical falsehoods are not regarded as contradictions – since the latter are "analytic", the former "synthetic" – this is just a mistake. Someone may indeed reject a correct method of construction for a perpendicular to a given line, but if he does, his position is contradictory, in the sense that it is necessarily false.

This criticism of Kant seems mistaken. For, whether there actually are certain ruler and compass constructions depends upon the actual geometry of space-time: Given the appropriate geometry, it may not be possible to use a ruler and compass to construct a perpendicular to a given line. Moreover, it is germane that Kant did not take mathematical falsehoods to be contradictions – for the notions of necessary falsehood and contradiction should be carefully distinguished. If I insist on prefacing all remarks about numbers with the claim 'According to number theory . . .', and refuse to accept any atomic remarks about numbers that are not thus prefaced, I may be rejecting some necessary truths – but it doesn't seem that there will be anything contradictory in my position.

The third Kantian objection is closely related to an objection made by Caterus to the argument of *Meditation V*. The Caterus objection – in the formulation of Forgie (1990:81) – is "The first premise of the argument is a conceptual truth. It expresses a relation between concepts.... Accordingly, that premise is really a disguised conditional statement.... But then the argument ... yields a conclusion which lacks existential import. For its conclusion ... is also a disguised conditional statement." The truth in this claim is that an atheist or agnostic will be prepared to accept the first premise of the argument – 'God is F' – if it is interpreted as a disguised conditional, but not if it is interpreted as a simple categorical statement. However, a defender of the argument can insist that it is the categorical interpretation that is intended; and, moreover, the defender can also insist that the premise is true under this interpretation.

Forgie (1990:83) suggests that the Caterus objection could only be circumvented by a strategy of "subjectising" – that is, of finding a suitable interpretation for the subject term in the first premise of the argument that is acceptable to an atheist or agnostic. Essentially, he makes two suggestions: (i) Introduce a theory of items, that is, Meinongian objects; (ii) treat the premise as a secondary assertion, that is, an assertion about what is true according to a certain story – fiction, theory. However, we have seen – in our discussion of definitional and Meinongian ontological arguments – that neither of these attempted circumventions will work. Moreover, we have also seen that a defender of the argument will do best (i) to insist on the original categorical interpretation, but (ii) to concede that the argument, as thus construed, is bound to be dialectically inefficacious.

Williams (1986) makes the interesting observation that Kant's claim – in the 'Transcendental Dialectic' – that there can be no being whose nonexistence is impossible seems to conflict with earlier remarks – in the 'Transcendental Aesthetic' – that seem to entail that space is a necessarily existent being. Williams claims that the difficulty is best resolved by holding that the sentence 'Space does (not) exist' is a meaningless string of words. Perhaps this is correct; but it seems to me at least as plausible to suggest that Kant should just have retracted his claim about the status of space; after all, it does seem to be intelligible to suppose that there might have been no universe, and hence no space-time manifold. Moreover, Kant himself may well have happily embraced another antinomy: Space is a necessary presupposition of experience and hence, in this sense, necessarily exists; but there might have been no things in themselves, nor any space to which they belong.

1.7. THE LOGICAL POSITIVIST CRITIQUE

The argument against the claim that a statement is meaningful iff either (i) it is analytic, (ii) it is falsifiable, (iii) it is verifiable, or (iv) it is a logical consequence of a statement that is meaningful – essentially the proposal of the preface to the second edition of Ayer (1948/1930) – is due to Church (1949).

1.8. CONCLUDING REMARKS

A much more detailed discussion of certain aspects of the history of ontological arguments may be found in Hartshorne (1965). In particular, Hartshorne provides a discussion of responses to the *Proslogion* proofs in the works of Gaunilo, St. Thomas, William of Auxerre, Richard Fishacre, Alexander of Hales, St. Bonaventure, Matthew of Aquasparta, Johannes Peckham, Nicolaus of Cusa, Aegidius of Rome, William of Ware, Duns Scotus, Albertus Magnus, Peter of Tarentaise, Henry of Ghent, Richard Middleton, Descartes, Gassendi, Hobbes, Spinoza, Cudworth, Leibniz, Hume, Kant, Hegel, Feuerbach, Flint, Hocking, Royce, Santayana, Collingwood, Reichenbach, Findlay, Malcolm, Rescher, Hartman, Berg, Shaffer, Scholz, and Fitch. It is probably worth noting that one of Hartshorne's main concerns it to document cases in which the *Proslogion* is not given the interpretation that he favors.

2. DEFINITIONAL ARGUMENTS

Linsky (1967:126) writes, "In speaking about movies, plays, novels, dreams, legends, superstitions, make-believe, etc., our words may be thought of as occurring within the scope of special 'operators'." This is the earliest reference that I have been able to find to the main idea behind the analysis in the text – though compare Charlesworth (1965:66).

Scriven (1966:141ff.) provides a careful treatment of definitional ontological arguments:

If God is defined as an absolutely perfect existing Being, it would be possible to say that God necessarily exists but that we didn't know if he really or actually existed. We could perhaps put this point less misleadingly by saying that he exists definitionally, but it has not been shown that the definition applies to anything. . . . When we put existence into the definition (implicitly or explicitly), we make it part of the concept, and this makes it very tricky to express the distinction that we normally make between the existence of a concept and the existence of the thing to which the concept refers (we have the concept of Martians but, thus far, no Martians). But the distinction is there, however tricky it is to express.

This seems to me to be more or less right, though I would demur at the claim that existence must be "put" into definitions in all definitional ontological arguments.

Reichenbach (1951:39) provides a clear example of a definitional interpretation of *Proslogion 2*:

[Anselm's] demonstration begins with the definition of God as an infinitely perfect Being; since such a being must have all essential properties, it must also have the property of existence. Therefore, so goes the conclusion, God exists. The premise, in fact, is analytic, because every definition is. Since the statement of God's existence is synthetic, the inference represents a trick by which a synthetic conclusion is derived from an analytic premise. . . . Logically speaking, the fallacy consists in a confusion of universals with particulars. From the definition we can only infer the universal statement that . . . if something is an infinitely perfect being it exists, but not that there is such a being.

Ferguson (1992) also supposes that the argument of *Proslogion 2* proceeds from a definition, or perhaps a conceptual truth.

Brecher (1985:36ff.) claims that the argument of *Proslogion 2* should be interpreted as a definitional argument. However, it seems doubtful that he supposes that the argument proceeds *from* the definition. Rather, he supposes that the definition picks out an antecedently specifiable object, namely, that object that occurs at the apex of the Platonic scale of being. If this is right, then the argument is immediately subject to the following difficulties: (i) The doctrine of the Platonic scale of being is very controversial; (ii) the assumption that there is a single object at the apex of the Platonic scale of being is controversial even granted that there is such a scale; and (ii) given that 'greater' means 'higher in the Platonic scale of being', it must be a mistake to suppose that 'greater' can be used as a characterizing predicate in definitions. Compare the subsequent objections to Meinongian ontological arguments.

Werhane (1985:59) provides a bizarre defense of a definitional ontological argument (OA), which she formulates as follows: "God (by definition) has all perfections, therefore, God is eternal." She writes:

"This formulation of the OA might appear to lead one to an agnostic position, but it does not. Rather, this sort of argument suggests that God is a unique kind of nonmortal, nonhuman being for whom ordinary anthropomorphic predicates such as existence and nonexistence do not and should not make sense." One wonders what conditions must be satisfied by a predicate that is nonanthropomorphic; moreover, one wonders how these conditions will entail that one can understand the claim that God is eternal, given that one cannot understand the claim that God exists. And, given that it makes no sense to say that God 'exists', one wonders how it can make sense to refer to God as a 'being'. Finally, given that it will make no sense to suppose that God is good, compassionate, creative, and so on, one also wonders why anyone would be interested in such a 'being'.

The distinction between "true" and "false" definitions in the text alludes to the traditional distinction between real and nominal definitions. For the classic discussion of the nature of definitions, see Robinson (1950). For more recent treatment, see Cargile (1991) and the other articles in Fetzer, Schatz, and Schlesinger (1991).

2.1. BEGGING THE QUESTION

Among those who have alleged that ontological arguments beg the question, there are the following: Basham (1976), Gale (1991), MacIntosh (1991), McGrath (1990), Plantinga (1974a), Platt (1973), Purtill (1975), and Rowe (1976a) (1976b). Perhaps Hartshorne (1965) should also be included in this list – for he certainly concedes that there is nothing in ontological arguments that need perturb a positivist. Defenders of the more subtle view that many ontological arguments have a reading on which they beg the question, include Forgie (1991), Lewis (1970), and Spade (1976).

Forgie (1991:139) claims that an argument is epistemically circular if one cannot get into some desired epistemic position with respect to a key premise without first getting into the same epistemic position with respect to the conclusion. He then claims that modal ontological arguments are epistemically circular. But this seems wrong. One could be justified in believing the premise of a modal ontological argument before one believes the conclusion of the argument, and then go on to infer the conclusion – for example, one might come to believe the premise on the basis of the testimony of someone whom one trusts. So modal ontological arguments are not epistemically circular, under Forgie's account. Forgie also suggests that epistemic circularity entails didactic impotence. However, as I have argued, the truth is that the crucial defect in ontological arguments is their "didactic impotence"; and this property can be established independently of considerations about the epistemic circularity of those arguments.

McGrath (1990:201) – foreshadowed in McGrath (1986) – claims that all ontological arguments beg the question. He writes, "If it is correct to say that the existence of the greatest conceivable being is logically possible only if it actually exists, then one would need to know that it actually exists in order to know that its existence is logically possible." This is surely wrong. There are all sorts of ways in which one might come by knowledge – for example, on the basis of divine revelation, the testimony of others. So one *could* first come to know that it is possible that there is a greatest conceivable being, and then infer that such a being actually exists. The problem is that McGrath tries to interpret the deficiencies of ontological arguments – that is, the fact that they are question begging – in terms of epistemic circularity, rather than in terms of dialectical inefficacy. It should also be noted that McGrath insists – for example, pp. 199, 202, 205, 208 – that the internal coherence of a notion cannot depend upon its possession of a referent, and, indeed, that it *makes no sense* to suppose that there could be such a dependence. This is not obviously correct. There might be some temptation to say that the coherence of mathematical descriptions – for example, the greatest prime – depends upon possession of a referent. One difficulty is to know how to interpret the notion of internal coherence. And another difficulty is that it is unclear whether we should say that mathematical terms do refer.

MacIntosh (1991:537) writes:

There is a distinction between those arguments which are such that, if their soundness is accepted their conclusion may be seen to be logically equivalent to a premise or conjunction of premises, and those arguments of which this is not true. I do not think that anyone with normal logical acuteness could be convinced by arguments of the first sort.

This distinction is then applied to a modal ontological argument involving necessity: "Given the first premise, we may see that modal operators are irrelevant to the claim that God exists. So finding evidence for God's possibility just is finding evidence for God's existence. But that was what the argument was meant to *prove*." But, *contra* MacIntosh, one *could* be led to accept the conclusion that God exists on the basis of reasoning from the independently established claims (i) that if it is possible that God exists, then God exists; and (ii) that it is possible that God exists. Suppose, for example, that one comes to accept (i) and (ii) on the basis of the testimony of distinct persons, and then draws the obvious inference. In these circumstances, even if one is only minimally logically acute, one *will* be convinced by the argument, that is, led to the conclusion by one's acceptance of the premises. Note, too, that MacIntosh is wrong to claim that there are instances of *modus ponens* that do not fit the condition that, given one premise, the remaining premise is logically equivalent to the conclusion – at least on some well-known accounts of logical equivalence. Since H strictly implies the material equivalence of C and $(H \rightarrow C)$, there is at least one good sense in which, given H, C and $(H \rightarrow C)$ are logically equivalent. Curiously, Doney (1978:17) seems to use the same criterion as that proposed by MacIntosh in arguing for the view that a Cartesian ontological argument begs the question.

Devine (1975c:281) defends ontological arguments against the charge that "by their very form," they beg the question. He claims that since it is possible to use the name 'God' in a sentence without assuming that God exists, it follows that ontological arguments do not, "by their very form," beg the question. However, even if Devine is right that ontological arguments do not beg the question merely because they contain occurrences of the word 'God', his argument hardly suffices to show that ontological arguments are not question begging. In particular, there is nothing in the considerations that he mentions that counts against the view that valid ontological arguments inevitably have question-begging, or manifestly false, premises. The point of the objection could be reput as follows: Any valid ontological argument requires an ontologically committing use of the word 'God' – and, hence, any valid ontological argument is question begging. Of course, this objection is not strictly speaking correct – but this fact is not revealed by anything that Devine says.

The question of the correct characterization of the fallacy of begging the question has been much discussed outside the context of the evaluation of ontological arguments. In particular, the interested reader might consult Barker (1976) (1978), Biro (1977) (1984), Dauer (1989), Hamblin (1970), Hoffman (1971), Jackson (1987), Jacquette (1994, "Logical Dimensions"), Jevons (1895), Johnson (1967), Joseph (1916), Joyce (1949), Lotta and MacBeath (1956), MacKenzie (1979a) (1979b) (1980) (1984a) (1984b), Noxon (1967), Palmer (1981), Rescher (1964), Robinson (1971), Sanford (1972) (1977) (1981) (1988), Sidgwick (1910), Stebbing (1948), Walton (1980) (1985) (1987), Walton and Batten

(1984), Whately (1864), Williams (1967), Wilson (1988) (1993), Woods and Walton (1975) (1978) (1979) (1982a) (1982b), and Ziembinski (1976).

Much of the literature on begging the question has been concerned with the following sorts of cases: (i) arguments in which the conclusion appears as a premise, or as a conjunctive component of a premise; (ii) arguments that move in circles; (iii) arguments in which the conclusion is (must be) epistemically prior to at least one of the premises; (iv) arguments that could not increase a fully rational person's degree of confidence in the conclusion. Cases (i) and (ii) provide purely formal sufficient conditions for dialectically ineffective arguments. However – leaving aside cases that involve claims of analytic equivalence – it seems to me that actual allegations of begging the question rarely involve cases of this sort. Cases (iii) and (iv) are more difficult to assess. As we have already seen, it seems that cases of inference from testimony provide counterexamples to alleged cases of question-begging arguments according to criteria (iii) or (iv) except in those cases where the arguments conform to (i) or (ii). So – even leaving aside difficult questions about the interpretation of (iii) and (iv) – it seems doubtful that (iii) and (iv) represent any advance over (i) and (ii).

Perhaps some people will suggest that the label 'begging the question' should be reserved for those infrequent cases in which arguments are viciously circular. However, it seems to me that the common usage of that label accords better with the suggestion made in the text. Woods and Walton (1982a:264ff.) introduce the term 'challenge busting' to describe situations in which one uses an assumption that one knows that one's opponent is not prepared to grant in order to answer a challenge. They suggest that while challenge busting is bad dialectical strategy, it is not necessarily circular, and hence not properly a case of *petitio* or begging the question. However, it seems to me that we would ordinarily say that such a reply is question begging – that is, it begs the question against one's opponent. Perhaps it might be granted that the term *'petitio'* carries connotations of circularity – but, if so, this is merely grounds for distinguishing between *petitio* and begging the question. Of course, nothing really substantial hangs on this point, for the purposes of the present work. Those who disagree should simply take it that I am using the expression 'begging the question' in an idiosyncratic way.

Jackson (1987:112) provides the following characterization of begging the question:

Propounding an argument may be part of an epistemological division of labour, and so provide evidence [via the presentation and selection of premises] . . . for borrowing. Nevertheless, some valid arguments are such that were they propounded, the extra evidence would be ineffective; and some will, moreover, be such that this is not an accidental feature of the particular audience but a pretty much inevitable feature for any audience in doubt of the conclusion. It is these latter arguments that beg the question in the most proper sense.

It seems to me that this is a good partial characterization of begging the question in the case of arguments directed toward an audience that is merely *in doubt* of the truth of the conclusion. However, the account in the main text attempts to (partially) characterize begging the question in the case of arguments directed toward an audience that positively *disbelieves* the conclusion. Jackson is interested in the cooperative aspect of argument: But some arguments seem to be merely confrontations; and there is also the case of arguments directed toward an audience that has no prior attitude toward the conclusion. I suspect that a complete account of begging the question is likely to be very complicated.

3. CONCEPTUAL ARGUMENTS

Scriven (1966:146ff.) provides a partial analysis of conceptual ontological arguments:

There is a logical slip in the argument. 'The concept of the fully perfect being exists'. Correct. '. . . such a Being cannot have merely conceptual existence but must have real existence'. Correct – meaning that the concept . . . involves the notion of real existence and so cannot correctly be applied to anything that has only conceptual existence. But what follows is only that we cannot *say* the perfect Being exists as long as all we know is that the concept exists, since conceptual existence is *not* enough for a perfect Being.

Scriven's intuitions seem to me to be sound; but what is lacking is a discussion of (i) the dialectical context in which ontological arguments are typically propounded; and (ii) an account of how the propriety of making certain assertions – for example, assertions about characters from fiction – can vary across contexts, so that, in some contexts, strict speech requires the inclusion of appropriate sentential operators such as 'according to the fiction', and so on.

Martin (1970:299ff.) provides a clear example of a conceptual ontological argument that fails because of confusions about the logic of propositional attitude ascriptions. Without any injustice, the argument may be paraphrased as follows: (i) Everyone conceives the null entity under the description of there being something greater than it; (ii) there exists a conception of something – perhaps (for all that we yet know) the null entity – under the description of being unsurpassable; (iii) no one can conceive of entities – not even the null entity – under contradictory predicates; (iv) (hence) it is not the null entity that is conceived under the description of being unsurpassable; (v) (hence) there is an unsurpassable being. I shall not bother to catalog the faults in this argument. For those who wish to look at the original, it should be noted that premise (5) is not true without qualification, that premises (9) and (10) can be disputed, and that premise (13) is evidently false (see pp. 300, 302).

Davis (1982:223) commits what appears to me to be a clear example of the equivocation that undermines Makin's argument (my italics):

What emerges [from previous considerations] is that we can conceive of a being greater than any being which in fact does not exist. We can conceive of a greater being even if the being is conceived (by someone or other or even by everyone) as existing. *Let us then imagine a being* B *which could possibly exist but does not. Now let us conceive of* B *as existing, or even insist that* B, *for some reason, must be conceived as existing. It still follows, given Anselm's assumptions, that I can conceive of a being greater than* B, *viz. one just like* B *in as many ways as possible except that it (unlike* B) *really does exist.*

And Davis (1984:247) makes explicit commitment to a principle that turns on the same point: "If the being than whom no greater can be conceived doesn't exist, then, if we can conceive of a unique being than whom no greater can be conceived, where that being is conceived also as existent, we will have conceived of a being greater than a being than whom no greater can be conceived." As Lopston (1986) observes, there is no contradiction or oddity in the thought that while existence is one of the defining characteristics of a being than which no greater can be conceived – so that a being than which no greater can be conceived must be 'conceived as existent' in an ontologically noncommitting sense – nonetheless there is no being than which no greater can be conceived. To suppose otherwise is just to confuse the ontologically committing and ontologically neutral senses of 'conceive of'.

Sproul, Gerstner and Lindsley (1984) – as reported by Yates (1986) – seem to be guilty of a confusion about the sense of the expression 'think of'. They write: "We can think of the non-existence of a perfect triangle, but we cannot think of the non-existence of a perfect being. We cannot think of the non-existence of a perfect, necessary being. Therefore, that being must exist. We simply cannot think of its not existing. We yield by necessity to the impossibility of the contrary." Of course – as Yates in effect points out – we *can* think that there is no existent, perfect, necessary being. Naturally this does not mean that we think that the perfect necessary being both exists and fails to exist. Rather, it means that we suppose (i) that existence is part of the definition (thought$_1$) of a perfect necessary being; but (ii) that we can still form the thought$_2$ that no existent thing falls under the definition – and hence can think$_2$ of a perfect necessary being that it does not exist.

Carnes (1964:510) provides an analysis of the Cartesian ontological argument that focuses on the use of the expression 'concept of' in that argument. Carnes claims that the Cartesian argument is valid, but that "the ambiguity connected with the term 'concept' hides its circularity." It seems to me that this is very nearly right: The truth is – as I have argued in the main text – that the slipperiness of the expression 'concept of' can serve to obscure the dialectical inefficacy of the argument. Of course, this analysis need not require that there is an ambiguity in the use of the term 'concept of' in the Cartesian ontological argument.

Anscombe (1993:501) offers a conceptual ontological argument as the canonical formulation of the argument of *Proslogion* 2; I have altered Anscombe's presentation:

1. That than which no greater can be conceived exists in the mind, at least, since it can be conceived – even by a fool. (Premise)
2. (Suppose) One conceives that than which no greater can be conceived to exist only in the mind. (Assumption for *reductio*)
3. (Clearly) One can conceive that than which no greater can be conceived to exist in reality. (Premise)
4. (But) For any object, to exist in reality as well as in a mind is greater than for it to exist only in a mind. (Premise)
5. (So) To conceive that than which no greater can be conceived to exist only in the mind is to conceive that than which no greater can be conceived to be that than which a greater can be conceived – which is evidently absurd. (From 2, 3, 4)
6. (So) One cannot conceive that than which no greater can be conceived to exist only in the mind. (From 2, 5)

7. (Hence) One must conceive that than which no greater can be conceived to exist in reality as well as in mind. (From 6)
8. (Hence) That than which no greater can be conceived exists in reality. (From 7)

The fool can make the following response: Either 'conceive' is used in an ontologically uncommitting way, in which case conclusion 7 is acceptable, but does not entail 8; or else, 'conceive' is used in an ontologically committing way, in which case premise 1 is simply question begging – compare the general analysis in the main text.

Parsons (1980:215) suggests that the persuasiveness of Anselm's ontological argument hinges on a double ambiguity in the use of the word 'conceive'. On the one hand, 'conceive' has a propositional sense: 'conceive that'; on the other hand, it also has a direct object sense: 'conceive of'. Moreover, each of these senses can be taken either *de dicto* or *de re*. Parsons says, "However the argument is construed, I suspect that it will either rely on fallacious reasoning, as in the . . . transition from a *de dicto* to a *de re* reading . . . , or it will employ assumptions about the relationships between these readings which are not viable." I think that the preceding discussion of conceptual ontological arguments vindicates this claim for those versions of the argument that make essential use of hyperintensional terms such as 'conceives', although there are other readings of Anselm's argument – for example, as a modal ontological argument involving actuality – on which all such vocabulary is eliminated.

Brecher (1985:105) provides the following argument:

Suppose that *x* is a possible fiction; then it cannot be a necessary existent, since, precisely because it is a fiction, it is logically possible that it should not have been conceived, and thus that it should not exist, for the existence of fictions is contingent upon their being conceived. But God is a necessary existent: therefore he cannot be a possible fiction.

This argument seems to rely on a confusion between vehicles of representation and their contents: While the existence of the vehicles of representation of fictions are clearly contingent upon their being conceived, it is much less clear that the content of those vehicles of representation is thus dependent. However, perhaps the argument is meant to go like this: If *x* is a merely possible fiction, then *x* is not a necessary existent. But God is a necessary existent. So *x* is not a merely possible fiction. But the problem is that an atheist or agnostic will only agree that according to a relevant fiction, God is a necessary existent.

Hence, all that can be established by the argument is that, according to the fiction, God is not a merely possible fiction. It is quite compatible with this conclusion that, in Brecher's terms, God *is* a mere fiction – and, given suitable assumptions about the modal logic involved, that God is a merely possible fiction.

The argument in Makin (1988) (1992) has been discussed by a number of writers – see Leftow (1989), McGrath (1988), Oppy (1991)(1993a), and Pearl (1990). Much of the discussion has focused on the question of the acceptability of the claim that if 'F' is an exemplified concept, and 'G' is not, then Fs are greater than Gs – and, in particular, on the need for a *ceteris paribus* qualification. Leftow and McGrath both urge the case against the unqualified claim; and Makin (1992) accepts this criticism. Leftow also claims that the qualified claim is insufficient for Makin's purposes: But this is only because Leftow misrepresents the actual argument that Makin gives. If one compares the presentation in Leftow (1989:13) with the argument in Makin (1988), one can see that there are numerous differences.

4. MODAL ARGUMENTS

One of the best-known modal ontological arguments is that defended by Malcolm (1960). I have not bothered to discuss this argument because I have nothing to add to the criticisms that have been made of it by Kenny (1968a), Plantinga (1961) (1967), and Gale (1986) (1991). In particular, I think that it is quite clear that Malcolm's modal ontological argument is undermined by its dependence upon the implicit assumption that no omnitemporal eternal being can be logically contingent. This premise is one that no opponent of the argument need grant. Brecher (1985:102) defends this assumption with the following argument: "Eternal existence can be ascribed only necessarily, since, if it were contingently true that x is eternal, then it would be possible that x should cease to be eternal – but then x would not be eternal at all. And if 'x exists eternally' must be a necessary proposition, then so must 'x exists', since the former implies the latter." This argument just reproduces Malcolm's error. Even if 'eternal' means "necessarily, that is, essentially, everlasting" – so that an eternal object is one that is everlasting in every world in which it exists – it might be that there are eternal objects that exist in some worlds but that fail to exist in other worlds. For such objects, the following claims will all be true: (i) They exist contingently; (ii) they are necessarily eternal; (iii) it is not possible for such objects to cease to exist – that is, not to cease to be eternal – though it is possible that they should never have existed.

I have also chosen not to discuss the arguments defended by Hartshorne (1941) (1945) (1961b) (1964) (1965) (1967b). Here, my reason is that when all of the confusions and false leads are eliminated, there is nothing in the best formulation of Hartshorne's argument that is not incorporated in Plantinga's "victorious" modal argument. Of course, there is much that could be said about the various debates about Hartshorne's arguments: But there is almost nothing that would not be of a merely historical interest. For an excellent account of Hartshorne's views, see Pailin (1969b).

It *is* worth remarking on a curious irony in Hartshorne's work. Hartshorne contended that St. Anselm's argument demonstrates that there are only two viable options, namely, (i) theism and (ii) positivism, that is, the view that theism is unintelligible, meaningless, and necessarily false. But it is only the adoption of characteristic *positivistic* conflations – namely, (i) the failure to distinguish between the analytic, the necessary, and the *a priori;* and (ii) the failure to distinguish between the incoherent, the unintelligible, the meaningless, the repugnant to commonsense, the *a priori* false, the analytically false, and the various senses of the necessarily false – that lend any plausibility to this contention. Of course, Hartshorne was himself alive to the need to draw distinctions here – see, for example, Hartshorne (1965:47); though compare Hartshorne (1961:111) – but these distinctions are ignored in his assertions about the *Proslogion* arguments. Hartshorne (1991a:18) observes that "if there is no *a priori* metaphysical knowledge, then I think agnosticism is the right conclusion." But, of course, one hardly needs to be a positivist to deny that there is *a priori* metaphysical knowledge, of the kind that Hartshorne has in mind. A similar line of criticism of Hartshorne may be found in Campbell (1976:108).

Hick (1967a:341) – repeated in Hick (1970) – contends that both the proof offered by Hartshorne and the proof offered by Malcolm are vitiated by "a shift in mid-course" between two importantly different concepts of necessary being. However, while there is some justice in this as a criticism of Malcolm's argument, it is less clear that it is a reasonable criticism of Hartshorne. Like Plantinga, Hartshorne is very clear that it is *logical* necessity that is supposed to be one of the divine attributes. However, unlike Plantinga, Hartshorne persistently construes logical necessity as truth in every alternative future state of the actual world, where the alternative future states of the world are nomically or causally constrained. Hick – and many others – have contended that the supposition that God is a logically necessary being in Plantinga's sense is manifestly absurd, mistaken, in conflict with traditional religious doctrine, and so on. But it is clear that no other kind of necessity will suffice for the production of an even *prima facie* plausible ontological argument; in particular, it is clear that Hartshorne's ontological argument simply begs the question against one who denies that God exists in any alternative future state of the actual world.

Finally, I have also chosen not to discuss the famous ontological disproof of the existence of God in Findlay (1948a). Again, the reason is simply that – after the discussion of Plantinga's modal ontological argument – there is nothing important left to say. Puccetti (1964) suggests that he may have constructed an alternative ontological disproof – namely, a proof that draws on those considerations normally adduced in discussions of arguments from evil. I shall discuss Puccetti's argument when I turn to that topic.

4.1. MODAL ARGUMENTS INVOLVING ACTUALITY

Spade (1976) suggests that the two-fold ambiguity that Lewis finds in the modal ontological argument involving actuality doesn't do justice to the case: There is a further ambiguity in the notion of having a property that also needs to be taken into account. However, (i) if we hold, with the later Lewis, that it is a mistake to suppose that there are conceptually possible worlds that are not logically possible worlds, then there is no need for Spade's further distinction; and (ii) if we hold that it was not a mistake to suppose that there are conceptually possible worlds that are not logically possible worlds, then in effect we shall be giving a Meinongian interpretation of the argument. Spade's analysis is discussed further in the notes on Meinongian arguments.

Baumer (1980) suggests that there is an argument for the existence of God in Duns Scotus that is vitiated by a modal error about actuality. Since the argument proceeds entirely *a priori*, it should be mentioned here, even though it has some similarity to the Thomistic ways of proving the existence of God. Scotus also defends a more familiar ontological argument – compare Doyle (1979) and Kielkopf (1978). It should be said that, on Kielkopf's interpretation, the arguments attributed to Scotus have unintelligible premises – for example that natures properly contain themselves – and the final position ascribed to Scotus is quite implausible.

4.2. MODAL ARGUMENTS INVOLVING NECESSITY

Hartshorne first enunciated his defense of modal ontological arguments involving necessity in Hartshorne (1941). However, other people seem to have made a more or less simultaneous discovery of the alleged importance of "Anselm's principle" – compare MacIver (1948).

Many attempts have been made to formalize modal ontological arguments involving necessity in systems of modal logic. I comment on some of those attempts here. In making these comments, I presuppose some familiarity with the wider literature on modal logics. Novices might like to consult Bull and Segerberg (1984), Chellas (1980), Forbes (1985) (1989), and Hughes and Cresswell (1968) (1984).

Maydole (1980) provides a proof that he claims can be carried out in the system LPC + S5 of Hughes and Cresswell (1968). Since LPC + S5 contains both the Barcan formula (BF) and the converse Barcan formula (CBF) as valid theorem schemata, and since it also incorporates the classical assumption that there are no nondenoting terms, it is obvious that it will be a theorem of LPC + S5 that God (necessarily) exists. Consequently, Maydole's claim that there is a "proof" is clearly correct – though, of course, the probative value of the demonstration is rather undermined by the assumptions that are required for the acceptance of LPC + S5; as Rosenthal (1976:187) points out, Fred Sommers's proof of the claim that if something is possible then something is actual, encounters a similar problem *via* its question begging reliance on BF. However, the proof that Maydole gives – in a system from Copi (1972) – seems to involve a mistaken application of the rule for the introduction of the necessity operator, that is, an application to a formula that is not completely modalized. It should be said that Maydole recognizes that BF and CBF are controversial – though he claims that Plantinga's well-known argument against BF is not decisive.

Pottinger (1983:46) canvasses a number of formulations of ontological arguments in logical systems, leading to a final version in free quantified modal logic. This final version contains, as a premise, the claim that it is possible that God exists. As he notes, the epistemological status of this claim is controversial. However, his further contention that "although the theist has not made his case, it is clear that the atheist has a very tough row to hoe" is entirely gratuitous: For the claim to have demonstrated that the existence of God is either necessary or impossible offers no particular comfort to either camp. Pottinger's discussion strongly suggests that if pains are taken to avoid question-begging uses of singular terms, modal ontological arguments must be formulated using question-begging possibility premises.

Sayward (1985:152) examines two different semantics for quantified modal logics – and, in particular, for two different versions of quantified S5. On one of these semantics, objects can possess properties even in worlds in which those objects do not exist; but in the other case, objects can only possess properties in worlds in which they exist. Sayward alleges that Plantinga's ontological argument is only valid on the second of these accounts – and he then claims that "Plantinga would need to show that [the second account] is preferable [to the first]; [but] far from doing this, it is not even clear that Plantinga sees the two accounts as viable alternatives; and [therefore] Plantinga's argument is a bad argument." In fact, in a series of articles, beginning with one in (1979), Plantinga has tried to argue the case for the second account ("serious actualism"); so there is no question that Plantinga had long been alive to the difficulty. Moreover, it seems to me that some version of the modal ontological argument involving necessity might survive the demise of serious actualism – that is, it is not clear to me that the two semantic theories that Sayward discusses exhaust the field. One might hold that even though there are some properties that can be possessed in a world by objects that do not exist in that world – for example, the property of not existing – so that serious actualism is false, nonetheless, there are other properties – for example, the property of being maximally excellent – that can be possessed in a world only by objects that exist in that world. Hinchcliff (1989) presents a plausible case for the view that Plantinga's defense of serious actualism is inadequate; however, if I am right, Plantinga could take the demise of serious actualism in his stride.

Rosenberg (1981) suggests that a proper formalization of modal ontological arguments involving necessity requires recognition of a typical ambiguity in the modal operators involved. In particular, he suggests that we must distinguish between (i) logical or conceptual possibility and (ii) theological necessity – and then suggests that each of (i) and (ii) is appropriate for different premises in the argument. A defender of the argument should, I think, deny the need for the distinction: The modal ontological arguments are solely concerned with broadly logical necessity. Interestingly, Plantinga changed his mind on this issue. In Plantinga (1964), the view that the existence of God is broadly logically necessary is attacked; but, in Plantinga (1974a) that very same view is defended. For further discussion of the alleged need to discriminate between broadly logical necessity and theological necessity, see Hartshorne (1977), Hick (1961), Humber (1974), and Nasser (1971) (1979).

Brown (1978:592) provides what purports to be a formal demonstration of the claim that "we are forced . . . into the dilemma of, on the one hand, questioning Non-Contradiction, Identity and Excluded Middle, . . . or, on the other hand, accepting the implication of a thing's necessity from its existence or mere possibility, and the credibility of the Ontological Argument." However, his "formal demonstration" is vitiated by a confusion between (i) theorems and (ii) formulas that occur as items in proofs with hypotheses. Since there are worlds in Kripke models for T in which Brown's alleged theorem is false, there must be some such fairly gross error in his "demonstration."

Basham (1976:673) claims that St. Anselm's modal ontological argument has the invalid form $\Box((P_1 \& P_3 \& P_4) \to (Eg \to \Box Eg))$, P_1, P_3, P_4, therefore $\Box(Eg \to \Box Eg)$. However, what he fails to notice is that St. Anselm would have accepted the claims $\Box P_1$, $\Box P_3$ and $\Box P_4$ – and, given that these replace P_1, P_3, and P_4, the argument in question is valid.

Mackie (1982) claims that Plantinga's ontological argument is vitiated by its use of modally improper world-indexed properties, that is, properties expressible by predicates of the form 'P in W', where 'P' expresses a standard property, and 'W' denotes a possible world. However, Sennett (1991) suggests that this criticism is mistaken: In his view, there is nothing wrong with world-indexed properties; and, in any case, Plantinga's argument makes no use of world-indexed properties. What Plantinga's argument does rely upon is the acceptability of universe-indexed properties – that is, properties that are defined in terms of the entire set of possible worlds – but, Sennett suggests, the introduction of these properties fouls up modal intuitions about the independence of possible worlds. I think that Sennett is only partly right here. Both universe-indexed properties and properties indexed to the actual world *can* foul up modal intuitions, hence the problems that confront modal ontological arguments involving necessity *and* modal ontological arguments involving actuality. But, when treated with proper care, both universe-indexed properties and properties indexed to the actual world are perfectly acceptable. However, as Sennett correctly notes, in Plantinga's ontological argument, universe-indexed properties are not obviously treated with the right measure of respect. Maloney (1980) contends that if one admits world-indexed and universe-indexed properties, then one must hold that one can have no knowledge about what is possible other than that knowledge that is obtained by inference from knowledge of actual states of affairs. However, it is clear that one needn't be driven to this conclusion provided that one treats the properties in question with appropriate circumspection. Finally, Plantinga (1986) provides a convincing critique of Mackie's remarks about world-indexed properties.

Tichy (1979:419) claims that St. Anselm's ontological argument is best represented in a "transparent intensional logic." In this formulation, there are three premises: (i) An individual office that instantiates necessary existence is greater than any other that does not. (ii) Necessary existence is a requisite of H, that is, that second-order office which is the greatest individual office. (iii) H is occupied, that is, there is a unique individual office than which no greater individual office can be conceived. Tichy claims that (i) is the suspect premise. However, his argument against (i) suggests that it is stronger than anything that St. Anselm's argument requires. He writes:

To see that necessary existence is a liability, rather than an asset, even to fairly great offices, consider the office of the holder of the greatest occupied office, L^*. L^* too instantiates necessary existence and is undeniably greater than the office L of the holder of the lowliest occupied individual office. Yet it is not a particularly great individual office as individual offices go. It is readily seen that no particular perfection is a requisite of L^*.

This seems to me to be a demonstration that Tichy has misrepresented St. Anselm's argument. What Anselm invites us to compare is two offices, one of which is the greatest conceivable office and the other of which is this office minus necessary existence. The Anselmian intuition is that, *in this case*, the latter office is lesser. Hence, the correct formulation of the first premise is: (i') An individual office that instantiates H is greater than an individual office that only instantiates the office H-minus-necessary-existence. It should be noted that Tichy really ignores the difficulties that confront premise (iii), that is, the difficulties that confront the claim that it is possible that there is a being than which no greater can be conceived. In my view, this is the most problematic premise of the argument. Also, it should be noted that Hugly and Sayward (1990) have criticized Tichy for misrepresenting St. Anselm's view, principally in his identification of Anselm's "natures" with his own "individual offices." I think that this identification may be implausible, but that it doesn't do any damage to the argument.

Lucas (1985) offers a formalization of an "epistemic existence argument" that purports to prove the existence of an omniscient being. His argument has three premises: (i) Necessarily, for any x, if x is epistemically unsurpassable, then it is not possible that there is a true proposition that x does not know; (ii) anyone who knows all true propositions is omniscient; and (iii) it is possible that there is an epistemically unsurpassable being. Lucas says that the derivation is in a system QB$^-$, for which no semantics are provided; however, since BF and CBF would appear to be derivable in QB$^-$, it should come as no surprise that the argument is derivable. After all, (i) says that for any world in which there is an epistemically unsurpassable being, it is true in every accessible world that that being knows every true proposition – and BF and CBF entail that the being in question exists in those accessible worlds; and (iii) says that there is a world in which there is an epistemically unsurpassable being. So, if the actual world is accessible from every world, (i) and (iii) entail that, in the actual world, there is an epistemically unsurpassable being. Lucas's argument is a close cousin of the argument defended by Plantinga: The choice of the expression 'epistemically unsurpassable' – which roughly means 'exists necessarily, and is necessarily omniscient' – is clearly apt. Lucas also claims that there is a version of the argument that is valid in a free-logic version of QB$^-$, since one can replace (iii) with (iii'): For some specific individual a that is known to exist, it is possible that 'a' is epistemically unsurpassable. Of course, there is a sense in which this is correct, namely, that the argument is clearly valid. But it is also clear that the argument is dialectically useless, since – by (i), as the argument shows – the concession of (iii') is tantamount to the concession that 'a' is an epistemically unsurpassable being.

Nasser and Brown (1969) provide a formalization of a proof that is similar to the one provided by Lucas. Their proof has two premises, namely, (i) $\Box(-(\exists y)Oy \rightarrow (x)\Box(Ox \rightarrow K[x, -(\exists y)Oy]))$ and (ii) $-\Diamond(x)\Box(Ox \rightarrow K[x, -(\exists y)Oy])$. From these premises, it follows that (iii) $\Box(\exists y)Oy$. However, the problem – as Nasser and Brown in effect note – is that (i) is evidently false, since a being that is possibly but not actually omniscient will know that it is omniscient in those worlds in which it is, but will not believe that it is omniscient in those worlds in which it is not omniscient. However, if we omit the offending modal operators, the resultant premise (ii) – $-\Diamond(x)(Ox \rightarrow K[x, -(\exists y)Oy])$ – won't suffice for the argument, since this will be false if there is no omniscient being, because the embedded conditional will then be vacuously true.

Hanson (1961:458) provides a curious analysis of the fault in ontological arguments, namely, that it involves a "cross-type inference from the necessary to the contingent." As he notes, it is absurd to suppose that there can be a strict entailment from a necessary proposition to a contingent proposition. However, it is unclear how this is supposed to bear on the ontological argument that he formulates as follows: "*G* necessarily has properties *a, b, c, d,* and *e* (for existence); therefore, in fact, *G* has the property *e.*" For, of course, the conclusion of this argument is not that as a matter of contingent fact, *G* has the property *e;* rather, the conclusion is just that it is true – because necessarily true – that *G* has the property *e.* And this does not involve anything that might be construed as a mistaken crosstype inference.

Clarke (1971:254) discusses the following three principles: (i) It is not contingent whether God exists (Anselm's principle). (ii) Given a definiens Dx for some definiendum Qx, if Dx is not tautologous, then it is possible that $-(\exists x)Qx$ (Rule A); (iii) Given a definiens Dx for some definiendum Qx, if Dx is not contradictory, then it is possible that $(\exists x)Qx$ (Rule B). He claims that there are just three options: "Either (1) we reject Anselm's Principle; or (2) we find some justification for choosing between Rule A and Rule B; or (3) we find some justification for rejecting both Rule A and Rule B." However, it seems to me that there is another option, namely, keep Rule A and Rule B, but restrict the vocabulary that can appear in the definitions to which they advert. In particular, modal and nonnuclear vocabulary should be excluded. Clarke's own solution involves an implausible relativization of possibilities to languages.

Hasker (1982:93) provides a very dismissive treatment of modal ontological arguments – in his view, they may be "fairly summarised in the following statement: 'God exists necessarily' has not been proved false." However, this "summary" relies on a conflation of two things: (i) the content of the premises and conclusion of modal ontological arguments, and (ii) the dialectical efficacy of modal ontological arguments. One might agree that for an atheist or agnostic, modal ontological arguments achieve nothing – that is, they show no more than the claim that there is no proof that it is false that God exists necessarily – but one should not conclude from this that the content of the premises and conclusion of the argument are adequately captured in this slogan. And it is even worse to suppose that the dialectical inefficacy of the arguments shows that "there are no such arguments"; for then what is there that fails to be dialectically efficacious?

Chellas and Segerberg (1994), following MacIntosh (1991:546n33), examine modal logics in which the following modal ontological argument involving necessity is valid:

1. $\Diamond P$ (Premise)
2. $P \to \Box P$ (Premise)
3. $\Diamond P \to P$ (From 2, MacIntosh rule)
4. P (From 1, 3 by *modus ponens*)

More exactly, they examine modal logics that have the MacIntosh rule: If $\vdash P \to \Box P$, then $\vdash \Diamond P \to P$. Chellas and Segerberg establish various technical results about modal logics that have this rule, including an identification of the smallest such logic. These results do not contradict my suggestion that virtually any modal logic can sustain modal ontological arguments *provided that one is prepared to add further, perhaps even infinite, sets of premises when working in systems with very weak rules;* however, these results do provide important information about the logical resources required for standard kinds of modal ontological arguments involving necessity.

My dismissal of other senses of 'necessity', apart from broadly logical or metaphysical necessity, applies only to the context of modal ontological arguments – that is, it is not a dismissal of the idea that God is best taken to be 'necessary' in one or more of these other senses. The question of how best to construe God's 'necessity' – especially in the case of particular writers such as St. Anselm and St. Thomas – has been much discussed. See, for example, Brown (1964), Daher (1971), Franklin (1964), Howe (1971), Humber (1974), Kenny (1962), Malcolm (1960), Hick (1961) (1967a), Martin (1976), Morreall (1984), Nasser (1971), Penelhum (1960), Plantinga (1964) (1974a), Rainer (1948), Rice (1964), Schrader (1991), and White (1979).

There have been many attempts to show that the crucial possibility premise in Plantinga's modal ontological argument should be rejected. Gale (1990:227ff.) suggests that there are more plausible premises that are incompatible with the claim that it is possible that unsurpassable greatness is instantiated – for example, that it is possible that there is morally unjustified evil, or that it is possible that every free person always freely does what is morally wrong. However, Gale's argument is subject to a dilemma: Either these alleged possibilities are compatible with the existence of God, or they are not. If they are, then a theist can accept them; but if they are not, then a theist will reject them. Moreover, a theist who rejects these possibilities need not be obviously irrational: For, if I hold that God exists and that the existence of God is incompatible with the existence of morally unjustified evil, then of course I will hold that it is not possible that there is morally unjustified evil. But why couldn't it reasonably turn out that I have a *very strong* intuition that it is possible that unsurpassable greatness is instantiated? Gale claims that the very same intuitions that support the claim that it is possible that unsurpassable greatness is instantiated also support the claim that it is possible that every free person always freely does what is wrong. But his argument for this claim relies on the assumption that if it is true for *any* free person that there is a world in which he always freely does what is morally wrong, then there is a world in which *every* free person always does what is morally wrong. This assumption could be reasonably rejected by a proponent of ontological arguments – that is, one who could hold that this assumption conflicts with the further fact that unsurpassable greatness is instantiated. Reasonable modal intuitions are systematic; but they can also be primitive. Gale (1990:236ff.) also suggests that (i) the relative simplicity of the nontheistic intuitions and (ii) the need that theists have to justify their intuitions both provide reasons for rejecting the theistic intuitions. Neither of these suggestions can pass unchallenged. Judgments about simplicity are notoriously subjective: It is not at all clear that theists could not reasonably maintain that, from a theistic perspective, their intuitions favor the more simple possibilities. And the fact that theists seek to construct theodicies has many potential explanations apart from the claim that they are lacking in confidence in their modal intuitions – for example, that they seek to demonstrate the reasonableness of their beliefs in the hope of winning converts, that they seek a systematic formulation of what they regard as an important area of knowledge, and so on. Of course, there is also the point that faith can wax and wane. One might be fully confident in one's intuitions, and yet regard the construction of a theodicy as insurance against the pitfalls that faith may encounter. One's beliefs can be undermined by mere causes as well as by reasons. See, also, Gale (1988) for an earlier formulation of the same critique of Plantinga.

Strasser (1985:154) suggests that Tooley's criticism of Plantinga – and, in particular, his claim that the only way to defeat a base-level modal claim is by showing that it entails a contradiction – can be turned to Plantinga's advantage: "As 'there is a maximally great being' does not entail a contradiction, one is justified in claiming that some possible world contains a maximally great being. However, if there is a possible world which contains a maximally great being, then all worlds contain a maximally great being." But, of course, the claim that there might be a maximally great being is not a base-level modal claim, since the notion of a maximally great being is defined with respect to the entire "universe" of possible worlds. As I argued in the main text, if Tooley were right about the nature of logical space, then Plantinga's view would be defeated.

Morris (1985:269) claims:

The Anselmian ... does have available the elements of an account of [her modal intuitions]. For the Anselmian's intuitions about God ... generate without intentional contrivance an overall belief-set in which it makes sense that there should be some such intuitions and that they should be, at least a core of them, reliable. For if an Anselmian God exists and creates rational beings whose end is to know him, it makes good sense that they should be able to come to know something of his existence and attributes. It makes sense that he create them capable of recognizing important truths about him as well as about themselves.

But (i) nontheists will reasonably object that it doesn't make sense that it should be so difficult to come to have the intuitions in question; and (ii) this kind of bootstrapping can be used to justify all kinds of competing conceptual schemes. It makes sense that, if there is no necessarily existent God, a great many people will have the intuition that it is not possible that there is a necessarily existent God.

Many defenses of ontological arguments – or of key premises that are required for ontological arguments – are vitiated by a slide between, or by a conflation of, (i) logical or metaphysical necessity and (ii) doxastic necessity. A clear example is provided by Ward (1982:26):

I think what we have to say is that we do not know whether it is necessarily true that there could be no being which could be actual but not simply possible and not-actual. In the absence of a proof of that proposition, we are compelled to admit the possibility of the notion of a being which, if it is possible, is actual. But it follows immediately that it is actual.

All the absence of a proof can require is the concession that it is doxastically possible that there is a necessary being. But it is only the logical – or metaphysical – necessity of a being that entails that it actually exists. A clear grasp of the required distinction would have made it much easier for earlier writers to find an adequate response to Findlay (1948a) – see, for example, the tortured discussion in Hutchings (1964). This conflation is discussed by Leslie (1980:210).

The debate between Beard (1980) and Clarke (1980) is also marred by a failure to distinguish between epistemological and metaphysical questions. Beard (1980:251) claims to be able to show that "the theist and atheist can hold precisely the same notion of God, and yet the former can claim that his existence is necessary while the latter holds that his existence is impossible." His method is to provide two models of logical space, one that contains God and one that does not. To this, Clarke (1980:503) objects that Beard's second model "stacks the deck" – that is, it presupposes that it is possible that God does not exist. But this objection involves a misunderstanding: The point of the two models is just to establish a common epistemological footing for the ontological debate between the theist and the atheist. It should not be supposed that the two models are meant to show to the theist that it is *logically* – or *metaphysically* – possible that God does not exist; and perhaps – *contra* Beard – it should not even be supposed that they are meant to show to the theist that it is *conceivable* that God does not exist, certainly not in any sense in which conceivability is intimately related to logical possibility. Rather, the models are meant to show that part of what is at issue between theists and atheists is the nature of logical space – that is, the nature of logical (or metaphysical) possibility and of conceivability. Consequently, the models can be used to point up the dialectical impotence of modal ontological arguments – compare Oppy (1993b) for further discussion of the bearing of conceptions of logical space on modal ontological arguments. Moreover, the models do establish a sense in which theists and atheists have the same notion of God – since both can concede, for example, that it is clear that one who opts for the theistic model of logical space will be committed to the claim that it is not logically possible that God does not exist, and that one who opts for the atheistic model of logical space will be committed to the claim that it is not logically possible that God does exist.

For an attempt to defend a modal ontological argument that was published as this book was going to press, see Steinitz (1994a,b). Steinitz claims that those who deny that there are necessarily existent nonabstract beings are obliged to hold that the concept of a necessarily existent nonabstract being is incoherent and self-contradictory. But, despite Steinitz's disclaimers, it *is* open to such people to argue as follows: There *are no* necessarily existent nonabstract beings – a premise supported by experience and global theoretical considerations – so there *can be no* necessarily existent nonabstract beings. A nontheist who argues in this way need not suppose that the concept of a necessarily existent nonabstract being is incoherent or self-contradictory; rather, she just thinks that it is uninstantiated, and *hence* necessarily uninstantiated. Of course, when she claims that the concept is uninstantiated, she means just that; that is, she does not suppose that it is *merely contingently* uninstantiated.

4.3. MODAL ARGUMENTS INVOLVING EXPLICABILITY

Ross's argument is discussed in Zeis (1986). On Zeis's formulation of the argument, it involves three crucial premises: (i) It is possible that there is an explanation of God's nonexistence; (ii) God's existence is neither inconsistent nor incompatible with the principle of explicability, namely, that any logically consistent state of affairs has a possible explanation for its being the case; and (iii) given that 'God' means 'uncausable' and 'unpreventable', it is not possible that there be something else that could prevent God's existence. Moreover, Zeis suggests that premise (ii) is the weakest point in the proof – since there seem to be equally good grounds for the claim (ii') God's nonexistence is neither inconsistent nor incompatible with the principle of explicability; and yet (ii') can be used to construct a precisely parallel argument for the conclusion that God does not exist. Zeis's suspicions about (ii) certainly seem well founded – an atheist or agnostic could surely be quite reasonable in rejecting (ii). However, (i) and (iii) also deserve suspicion. As it is formulated, (iii) is absurd: All sorts of things have inappropriate names, so the fact that 'God' means 'unpreventable' does not entail that it is impossible that there is something else that prevents God's existence. Presumably, what is intended is something like this: If 'God' refers at all, it refers to a being whose existence is unpreventable. But, in order to accommodate this variant, other parts of the argument need to be reformulated. The chief difficulty that I see for (i) is explained in the main text.

Ross's argument is also criticized in Hick (1970:97ff.), Mavrodes (1970:93ff.), and Nathan (1988). Hick argues – mistakenly – that the argument fails because there is no suitable conception of logical possibility – compare my earlier discussion of modal ontological arguments involving necessity. Mavrodes provides a penetrating discussion of the different interpretations that might be put on the notion 'self-explanatory being' in Ross's argument; among other things, he makes the correct observation that Ross's own statements of his arguments are unnecessarily complicated. Nathan discusses a number of related arguments, including the following pair:

1a If a proposition is false, then it is possible that there is an explanation of its falsity. (Premise)

2a All explanations of a proposition's falsity are either internal (in terms of the inconsistency of the proposition) or external (in terms of something's preventing the proposition from being true). (Premise)

3a 'There is an unpreventable being' is consistent. (Premise)

4a It is impossible that anything should prevent the existence of an unpreventable being. (Premise)

5a If 'There is an unpreventable being' is false, it is impossible for its falsity to have an internal explanation. (From (3a))

6a If 'There is an unpreventable being' is false, it is impossible for its falsity to have an external explanation. (From (4a))

7a If 'There is an unpreventable being' is false, it is impossible for its falsity to have an explanation. (From (2a), (5a), (6a))

8a There is an unpreventable being. (From (1a), (7a))

1b If a proposition is true, then it is possible that there is an explanation of its truth. (Premise)

2b All explanations of a proposition's truth are either internal (in terms of the inconsistency of the proposition's negation) or external (in terms of something's causing the proposition to be true). (Premise)

3b 'There is no uncausable being' is consistent. (Premise)

4b It is impossible that anything should cause the existence of an uncausable being. (Premise)

5b If 'There is an uncausable being' is true, it is impossible for its truth to have an internal explanation. (From (3b))

6b If 'There is an unpreventable being' is true, it is impossible for its truth to have an external explanation. (From (4b))

7b If 'There is an unpreventable being' is true, it is impossible for its truth to have an explanation. (From (2b), (5b), (6b))

8b There is no uncausable being. (From (1b), (7b))

Nathan claims that the premises of these arguments are "rather plausible," but that they are of no use to the natural theologian, since they entail that no unpreventable beings are uncausable. However, while I agree that Nathan's construction of parallel arguments shows that Ross's argument is dialectically ineffective, I do not think that it ought to be conceded that the premises of that argument are rather plausible. In particular, one should ask for more information about the notions of '(propositional) consistency' and 'something's preventing a proposition from having a given truth-value' that are invoked in premises (2) and (3): Can one explain the truth of a proposition *via* the observation that its negation is false? Can one explain the truth of the claim that *a* is not red *via* the observation that *a* is green? Can one explain the nonexistence of a particular unpreventable being *b via* the observation that there are no unpreventable beings? And so on.

Ross (1969b:50–8) provides a simplified presentation and defense of his argument. In defense of the principle of hetero-explicability, he writes, "A brief examination of our ordinary discourse and of scientific discourse, too, will disclose that any proposition which we are willing to call logically contingent expresses a state of affairs which we can readily see to be causable or preventable, at least in principle." What does "preventable" mean here? If it means merely that there are worlds in which the proposition does not obtain, then it will be question begging to insist that God's existence is unpreventable; and moreover, the principle of hetero-explicability will be trivially true. But what else could it mean? We seem to be able to make more sense of the idea that logically contingent propositions express causable states of affairs – since, for example, for any world in which there are uncaused contingent propositions, we can imagine a similar world in which the counterparts of those uncaused contingent propositions are caused to obtain by the will of an external agent – but this part of the principle is insufficient for Ross's purposes. Moreover, there are still problems: for example, if it is true but contingent that a certain subatomic particle was subject to uncaused decay, then it cannot be the case that there is another world in which there is a cause for that particle's uncaused decay, though it may be true that there is a cause for the particle's decay. So we need some restrictions on the vocabulary that can be used to specify propositions and states of affairs in order to guard against counterexamples. But perhaps this can be done.

4.4. MODAL ARGUMENTS INVOLVING INCOMPREHENSIBILITY

Friedman has discussed other ontological arguments. In Friedman (1980) he discuses (Hartshorne's) modal ontological arguments involving necessity. And, in Friedman (1978)(1982), he discusses Spinoza's ontological argument.

Friedman (1980) distinguishes six senses of necessity and argues that on none of them is Hartshorne's ontological argument both valid and uncontroversially sound. There is much in this article of interest; I shall mention just one point here. According to Friedman (1980:309), there is an issue about whether God comprehends all the logical types in the Russellian hierarchy. However, I suspect that this is not so. We should not suppose that there are recursive procedures whereby God records or collects information: Nothing can get to be omniscient that way. Rather, God has a nonlinguistic, nonrecursive means of accessing and recording the facts. Consequently, the results of Russell, Tarski, Church, Godel, et al. are simply irrelevant – for all of these results are essentially connected to the recursive nature of language. Goodwin (1983) provides a critique of Freidman's criticisms of Hartshorne.

Basson (1957) purports to provide an argument that shows that there could not be a being with a nonlinguistic, nonrecursive means of accessing and recording all the facts – for, if there were such a being, then there would be a method for determining all the facts, namely, consult the being in question. However, as Matson (1958) points out, the direction "consult the being in question" does not provide a *method* for determining all the facts. The being in question could not provide a recursive account of the "method" that it uses for accessing and recording the facts – for, *a fortiori,* there is no method that it follows. The error that Basson makes clearly bears on the argument that tempts Friedman and that was discussed in the preceding paragraph.

Friedman (1982) contains a detailed examination of Spinoza's ontological argument. According to Friedman, the essential flaw in the argument is that it involves a conflation of causal necessity with logical necessity – that is, it shares the main flaw of Malcolm's reconstruction of St. Anselm's argument. I think that this critique is probably unfair to Spinoza – that is, I doubt that Spinoza does make this conflation – and, more importantly, this critique misses the fact that one of the premises of the Spinozistic argument is that it is possible that God exists. This premise is one that no opponent of modal ontological arguments will grant. Nonetheless, there is an interesting argument that is suggested by the "combination" of the Spinozistic argument and Friedman's mystical ontological argument, as follows: I know *a priori* that at least one thing exists, since I know *a priori* that I exist. Moreover, I know *a priori* that mereology is an ontological free lunch – so I know *a priori* that there is a mereological sum of all the things that exist. So I know *a priori* that there is a mereologically greatest being – and this thing I shall call 'God'. This argument seems plausible to me – except for the decision to call the mereologically greatest being 'God'. As far as I can see, there is no reason to think that there is anything religiously significant about the mereologically greatest being. Certainly, there is no sense in which this being is the creator and sustainer of all things. Perhaps it is just the physical universe. A closely related argument is discussed in Johnson (1965:333). The most important difference is that Johnson defines 'God' to be "the being which possesses the most predicates." This definition is of very doubtful intelligibility, since it seems plausible to suggest that all beings will have infinitely many properties and, moreover, that it will be the same infinity in each case. A similar argument is also presented by Galloway (1950:386). Mijuskovic (1973:23) claims that Spinoza provides a "conclusive and irrefutable" proof of the existence of a being that may be called indifferently "God, nature, Manna, the greatest being, the most perfect being, absolute being, *ens, res, aliquid,* etc."; once again, the proof in question seems to be intimately related to the one sketched earlier.

Hoernle (1922:30) cites Bosanquet quoting Stout: " ' "I believe in the totality of being, and it is nonsense to say that I might be deceived. . . . Whatever point there may be in the ontological argument for the existence of God is this." ' " This suggests that the argument that I have sketched earlier is also neo-Hegelian; the main difficulty is to understand how anyone could have supposed that it constitutes a proof of the existence of *God*.

There have been numerous attempts to formalize Spinoza's *Ethics* – and, hence, to formalize his ontological argument. Jarrett (1978) describes a derivation of forty propositions from eleven definitions, seven axioms, and fifteen extra axioms, which he thinks can be reasonably attributed to Spinoza. In the informal discussion, Jarrett (1978:42–5) notes that in order to produce a valid ontological argument, Spinoza needs to assume that it is possible that God exists – and, indeed, this claim is one of the fifteen extra axioms that Jarrett introduces. However, in the formal treatment, Jarrett (1978:52) does not include this extra axiom among those that are needed in the derivation of the claim that God exists. Moreover, the axioms and definitions that he does include do not seem to be sufficient; perhaps there was a typographical error at this point? Friedman (1978:104n3) claims to have formulated Part I of the *Ethics* using 165 extra premises, of which 32 are neither analytic nor logically necessary. However, he suggests that the formulation could be simplified. Friedman (1978:78) also notes the need for the assumption that "there is exactly one possible substance" – that is, it is possible that God exists.

The earlier suggestion that there is a sound ontological argument that is suggested by the argument of Spinoza's *Ethics* needs to be treated with some care. In particular, it should be noted that it is quite implausible to identify Spinoza's God (Nature) with the physical universe – for, according to Spinoza, God is that being that possesses all attributes, and of which all other beings are merely modes. But it seems to me to be clearly wrong to suppose that physical objects are modes of the physical universe; rather, as the earlier argument required, physical objects are *parts* of the physical universe. The question of the interpretation of Spinoza's metaphysical system – and of the interpretation of his basic vocabulary of substance, mode, attribute, and so on – is very complex. Fortunately, we need not pursue it here.

Joachim (1901:50) summarizes the Spinozistic argument as follows:

It belongs to the nature of Substance to exist: a Substance which is not, is not Substance at all. . . . Either then, you must give up the idea of Substance, or you must admit that Substance – i.e. God – necessarily exists. But, if you give up the idea of Substance, you must give up the idea of mode as well. Either, therefore, nothing exists, or God exists of necessity.

One error here is patent: One who gives up the idea of Substance will surely give up the idea of mode as well, but such a one will not accept that this amounts to drawing the conclusion that nothing exists. Also, the argument appears to involve a modal fallacy: At best, the conclusion to be drawn is that either nothing actually exists, or that God actually exists. But, in any case, this argument seems to bear little resemblance to the text of the *Ethics*. Compare Hallett (1957:24), Harris (1973:40), McKeon (1928:176), Parkinson (1954:46), Saw (1951:63), and Wolfson (1934:184) for vastly different readings of the proof. Many of these readings seem equally fanciful.

Young (1974:191) claims that in order to assess "the full force" of Spinoza's ontological argument, one needs to decide whether the metaphysical view on which his system rests is the correct metaphysical view. But this is surely a confusion. If there are alternative metaphysical systems that can be reasonably accepted, and on which Spinoza's ontological argument is unsound, then it is perfectly clear that Spinoza's ontological argument is not dialectically effective. Of course, we may concede that given Spinoza's metaphysical system, his ontological argument is sound – but that is a very weak concession. In particular, this concession does not yield any interesting sense in which Spinoza's ontological argument is a good argument.

Findlay (1948a) embeds the discussion of the attributes of a being that is worthy of worship in an extended defense of the claim that there is a modal disproof of the existence of God. The arguments that Findlay gives for the claim that it is not possible that God exists are weak, since they rely on a conventionalist account of necessity. Some difficulties for this view were noted by Hughes (1948), in his critique of Findlay (1948a). Both Hughes (1948) and Rainer (1948) take the view that the existence of God is not logically necessary, and that some other understanding of God's unique necessity is required; a similar view is expressed by Hick (1967:343). Rainer suggests: (i) *complete actuality* – but actuality does not come in degrees; (ii) *indestructibility* – but mass-energy is indestructible; (iii) *aseitas* – but the universe is very likely self-existent, at least according to agnostics and atheists; and (iv) *independence of limiting conditions* – but even God is subject to the laws of logic, that is, his nature must impose some limitations upon him. The difficulties in explaining the nonlogical sense in which God is necessary suggest that what is really required is a nonconventionalist account of logical necessity. Nonetheless, it is clear that the argument that Findlay endorses is valid, and that the conflict between his argument and the one defended by Hartshorne will come down to a clash of intuitions.

5. MEINONGIAN ARGUMENTS

Meinong's theory of objects has been much discussed in recent times. The three major studies are Findlay (1963), Routley (1980), and Parsons (1980). The essays in Haller (1986) are also useful, as is Lambert (1983a).

Meinong's name is often mentioned in connection with ontological arguments – see, for example, Brecher (1975b), Campbell (1976), Davis (1982) (1984), Devine (1975c:280), Hinton (1972), Kenny (1968a) (1968b), King (1984), Lopston (1980) (1984) (1986), Parsons (1980), Routley (1980), and Woods (1986).

It should be noted that Meinong himself rejected the Meinongian ontological argument – compare Brecher (1975b:14). Brecher claims that a Meinongian interpretation of the Cartesian ontological argument can be used to overcome some of the difficulties that confront that argument – and, in particular, to answer some of the hard questions about existence and predication.

Parsons, Routley, and most other Meinongians would agree that, somehow, a Meinongian theory must not allow the claim that, for any F, the existent F exists. There are various means of achieving this end. Routley distinguishes between characterizing and noncharacterizing properties, and allows that only the former are assumptive. Parsons distinguishes between nuclear and extranuclear properties, and holds that it is only true for properties F from the former class that the F is F. Other theorists have tried to use Meinong's doctrine of the modal moment to secure the same result: Effectively this leads to the denial of the claim that the existent F exists; however, as Routley argues, it seems that this doctrine alone cannot suffice. Given the need for some restriction of this type – to prevent an objectionable proliferation of objects that actually exist – no acceptable recent formal development of Meinongianism allows a non-question-begging derivation of any ontological argument. For an independent discussion that reaches the same conclusion, see Jacquette (1994, "Meinongian Logic").

Hinton (1972:108) suggests that "faced with the choice between forcible conversion to theism or to Meinongism, many an atheist would choose theism." Perhaps, but many atheists will hold that Meinongian theory is not that bad. In particular, it is worth noting that much of it can be reconstrued by non-Meinongians: Where the Meinongian talks about objects, the non-Meinongian thinks in terms of, for example, collections of properties or – for the more resolutely nominalistic – collections of predicates. Some might try to opt for reconstrual in terms of classes: But there won't be enough objects to allow all of the required distinctions to be drawn, at least if the classes are extracted from the extensions of predicates in the obvious way. I have tried to remain neutral on the question of the acceptability of a Meinongian theory of objects; no doubt some will think that this concedes too much to the proponent of Meinongian ontological arguments.

The main thought behind my objection to Meinongian ontological arguments is substantially the same as – though it was derived independently of – an idea that Plantinga (1966) develops in his discussion of the Kantian claim that existence is not a predicate. Plantinga introduces (i) the notion of a *maximal concept*, that is, a concept that is such that, for any property P, either P or the complement of P belongs to the concept; and (ii) the notion of a *whole concept*, that is, a concept whose content includes all and only the properties possessed by some particular object. Moreover, he makes the assumption that every maximal concept corresponds to an existent being, while allowing that

266

whole concepts may correspond to nonexistent beings. He then writes, "We cannot construct a maximal concept by adding non-existence to a whole concept diminished with respect to existence." The point on which my argument turns is roughly the converse of Plantinga's, namely, that it is not true in general that we shall construct a maximal concept if we add existence to a whole concept diminished with respect to nonexistence; consider what happens if we add existence to the whole concept of Bugs Bunny diminished with respect to nonexistence. So there is no guarantee that the concept 'being than which no greater can be conceived' is maximal. Indeed, more directly, an opponent of the argument has been given no reason at all to think that the concept 'being than which no greater can be conceived' is maximal.

Spade (1976) analyzes an interpretation of St. Anselm's argument in which logically impossible but understandable beings are taken to exist in logically impossible but understandable worlds. Spade suggests that we need to distinguish between two senses in which something may be said to have a property: (i) x r-has q in w provided that x exists in w and has q in w; and (ii) x c-has q in w provided that x r-has q in every world in which x exists. However, there is a problem that arises immediately: Since, for any x, x r-has existence in every world in which it exists, it follows that, for any x, x c-has existence – that is, existence is part of the essence of every understandable being. This is a very unpromising basis for ontological arguments, since it fails to preserve one of the central intuitions behind the argument, namely, that God is unique in that his essence involves existence. Since Spade (1976:436) glosses c-having with the statement, "An individual may be said to c-have a property if ... it would r-have that property if it did exist," I have amended the text a little, but without changing its sense; and since he accepts that existence is a property (1976:436n7), it seems that he is committed to the view that all understandable beings c-exist.

Woods (1986:195) seems to suggest that even though a naive Meinongian ontological argument leads to "an unstoppable polytheistic flood of Gods," there is nonetheless something "dogmatic" in a restriction of the class of assumptive properties that excludes existence and other existence-entailing attributes. But, without such a restriction, one can "prove" the existence of all kinds of things that are known not to exist – for example, the leprechaun that has lived behind my left ear ever since I was born. That God – "God-plus" – actually possesses properties that "involve genidentity or C-connections with us" is not something that is guaranteed by any reasonable formulation of the theory of objects – for genidentity and C-connections cannot be taken to be assumptible, on pain of absurdity.

Tomberlin (1972b) discusses the following argument:

a. There is a being greater than the greatest possible being. (Assumption for *reductio*)
b. Necessarily, if the greatest possible being exists, then it is impossible that there be a greater being than it. (Premise)
c. Necessarily, if there is a being greater than the greatest possible being, then the greatest possible being exists. (Premise)
d. The greatest possible being exists. (From (a), (c))
e. But it is impossible that there be a being greater than the greatest possible being. (From (b), (d))
f. (Hence) (a) is necessarily false. (From (e))
g. The greatest possible being does not exist. (Assumption for *reductio*)
h. For any object x, if x does not exist, then it is possible that there is a being greater than x. (Premise)
i. If the greatest possible being does not exist, then it is possible that there is a being greater than the greatest possible being. (From (h))
j. It is possible that there is a being greater than the greatest possible being. (From (g), (i))
k. (Hence) The greatest possible being exists. (From (f), (g), (j))

He suggests that the sole fault of the argument lies with premise (c), which he claims would be justified if it were true that 'being greater than' is an e-attribute – compare the discussion of e-attributes in Section 10.3. However, it seems to me that if being greater than is an e-attribute, then (h) is clearly false – since no nonexistent object can be a term of an e-attribute. Nonetheless, Tomberlin is right to worry about the status of the relation 'being greater than'. If it is concerned only with nuclear properties, then there is no non-question-begging reason to suppose that (c) is true; and if it is also concerned with extranuclear properties, then there is no non-question-begging reason to suppose that (h) is true. So, however the argument is interpreted, it fails.

Oppenheimer and Zalta (1991) suggest that St. Anselm's ontological argument should be given a Meinongian – that is, object-theoretic – formulation, as follows:

1. There is a conceivable being that is such that nothing greater can be conceived. (Premise)

2. (Hence) There is a unique conceivable being – which we shall call 'God' – than which no greater can be conceived. (From 1)
3. If that than which none greater can be conceived, that is, God, does not exist, then something greater can be conceived. (Premise)
4. (Hence) God exists. (From 2, 3)

In the system in which this argument is formalized, the existential quantifier is supposed not to be existentially committing, and there is enough apparatus to justify the inferences from premises 1 and 3. However, no agnostic or atheist who is prepared to grant the formal system to St. Anselm is obliged to accept both of the premises: Either there is no being than which no greater can be conceived – perhaps because there is an endless hierarchy of conceivable beings – or the being than which none greater can be conceived does not exist – which is permissible, say, because nonnuclear or noncharacterizing properties must not be taken *a priori* to contribute to greatness, on pain of admitting absurdities such as the existent greatest conceivable round square. Moreover, there are aspects of the formal system – for example, the assumption that the 'greater than' relation is connected – that can reasonably be disputed.

6. EXPERIENTIAL ARGUMENTS

Rescher's experiential argument is criticized by Gunderson and Routley (1960), Ruja (1963), and Wald (1979). A similar argument is defended by Rynin (1963); it, too, is criticized by Wald (1979). McGill (1967:71ff.) discusses a range of "realistic" – that is, experiential – interpretations of the arguments of the *Proslogion*. As he notes, the main difficulty that confronts this interpretation of St. Anselm's thought is that St. Anselm explicitly denies that one can have the experiences that would be required.

Rescher's experiential argument is very similar to the argument of Hocking (1912) and of other contemporaneous idealists. Mecklin (1917) provides an interesting critique of Hocking's argument that shares some of the features of our critique of Rescher's argument.

Pap (1946:240) claims that "unless red patches existed, the word 'red' would be devoid of meaning" and hence that "unless at least one red surface existed . . . the statement 'there exist red surfaces' would be unintelligible." Of course, this is obviously wrong: What Pap ought to have said is that unless red patches existed, the word 'red' would not have meant what it actually means. But – even if this reformulated claim is true – it is hard to see how to infer any conclusions about the indubitability of the claim that there are, or have been, red patches. For – to take a somewhat far-fetched example – suppose that a demon has just created a copy of the actual world, complete with speakers who have the actual speech dispositions that we have, but in which there are no red patches. Even if we want to say that the speakers in such a world do not mean the same things by their words as we do, it is hard to see that we are any better placed than they are to make *a priori* judgments about the existence of red patches – for it is not beyond doubt that we share their plight. Perhaps this is just to say that we cannot know *a priori* what we mean when we say there are red patches – and, moreover, that we cannot even be sure, *a priori,* that we mean anything at all; for the imagined creatures, the sentence 'There exist red surfaces' would certainly seem to be intelligible; the hard questions concern the content that is to be assigned to their utterances of it. Clearly, the issues here are complex: The only point I wish to insist on is that it is far from obvious that Pap is right to claim that we know *a priori* that we can make *indubitably* true existential statements using sentences like 'There are red patches'. Pap rejects the extension of his argument to the case of God, on the grounds that it applies only to primitive – that is, verbally undefined – predicates and terms. But Rescher claims that 'God' is no less primitive than 'red', and, hence, would claim to be able to adapt Pap's argument to his case. This looks like a dispute that it is best to avoid.

Schufreider (1983:404) is one of many recent interpreters of the *Proslogion* who suggests a point of contact with Rescher's experiential ontological argument:

The actual conclusion being drawn here is that only one who really understands, who does not just think the words signifying the thing, but thinks his way through to the thing itself, cannot think that it does not exist precisely because the nature of the existence of the thing itself is such that its non-existence, even for thought, is impossible.

Of course, the fool will reply that in the nature of the case, there can't be anything more than "thinking words," since there is no "thing in itself" – compare the discussion in Chapter 12, Section (2), in the main text.

Dore (1975:350ff.) suggests that one can defend claim (i) that it is possible that there is a divine being – that is, a being that exists necessarily, and that is necessarily omnipotent, necessarily omniscient, necessarily omni-good, and so on by defending claim (ii) that we have evidence that experiences of a divine being have occurred. Moreover, he suggests that the defense of (ii) consists in appeal to the fact that many people have sincerely reported that they have had experiences of a divine being. But the difficulty in this suggestion is that it is quite unclear why we should suppose that it is part of the *content* of the experiences in question that the being that is allegedly encountered exists *necessarily*, and possesses certain properties *necessarily*. How *could* it be part of the content of an experience that certain properties are possessed necessarily? Surely, necessity just isn't the kind of property that can be given in experience – compare Hick (1967a:345) for the expression of a similar view. But if so, then Dore's defense of (i) is inadequate – for, at most, the experiences in question establish that it is possible that there is an omnipotent, omniscient, omni-good being; but this is insufficient for the development of a valid modal ontological argument. Dore suggests that the way to discover whether something can be experienced is to determine whether people have reported experiencing it: But, to my knowledge, it is almost never claimed that it is part of the *content* of a religious experience that the being encountered exists necessarily. And, if such claims were made, we would have good reason to think that those making the claims were confusing properties given in experience with properties ascribed on the basis of prior theory.

Baker (1983:229) criticizes Dore (1975) on the grounds that he fails to justify his contention that no experiences of what is logically impossible are possible. Dore (1984a:253) claims this contention is justified as a generalization of the claim that it is not possible for anyone to have an experience of a square circle, the sound of one hand clapping, a person who is a nonperson, Russell's barber, and so on. But couldn't one have a hallucination whose content is, in part, that water is not H_2O? Surely so. But then, even if we grant that there are people who have experiences of divine beings, we need not grant that this shows that it is possible that there are divine beings. And why couldn't one have a hallucination of one hand clapping, and so on? Perhaps one can't have experiences whose *sensuous* content is inconsistent – but experiences also have *cognitive* content, and alas it is a well-known fact that cognitive content can be inconsistent. Consider, for example, the case of Escher's drawings of impossible objects. And recall that one can certainly experience what one takes to be a demonstration of something that is logically impossible – for example, a proof that the circle can be squared. Moreover, it may even be that one can have experiences whose sensuous content is inconsistent. Gregory (1966:107) notes:

If the after-effect from the rotating spiral is examined carefully, two curious features will be noticed. The illusory movement may be paradoxical: it may expand or shrink, and yet be seen not to get bigger or smaller, but to remain the same size and yet to grow. This sounds impossible, and it is impossible for real objects, but we must always remember that what holds for real objects may not hold for perception once we suffer illusions.

Dore (1984b:74ff.) contains a further defense of his claim that one cannot experience the logically impossible – but without managing to pay any better attention to the slipperiness of talk about "experience of." And his views are further discussed in Dore (1984c)(1990) and Downer (1987).

7. "HEGELIAN" ARGUMENTS

Collingwood (1933), Ryle (1935) (1937), and Harris (1936) (1972) debated the merits of Collingwood's Hegelian ontological argument. It is tempting to suggest that Ryle and Harris really talk right past each other. Ryle (1935:255) is determined to defend the view that there is no way of demonstrating *a priori* particular matters of fact. Harris (1936:265) is determined to defend the view that if the world of everyday experience is ultimately intelligible, then it must be regarded as a part of an Absolute Whole that transcends the experience of finite beings. Perhaps they are both wrong. It is tempting to suppose that there are some particular matters of fact – for example, that I exist – that I can know *a priori*. Moreover, roughly following Spinoza, it is tempting to argue that there must be an Absolute Whole, namely, the mereological sum of all the things that there are. However, *pace* Harris, this argument does not depend upon the view that the world of everyday experience is "ultimately intelligible" – and, indeed, it is very controversial whether one should want to hold that view. Perhaps the dispute between theists and atheists is best understood as a dispute about whether the world is ultimately intelligible. The point is that to the extent that there is anything to the Hegel–Collingwood–Harris argument, the argument has no religious significance – or, at least, so an atheist or agnostic can reasonably contend.

7.1. THE NEO-KANTIAN ARGUMENT

Baumer (1966:141) notes that Kant propounded a Spinozistic ontological argument in *The One Possible Basis for a Demonstration of the Existence of God.*

In this argument things are held to be internally impossible when their descriptions constitute self-contradictions. . . . The argument then proceeds: if nothing exists, there is nothing to be thought; and consequently nothing to be thought as possible. Therefore it is materially impossible that nothing exists, that is, there is an absolutely necessary being, the ground of all thought.

This argument involves at least one modal fallacy. Suppose that I can know *a priori* that I exist. Then I know that it is not the case that there is nothing. But this does not show that it could not have been the case that there is nothing – that is, it does not establish that it is necessary that something exists. Moreover, even if it did show that it is necessary that something exists, it would not establish that there is a being that exists necessarily – for all that has been said to far, it could be the case that every being fails to exist in at least one possible world – compare the discussion of the Spinozistic argument in Section 4.4.

Wolz (1951:359) attributes a version of the neo-Kantian argument to St. Anselm:

Anselm sets out from an empirical fact, the knowledge process. Through an analysis of that process, he discovers a factor, the idea of a perfect being, without which the knowledge process would not be possible. The discovery of that principle confronts him with an alternative: either to attribute objective validity to that idea, or to deny the ability of the mind to know reality.

The attribution of this argument to St. Anselm seems implausible; moreover, the alleged dilemma is easily evaded – compare the discussion in the main text.

Verweyen (1970:395) claims that the argument of the *Proslogion* should be interpreted along neo-Kantian lines: "[The] proof can be understood by the philosopher [i.e., fool] if he takes into consideration the transcendental conditions of possibility of the idea of 'that than which nothing greater can be thought', not only its logical implications, as the form of the argument suggests." Again, the attribution of this argument to St. Anselm is implausible; and, more importantly, there is no non-question-begging sense in which the fool *can* "take into consideration the transcendental conditions of possibility of the idea," since the fool denies that there are any such conditions, at least of the kind to which Verweyen adverts. To think otherwise is just to misunderstand the position of the fool.

Hartshorne (1965:95) writes:

In spite of Kant, I do not believe an ideal can have a clear and consistent meaning, yet be (for all we can know) incapable of existing. I believe that there are ambiguities or inconsistencies even in the regulative use of the classical idea of God which cannot be overcome without at the same time removing the grounds for denying a constitutive use also.

As I have argued in the main text, this seems right to me – though it must be conceded that, for example, constructive empiricists would see no difficulty in the position that Hartshorne and I have rejected.

Flimons (1923:33), in an article that is largely worthless invective, emphasizes the difficulties in the Kantian view that God is a necessary regulative ideal that it would be illegitimate to hypostasize. What reason could there be for the Kantian supposition that God *is* a necessary regulative ideal? Surely, once the hypostasization is given up, there need be no reason at all to suppose either (i) that nature is "ultimately intelligible", or (ii) that we ought to conduct our enquiries as if nature is "ultimately intelligible."

7.2. THE NEO-PLATONIC ARGUMENT

Crocker (1972:44) writes as follows:

The fact is that we do make ontological comparisons, and we do attempt to get at the most fundamentally real facts. If we do this in accordance with the exigencies of rational thought we will not stop until thought has come to rest in something it cannot go beyond: something which cannot possibly be destroyed and could not possibly have been created, and which is therefore capable of explaining the existence of the facts of the world.

This illustrates the fundamental neo-Platonic assumption, namely, that there must be an ontological ground, on which a complete rational explanation of the world can be based. However, "the exigencies of rational thought" do not require this assumption: One can perfectly reasonably suppose that there are facts for which there is no explanation. And, even if one supposes that, in principle, every fact does have an explanation, one might hold that it is a constraint on any rational finite being that it recognizes that there will be some facts for which it can provide no explanation; for example, one might hold that there is an unending hierarchy of facts, each of which is explained in terms of the next. These questions will be pursued when we take up our investigation of cosmological arguments.

Crocker (1976) contains a similar kind of neo-Platonic claim:

If we deny that something has always existed, and in some sense necessarily, we then have to say that reality came into being absolutely *ex nihilo* and radically, i.e. without reason and at once; and that all of reality might, without warning, destroy itself and be gone without a trace. Both of these . . . are thoughts from which the mind recoils.

Some minds are more easily repelled than others, and in any case, there are many other options.

Many people have defended a Hegelian account of the ontological argument. Typically, such defenses take one of two forms. On the one hand, there are those who concede that what Hegel offers is not, strictly speaking, an argument: Rather, he provides expression of a fundamental truth about the world – see, for example, Caird (1880:159), Tillich (1951:230–1), and Webb (1915:151ff.). On the other hand, there are those who claim that Hegel offers an interpretation of "the ontological argument" that reveals that the argument is sound. In general, such claims entail that further premises must be added to the argument; and, in particular, such claims usually require the addition of premises that capture the fundamental truth referred to in the first kind of defense – see, for example, Hodges (1979:74).

Laird (1941:46–56) provides a nice discussion of the distinction between "the ontological argument" and "Hegel's Grand Ontological Assertion." The latter is the claim that "truth, reality, and thought are one and the same. . . . [F]ullness of being cannot be distinguished from fullness of conceived being." Somewhat more intelligibly, it is the claim that "what is central in thought must be central in reality. . . . [T]hought's ideal is also reality's goal." It is clear from this distinction that "the Hegelian ontological argument" is really nothing more than Hegel's grand ontological assertion – compare the debate between Collingwood (1933), Ryle (1935) (1937), and Harris (1936) (1972).

7.3. HAIGHT'S ARGUMENT

Dupre (1973:271) makes a good point against phenomenological ontological arguments:

A phenomenological analysis . . . may reveal the existence of a being of perception, which is ideally, that is, intentionally, present to the act, but it cannot reveal the existence of a being beyond perception. Much less can the reality of the transcendent terminus be proven by consideration of the psychological reality of the act, for the intentional object is not part of the real act at all: it is only ideally present to it.

The point is that given the nature of phenomenological analysis, there is no way that such an investigation can yield ontological conclusions. It is clearly wrong to suppose that the justification for Haight's story could draw solely on the results of phenomenological analysis.

8. APPLICATION TO HISTORICAL ARGUMENTS

In giving the application of the analytical chapters to historical arguments, I have ignored the fact that some people choose to give definitional, or experiential, or Hegelian interpretation of the Anselmian and Cartesian arguments. In the case of St. Anselm, there is some plausibility for each of these interpretations; however, the considerations adverted to in the relevant analytical chapters show that such interpretations cannot yield good arguments. In the case of Descartes, there is little justification for the experiential or Hegelian interpretations; but, in any case, such interpretations would be doomed to yield bad arguments. The interpretations discussed in the main text are the ones that have the best chance of creating the appearance of cogency.

8.1. THE ARGUMENT FROM *PROSLOGION* 2

Campbell (1980:189) suggests that there are just two choices in the interpretation of *Proslogion* 2: Either (i) treat it as an argument by definition, or else (ii) adopt Campbell's suggestion that *Proslogion* 2–3 is to be read as a continuous three-stage argument. Clearly, this is a gross underrepresentation of the available options: For one could suppose that there is an independent argument in *Proslogion* 2, yet treat it as a conceptual argument, or a modal argument, or a Meinongian argument, or an experiential argument, or a Neoplatonic "Hegelian" argument.

Schufreider (1981:93) suggests that a critical point in the understanding of the argument in *Proslogion* 2–3 concerns the question of what it is for God to exist: "Anselm argues that something than which a greater cannot be thought truly exists in that way which is God's own and God's alone, a way in which nothing else *can* exist: He so exists that He cannot be thought not to exist." Apart from doubts that one might have about the idea – that the alleged fact that God cannot be thought not to exist shows that God has a special way of existing – there are many putative counterexamples to the alleged uniqueness of God's "way of existing." For instance, (i) if numbers exist, then surely they cannot be thought not to exist in any sense in which God cannot be thought not to exist; (ii) as Descartes discovered, I cannot think that I do not exist; (iii) given that "the Universe" denotes everything that there is, then the Universe cannot be thought not to exist.

8.2. THE ARGUMENT FROM *PROSLOGION 3*

Some writers have distinguished other arguments inspired by *Proslogion 2–3*. Nakhnikian (1967) distinguishes four different arguments. The third argument is essentially Malcolm's interpretation of *Proslogion 3*, and Nakhnikian provides an adequate response in terms of the standard objection; the other arguments require further comment.

The first argument is a modal argument, which is given three distinct formulations, each with a badly formulated premise. The first formulation contains the following premise: For any property F, if nothing is F although it is possible that something is F, then it is possible that: there exists something that is F, and there exists something that is greater than the thing that is F. Consider the property of being the only object that exists in a world. It seems plausible to think that it is possible that there is a one-object world – but it is certainly not possible that one object is greater than another in a one-object world. The second formulation contains the following premise: If God does not exist, but it is possible that God exists, then it is possible both that God exists and that a being greater than God exists. One major problem with this premise is that it is plausible to think that God will be the greatest being in any world in which God exists. The third formulation contains the following premise: If in the understanding there exists a thing that is God, and outside the understanding no God exists, while it is possible that outside the understanding God exists, then it is possible that outside the understanding God exists and also that outside the understanding there exists a thing greater than God. Here, again, a major problem is that it is plausible to think that if it is possible that God exists outside the understanding, then it is not possible that a being greater than God exists outside the understanding.

The second argument is also a modal argument that explicitly invokes the notion of a necessarily existent being. Here, Nakhnikian objects (i) that, even if existence is a property, necessary existence is not a property, and (ii) that, even if necessary existence were a property, it would not be an absolute great-making property, since, for example, numbers and properties exist necessarily, but there is no sense in which they are great. Both objections are unnecessarily controversial – that is, an opponent of the argument could concede that necessary existence is an absolute great-making property, while yet maintaining that there is no supremely perfect being.

The fourth argument – due to R. M. Chisholm – begins with the following premise: If a being than which no greater can be conceived does not exist, then a being than which no greater can be conceived is not a being than which no greater can be conceived. It then notes that since the consequent of this true conditional is contradictory, the antecedent must also be contradictory. As Nakhnikian notes, the main question concerns the interpretation of the indefinite descriptions in the first premise. One plausible interpretation is to treat them as denoting expressions. On this interpretation, the premise is arguably true – for all sentences of the form 'If *a* does not exist, then *a* is not identical to *a*' are theorems of many free logics – but it does not have a contradictory consequent. Since other plausible interpretations are hard to find – compare the attempts by Nakhnikian – it is tempting to suggest that the preceding observation suffices to undermine the argument. If one allows one's quantifiers to range over nonexistent items – that is, if one shifts to a Meinongian interpretation of the argument – then the earlier discussion of Meinongian arguments in the main body of the text shows that the argument is bound to be unsuccessful.

8.3. THE CARTESIAN ARGUMENT

Dore (1984b) provides an interpretation of the Cartesian ontological argument as a conceptual ontological argument – that is, as an argument that has the following form: (1) The concept of God is the concept of a supremely perfect being; (2) the concept of actual existence is the concept of a perfection relative to God; (3) (hence) it is a conceptual truth that God has actual existence; (4) (hence) God exists. Dore maintains that this argument does *establish* that God exists. Moreover, he claims that the crucial issue is that whereas he holds that (4) follows from premises (1) and (2), opponents hold that all that follows from (1) and (2) is: (4') If God exists, then God exists. However, this claim misrepresents the main point at issue, namely, the question of the interpretation of the premises of the argument. On one interpretation – favored by theists such as Dore – (4) does follow from (1) and (2); but, of course, from an agnostic standpoint, this interpretation is question begging. On the other interpretation, favored by everyone else, all that genuinely does follow from (1) and (2) is (4'), or something suitably like it – for example, that according to certain conceptions (theories, etc.), it is an *a priori* truth that God exists. Dore's argument (i) involves an equivocation of the meaning of the expression 'conceptual truth', since there is a sense in which, even if God does not exist, it is nonetheless a conceptual truth that God exists, and (ii) misrepresents the views of his opponents in attributing to them a thesis about meaning equivalence – namely, that 'God exists' means the same as 'If God exists, then God exists' – when, in fact, their main concern is the question of what actually follows from claims that can uncontroversially be conceded to be true.

Forgie (1976:113) defends the view that the Cartesian ontological argument is vitiated by a distinction between different kinds of assertions: (i) *primary assertions,* which make a claim about how things are in our world, and (ii) *secondary assertions,* which make a claim about how things are in the world of a work of fiction. He notes that if the Cartesian argument is to succeed, then grounds must be found to support that claim that it is primarily assertable that God is a supremely perfect being. However, "It is difficult to see how that premise ... could be anything but a secondary assertion." I think that Forgie slightly overstates the case. A theist might, with perfect reason, take himself to be able to primarily assert that God is a supremely perfect being. However, an agnostic or atheist will only be able to interpret her claim as a secondary assertion, that is, as a claim about how things are according to a certain story. What is missing from Forgie's analysis is attention to the way in which assertions are used and understood in dialogue. See also Forgie (1990), in which the same analytic framework is invoked.

Forgie (1976) also makes the interesting observation that one might respond to a Meinongian version of the Cartesian argument with the claim that, at best, the argument shows that in the world of Meinongian objects, God exists. This comes close to a view that I would endorse, namely, that all that the Meinongian ontological argument establishes is that according to some versions of Meinong's theory of objects, God exists. But one can, with perfect reason, reject those versions of Meinong's theory of objects. So, one can, with perfect reason, refuse to accept the claim that the Meinongian ontological argument establishes the existence of God.

Nakhnikian (1967:225) discusses a series of formulations of the argument of *Meditation V*. His main objections turn on the use that is made of proper names and definite descriptions in the statement of the argument. In his conclusion, he suggests that the case against the Cartesian argument is not definitive: "Perhaps a more suitable logic can be constructed in which talk about the so-and-so commits us neither to presupposing nor to asserting the existence of the so-and-so in question." Of course – as the work of Routley and others clearly demonstrates – such logics are readily constructed. However, the assessment of the Cartesian ontological argument needn't await the final formulation of such logics – compare the discussion of the general objection in the main part of the text.

8.4. GENERAL REMARKS: THE GENERAL OBJECTION

The general objection bears some relation to an objection that Gassendi made to Descartes namely, that existence is not a perfection but rather the precondition for the possession of perfections. The point is not that there is no sense in which nonexistent objects can have properties – for, while this may be true, it is nonetheless too controversial for my purposes. Rather, the point is that one cannot seriously and strictly use an *atomic* sentence of the form '*Fa*' to make a statement unless one supposes that the term '*a*' refers to an item of an appropriate existential category: present existents, possible existents, Meinongian objects, and so on. Of course, there may be all kinds of linguistic conventions that make utterances of sentences of this form appropriate even when one does not suppose that the term in question refers to an item of a given existential category – for example, circumstances in which it is correct for one to say that Santa Claus lives at the North Pole even though one believes that the term does not refer to an item in any existential category. But then, when one is speaking strictly, one ought not to claim that Santa Claus lives at the North Pole – since, by one's lights, there isn't anything to which the name 'Santa Claus' refers; rather, all one ought to claim is that according to the well-known story, Santa Claus lives at the North Pole. Exactly similar considerations about the use that nontheists can make of theistic vocabulary serve to expose the dialectical failings of ontological arguments.

Smiley (1960:132) describes a logic system that is well suited for the characterization of disputes between those who disagree in their ontologies:

The whole point of the logic here proposed is to allow different and even incompatible theories to be formulated simultaneously in one and the same language. In particular, we can all draw on a common vocabulary of names without being committed to some all-inclusive ontology. But unless we are willing to assert that a particular name has a bearer we cannot use that name as a name ... for as soon as we do this we are logically committed to the existence of something denoted by it.

In my view, this is not quite right: If we are unwilling to assert that a particular name has a bearer, then we cannot use that name as a name *in atomic sentences*, though we can use it as a name in embedded contexts. But, otherwise, this viewpoint expresses a position that is fully consonant with my general objection to ontological arguments: For how one is prepared to use certain vocabulary is consequent upon the ontological commitments that one has. Consequently, any ontological argument that rides roughshod over differences in preparedness to use certain vocabulary – and, in my view, this includes *all* ontological arguments – fails.

Shaffer (1962:321ff.) seems to approach the general objection in his discussion of Carnap's distinction between internal and external questions. However, because he rejects the Carnapian distinction, Shaffer fails to realize that the general form of the Carnapian thought does provide a recipe for constructing general objections to ontological arguments. It is noteworthy that Plantinga (1967) fails to pick up this strand of Shaffer's discussion in his critique of Shaffer (1962). Plantinga claims that Shaffer overlooks the fact that there are existence statements in mathematics that are necessarily true. But, following Carnap, Shaffer could reply that this is merely an internal feature of mathematical talk. The external question, whether there are numbers, is only settled by pragmatic considerations. And, of course, while very few people would wish to reject mathematical talk, the analogy makes it clear that people might reasonably discover that they have no use for God talk.

Hartshorne's contention that St. Anselm's ontological argument forces a choice between positivism and theism can be construed as a recognition of the force of the general objection. The point is that where there is a clash of ontological commitments, it is very implausible to suppose that *a priori* considerations can be adduced that will resolve the clash – compare Geach (1951:136): "It may be laid down as a rule of method that no direct deductive proof is any good against somebody who rejects your ontology." For, anything that one party says that presupposes disputed ontology will be taken up by the other party under the protection of intensional operators. For example, suppose that I dispute that there are any numbers – say, because I am a fictionalist, *a la* Wagner (1982). Then it will be useless to say to me that since it is true that there is a prime number between 6 and 10, it is true that there are numbers. For, of course, all I would take up from this assertion is that according to the mathematical fiction – or, perhaps, according to you – there are numbers. And that brings me not one bit closer to the concession that there are numbers. Yet this remains the case even if it is true that numbers necessarily exist.

Kalin (1982:83) claims that there are three fatal hurdles to theistic proofs, namely, (i) no theistic proof can have persuasive true sentences as premises; (ii) no proof without premises can yield more than a definitional claim; and (iii) no proof that establishes the existence of a being can persuade that this being is God. But (i) there are theistic "proofs" that have persuasive true sentences as premises; (ii) perhaps not all *a priori* claims are matters of definition; and (iii) if successful, some theistic "proofs" would show that God exists. What is right in Kalin's claim is that his three allegedly fatal hurdles together constitute a single impassable obstacle to ontological arguments: There is no *a priori* argument from uncontroversial premises that will persuade any reasonable nontheist that God exists.

9. ARE THERE (OTHER) GLOBAL OBJECTIONS TO ONTOLOGICAL ARGUMENTS?

Fitch (1963:469) provides a very curious argument, which is, I think, intended as a global objection to ontological arguments – though it might also be construed as a form of acceptance of some ontological arguments. What Fitch does is to provide a "proof" that the attribute of perfection is satisfied by exactly one entity, namely, the attribute of perfection itself. Moreover, he concludes that the attribute of perfection can't be *merely* an attribute – that is, "It must be whatever else is required of it in order to be perfect." So, "The perfect being, among its other attributes, has the attribute of being itself an attribute." I think that if Fitch's argument succeeded it would be a *reductio* of the suggestion that attributes – properties – are entities that lie in the range of first-order quantifiers. What ontological arguments purport to show is that there is an *individual* that falls under the description 'being than which no greater can be conceived' – and hence it is an egregious error to suppose that ontological arguments are best construed as attempts to prove that there is an attribute – or an attribute-cum-individual – that falls under that description. Leftow (1990) presents a related argument for the view that a thing than which nothing greater can be thought is the property of being a thing than which nothing greater can be thought. To those who like well-founded ontologies – in which individuals and attributes occur at distinct levels – such claims are bound to appear manifestly false. Moreover, such claims are not obviously nominalistically acceptable, despite Leftow's explicit disclaimer: For the crucial relevant feature of nominalist views, on one well-known construal of those views, is their acceptance of only one ontological category, namely, individuals. True, some nominalists also allow sets or classes as a second admissible ontological category; and others who call themselves "nominalists" admit tropes; but there is at least room for debate about which usage should be preferred.

Kiteley (1958) also considers the suggestion that ontological arguments might be recast as a higher-order argument. He considers three arguments, which he calls the *septic,* the *aseptic,* and the *antiseptic,* and which I label (a), (b), and (c), respectively:

1a God is perfect.
2a Being perfect entails being existent.
3a (Hence) God exists.
1b Whatever is divine is absolutely perfect.
2b Were nothing divine, divinity would be imperfect.
3b (Hence) Something is divine.
1c Divinity is perfect.
2c Were nothing divine, divinity would be imperfect.
3c (Hence) Something is divine.

He claims (i) that the major premise of the septic argument is a logical solecism; (ii) that the aseptic argument is simply invalid, since an existential conclusion cannot follow from two universal premises; and (iii) that the minor premise of the antiseptic argument is simply false, since the concept of divinity is not analytically homological. However, an atheist or agnostic could grant that the concept of divinity is analytically homological without cost – for then the atheist or agnostic need not deny that there is something that is divine, namely, the concept of divinity. But, of course, in this case, the major premise in the antiseptic argument is redundant.

9.1. THE MISSING EXPLANATION ARGUMENT

In Johnston (1992), the missing explanation argument is presented as a general refutation of any view that for some S and S^*, is committed to the following pair of claims: (i) It is knowable *a priori* that S iff S^*; (ii) the claim that S because S^* is not an explanatory solecism. In particular, Johnston claims that the missing explanation argument refutes response-dependent analyses of concepts – for example, the analysis of color terms according to which (i) it is knowable *a priori* that something is red iff it looks red to standard observers under normal conditions, and (ii) the claim that things look red to standard observers under normal conditions because they are red is not an explanatory solecism.

Menzies and Pettit (1993) hold that the missing explanation argument is a good argument, but that it fails to apply in many cases, where one might think that it would apply, because of a subtle equivocation in the use of S and S^*. Thus, for example, they hold that one can consistently endorse the following pair of claims: (i) It is *a priori* that Xanthippe became a widow iff her husband died; and (ii) the claim that Xanthippe became a widow because her husband died is not an explanatory solecism. The trick is to read (i) as 'It is *a priori* that Xanthippe became a widow iff she had a husband and that husband died' and to read (ii) as 'Xanthippe became a widow because that particular person who happens to be identified as "her husband" died'. Menzies and Pettit contend that a similar story can be told about response-dependent analyses of concepts. However, it seems clear that this strategy cannot be used to save ontological arguments. So – even if one thinks that the Menzies and Pettit strategy works in some cases – defenders of ontological arguments will need some other account of the failure of the missing explanation argument.

In fact, I think that the claim made by Menzies and Pettit can be disputed. There are a number of different kinds of claims that can be expressed by sentences of the form 'S because S^*'. Johnston himself distinguishes between (i) expressions of logical, or logicomathematical, inference; (ii) expressions of conceptual articulation – for example, 'x is a bachelor because x is an unmarried adult male'; and (iii) expressions of causal/explanatory dependence. We can also distinguish (iv) expressions of constitutive dependence and (v) expressions of evidential dependence – this last supplying one natural reading of the claim 'God knows that p because p'. (Note that a sentence of the form 'It is *a priori* that S iff S^*' carries no implications about the truth of either S or S^*; it is compatible with the truth of this sentence that neither S nor S^*. On the other hand, a sentence of the form 'S because S^*' does carry implications about the truth of S and S^*; the truth of this sentence requires the truth of both S and S^*. So, an utterance of a sentence of the form 'S because S^*' is bound to convey information that is not conveyed by an utterance of the form 'It is *a priori* that S iff S^*'.) More importantly, we can distinguish different kinds of expressions of causal or explanatory dependence. In particular, sentences of the form 'S because S^*' can be used to express the fact that S is a relational – noncategorial – fact whose obtaining depends upon the obtaining of a nonrelational – categorial – fact. For example, Xanthippe's becoming a widow is a relational – noncategorial – fact whose obtaining requires a categorial basis, namely, the death of a suitably related person. Similarly, John's becoming an uncle requires the production of a child by a suitably related person. And a thing's becoming disposed to look red to normal observers under standard conditions requires that the thing acquires a suitable categorial property to serve as the basis for that disposition, namely, the property of being red. So, that one can know *a priori* that S iff S^* is no barrier to the truth of the further claim that the – noncategorial – obtaining of S depends upon the – categorial – obtaining of S^*; for, in the relevant sense, one can also know *a priori* that, if S, then S *because* S^*. The noncausal dependence in question is simply the dependence of the noncategorial on the categorial – a dependence that it is plausible to suggest can be recognized *a priori*. Of course, as Menzies and Pettit suggest, there will always be some particular instantiation of the categorial basis for a relational property – for example, there will be a particular person who dies in order to make Xanthippe a widow, a particular person who gives birth in order to make John an uncle, a particular change in the categorial structure of a thing that makes it disposed to look red to normal observers under standard conditions – but it seems to me that the explanatory claims under consideration do not, or at least need not, advert to these particular instantiations. It is at least tempting to suggest that this further order of dependence is irrelevant to Johnston's missing explanation argument.

There is at least one qualification that should be added to these comments. It is well known that questions about explanatory dependence are highly sensitive to matters of context. Recall the well-known case of the flagpole in the courtyard. It is easy to imagine contexts in which we would say that the length of the shadow cast by the flagpole is explained – at least in part – by the height of the flagpole. However – as demonstrated by van Fraassen (1980) – it is also possible to imagine contexts in which we would say that the height of the flagpole is explained by the length of the shadow. Consequently, it may be that – in some contexts – we are prepared to allow that possession of relational, noncategorial properties can explain the possession of nonrelational, categorial properties. This does not affect the main point of the preceding paragraphs, for it remains true that there is a clear metaphysical sense in which possession of relational, noncategorial properties depends upon possession of nonrelational, categorial properties.

9.2. THE THOMISTIC OBJECTIONS

Duncan (1980) defends the second Thomistic objection. He suggests that roughly what St. Thomas says is that while it is necessarily true that God exists, it is neither analytic nor knowable *a priori* that God exists. Moreover, it is our inability to comprehend – grasp, understand – the essence of God that prevents us from attaining *a priori* knowledge of God's existence. As I mentioned in the main text, a defender of ontological arguments could reasonably object that this response begs the question: For what ontological arguments purport to show is precisely that we do know *a priori* that God exists. It should also be noted that it need be no part of ontological arguments that we have much comprehension of the essence of God: All that is required is, for example, that we know that God is a being than which no greater can be conceived.

Rousseau (1980:24) claims that there is a great deal of convergence in the thought of St. Anselm and St. Thomas. In particular, he claims that St. Thomas was the first interpreter of St. Anselm to correctly observe that "the so-called proof is ... no proof at all, but an attempted unfolding of a supposedly self-evident proposition." However, while it is true that St. Thomas agreed that the existence of God is "self-evident in itself," it is surely wrong to suppose that St. Anselm did not take himself to be providing a demonstration of the existence of God – compare the earlier discussion in the notes to Chapter 1.

Matthews (1963) claims that St. Thomas presents a cogent objection to St. Anselm's argument in the *Summa contra Gentiles.* In that work, St. Thomas observes: "No difficulty befalls anyone who posits that God does not exist. For that, for any given thing either in reality or in the understanding, something greater can be conceived, is a difficulty only to him who concedes that there is in reality something than which a greater cannot be conceived." Matthews (1963:475) suggests that the significance of this objection lies in the correct observation that the atheist's view is correctly expressed by the claim that for any given thing, a greater thing can always be conceived. However, (i) it is not clear to me that this observation is even implicitly present in the passage from Aquinas; and (ii) one need not accept the claim in question in order to reject ontological arguments. In my view, St. Thomas's observation is correct, but unhelpful – for it fails to explain where St. Anselm's *reductio* argument goes wrong. Compare Cosgrove (1974:525ff.), who also makes use of Matthews's defense of Aquinas. It should be conceded that if the interpretation that Matthews and Cosgrove give to the passage in the *Summa contra Gentiles* is correct, then Aquinas did provide a good reason for thinking that St. Anselm's argument is not dialectically effective against all possible reasonable opponents.

Brecher (1985:55) claims that the objection that Matthews attributes to Aquinas – namely, that an atheist could hold that for any given thing, a greater can always be conceived – is "crucially ambiguous. Does it mean that it is impossible to conceive a specific entity that is unsurpassably great, or that it is impossible to conceive that there is an unsurpassably great entity?" In Brecher's view, only the latter claim would hurt Anselm's argument, while only the former claim is plausible. But this is surely a mistake. If for any given thing, a greater can always be conceived, then the description 'entity than which no greater can be conceived' necessarily applies to nothing. Hence, Aquinas could be taken to have anticipated the main criticism that Brecher himself wishes to make of Anselm's arguments – compare Brecher (1985:114ff.).

Crawford (1966:116ff.) criticizes Matthews (1963) for making the claim that atheism can be given a consistent statement. She holds – in effect – that any statement of atheism is inconsistent because, in fact, a being than which no greater can be conceived is one of the entities that lies in the domain of those quantifiers that are used in the statement of the atheistic position. But, of course, this is to give a rather uncharitable interpretation of the atheistic position: For part of the view that the atheist defends is that it is not the case that a being than which no greater can be conceived is one of the entities that lies in the domain of those quantifiers that are used in the statement of the atheistic position. Perhaps St. Thomas should be given some credit here; certainly, he seems to have had a much better grasp of the content of atheism than many more recent commentators.

Strictly speaking, it would be wrong to say that St. Thomas held that God's existence is necessary *a priori*, since – as Brown (1964:82) emphasizes – for St. Thomas, "necessary beings" are beings that cannot undergo any essential change in any of the ways permitted by Aristotelian theories of matter. Relatedly, for Geach (1968), "actually existent beings" are beings that do act or undergo essential changes.

For a recent broadly Thomistic discussion of ontological arguments, and theistic arguments in general, see Davies (1985).

9.3. THE USE OF SINGULAR TERMS

One of the earliest suggestions that ontological arguments fail in their use of singular terms is due to Gregory of Rimini – compare the extract from his writings in Weinberg and Yandell (1971); Streveler (1976:62) claims that a related suggestion may also be found in the work of Robert Holcot. Rimini contends that it is not true that when someone understands the word 'God', there is some *thing* in his understanding in virtue of which he understands the word. For, first, there are necessarily nondenoting phrases – for example, 'the round square' to which no *thing* can correspond; and, second, there are denoting expressions – for example, 'the number one higher than the greatest number ever specifically thought of by any human being' – that necessarily do not denote a *thing* that exists in any human understanding. Meinong would have taken a keen interest in Rimini's first example, and Russell – with his well-developed sense for paradox – would have taken a keen interest in the second.

According to Streveler (1976), another early criticism of the reasoning that underlies ontological arguments may be found in the work of William of Occam. Streveler claims that Occam held that sentences of the form '*T* is *T*' – for example, 'God is God', 'That than which no greater can be conceived is that than which no greater can be conceived' – are not tautological, but rather entail the existence of that which is referred to by '*T*'. In other words, Occam had noticed that the use of singular terms in arguments that purport to establish existence claims may well leave those arguments open to the charge of begging the question.

Plantinga (1975:585) criticizes Barnes's claim that ontological arguments fail because there is no reason to believe that there is just one thing than which nothing greater can be imagined: "Given his own views about quantification and things that do not exist, I think Barnes is mistaken; there is reason to believe that there is just one [thing than which nothing greater can be imagined]." Just as Barnes allows that one can refer to the hero of Hamlet, it seems – at least according to Plantinga – that he should allow that one can refer to the being than which no greater can be conceived. This question is controversial: It depends upon the theory of items that one is prepared to countenance. If one is prepared to countenance incomplete and inconsistent items, then Plantinga is obviously correct; but if one restricts oneself to complete and consistent items, then matters are less clear. Since Barnes does not address this issue – and since he also fails to address the related issue of characterization principles – it does not seem to be a question that is worth pursuing.

Purtill (1975:110) claims that any ontological argument can be re-futed by the observation that "no matter how much we pack into the definitions of our terms, it is always possible to simply raise the possibility that these terms fail to have a referent." The sense in which this claim is correct is the following: There is no *a priori* argument that must convince someone, who reasonably doubts that a certain theoretical vocabulary applies to anything, that that vocabulary does apply to anything – for the doubt can reasonably extend to anything that might be offered as an *a priori* justification for the claim that the theoretical vocabulary does apply. As I have remarked elsewhere, arithmetical Platonism cannot be conclusively justified on simple *a priori* grounds.

Berg (1961) tries to use Russell's theory of descriptions in the analy-sis of St. Anselm's ontological arguments. Not surprisingly, he finds it difficult to produce a formulation of the argument that is not obvi-ously question begging. Two points are particularly salient: (i) It is hard to see how to formulate the claim that God is the being than which no greater can be conceived in classical logic without presup-posing that God exists, because of the way that names function in classical logic; and (ii) it is hard to see how to formulate the pair of claims (a) that if the being than which no greater can be conceived does not exist, then the being than which no greater can be conceived is not a being than which no greater can be conceived; and (b) that the being than which no greater can be conceived is a being than which no greater can be conceived in such a way that both can be thought to be true without begging the question. Hochberg (1959) contains a similar analysis of St. Anselm's ontological arguments. Hochberg claims that the Russellian analysis vindicates the criticisms of ontolog-ical arguments made by Aquinas and Kant.

Mann (1967) notes some of the obvious difficulties with Berg's

Russellian treatment of definite descriptions in the analysis of ontological arguments in Berg (1961). Mann suggests that a "valid, non-circular" interpretation of St. Anselm's argument can be obtained by using a free logic devised by Lambert. This argument has three premises: (i) God is *the* being than which no greater can be conceived; (ii) if there is no being that is *the* being than which no greater can be conceived, then it is not the case that *the* being than which no greater can be conceived is such that nothing greater can be conceived; and (iii) *the* being than which no greater can be conceived is such that nothing greater can be conceived. Given that the descriptions are not supposed to carry existential commitments, it seems that an opponent of the argument can reasonably object to the conjunction of premises (ii) and (iii). For, given that the descriptions carry no existential commitments, (iii) will only be conceded if it is allowed – roughly – that things that do not exist can have properties; whereas (ii) will only be conceded if it is maintained – roughly – that things that do not exist cannot have properties. Consider this question: Should we agree that whether or not there is a unique being than which no greater can be conceived, *the* being than which no greater can be conceived is such that nothing greater can be conceived? If we should, then we shall deny (ii); if we should not, then we shall deny (iii).

McGill (1967:74n144) cites a version of St. Anselm's argument – due to William of Auxerre and Richard Fishacre – that clearly involves a mistreatment of definite descriptions:

Existence is included in what is good. But existence is such a great good that everything seeks it. Therefore existence is included in our understanding of what is best. Therefore, just as snub-nosed cannot be understood without nose, so what is best cannot be understood without existence. Therefore, if [what we are thinking about] is the best, then it exists. But the best [which we are thinking about] is the best. Therefore, [that which we are thinking about] does exist.

The point is that the insistence that "the best is the best" is not one that should be granted lightly – for, at least on a Russellian treatment of definite descriptions, it may well be false.

Sobel (1983:197) claims that "most ontological arguments are compromised if not vitiated by premature introduction of 'God' and elementary and uninteresting occasions for quantifier-equivocations." In particular, he suggests that the argument of Kordig (1981) is marred by an equivocation in its use of indefinite descriptions. However, it seems to me that the equivocation that Sobel detects is not essential to

Kordig's argument, which can be recast as follows: "A (unique) perfect being would be deontically perfect. (Hence) It ought to be the case that there is a (unique) perfect being. (Hence) It is logically possible that there is a (unique) most perfect being. (Hence) It is the case that there is a (unique) most perfect being." Similarly, while I grant that many ontological arguments have been compromised by equivocations on the use of indefinite descriptions, and so on, I would also hold (i) that, as Sobel acknowledges, many ontological arguments have not been thus compromised; and (ii) that when arguments have been thus compromised, there have usually been easy reformulations that avoid the difficulty. Of course, new difficulties will turn up – so Sobel's point can continue to hold, as part of a more general objection. Perhaps the defenders of ontological arguments are in the position of one who is trying to cover a floor with a rug that is too small for the purpose: No matter in which direction the rug is pulled, portions of the floor remain visible.

Bednarowski (1976:288) claims that "the ontological proof" is vitiated by its use of the singular term 'God', which requires the question-begging assumption that this term is nonempty. As I explained in the main text, there are various reasons why this won't do as a general refutation of all ontological arguments.

9.4. FURTHER ATTEMPTS

Hardin (1961) provides an "empirical" refutation of ontological arguments, which I frame as follows:

The ontological argument amounts to the claim that the sentence 'God exists' is analytic. This argument relies on the assumption that existence is a predicate. Suppose it is granted that existence is a predicate. Then the sentence 'the existent unicorn which I shall see in the next thirty seconds exists' is analytic. Hence, the sentence 'there is a unicorn which I shall see in the next thirty seconds' is analytic. But this sentence is false, and no analytic sentences can be false. So existence is not a predicate – i.e. no existence statements are analytic. Hence the ontological argument fails.

There are a number of replies that defenders of ontological arguments could make. Most notably, they could insist that Hardin's argument involves a misunderstanding of the analysis of definite descriptions that is proposed by defenders of ontological arguments. On the one hand, if definite descriptions are given a Russellian analysis, then the sentence in question will not be judged analytic – yet Hardin offers no argument to show that defenders of ontological arguments cannot adopt a Russellian analysis of definite descriptions. On the other hand, if definite descriptions are given a non-Russellian analysis, then the sentence in question may well be judged analytic – but not if that non-Russellian analysis is embedded in a suitable free logic. Since sophisticated defenders of ontological arguments will opt for the free-logic analysis, Hardin's argument does nothing to undermine those arguments. More controversially, defenders of ontological arguments might also insist that there is a disanalogy between 'God' and 'the existent unicorn' because there is no sense in which 'existence' is explicitly built in to the former. Hardin's argument generated some subsequent discussion – see Resnick (1962) (1963), Hardin (1962), and Keyworth (1962). However, this discussion fails to question Hardin's key assumptions: (i) that defenders of the view that existence is a predicate cannot also espouse a Russellian analysis of definite descriptions, and (ii) that if defenders of the view that existence is a predicate do not espouse a Russellian analysis of definite descriptions, they will then be obliged to concede that all sentences of the form 'The F is F' are analytically true.

Srzednicki (1965:28) claims that ontological arguments all "rest on a logical trick [which] turns on the application of the concepts of 'absolute' and 'perfection'." He suggests that successful ontological arguments require that the following conditions obtain: (i) Existence is a perfection; (ii) perfections are intensified by existence; (iii) perfections are all compatible; and (iv) the specification of a maximally perfect being is coherent. Moreover, he suggests that claims (i), (iii), and (iv) must all be rejected. I think that he is right to this extent: There are ontological arguments that rely on one or more of (i)–(iv); and one could reasonably reject those arguments because one reasonably rejects the relevant members of (i)–(iv). However, there are many ontological arguments that do not rely on these assumptions; and there are more obviously acceptable objections that can be made to all ontological arguments.

Geisler (1973) claims (i) that the ontological argument requires a further premise, namely, that the rationally inescapable is real; (ii) that even with this additional premise, the ontological argument is not rationally inescapable; and (iii) that the addition of a further premise – which is borrowed from the cosmological argument, and which converts the argument into a cosmological argument – does produce a rationally inescapable argument. Of these claims, (i) and (iii) are evidently incorrect. In particular, claim (i) is absurd – the additional premise does nothing at all toward improving "the ontological argument." A somewhat similar view to that espoused in (iii) is defended by Charlesworth (1965:77) and Hughes (1990). I shall discuss this argument in my examination of cosmological arguments.

Devine (1975a:110) suggests:

Despite the ontological argument the atheist option remains open.... Although the ontological argument establishes that 'God exists' is necessarily true, given the coherence of the concept 'God', to establish that the concept, and hence the statement itself, is coherent requires a context of belief in God which the ontological argument alone is impotent to supply. Without such context the concept of 'God' is otiose and for that reason meaningless.

This is wrong. The atheist or agnostic does not need to hold that the concept of God is incoherent, or meaningless, or otiose, in order to reject ontological arguments; all she needs to deny is that there is anything that falls under the concept. Moreover, the idea that the question of the coherence of a concept should be relativized to contextual matters – for example, background beliefs – is a mistake: It is a factual matter whether a given concept is coherent, just as it is a factual matter whether a given concept has application to anything. Devine's argument confuses epistemological and ontological categories: For, as I have argued, it is quite likely rational for theists to believe that some ontological arguments are sound; but this is not to say that they should think that those arguments establish – prove, demonstrate beyond reasonable doubt – that God exists.

Kuhn (1959:612) writes: "It was Anselm's error to try to find, on the basis of a strictly logical argument, the answer to a metaphysical question. [Broad], while rejecting Anselm's conclusion, shares his fundamental mistake." This seems partly correct. It may be reasonable to think that one can have metaphysical knowledge *a priori*; but, as noted earlier, it seems very doubtful that there can be effective *a priori* arguments for changes in ontology, except in cases where questions of consistency, simplicity, explanatory power, and so on intrude.

Hintikka (1969:54n4) claims that "the basic difficulty about the ontological argument is that . . . the argument is not readily seen to be the tautology which it is." However, Hintikka's claim that proponents of ontological arguments conflate (i) the claim that $\Box(\exists x)[(y)(y$ exists $\to x$ exists$)]$ with (ii) the claim that $(\exists x)\Box[(y)(y$ exists $\to x$ exists$)]$ is quite implausible. No one who is capable of understanding (i) could possibly think that it "seems to express quite well the Anselmian idea that the most perfect being must necessarily exist" (1981:129). Indeed, an atheist who holds that numbers are necessary existents will hold that both (i) and (ii) are true. Note, too, that it is controversial to claim that (i) is tautological; it is not clear that there isn't an empty possible world. Hintikka's further claim that attempts to justify the inference of (ii) from (i) presuppose a question-begging premise may be correct – but it seems to be misguided to suppose that the necessity operator in (i) and (ii) is well interpreted as an epistemic operator: 'it is known that'. That the inference from (i) to (ii) fails under this interpretation seems to be irrelevant to the success or failure of ontological arguments. (Compare Tomberlin (1974) and Vallicella (1989) for similar criticisms of Hintikka's views.)

Anscombe (1959:15) claims that the Cartesian ontological argument is best symbolized as follows: $(x)(Fx \rightarrow Gx)$, therefore $(\exists x)Fx$, where 'Fx' reads 'x is God' and 'Gx' reads 'x has eternal existence'. She then has no difficulty in invoking the classical first-order predicate calculus in order to refute the argument. This is a travesty: No defender of ontological arguments will concede that the argument has this form, though some opponents of the argument may insist that this formulation incorporates the only kind of premise that they are prepared to concede to the defenders of the argument.

Kellenberger (1970:282) claims that ontological arguments are vitiated by their failure to conform to "the ontological principle," namely, that "no concept can carry within itself a guarantee of its application . . . for the meaning of any term that can apply to something is compatible with that meaning in fact applying to something or to nothing." The content of this principle is not transparent, but it seems (i) that it may well be false, and (ii) that it is at best question begging. Given the actual meaning – that is, conceptual role – of the concept 'prime number', is there a possible world in which it fails to apply to anything? Given the actual meaning of the concept 'possible world', is there a possible world in which it fails to apply to anything? And so on. Even if these counterexamples are denied, a defender of ontological argument can still insist that 'God' is the unique concept that "carries within itself a guarantee of its application." At best, Kellenberger's "ontological principle" leads to dialectical deadlock.

Walters (1973:396) claims that it is possible to demonstrate that no perfect being can exist, and, hence, that all ontological arguments are unsound. The core of his argument is the contention that there is a contradiction that is generated by the thought that knowledge is a characteristic of perfection: "For that which can be pursued with the intent of knowing is by nature unlimited and the perfection of knowledge can only mean the completion of the uncompletable. Because knowledge is by nature always unfinished, there cannot be a greatest possible being." This is an interesting argument that I hope to take up again in a later work. For now, I shall merely note that it seems to be question begging: For the defender of an ontological argument will hold that while (i) that which can be pursued with the intent of knowing is, by its nature, such as to elude complete possession by finite agents; nonetheless, (ii) that which can be pursued with the intent of knowing can be completely possessed by an infinite agent. Moreover, the defender of an ontological argument will not concede to Walters that there is anything wrong with the notion of an actual infinity.

Pollock (1966:195) claims (i) that it can be shown that "the ontological argument" is invalid and (ii) that the argument for (i) can be used to generate a demonstration that God does not exist. Here is Pollock's demonstration. I have used my own labeling: 'g' is 'God'; 'Ex' means 'x exists'; 'Px' means 'x is perfect'; '$\rightarrow$' is entailment; and '$\supset$' and '$\equiv$' are truth-functional:

1. $((g =_{df} (\text{the } x \text{ such that } Px)) \rightarrow \Box(Eg \supset \Box Eg))$ (Premise)
2. $-[(g =_{df} (\text{the } x \text{ such that } Px)) \rightarrow Eg]$ (Premise)
3. $(\Box Eg \equiv [(g =_{df} (\text{the } x \text{ such that } Px)) \rightarrow Eg])$ (Premise)
4. (Hence) $-\Box Eg$ (From 2, 3)
5. (Hence) $((g =_{df} (\text{the } x \text{ such that } Px)) \rightarrow -Eg)$ (From 1, 4)

There are a number of questions that one might ask about this argument, for example: (i) Are the definitions in question intended to be reference fixing, or are they merely abbreviatory? (ii) What is the scope of the "definition" operator in the premises and conclusion of the argument? (iii) How could this argument be extended to cover ontological arguments that do not involve definitions, or names, or descriptions? However, I shall just focus on one question, namely, why should a theist accept premise (3)? Pollock suggests that (3) is an instance of a more general principle, namely, "that a proposition is necessarily true iff it is true by virtue of the meaning of its constituent terms" (1966:) – that is, $(\Box Fa \equiv [(a =_{df} (\text{the } x \text{ such that } Gx)) \rightarrow Fa])$. But this principle is massively implausible. Consider the substitution instance in which 'a' is 'God', 'Gx' means 'x is a perfect being', and Fx means 'x knows that, in the actual world, Graham Oppy has a son named "Gilbert" '. A theist may well hold that, necessarily, God knows that, in the actual world, Graham Oppy has a son named

'Gilbert', since (i) it is true that I do actually have a son named 'Gilbert', and (ii) the theist in question will hold that it is a necessary truth that God knows all truths. However, it is quite implausible to suggest that the definition of God entails – all by itself – that God knows that, in the actual world, I have a son named 'Gilbert'; if Pollock replies that by entailment he means strict implication, the theist will then respond that premise (2) is obviously question begging. I conclude that Pollock certainly has not managed to demonstrate that God does not exist. Moreover – although I haven't argued for this – I think that, at best, Pollock could only hope to show that there is something amiss with definitional ontological arguments.

Brunton (1970:282) claims that ontological arguments – and, indeed, all theistic arguments – fail because the concept of spatiotemporal limitation is "essential to our logical vocabulary and understanding." I think that this claim can be reasonably denied – since, for example, it seems that one could learn number theory without having the concept of spatiotemporal limitation. More importantly, I think that proponents of ontological arguments could accept the claim with equanimity – provided that it is taken to allow for the possibility that God exists in a higher-dimensional space. And if the claim is restricted to *actual* spatiotemporal limitation, then it is surely just question begging.

Korner (1979:228–9) claims that St. Anselm's argument can be refuted by attention to a distinction between two different senses of 'understanding'. On the weaker sense, '$P(x)$' is understood if "the hearer is able to define '$P(x)$' in familiar terms and acknowledges that the speaker has – correctly or incorrectly – applied '$P(x)$' to something that may be unknown to the hearer." On the stronger sense, "$P(x)$" is understood if " '$P(x)$' is understood in the weak sense, and '$P(x)$' is acknowledged to apply to something (i.e., is non-empty)." Korner then claims that "we need concede no more than that we understand Anselm in the weak sense. It is at this point that his ontological argument breaks down." There are numerous objections to Korner's claims. First, St. Anselm has an argument that, if successful, would show that if one understands the expression 'being than which no greater can be conceived' in Korner's weak sense, then, if one is reasonable, one must also understand it in Korner's strong sense. Consequently, Korner's further assertion is merely question begging: It may be true that one need concede no more than that one weakly understands the expression 'being than which no greater can be conceived', but why doesn't St. Anselm's argument succeed in showing that this isn't so? Second, St. Anselm holds that one can understand a term in a suitable but weak sense even if one cannot define it, and even if one does not think that there is anything to which it is either correctly or incorrectly applied. Consider the sense in which a materialist understands the vocabulary of a dualist: Such a materialist might insist that there isn't anything to which the soul-describing vocabulary of the dualist either correctly or incorrectly applies. So St. Anselm needn't concede that he requires that an atheist weakly understand the expression 'being than which no greater can be conceived'.

Leonard (1956:58) claims that ontological arguments – at least those of St. Anselm and Descartes – are refuted by the observation that analysis reveals that to exist is to possess contingent properties. One obvious response to make to this claim is that it is question begging: Why not say instead that to exist is either to possess contingent properties or to be God? Alternatively, one could deny that God possesses only necessary properties. Suppose that I freely think about God. Does God then have the property of being freely thought about by me? At the very least, we are off on a tricky investigation of the characterization of properties.

Esmail (1992) claims that the reformulation of St. Anselm's argument in Plantinga (1967) is readily refuted by the observation that there are forms of existence other than existence in the understanding and existence in reality: for example, existence in fiction. However, the argument is readily repaired to overcome this difficulty:

1. Suppose that God exists in one or more forms that do not include existence in reality. (Assumption for *reductio*)
2. To exist in one or more forms that include existence in reality is greater than to exist in any combination of forms that does not include existence in reality. (Premise)
3. It is possible that God exists in one or more forms that includes existence in reality. (Premise)
4. A being having all of God's properties plus existence in reality is greater than God. (From (1), (2))
5. It is possible that there is a being greater than God. (From (3), (4))
6. It is false that it is possible that there is a being greater than God. (Premise)
7. Hence it is false that God exists in one or more forms that do not include existence in reality. (From (1), (5), (6), by *reductio*)
8. But God does exist in the understanding. (Premise)
9. So God does exist in reality. (From (7), (8))

Dummett (1993:278ff.) claims that the ontological argument has the general form:

1. Whatever is God has the property X. (Premise)
2. Anything that has the property X has also the property of existing. (Premise)
3. (Hence) God exists. (From 1, 2)

He then observes:

The proponent of the ontological argument has . . . to do more than make out that there are objects which do not exist. . . . Even if 'exists' is regarded as a predicate . . . it must be one of a very peculiar sort; and if we so regard it, we shall be hard put to explain this peculiarity. . . . The proponent of the ontological argument faces the fact of explaining why existence cannot be one of the properties by which a possible object is specified. . . . No plausible solution . . . has ever been offered by the friends of non-existent objects.

However, (i) not all ontological arguments are Meinongian ontological arguments of the form that Dummett presents; and (ii) it is not clear what Dummett's objection to Meinongianism is supposed to be. After all, a Meinongian can quite properly say that existence cannot be a characterizing property on pain of absurdity. Meinongians suppose that there are theoretical advantages to be purchased by investment in a theory of objects that relies upon a distinction between characterizing and noncharacterizing properties; it is no overwhelming objection that no one has yet found an independent account of that distinction. On the other hand, as I have already explained, Meinongian ontological arguments are bound to fail, since noncharacterizing properties must be attributed in the premises, in order to get the attribution of noncharacterizing properties in the conclusion.

Zemach (1993:151) claims that "the ontological argument" runs as follows (I use Zemach's commentary in providing annotation):

1. God is the greatest being. (Premise, true by definition)
2. "The greatest being" is noncontradictory. (Premise, obviously true)
3. The greatest being is in the understanding, i.e., in some conceivable world. (From 2)
4. One who is in reality too is greater than one who is only in the understanding, i.e., in some merely conceivable world. (Premise, obviously true)
5. (Hence) God is in reality. (From 3, 4)

Zemach claims that this argument goes wrong only in the move from 2 to 3. Given his Meinongian assumptions, this is perhaps correct: Given that greatness is existence entailing, and hence nonnuclear, freedom from internal contradiction is certainly insufficient to guarantee reference for descriptions that invoke greatness. However, the argument clearly admits of other readings for which other challenges are appropriate – for example, the first premise begs the question on any non-Meinongian reading of the argument – and even a Meinongian might dispute 4.

Kelly (1994) offers a syllogistic analysis of the proofs in *Proslogion 2* and *Proslogion 3*. He claims several advantages for this approach, namely, (i) that it makes use of patterns of argument that St. Anselm would implicitly recognize; (ii) that syllogistic is free from various difficulties that beset predicate calculi; and (iii) that the syllogistic analysis provides a clearer view of the circularity and amphiboly that plague ontological arguments. All of this seems very dubious: For (i) I see no reason to think that St. Anselm would have recognized syllogistic dressed-up to compete with predicate calculi; (ii) the alleged difficulties of predicate calculi seem to me to be specious (and the syllogistic alternative has genuine problems of its own); and (iii) the circularity and amphiboly that allegedly plague ontological arguments, to the extent that they really do so, are just as visible from the standpoint of predicate calculi. Nonetheless, it is worth noting that Kelly's syllogistic formulations bear out my general objection to ontological arguments: Either the arguments are invalid or else they contain premises that atheists and agnostics will reasonably reject.

10. IS EXISTENCE A PREDICATE?

The claim that existence is not a predicate has seemed incontestable to many philosophers; for example, the very first sentence of Hutchings (1963) reads, "Of course existence is not a predicate!" This confidence in a claim of such doubtful intelligibility was surprisingly prominent among extraordinary language philosophers of the Wittgensteinian persuasion. For other confident avowals of the claim that existence is not a predicate, see Charlesworth (1965:65), Hartshorne (1962:7), Hick (1961:355) (1970:83), Hodges (1979:72), Hospers (1967:428), Kneale (1936:156), Malcolm (1960), Mitchell (1962:75), Morreall (1984:41), Pailin (1986:177ff.), Penelhum (1960:180) (1971:16), Ryle (1951:15), Sen (1983:238), Smart (1955:503), Webb (1989:463), and Williams (1984:284).

Hospers (1967:428) defends the claim that existence is not a predicate with the following argument: "If I imagine a horse and then imagine the horse as existing, what I imagine is no different in the two cases; if it were different, if something were added in the second case, then I would not be imagining as existing the same thing that I had previously imagined." But – following Shaffer (1962) – we can construct a parallel argument: If I imagine a blue ball, and then imagine the very same ball colored red, what I imagine is no different in the two cases; if it were different, if something were added in the second case, then I would not be imagining as colored red the very same ball that I had previously imagined. So, amazingly, color terms are not predicates. Many other philosophers have espoused the kind of argument that Hospers uses.

Forgie (1974) provides a short argument for the claim that the Cartesian ontological argument is not refuted by the observation that existence is not a property. He begins by distinguishing two "criteria for propertyhood": (i) the *ontological criterion*, according to which F is a property iff we can sensibly distinguish between things having F and things lacking F; and (ii) the *semantic criterion*, according to which F is a property iff in making assertions of the form 'N is (not) F', we can plausibly be regarded as referring to N, and ascribing to (denying of) it 'being F'. He then claims that, on the ontological criterion, Descartes can reasonably accept that existence is a property; whereas, on the semantic criterion, there is no reason for Descartes to suppose that existence is a property, since his argument does not require this assumption. Forgie's argument is too quick: For his defense of the claim that it is compatible with the ontological criterion to hold that existence is a property relies on the claim that it is literally true that Fafner is a dragon – that is, nonexistent entities can have properties. This is a controversial question that requires further investigation. Forgie suggests that adoption of the ontological criterion is compatible with the view that in making existence assertions of the form 'x exists', one is saying of the property 'being an x' that it belongs to something that also has the property of existence. But, when I say 'George Bush exists', I am not saying that the property of being a George Bush belongs to something that also has the property of existence – indeed, I dispute that there is a property 'being a George Bush', even though there is the property 'being George Bush'. And, when I say 'Santa Claus does not exist', I am certainly *not* saying that the property 'being (a) Santa Claus' belongs to something that also fails to have the property of existence.

10.1. REAL PREDICATES

Many have claimed that it is all but impossible to understand what might be meant by the claim that existence is (not) a predicate – see, for example, Ebersole (1963), Mackie (1976), and Shaffer (1962). Kiteley (1964) provides a careful account on which, although 'exists' clearly functions as a predicate in many uses, it has distinctive features that is does not share with other predicates.

Rescher (1960) claims that the view that existence is not a predicate is explicit in the writings of al-Farabi (c. 870–950) and his successor ibn-Sina. Moreover, he claims that there is nothing in the Arabian distinction between *mahiya* (essence) and *huwiya* (existence) that "could not arise naturally out of explicative glosses on [a] passage of [Aristotle's] *Posterior Analytics.*" Wolter (1990:283) claims that the Kantian discussion was anticipated by Duns Scotus.

10.2. ATTEMPTED DEFENSES 1: PROPOSITIONS AND SINGULAR TERMS

Broad's argument is similar to arguments given by Ayer, Wisdom, and others. Baker (1978) provides an interesting analysis of the following formulation of their main argument:

1. If existence is a predicate, all positive existential statements are tautologous, and all negative existential statements are self-contradictory. (Premise)
2. It is false that all positive existential statements are tautologous, and all negative existential statements are self-contradictory. (Premise)
3. (Hence) It is false that existence is a predicate. (From 1, 2)

According to Baker, there is no plausible interpretation on which both (1) and (2) can be alleged to be true without begging the question. This seems correct; but any interpretation on which (1) is true is massively implausible – compare the discussion in the main text.

Moore's examination of the "tiger" sentences has been variously discussed – see, for example, Bennett (1974), Pears (1967), Peetz (1982), Smart (1955), and Tully (1980). Peetz (1982) makes some very interesting points by comparing the sentence 'Rain fell in Nottingham today' with the sentence 'Tame tigers growl'. In particular, she notes that the former sentence shares many of the alleged peculiarities of 'Tame tigers exist'. This suggests that Moore's arguments may have developed from a poorly chosen example. Among other things, Peetz contends (i) that 'exists' cannot be used to describe a characteristic or habit that something has, and (ii) that in order to predicate something of X, we must first of all assume that X exists. Both of these contentions seem false, if extended to modifications of existence, namely, 'actually exists', 'presently exists', and so on.

10.2(a) *All genuine propositions are about their subjects*

Many people have noted the superficial point that we can, with perfect propriety, claim to be talking about nonexistent objects – for example, Shaffer (1962:313ff.). However, many people have confused this (superficial) point with the further, extremely controversial, suggestion that, when we do metaphysics, we should use the surface forms of ordinary language as an incontrovertible guide. Recall Quine's point about 'sakes'.

Devine (1975c:279) claims that "both in the case of negative existential statements and in the case of fictional discourse, one can talk about non-existent things, and do so truly." However, his claim is entirely based on observations about the surface forms of ordinary language – for example, on the observation that there are contexts in which we shall say that it is true that Pegasus has wings. As I have argued in the main text, these observations are entirely compatible with the view that contexts of utterance can be governed by conventions in which sentences are appropriately interpreted as if they incorporated certain implicit operators – 'according to the story', and so on. Moreover, these observations are also entirely compatible with the view that there are other contexts – for example, those of serious metaphysical and ontological enquiry – in which we should not want to say, for example, that Pegasus has wings.

Maloney (1981:10) writes, "It strikes me as evident that when responding to your denial of God's existence, I say that God does exist, we have different thoughts about God and are trying to change each other's thoughts of God." This claim needs to be handled with care. In one sense, I – pretend that I am an atheist – shall certainly deny that we have thoughts about God: For there is no God for us to have thoughts about. In another sense, I shall agree that we can *say* that we have different thoughts about God: But, if pressed, I would want to recast this statement as a claim about differences in our theories of the world. You say it is a dispute about God; but I say it is better characterized as a dispute about 'God' – for, while you think that this characterization leaves something out, we can both agree that it doesn't include anything that ought not to be included.

Ryle (1951:18) discusses a list of sentences, among which are 'Mr. Baldwin is a being' and 'Mr. Pickwick is a nonentity'. He writes: "None of these statements is really about Mr. Pickwick. For if they are true, there is no such person for them to be about. Nor is any of them about Mr. Baldwin. For if they were false, there would be no one for them to be about." The second claim is particularly dubious: Surely one could hold that exactly if Mr. Baldwin exists, the claims in question are about him. Perhaps we might nonetheless agree with Ryle that there is something systematically misleading about claims of the form '*a* does [not] exist'.

10.2(b) *All genuine singular terms refer*

Campbell (1976:111) writes as follows:

There is a sense in which it cannot be thought of the present King of France that he does not exist, but it does not follow that such a person exists. This is so no matter what analysis we give of statements ostensibly about the present King of France. If, in a neo-Meinongian way, we take it that such statements are about some object that is essentially described as 'the present King of France', we will be committed to thinking that this object exists. So thinking that this object does not exist will involve thinking a contradiction. . . . On the other hand, this outcome might lead us to deny that statements ostensibly about the present King of France are about any such object, and to analyse these statements along the lines of Russell's theory of descriptions. Then the thought that the present King of France . . . is not about the present King of France at all.

Although Campbell is wrong to suggest that a neo-Meinongian will hold that pure objects exist, it is true that a neo-Meinongian can hold that many "empty" singular terms refer – compare Routley (1980). Compare, too, the discussion of Salmon (1987) in Chapter 10, Section (2) (5), in the main text.

Gale (1966) relies on the Strawsonian claim 'A subject-predicate sentence can be used to make a statement [i.e., to say something that is either true or false] only if its subject expression refers successfully' in order to argue for the conclusion that existence is not a logical predicate. But his argument can be resisted if one accepts instead the claim that an atomic subject-predicate sentence can be used to make a true statement only if its subject expression refers successfully, or, more radically, if one accepts that sentences that involve nonreferring terms can be used to make statements. The point is that one could then say, for example, that 'Santa Claus exists' is false precisely because the subject term is nonreferring – but without denying that existence is a logical predicate. Recall the discussion of gappy propositions in the main text.

Mitchell (1962:75) argues for the claim that existence is not a predicate *via* consideration of the sentence 'God exists'. He claims that if this sentence expressed a predicative proposition, then "the function of the word 'God' would be to refer to an existing being" – and, in that case, the sentence would be an empty truism. But, of course, this argument simply overlooks the fact that there is at least one conception of propositions on which the sentence can succeed in expressing a proposition even if the subject term fails to refer to anything.

Fictionalist proposals are not without difficulties. Perhaps the most obvious objection to the theory of gappy propositions that was hinted at in the texts is the claim that it cannot be extended to provide a correct analysis of, for example, propositional attitude ascriptions and fictionalist claims. However – as the argument of Oppy (1990)(1992a) (1992b) shows – this claim is simply mistaken. Provided that one allows that there can be a *further* component to the semantic content of embedded singular terms that is not present in the case of unembedded occurrences of those terms, then there is no obvious difficulty in the provision of an analysis of propositional attitude ascriptions and fictionalist claims that is consistent with the theory of gappy propositions. Of course, this means that the fictionalist trades off ontological simplicity for semantic complexity. I think that there are many cases in which the trade is worth making; and I also think that the semantic account that I prefer can be defended on independent grounds. However, these are not points upon which I wish to insist here.

Vision (1993) offers a global argument against "fictionalism," which he interprets as the strategy of avoiding ontological commitments by prefacing all statements in certain areas of discourse with protective operators – for example, 'according to such-and-such a story' – and draws obvious consequences for mathematical and modal fictionalisms. However, no fictionalist should espouse the pure strategy that Vision offers: False atomic sentences in the discourse to be "fictionalized" can be traded in for truths *via* prefixing: But in more complicated cases, or when one has other purposes in mind, different strategies of paraphrase may be required – compare my discussion of fictional claims in Chapter 10, Section (3)(6). A mathematical fictionalist can hold (i) that it is strictly speaking false that $2+2=4$; (ii) that it is true that, according to number theory, $2+2=4$; and (iii) that if one has two distinct things, and two further distinct things that are each distinct from each of the first two, then one has four things. Of course, it might be that mathematical fictionalism is untenable because paraphrases like (iii) are not generally available: But that is quite a different issue.

10.2(c) *All genuine singular terms purport to refer*

Smiley (1960:131) describes a logic in which there are nonreferring terms, in which there is a general distinction between internal and external negation, and in which 'exists' functions as a genuine predicate. He notes that, in his system, there is no distinction between internal and external negation in the case of 'exists' – and then adds: "Philosophers might find [this] a reason for continuing to say that existence is not a property. What there is definitely no cause to say, however, is that 'exists' is not a (genuine, logical) predicate." However, I can see no reason why one might wish to use openness to internal negation as a criterion for propertyhood. Note, too, that this question seems to have no bearing at all on the success or failure of ontological arguments. I should also add that one might motivate acceptance of the account of gappy propositions introduced in the text by referring to Smiley's logic; there is at least a loose sense in which gappy propositions provide a natural propositional semantics for Smiley's system.

10.2(d) *There are no genuine singular terms*

Quine's proposal for the elimination of singular terms has been much discussed. See, in particular, Williams (1981), for a vigorous critique. The classical critique of the quasi-Russellian proposal for elimination is provided by Kripke (1980).

Mendelsohn (1989:613) offers a formalization and defense of a logical system in which the proper names of ordinary language are represented as singular predicates. He claims that it is a virtue of his notation that it "enables us to fudge the issue of truth value for statements containing non-denoting singular terms." However, it seems to me to be at least equally virtuous to provide a fictionalist analysis of the use of nondenoting singular terms – compare Bertolet (1984) and Smiley (1960). In my view – though I don't need to insist on this here – we should look to *pragmatics* for some of the crucial ingredients of a correct treatment of nondenoting singular terms.

10.3. ATTEMPTED DEFENSES 2: EXISTENCE

Perhaps the most sustained recent defense of the view that existence is not a predicate is that of Williams (1981). I cannot hope to do justice to his views here, but I would like to indicate why I think that his arguments are not persuasive.

First, Williams makes much of the contrast between the sentences (1) 'Aristocratic Australians exist' and (2) 'Aristides exists'. He claims that (1) obviously makes good sense, but that (2) does not. My intuitions run roughly counter to those of Williams. Sentence (2) seems to me to be all right on its face; whereas (1) is only all right if it is taken to mean 'There are Aristocratic Australians'. Similarly, it seems to me that 'Aristocratic Australians are numerous' is only all right if it is taken to mean 'There are many Aristocratic Australians'. Since the point at issue is whether there is anything more to existence than is given in existential quantification, there is clearly a good question to ask here about the warping of intuitions by prior theory. It should also be noted that interpretation of sentences of the form '*Fs G*' is not easy. One tempting suggestion is that they are elliptical and require completion from context: 'Some *Fs G*'; 'All *Fs G*'; 'Typical *Fs G*'; and so on. But it is not plausible to suggest that (1) is elliptical in this way, since none of the suggested completions is assertible in the way that (1) is supposed to be.

Second, Williams claims (pp. 78–9) that sentences of the form '*a* exists', where '*a*' is a proper name, are not used – and have no proper use – outside of philosophy. But this is surely just wrong. It is easy to imagine contexts in which someone might quite properly say: 'Troy exists', 'Bourbaki exists', 'Homer exists', 'God exists'. Moreover, it is a commonplace that people do say these sorts of things all the time. Perhaps Williams might insist that people misspeak when they talk in this way: But that is surely no datum of ordinary language.

Third, Williams insists that for names of people to be genuine proper names, there must be unique persons answering to certain descriptions, since otherwise "the use of the name . . . could not have been taught" (p. 76). But this argument is a *non sequitur*. Clearly, if we assume that it is part of the use of a name, for example, 'Aristides', that it refers to a particular person, Aristides – that is, it is part of the identity of the name 'Aristides' that it refers to Aristides – then there is no question of the possibility that the use of that name might have been taught even if Aristides did not exist. But from this it simply does not follow that there are no genuine proper names that fail to refer to anything – for it does not rule out the possibility that there are genuine proper names – for example, 'Bourbaki', 'Santa Claus', 'Hercules', 'Vulcan', and 'Atlantis' – for which it is no part of their identity or their proper use that they refer.

Fourth, Given that he holds that sentences of the form 'a exists' make no sense, Williams is obliged to give a (complicated) account of the meaning of constructions of the following forms, which he concedes to have eminently sensible instances: (1) 'a no longer exists'; (2) 'a might not have existed'; (3) 'a never existed'; (4) 'x does not know that a exists'. After much consideration, he offers the following analyses, subject to the proviso that sentence (3) can only make sense in the case of names from fiction: (1') 'For some p, for some n, both it was the case n time units ago that a occupied p, and (now) it is not the case that, for some y, y has reached the place where it now is by a continuous route over n units of time from p, and y is suitably kind-related to a'; (2') 'For some F, both a alone Fs and it might not have been the case that, for just one y, Fy'; (3') 'No one was ever both called "a" and truly described by the descriptions in such-and-such a story'; (4') 'It is not the case that, for some F – whose unique instantiation is not deducible, with the help only of logical truths, from general knowledge – both a alone Fs and x knows that, for just one y, Fy'. All of these analyses appear subject to counterexample by conceivable cases. *Ad*(1): If noncontinuous time travel is, as it appears to be, a conceptual possibility, then it is conceivable that (1) might be false in circumstances in which (1') is true. *Ad*(2): Suppose that G is a necessarily existent being, and that G is the only being that occupies position p at the moment, and that it might have been the case that position p was unoccupied at the moment. Then (2) is false, and yet (2') is true. *Ad*(3): Suppose that, by an amazing coincidence, there is a distant planet part of whose history is truly described by *The Lord of the Rings*. Even though there is a creature called 'Bilbo' on that planet whose deeds are truly described by *The Lord of the Rings*, it seems to me that Tolkien's Bilbo never existed, that is, he was just a creature of Tolkien's imagination. *Ad*(4): As it stands, this analysis makes it impossible to know of the existence of anyone whose existence is general knowledge unless one knows something about them that is not general knowledge. But, as Williams acknowledges, the restrictions on F are essential to rule out other counterexamples; and, moreover, there

307

are hard questions about opacity that remain to be addressed – compare the following paragraph. Perhaps there might be ways of repairing all of these analyses to avoid the counterexamples. But, even so, it is important to emphasize the costs: It is hard to believe that there is so much complexity embedded in such simple utterances. At the very least, if an alternative theory that treats 'exists' as a first-order predicate can give a straightforward analysis of these kinds of examples, then that is a very big point in favor of those analyses.

Williams analysis of (4) has been criticized by Flint (1988:63), who presses an "opacity" objection:

Suppose that ... Reagan has installed an elaborate alarm system which informs him, wherever he happens to be, [of] the total number of people in the White House and the Capitol. When one light goes on, the President knows exactly one person is either in the White House or in the Capitol; two lights, two persons; and so on. Suppose that, having installed this system and tested it rigorously, President Reagan orders that the Capitol and the White House be evacuated. Within a few minutes, his alarm system tells him that his order has been carried out. Suppose that Reagan now sends Howard Baker to the Capitol. Five minutes later, one light on the President's alarm system goes on. Seeing this, the President forms the belief that, for just one x, x is either in the White House or in the Capitol, and also forms the belief that Baker has arrived at the Capitol. In this latter belief, though, he is mistaken; in fact, the light has gone on because the crafty David Pears has surreptitiously entered the White House.

In this case, it seems intuitively wrong to say that Reagan knows that David Pears exists, even though Williams's analysis of (4) entails that this is what we should say. Williams (1988:64) insists that Reagan does know that David Pears exists: "A president need not know a man's name in order to know that that man exists. ... It is no objection to saying that a President knows that a man exists if he confuses him with someone else." However, while these remarks are clearly correct, they do not suffice to overthrow the view that in a large range of ordinary contexts, it would simply be a mistake to say that, in the envisioned circumstances, Reagan knows that David Pears exists. What Williams needs to establish is that proper names cannot have contextually associated modes of presentation that enter into the determination of the truth conditions of sentences in which they occur. Nothing that he has written comes close to showing this to be so. I believe that Williams is simply wrong: Proper names do have contextually associated senses – compare Oppy (1990) (1992a) (1992b); however, since this view is controversial, I shan't insist on it here.

Fifth, Williams expresses controversial views on a range of other topics – for example, substitutional quantification, ontological commitment, opacity, modality, and fiction. I do not deny that his views form a more or less coherent and systematic whole. However, it seems to me that, at the very least, one could quite reasonably believe that there are other, quite different, packages that are no less coherent and systematic, and that are equally worthy of reasoned assent – and, moreover, that some of these alternative packages leave room for the claim that 'exists' is a first-order predicate. Certainly, the mere scope of William's discussion shows that there is no easy argument to the view that existence is not a predicate – and that is enough to justify the search for an alternative diagnosis of the failings of ontological arguments. See Lambert (1983b) for further critical discussion of Williams's views; also, see Williams (1992) for a more streamlined presentation of his views.

Tomberlin (1970) (1971) (1972b) discusses the following two-step analysis of existence, which is due to Arthur Prior:

i. x exists iff there is some e-attribute that x has.
ii. P is an e-attribute iff P entails existence.

Tomberlin, by discussing eight failed interpretations, suggests that it is very hard to provide a plausible interpretation of (ii). But a Meinongian would, I think, be puzzled by this fuss: For, on a Meinongian view, e-attributes are nothing other than extranuclear, or noncharacterizing, properties. And, while it is admittedly hard to provide a characterization of the nuclear–extranuclear distinction, it does seem that everyone understands it in more or less the same way. Moreover, it is clear that one who holds that only existent beings can have properties will not think that Prior's suggestion is even *prima facie* helpful – for, on this view, all attributes are e-attributes. As it happens, I suspect that Tomberlin actually dismissed at least one characterization for bad reasons. Consider:

D6. P is an e-attribute iff it is necessarily true that if x has P, x exists (where the domain of the variable 'P' is the set of logically possible properties, and where the domain of the variable 'x' is the set of existent and nonexistent objects).

Tomberlin claims that if being red is identical with the attribute I am thinking of, then (D6) entails that the sentence 'If the beast killed by Hercules has the property I am thinking of, the beast killed by Hercules exists' is necessarily true, because being red is an e-attribute. But all this argument shows is that we need to distinguish between (i) the attribute I am thinking of and (ii) the attribute I am actually thinking of. At best, only the latter is identical with the attribute of being red. Cochiarella (1968) (1969) provides a formalization of the logic of *e*-attributes.

Webb (1989:463) claims that " 'existent' is not a predicate of the sort that can be entailed by other predicates." But surely the inference from 'x is red and existent' to 'x is existent' is valid; and, more controversially, why shouldn't we suppose that the inference from 'x is red' to 'x is existent' is valid? After all, it seems *prima facie* reasonable to suppose that only actually existing things can actually be red.

10.3(a) *Existence is a second-order predicate*

Forgie (1972) makes the point that even if there is a second-order existence predicate, it does not follow that there is no first-order existence predicate. This parallels the point that even if existence is typically represented by existential quantification, it is nonetheless possible to introduce an existence predicate into standard first-order logic with property abstraction – compare Chapter 10, Section (3)(c).

Williams (1981) makes much of the point that if there were both first-order and second-order existence predicates, some reason would need to be provided for this duplication, and/or some account would need to be given of the connection between these two predicates. This point does not seem to be unanswerable; surely the need for the two kinds of predicates, and a suitable connecting link, is to be found in the difference between names and definite descriptions – that is, be-tween terms that refer and terms that have satisfaction conditions. At the very least, this seems to be a promising start toward an answer to Williams's worries.

Mavrodes (1966) defends the claim that the Fregean analysis of existence entails the rejection of known versions of ontological argu-ments. Thus, he seems to contradict the claim in Plantinga (1966) that Frege did not provide a decisive objection to St. Anselm. However, appearances are deceptive: For, while St. Anselm's argument cannot be translated directly into Frege's notation (Mavrodes's point), it may be possible to give a second-order formulation of the argument (Plan-tinga's point). In fact, though, it is not easy to give a second-order formulation of the argument. Consider the following attempt:

1. We conceive that the concept of God is not instantiated. (Assump-tion for *reductio*)

2. (Hence) We conceive that the concept of God is the concept of a being than which no greater can be conceived that does not instantiate the concept 'being than which no greater can be conceived'. (From 1)

3. We (can) conceive that the concept of God* is the concept of a being than which no greater can be conceived that instantiates the concept 'being than which no greater can be conceived'. (Premise)

4. If we conceive that a concept A is instantiated but that a concept B is not instantiated, then we conceive that A is greater than B. (Premise)

5. We conceive that the concept of God* is instantiated but that the concept of God is not instantiated. (From 2, 3)

6. We conceive that God* is greater than God. (From 4, 5)

7. We do not conceive that God* is greater than God. (Premise)

8. (Hence) We cannot conceive that the concept of God is not instantiated. (From 1, 6, 7 by *reductio*)

9. (Hence) We must conceive that the concept of God is instantiated. (From 8)

10. (Hence) The concept of God is instantiated. (From 9)

This argument involves an obvious equivocation on the notion of conceiving of a concept as instantiated: Does it mean that the concept says of itself that it is instantiated, or does it mean that the concept really is instantiated? However, there is a corresponding equivocation on the notion of conceiving of an object as existing in the related first-order argument. Perhaps the corresponding equivocation is less obvious – especially when suitably dressed up in ordinary language – so that the transition to the second-order version makes the flaw more apparent; but, nonetheless, it is the same kind of flaw. So it seems that we should side with Plantinga, and against Mavrodes and Frege: If there is something wrong with ontological arguments, it should be possible to demonstrate this without making use of the assumption that existence is a second-order property.

Dejnozka (1982) defends the view that "in Frege's philosophy existence may be and is best identified as identifiability." This claim is most implausible – not least because it requires the assumption that only existent beings can be identified. Even if it is true that only existent beings can be identified, it seems wrong to suggest that this putative fact is analytic and knowable *a priori*. Consider, for example, Geach's puzzles about intentional identity: It seems wrong to suppose that they rest on a mere mistake about the meaning of the words 'exist' and 'identify'. Moreover – as Dejnozka in effect acknowledges – the textual evidence for the attribution of such a view to Frege is very scant.

10.3(b) *Existence is a quantifier*

For endorsement of the Frege–Russell–Quine suggestion that existential quantification is the proper mode of expression of claims of existence, see Kneale (1936:164), Smart (1955:503), and Williams (1981).

Ryle (1951:22, 36) provides a clear account of the kind of rationale that might be given in defense of the analyses of fictive sentences provided in the main text:

Those who, like philosophers, must generalise about the sorts of statements that have to be made of sorts of facts about sorts of topics, cannot help treating as clues to the logical structures for which they are looking the grammatical forms of the common types of expressions in which these structures are recorded. . . . [Philosophers'] restatements are transmutations of syntax, and transmutations of syntax controlled not by desire for elegance or stylistic correctness but by desire to exhibit the forms of the facts into which philosophy is the inquiry.

As Routley (1980) emphasizes, this defense relies upon substantive philosophical assumptions – for example, that only existents can bear properties and be objects of reference – that is, it relies upon a particular conception of the nature of "the facts." In the main text, I have tried to remain neutral about this debate; for, no matter which way it is resolved, it turns out (i) that it may well be that existence is a predicate and (ii) that there is no solace for defenders of ontological arguments.

One important question addressed in this section concerned the bearers of properties: What kinds of things can have properties? A natural answer is all and only those things that tenselessly exist – though, of course, some will wish to add those things that might have existed and those things that could not have existed. Famously, Prior argued that only presently existing entities can have properties. For some properties, this seems evidently correct – for example, nothing can be red that is not presently red. But, as Walker (1969:55–6) points out, it certainly seems that merely past entities can presently have properties – for example, Julius Caesar now has the property of having been the first Roman emperor. More controversially, Walker also claims that fictional and mythical entities have properties – for example, that Pegasus is a winged horse of Greek mythology. In this latter case, a fictionalist will want to insist that all that is true is that, according to Greek mythology, Pegasus is a winged horse – and that this truth can be explained without supposing that the term 'Pegasus' refers to anything that bears properties. The important point is that the answer to the question, What are the bearers of properties? is identical to the answer to the question, What is there? – so we should expect to find the same range of reasonable opinion.

10.3(c) *Existence does not admit of analysis*

Alston (1960:471) famously defends the view that even if we distinguish different modes of existence, 'exists' is not a predicate. However, his claim is tempered by the concession that there are special contexts in which 'exists' is a predicate. And, once this concession is made, it is very hard to see why one should not then admit that, in fact, 'exists' is always a predicate – albeit one of a very special kind. Alston claims that there is a problem in construing the sentence 'King Arthur exists in legend' if we suppose that existence is a predicate – for "if we try to construe [the sentence] as the attribution of legendary existence to a subject presupposed to exist in the imagination, we run into the difficulty that no statement about what exists in the imagination can have the sort of implications about what goes on in legend-narrating activities that a statement of legendary existence must have." But surely a defender of "legendary existence" will hold that King Arthur exists in legend, as well as in the imagination: And there is no problem in explaining how existence in legend is germane to legend-narrating activities. Plantinga (1967:47ff.) provides a very careful critique of Alston's views.

Baier (1960:20ff.) defends the view that 'exist' is equivocal: It can be used to make (i) status explanations, which elucidate the logical status of concepts; (ii) actual instantiation claims, which make claims "concerning the world around us"; and (iii) conceptual instantiation claims, which make claims "whose truth or falsity is determined by consideration of concepts alone." Moreover, he uses this distinction to defend the Humean dogma that all genuine existence claims – that is, all actual instantiation claims – are contingent. However, his argument merely begs the question concerning the issue of what there is "in the world around us": according to some theists, God – a necessarily existent being – is in the world around us; and no mere redrawing of terminological boundaries can show that such theists are wrong. Moreover – as Quine argues – it seems wrong to suppose that there are different kinds of existence, in "special status worlds"; why not say instead that 'exist' is univocal, but that there are different kinds of things? Baier's arguments are well criticized by Williams (1969).

Fleming and Wolterstorff (1960) defend the view that neither 'exist' nor 'there is' is univocal, and that the proper uses for 'exist' and 'there is' are not coincident. However, the examples that they give all admit of pragmatic explanations – for example, in terms of contextual restrictions on the domain of quantification, or implicit qualifications of the mode of existence. The crucial point is that any interesting equivocation would need to occur at the semantic level – but it is far from clear that there are any examples that demonstrate that either 'exist' or 'there is' is semantically equivocal.

10.3(d) *Existence is not a property*

Sometimes, the claim that 'exists' is a second-order predicate is construed as a deflationary account of existence. Thus, for example, Williams (1981) holds that existence is transcendental: In the case of the word 'exists', there is nothing but *syntactic* explanation of its functions. And he holds a similar account of the word 'true'. I think that he is wrong on both counts. The case for rejecting syntactic – or otherwise minimalist – accounts of truth is made in Jackson, Oppy, and Smith (1994). I suspect that a similar case can be mounted for rejection of minimalist accounts of existence, though I see no need to insist on this here. At the very least, I think that it should be clear that there is no easy argument for the claim that existence is not a substantial property, and that is really all that is required for the general position that I wish to take concerning ontological arguments. If it turns out that there is a surprising argument that shows that existence is not a property, then there will be an additional reason for rejecting many ontological arguments – namely, that they are unsound. However, it is much easier – and, I hope, less uncontroversial – to argue that ontological arguments are bound to be dialectically inefficacious; and, hence, it is possible to give a definitive thumbs down to ontological arguments without waiting for the results of what will clearly be a difficult, and no doubt controversial, investigation.

10.4. (MAYBE) EXISTENCE IS A PREDICATE

Nakhnikian and Salmon (1957) defend the view that 'exists' can be consistently treated as a *redundant* predicate – that is, a necessarily universal predicate that can be eliminated in favor of the existential quantifier. This seems partly correct: As I have argued, existence can be defined in terms of quantification and property abstraction. However, once the possibility of introducing different modes of existence is recognized, it may turn out that there is great utility in having both predicates and quantifiers – that is, 'exists' may only be theoretically redundant. Nakhnikian and Salmon also *illustrate* the correct point that the concession that 'exists' is a predicate does not reinstate ontological arguments by giving two examples of ontological arguments that can be refuted in other ways.

Basham (1977) claims that it is possible to give a metalinguistic analysis of singular attributions of existence on which (i) 'exists' can be regarded as a predicator of English, that is, as a predicate that is not true of everything; and yet for which (ii) one need not invoke an ontology of subsistent or nonexistent entities. On his account, 'a exists' is given the analysis '$(\forall d_i)$ ($\{(d_i$ is an $\cdot a \cdot) \supset$ $(E!\{(\iota x)(d_i$ designates $x)]\}$', where '$\cdot a \cdot$' is a distributive singular term formed using Sellarsian dot quotes, and 'd_i' ranges over the individual designators of the object languages of all natural languages. However, if 'd_i' ranges over the actually existing designators of the object languages of actually existing languages, then this analysis is massively implausible: It is platitudinous that many things are actually unnamed and undesignated. And if 'd_i' ranges over merely possible designators of the object languages of (perhaps) merely possible natural languages, then it is simply untrue that this analysis avoids nonexistent entities. In my view, those who wish to shun nonexistent objects should agree with Nakhnikian and Salmon (1957) that 'exists' is not a predicator; but – pace Basham – this agreement does not constitute a vindication of Kant's views about existence, and neither does it entail that existence is not a real predicate in any sense that it is damaging to defenses of ontological arguments.

Stirton (1995) defends the view that it is incoherent to suppose that 'exists' is anything other than a first-order predicate. Moreover, he claims that the admission that 'exists' is a first-order predicate requires rejection of at least one of the following two claims: (1) If a proper name occurs in a statement that is either true or false, then, in the context of that statement, it must denote an object; and (2) There are no nonexistent objects. While I have strong doubts about some of Stirton's claims and arguments, I am sympathetic to the general position he endorses. In particular, I am inclined to the view that those who wish to claim that 'exists' is a first-order predicate ought to reject (1).

The allusion in the main text to Wittgenstein's Tractarian discussion of identity raises some controversial questions. There seem to be close parallels between the idea that existence is not a predicate and the idea that identity is not a relation. Indeed, Williams (1980) provides a defense of the claim that identity is not a relation to accompany his sustained defense – in Williams (1981) – of the claim that existence is not a property; see also White (1978), upon which Williams draws. Williams suggests that the identity operator is most properly understood as an operator that forms a one-place predicable from a two-place predicable. His main reason for saying this is that he claims that it is required to block the fallacious inference from 'Mark believes that Abyssinia was once invaded by Mussolini and Ethiopia is now at war with Somalia' to 'Mark believes that a country once invaded by Mussolini is the same as one now at war with Somalia'. But – as the work of Salmon (1986) demonstrates – there are other ways to block the fallacious inference. Consequently, Williams's argument will only persuade those who favor his general approach to philosophy of language. That is, there is no short and simple argument to the conclusion that identity is not a relation; rather, at best, there are only general considerations about the simplicity and power of rival approaches to the philosophy of language – compare my earlier remarks about Williams's views on existence.

11. THE USES OF PARODY

La Croix (1972a:126) illustrates one kind of parody that I do not discuss in Chapter 11 of the main text, namely, parodies for which the conclusion is that God – a most perfect being, a being than which no greater can be conceived – does not exist. La Croix claims that the crucial issue is the acceptability of the following pair of claims: (i) It is possible that the being than which a greater cannot be conceived is thought to exist in reality; and (ii) it is possible that the being than which a greater cannot be conceived is thought not to exist in reality. Moreover, he claims that this issue mainly turns on the question of the intelligibility of the contents of the modal claims in (i) and (ii). What, for example, is the content of the claim that the being than which a greater cannot be conceived is thought to exist in reality? As we noted in our discussion of conceptual ontological arguments, this is a very difficult question.

La Fleur (1942) suggests that the R-being – that is, the being that possesses all (and only?) the qualities that, expressed in English adjectives, begin with the letter 'R' – can be used to construct an effective *reductio* of ontological arguments. While La Fleur's article is rather droll, it would cut no ice with those proponents of ontological arguments who undertake to show that the notion of, say, a perfect being, is consistent. Of course, the R-being would raise problems for naive proponents of Meinongian arguments, since one of the properties of the R-being is that it is real.

Smullyan (1983) contains a delightful presentation of an ontological argument, which he attributes to "the unknown Dutch theologian van Dollard." The argument relies on five premises: (i) The property of existence is a perfection; (ii) given any perfection P, if all things having property P also have the property of existence, then there is at least one entity having property P; (iii) given any class C of perfections, the property of having all the perfections in C is again a perfection; (iv) there is a class of perfections that contains all perfections; (v) for any god g, the property of being identical to g is a perfection. From these premises, it is easy to prove that there is exactly one God. Moreover, if we add the following premises – (vi) nonexistence is an antiperfection; and (vii) given any antiperfection A, if there is no existent entity having property A, then there is no entity at all having property A – we can prove that there is no devil – that is, no being that has all antiperfections – existent or otherwise. This is all good fun; the serious point is that Smullyan's arguments are as good as any genuine ontological arguments.

11.1. BEINGS OF KIND K THAN WHICH NO GREATER BEINGS OF KIND K CAN BE CONCEIVED

Cornman, Lehrer, and Pappas (1987:245) discuss parodies of ontological arguments that involve instances of the formula 'being than which no F'er being can be conceived', where 'F' is to be replaced by any predicate: 'great', 'dirty', 'absurd', 'evil', and so on. They note that most ontological arguments that involve the use of this formula are unsound – and hence that most claims of the form 'If a being than which no *F*'er can be conceived does not exist, then it is possible that there exists a being that is *F*'er than a being than which no *F*'er being can be conceived' are false. Moreover, they claim that this fact provides some reason for thinking that the particular instance 'If a being than which no greater can be conceived does not exist, then it is possible that there exists a being that is greater than a being than which no greater can be conceived' is also false: "If at this point Anselm were to reply to us, similarly to the way he replied to Gaunilo, that his argument applies only to the one adjective 'great', we could reply in turn that there seems to be no relevant difference between the adjective 'great' and many other relevant adjectives." But there are several reasons for disputing this view. (i) If one holds that there is a being than which no greater can be conceived, then one will hold that the relevant instance is true; and the fact that all of the other instances are false can be met with equanimity. There is simply *no* reason to hold that failure in all the other instances provides some reason for thinking that there will be failure in the particular case of 'great'. (ii) St. Anselm does think that there is a relevant difference between 'great' and other predicates, namely, that existence is a necessary condition for greatness. By contrast, nonexistent beings can fall under the other predicates: 'dirty', 'evil', 'absurd', and so on. One might dispute this view – for example, on the grounds that only existent beings can have properties – but, at the very least, some argument is required; why shouldn't the dirtiest possible being exist merely in the understanding? (iii) It may be that Cornman et al. are flirting with the following view: If an argument can be shown to instantiate an argument form most of whose instances are unsound, then the argument is very likely to be unsound. But (i) all arguments instantiate invalid argument forms; and (ii) many valid argument forms have countless instances that are unsound.

Hartshorne (1941:127) discusses the view that a perfect island might have God-like properties:

It is not apparent what would make such a world an island, if the "waters" that "washed" it never wore its shores, and if it were not a part of the surface of a body in space surrounded by other bodies capable of smashing it to pieces, and were not composed of particles capable of ultimately separating, etc. The question is if such a conception would in the end be distinguishable from the idea of a cosmos as the perpetually renewed body of God, that is, not an island in the least, but an aspect of the very idea of God whose self-existence is upheld by the argument.

Hartshorne's "question" is readily answered: It is no part of the traditional conception of God that his body is an island. Since there are numerous possible conceptions of the "body of God," there are numerous possible conceptions of God – and so the purpose of the parody is fulfilled.

Mann (1976) claims that Gaunilo's "perfect island" objection is "bogus." In particular, he suggests that the argument that involves the expression 'island than which no greater island can be conceived' is not parallel in form to St. Anselm's argument. However, this claim relies on an unsympathetic reconstruction of the parody that Gaunilo would offer. Mann claims – in effect – that Gaunilo will carry over the principle that for whatever is in the understanding only, and does not exist in reality, something greater than it can be conceived. But, of course, the parody requires the principle that for anything of kind K that is in the understanding only, and does not exist in reality, a greater thing of kind K can be conceived. Now it may be – as Mann suggests – that St. Anselm would not have accepted the principle that the parody requires. But this consideration is irrelevant. What matters is whether there is some non-question-begging reason that can be given for the acceptance of only the former of the two principles. If an agnostic or atheist can reasonably think that the two principles stand or fall together, then the purpose of the parody is achieved.

Downey (1986:48) claims that "no island can necessarily exist, since any material thing can be conceived not to exist, one way being by means of a thought that space does not contain it." But, of course, if there is a necessarily existent island, then it will be impossible for that island to fail to be contained in space – and the conception to which Downey refers will simply be necessarily mistaken. There is an important point here, namely, that in discussions about the existence of God, it must be a mistake for theists to rest their *arguments* on an identification of logical possibility with conceivability. For it is clear in advance that agnostics and atheists need not agree with theists about what is conceivable – and so, via the identification, may disagree about what is logically possible.

Preuss (1980:97) provides the following travesty of Gaunilo's argument:

Anselm claims to have discovered that there is a concept . . . which implies necessary existence. Gaunilo asks to make any change he pleases to this concept, in particular, one which turns it into a concept . . . which implies possible existence. Then he points out that the new concept does not imply necessary existence. The implicit argument is that since some concepts imply possible existence, no concept implies necessary existence.

This is outrageous. To mention just one point, Gaunilo's objection consists precisely in the thought that the concept of a perfect island implies necessary existence iff the concept of a perfect being does.

11.2 MOST PERFECT BEINGS OF KIND *K*

One issue that I have not discussed is the connection between the Christian doctrine of the Trinity and the claims mentioned in the text about the connections between greatness and (i) subjection to change, (ii) subjection to dissolution, (iii) possession of spatiotemporal parts, and (iv) possession of contingent parts. If Christ existed and conformed even roughly to the biblical story, then there is no doubt that his body was subject to change and dissolution, that it was contingent, and that it had spatiotemporal parts. Moreover, there is no doubt that his mind was also subject to change and possessed temporal parts. So the preceding claims would clearly seem to be threatening to orthodox Christian doctrine, even apart from considerations about the nature of mind and personal identity. Moreover, even if one drops the doctrine of the Trinity, there are still hard questions about the relationship between people and God, if God is unchanging and not possessed of temporal parts. I shall not worry about these issues here.

Scriven (1966:147) provides an argument for the view that perfection guarantees nonexistence:

In general, are there not physical limitations of some kind on any actual entity? Either it is not perfectly strong, or it is not perfectly formed, or it is not perfectly uniform, or it is not perfectly good. It seems that the exact opposite of the ontological argument's conclusion is the right one. Conceptions can be perfect; but that is just because they only exist in the mind or, to put it another way, it is just because they need meet only the requirements of a definition and not those of reality that they can be perfect. For the totally perfect Being, all the practical difficulties would be compounded, and it would seem to be even less possible that it should exist than that a being perfect in only one respect should exist.

This argument seems dubious on several counts. The most obvious point is that it is part of the conception of the totally perfect Being that it is nonphysical. Consequently, the inductive point about the imperfections of physical beings is simply irrelevant. That there are no perfect circles in the physical world provides not the slightest reason to suppose that there cannot be a nonphysical most perfect Being. Moreover, there is nothing in Scriven's argument that supports the view that nonexistence is one of the perfections of geometrical figures: For almost no one who wants to say that mathematical objects exist will concede that those objects are physical.

Laserowitz (1983:259) claims that the phrase 'most perfect being' is "a bogus description: it does no more than create the semantic appearance of describing an attribute of a kind of being." He supports this claim with the contention that the notion of the "extended infinite" is indefensible. I think that this is unfair to the notion of the extended infinite; however, I shall leave a defense of this contention until my investigation of the *kalam* cosmological argument. Tartarkiewicz (1981) provides an interesting account of the connections between the notions of 'perfection' and 'infinity' – it is not obvious that a theist need hold that a most perfect being is infinite in every, or indeed any, respect.

11.3. NECESSARILY EXISTENT BEINGS OF KIND *K*

Kane (1984) makes interesting use of LPNs, that is, less than perfect necessarily existing beings. He claims that consideration of LPNs shows that we must reject at least one of the following four claims: (i) God exists; (ii) the characteristic axiom of *B* is true; (iii) a perfect being is logically possible; (iv) LPNs are logically possible. This is clearly correct: Claims (i)–(iv) form an inconsistent quartet. Moreover, this fact justifies Kane's further claim that the defender of the relevant modal ontological argument must show that all necessary beings are perfect. However, it seems to me that such a defender could claim that the statement in question is a corollary of the argument; that is, once we use the ontological argument to demonstrate (i) from (ii) and (iii), it follows that (iv) is false. Of course, this won't convince an opponent of the argument – but so what? Morris (1985) makes much of this point.

Following Morris (1985), we can distinguish between abstract LPNs – numbers, propositions, other traditional abstract entities – and nonabstract LPNs – the alternative deities discussed in the text. Both classes of entities can be held to create problems for orthodox theism. For the purposes of the ensuing discussion, I ignore the possibility that one might espouse nominalism – that is, one might deny that there are any abstract LPNs: This is clearly one way to circumvent any difficulties that might arise in connection with abstract LPNs.

Morris (1985:267) suggests that "the claim that some non-abstract LPNs possibly exist has absolutely no support from the intuitions of most Anselmians." This claim is disputed by Leftow (1988). In Leftow's view, the crucial question is whether Anselmians share the intuition that the set of attributes that constitute God's divinity are not necessarily coexemplified. He provides three reasons for thinking that Anselmians must share this intuition: (i) We know that power, moral goodness, and knowledge are not necessarily coexemplified; and this provides us with compelling reason to think that it is possible that maximal power, maximal moral goodness, and maximal knowledge are not coexemplified. (ii) If maximal goodness and maximal power are coextensive, then maximal power entails goodness, and maximal goodness entails power; but surely we have good reason to think that maximal power and goodness, and maximal goodness and power are irrelevant to one another. (iii) If maximal goodness and maximal power are coextensive, then, since maximal goodness is a determinate of goodness, only good beings have maximal power; but there is no reason at all to think that beings with maximal power belong to the kind of good beings. Leftow thinks that these arguments do show that theists have the intuitions to which the arguments appeal; but this seems wrong. Anselmians will deny that they share the intuitions to which appeal is made in (ii) and (iii) – for example, they will deny that they share the intuition that maximal power and goodness are irrelevant. Moreover, they will deny that the inductive inference in (i) is correct: There are many cases in which properties only converge in a limit. Of course, Leftow is right that many of us do not share the intuitions of the Anselmian – even to the extent that it may be hard for us to understand, or empathize with, those intuitions. But it seems to me that it is simply a mistake to project our intuitions onto the Anselmian if our task is to try to understand her position. It is easy enough for the Anselmian to resist the move to polytheism; but the non-Anselmian has intuitions that would not provide for such resistance – hence the spate of parodies of ontological arguments. Compare the subsequent section on the question of what parody achieves.

Morris (1985:268) also writes:

A quite traditional Augustinian picture of the Platonic realm sees such items as concepts or thoughts in the mind of God, dependent for their existence on an eternal, creatively efficacious divine intellective activity. This picture is fully compatible with the modal status of such items being one of broadly logical necessity, as long as the causally productive divine activity responsible for their existence is assigned that status as well. . . . It is true that God would lack control of abstract LPNs, in the sense that he could not annihilate them, or bring new ones into existence, but it does not follow that any which do exist do not depend on God for their existence.

The main difficulty with this view is the interpretation of the notion of 'dependence' that Morris invokes. Ordinarily, one would suppose that *x* depends on *y* only if it is possible for *y* to exert some influence over *x*. But, in the case in question, it is denied that God can exert any influence over the abstract LPNs. Since, logically, it could not have failed to be the case that there are abstract LPNs, in what sense can it be true that the abstract LPNs depend upon God for their existence? Note that it is not clear that we can say 'If God had not existed, then the abstract LPNs would not have existed either' – for, at least on standard accounts of counterfactuals, this claim is vacuously true. And talk about God's creation of the abstract LPNs doesn't help – for what is at issue is precisely how we are supposed to understand the idea that God *created* the abstract LPNs. Note, too, that it isn't clear why God couldn't create copies of abstract LPNs, if LPNs are genuinely dependent upon God for their existence. Nothing in number theory is falsified by the existence of nonstandard models. For further discussion of the issues considered in this paragraph, see Davison (1991), Kelly (1986), and Werther (1989).

Kane (1984) and Morris (1985) are both discussed by McGrath (1986:375). Against Morris, McGrath claims that we should abandon talk of modal intuitions and modal beliefs, accepting instead that "we can have a positive warrant for judgments of broadly logical possibility only when the objects in question exist." Moreover, he suggests that Morris's strategy is self-defeating, since the argument is "powerless against anyone who says that he lacks an intuition that the existence of a perfect being is possible." And finally, against both Kane and Morris, he suggests that modal ontological arguments are plainly question begging, because "one could not know that the existence of a perfect being is possible without first knowing that it exists." It seems to me that each of these criticisms is mistaken since (i) there are many cases in which it seems clearly correct to make judgments of broadly logical possibility about nonexistent objects, for example, about what would have happened to the unfortunate driver coming the other way when I swerved onto the wrong side of the road; (ii) it is not clear that Morris's strategy will fail against those who are prepared to concede that one could reasonably have the intuition that the existence of a perfect being is possible; and (iii) it seems possible that one could come to know that the existence of a perfect being is possible via testimony – compare the discussion in the notes to Chapter 2. Nonetheless, I am sympathetic to McGrath's outlook: I agree with him that, in fact, all ontological arguments are *useless*; but I don't think that he manages to explain exactly why this is so.

11.4. ACTUALLY EXISTENT BEINGS OF KIND *K*

Kenny (1968a) contained a different formulation of the Cartesian distinction between real and fictitious essences, namely, that if F is part of the true and immutable essence of G, then it is impossible for us to conceive of a G that is not F. Of course, this principle is unsatisfactory, since it conflates ontological and epistemological categories – but the conflation can be easily repaired. For example, Sievert (1982:204ff.) suggests the following: The basic contrast is between *invariant complex ideas* – that is, complex ideas in which the component ideas are so united that one cannot think of all but one of the parts of the idea without also thinking of the remaining part – and *variable complex ideas* – that is, complex ideas in which the component ideas are not so united that one cannot think of all but one of the parts of the idea without also thinking of the remaining part. Kenny's reason for rejecting the ascription of this formulation of the principle to Descartes was that following the comments of Ernest Sosa, he came to think that his formulation clearly didn't capture the intuitive force of the Cartesian distinction. This just seems wrong to me, though I am prepared to allow that the matter is controversial. In any case, as Sievert notes, the distinction in question is of no use in meeting the most serious objections to the Cartesian ontological argument.

Cottingham (1986:63) discusses "the overload objection" to Descartes' ontological argument – that is, the objection that a parallel proof can be used to establish the existence of Superpegasus, that is, "the actually existing Pegasus." He suggests that Descartes hoped to meet this difficulty by relying on a distinction between analyzable and unanalyzable ideas, *via* the suggestion that only the latter depict true natures. But, says Cottingham, this hope was vain: For Descartes himself held that there are analyzable ideas that depict true natures, for example, the idea of a square inscribed in a circle. As Wilson (1978:172ff.) notes, there are really two distinct criteria to which Descartes adverts in trying to meet the overload objection. His first criterion involves the possession of unforeseen, and unwilled, implications; and his second criterion involves susceptibility to analysis by clear and distinct mental operations. Neither criterion meets the difficulty generated by the idea of a square inscribed in a circle.

Scriven (1966:146) claims:

> By giving (or finding) the property of real existence in a concept, you make it that much harder to apply it to anything; and if it also has the requirement of total perfection built into it, it is really going to be tough to find anything to apply it to. . . . A concept's chances of application to anything go down with the discovery (or addition) of "real existence" in its definition, as with the discovery of any further property.

This seems wrong. Since 'is F' and 'is an existent F' will apply to exactly the same class of existent beings, the inclusion of the property of real existence makes no difference to the ease of applicability of the predicate. What is true is that the inclusion of further properties cannot improve the chances that a concept will apply to something – but this does not entail that the inclusion of further properties will actually diminish those chances, since there is also the possibility that those chances will be unaffected, as in the case of 'real existence'.

Rowe's argument about 'magicans' has been much discussed. In addition to the works discussed in the main text, see Rowe (1988) (1989), Dicker (1988a)(1988b), and Dore (1986). One crucial point that many of Rowe's critics overlook is that his claim that God is not a nonexisting being must be coupled with the Meinongian insistence that existence is an extranuclear property. The point is that, according to Rowe, 'God' is simply a nonreferring term – that is, it does not refer to an item of any sort. The same would be true of the term 'magican' in a world in which there are no magicians.

11.5. MAXIMAL BEINGS OF KIND K

Gregory (1984:57) offers an argument that purports to show that for any suitable property E – that is, for any property that for any possible entity x, is possessed to a higher degree if x exists than if x does not – there is an ontological argument that establishes the existence of a being of any species that possesses E to that degree that is the highest logically possible degree for that species. Downey (1986:47) responds by claiming that there is only one suitable property, namely, 'greatness'. However, this response seems questionable. Surely it is not unreasonable to hold that things that do not exist lack power in just the same sense – if any – that they lack greatness. Perhaps defenders of ontological arguments can reasonably hold the opposite view: But that is insufficient for a defense of the argument. Gregory's claim is partly borne out by the fact that some people have defended ontological arguments that are not couched in terms of greatness – for example, Lucas (1985) defends an argument couched in terms of epistemic unsurpassability. Moreover, it seems independently plausible that the parodies that his argument licenses should be available to atheists and agnostics.

11.6. DEVILS, AND SO ON

Wilbanks (1973:363) offers a parody of St. Anselm's argument that begins with the premise that if a being than which nothing lesser can be conceived exists in the understanding, then that very being – than which nothing lesser can be conceived – is one than which a lesser can be conceived, and goes on to conclude that it is not the case that whatever is understood exists in the understanding. The initial premise is supported by the following consideration: "Suppose that it (i.e. a being than which nothing lesser can be conceived) exists in the understanding (at least); then it can be conceived to be nonexistent (i.e. to not exist at all in any realm); which is lesser." St. Anselm could reply to this as follows: (i) While it is true that existence in reality is a perfection, it is not true that existence in the understanding is a perfection; and (ii) it is question begging – if not downright unintelligible – to suppose that a being that exists in the understanding can be conceived not to exist in the understanding. Can I coherently suppose that something that I do suppose that I conceive is inconceivable? The first point is more or less forced by the text, since, in *Proslogion 15*, St. Anselm holds that we don't really understand God – that is, God doesn't really exist in the understanding – but that of course this is no sign of imperfection in God.

Johnson (1965:329) offers a parodic ontological proof of the existence of Satan – that is, of a being than which nothing more evil can be conceived. He claims that the availability of the parodic proof raises serious questions about the claim that existence confers value on an object. However, it seems to me that one could accept this claim while nonetheless rejecting both the original ontological argument and the parody – compare the discussion of St. Anselm's arguments in the main text.

Charlesworth (1965:70) discusses the arguments of Cock (1918) and Grant (1957). He accepts that there is a parallel proof that the least great being must exist in the mind alone, and then makes the obvious point that it is absurd to suppose that the devil of Christian tradition might be identified with this being.

Power (1992:672) claims that ontological arguments for devils fail for the same reasons as ontological arguments for any beings other than God fail, namely, (i) it is only in God's case that conceivability guarantees existence in reality; (ii) it is not absurd to deny the existence of any being, other than God, whose existence is allegedly established by an ontological argument; and (iii) concepts or definitions of beings, other than God, whose existence is allegedly established by ontological arguments, are all inconsistent. Of course, from the standpoint of the parodist, these objections are all question begging: Even if Power insists that God is of a different order from all other kinds of beings, the parodist will insist that he has still been given no reason to believe that there are no concepts that are relevantly similar to the concept of God, that is, similar for the purposes of the construction of ontological arguments. The parodist can concede that Power is rationally entitled to the view that the parodies are unsound and that Power's ontological argument is sound; but that concession has no implications for the success of the parodies. After all, it is the defender of ontological argument who claims to have a proof; what the parodist aims to show is that the arguments in question fail to be rationally compelling for many undoubtedly rational people.

11.7. WHAT DOES PARODY SHOW?

Haight (1974:153) suggests that the parody in Haight and Haight (1970) shows that the argument of *Proslogion* 2 only establishes the existence of some deity – "perhaps a morally neutral God" – rather than the existence of God. This is confused. The parodies show that there are numerous parallels to the argument of *Proslogion* 2 that purport to establish the existence of incompossible entities. It is not an adequate response to suggest that, in fact, all of these arguments establish the existence of the very same, morally neutral being – for, of course, most of the parodies, together with the original argument, deny that the being whose existence they purport to establish is morally neutral. Note, too, that it is hopeless to claim that all that the parodies show is that more premises need to be added to the argument of *Proslogion* 2 in order to vindicate the proof of the existence of God – at least until those further premises are produced. For, of course, everything turns on the nature of those additional premises. In particular, if they are clearly question begging, then an opponent will insist that the original argument failed to provide a sound demonstration of the existence of God.

12. ARE ONTOLOGICAL ARGUMENTS OF ANY USE TO THEISTS AND/OR ATHEISTS?

Devine (1975c:98, 101) contains an extended discussion of the religious significance of ontological arguments. He suggests that "while the ontological argument may establish God's existence, it is impotent, at least when taken alone, to uphold belief in God." This seems either manifestly wrong or else trivially true. If the soundness of the argument could be readily recognized by those who were not initially committed to the truth of its conclusion – that is, if the argument did establish God's existence – then only the very stupid would be atheists or agnostics, that is, only the very stupid would fail to have belief in God. But, of course, that one believes that God exists, does not guarantee that one will have other beliefs, desires, and intentions that are required for a properly religious life – so that, in another sense, it is obvious that no mere argument could serve to generate belief in God. Devine's observation that "it is impossible that an *a priori* theology, taken alone, should have the kind of practice-justifying power that is required" is obviously correct; but it is puzzling why anyone would think that a mere argument could serve to justify a practice, that is, to inculcate not merely beliefs, but also desires and intentions.

Platt (1973:461ff.) claims:

At the profoundest level, the ontological argument is a rational attempt to explicate and interpret the awe-inspiring impact with the divine dimension in experience.... It can not only provide an additional assurance to the man of faith, it can provide insight to the religious philosopher.... It can and does give rational expression to the deep faith of the believer.

Moreover, Platt (1973:463) adds, "I am arguing that the ontological argument is invalid, *period*, but that it is not therefore nonsense or pure sophistry." It seems to me that Platt confuses (i) *failed* attempts to give logically sound expression to reasonable beliefs and (ii) *well-reasoned* attempts to give logically sound expression to reasonable beliefs. Given that he thinks that ontological arguments are invalid, he ought to hold that there is no enterprise in which ontological arguments succeed; but this does not mean that he cannot also hold that there *are* genuine insights that ontological arguments aim, but fail, to capture. One might be very impressed by the sentiments to which St. Anselm gives expression in the *Proslogion*, while yet maintaining that the attempt fails to provide any vindication for the possession of those sentiments.

12.1. THE RATIONALITY OF THEISTIC BELIEF

DePaul (1981) discusses van Inwagen's objection to Plantinga. He suggests that Plantinga's initial argument required commitment to the following principle: For any proposition p such that it is necessarily true or necessarily false, a person could either rationally (reasonably) accept p or rationally not accept p, if it is epistemically possible that p and epistemically possible that not p. However, in the light of van Inwagen's objection, DePaul proposes the following modification of this principle: For any proposition p such that it is necessarily true or necessarily false, a person could rationally accept p or rationally not accept p if (i) on the assumption that p is true, it is necessarily epistemically possible that p and necessarily epistemically possible that not p; and (ii) on the assumption that p is false, it is necessarily epistemically possible that p and necessarily epistemically possible that not p. On this revised principle, one cannot reasonably believe that there are four consecutive sevens in the decimal expansion of pi since, if there are, it is in principle possible that we should find out that there are, by working through a sufficiently large amount of the expansion. DePaul discusses an objection to the revised principle raised by van Inwagen, which DePaul rejects on the grounds that it is doubtful whether it is possible to name possible worlds. This seems strange to me; I think that van Inwagen's objection is correct and that there is no difficulty in the thought that, for example, the name '@' can be used to name the actual world. But, in any case, there are objections to the revised principle that are just like the objection to the original principle. Consider the following claim: No finite sequence of digits occurs only once in the decimal expansion of pi. It seems to me that – on Plantinga's conception of reasonable belief – neither this claim nor its rejection is reasonably believed; and yet it satisfies the conditions for DePaul's revised principle. I conclude that one cannot use the revised principle to justify Plantinga's views.

Forgie (1991:131, 137) discusses Plantinga's claim that his modal ontological argument establishes the rationality of religious belief:

Because the possibility premise is *a posteriori,* a typical enquirer is not going to be able to determine that it is rational to accept that premise without first determining that it is rational to accept the conclusion of the argument. Thus, not only does the argument not establish the truth of theism, it doesn't even establish its rationality either.

Why does Forgie think that the possibility premise is *a posteriori?* Because either it is, or else it entails, a statement that involves properties that are non-idly indexed to the actual world. But how does this entail that the possibility premise is *a posteriori?* Because, for example, "the property 'being divine' . . . is not necessarily co-extensive with its indexed counterpart 'being divine in the actual world'." But this just begs the question: According to the theist, these two properties *are* necessarily coextensive, because God – and only God – is divine in every world. Of course, I think that Forgie misses the main point. No argument can *establish* that it is reasonable to believe its conclusion without the further assumption that it is reasonable to believe its premises. And nothing in the argument itself can establish that it is reasonable to believe its premises. So Plantinga's claim must be wrong – compare the discussion in the main text.

Gutting (1982:321) discusses Plantinga's claim that ontological arguments show that it is rational to accept their conclusions: "This claim is entirely acceptable as long as we agree with the assumption that it is rational to accept controversial premises that on reflection seem true to [us], even though [we] have no conclusive argument for them." As I have argued in the main text, Gutting's claim is mistaken: It may follow, from the assumption that it is rational to accept controversial claims that on reflection seem true to us even though we have no conclusive argument for them, that it is rational to believe in God – but Plantinga's ontological argument plays no part in, and adds nothing to, this observation. Gutting (1982:328) further claims that Plantinga's ontological argument is a genuine cognitive achievement: "[Plantinga's ontological argument] establishes or maintains the intellectual viability of an important philosophical picture." Not so. What would establish the viability of the picture is just that epistemological conservatism to which, in effect, both Plantinga and Gutting appeal. And – at least for the purposes of the present work – I am prepared to grant that epistemological conservatism is a very attractive doctrine.

Oakes (1980:214) presents what he calls "a new argument for the existence of God." It seems to me that his argument is not interestingly different from Plantinga's modal ontological argument – that is, that its validity turns on exactly the same modal principles. However, what is of note is his suggestion that (i) since it seems perfectly rational to accept the premises of the argument, it is perfectly rational to believe that the argument is sound; and hence, (ii) there is no reason for not regarding the argument as a "good argument for the existence of God," since it constitutes "a conclusive argument for the truth of the proposition that belief in God's existence is eminently rational." The argument in the main text suggests that the move from (i) to (ii) is a complete mistake. Oakes's argument is criticized by Kondoleon (1982). Zagzebski (1984) defends Oakes against Kondoleon's criticisms, and then – in effect, and with the approval of Oakes (1984) – emphasizes the dialectical inefficacy of the argument.

Vallicella (1993) defends the claim that Plantinga's ontological argument is a good argument, though not a successful piece of natural theology. He stipulates (i) that a deductive argument is *probative* iff (a) it is formally logically valid, (b) it has true premises, and (c) it is free from informal fallacy; (ii) that an argument is *normatively persuasive* for a person iff (a) it is probative and (b) it has premises that can be accepted, without any breach of epistemic propriety, by the person in question; and (iii) that an argument is *demonstrative* iff (a) it is probative and (b) it has premises that would be accepted by any reasonable person. Vallicella then claims that a reasonable position to take, vis-à-vis ontological arguments, is that they are probative and normatively persuasive, but not demonstrative. There are two questions to ask. The first is, What counts as an informal fallacy? If begging the question is an informal fallacy, then it seems to me that a theist should agree that ontological arguments are not probative – for whether or not an argument is probative, in this sense, will depend upon whether or not it is dialectically effective. Suppose, then, that the informal fallacies in question refer only to the assessment of the soundness of the argument – that is, such things as semantic equivocation, amphiboly, division, and composition. Then we should ask, Does the fact that a theist can reasonably regard ontological arguments to be both probative and normatively persuasive show that there is a sense in which ontological arguments are useful? Well, note first that I can only regard an argument as probative if I also regard it as normatively persuasive, on pain of falling victim to Moorean paradox. So the question is, Does the fact that a theist can reasonably regard ontological arguments to be probative show that there is a sense in which ontological arguments are useful? But, as I have argued in the main text, the answer to this question is clearly no. Of course, I have allowed that theists can properly think that some ontological arguments are probative – but I have also suggested that any enthusiasm that might be generated by this thought should be quashed by the further observation that the argument 'Either $2+2=5$ or God exists; it is not the case that $2+2=5$; hence God exists' can also reasonably be regarded as probative by some theists, and in exactly the same sense.

12.2. THE IRRATIONALITY OF NONTHEISTIC BELIEF

Hopkins (1978:74) has a nice discussion of St. Anselm's attempt to show that the atheist is a fool:

In the end, it is not the Fool who fails to comprehend what 'God' means but Anselm who fails to comprehend what the Fool means. The Fool may admit that God must be conceived of as existing; but he need not understand God to exist, i.e., he need not take it to be a fact that God, conceived of as having to exist, does exist.

Ignoring potential difficulties with talk about 'conceiving of' and 'conceiving of as', this might serve as an encapsulation of the view that I have defended.

Johnson (1973:57) also defends the view that St. Anselm misrepresents the view of the fool. According to Johnson, the atheist recognizes that she has no concept of God and that this is why she says, 'There is no God'. "What [she] is saying is something similar to the blind person who says 'There are no colours'. What the blind person is saying is that [he] has no concept of colours." The analogy with the blind person is unfortunate – for, typically, a blind person will acknowledge that there are colors, but that he cannot see them. On the other hand, the atheist denies that there is a God. Of course, the atheist will agree that she has no concept *of* God, because there is no God to have a concept *of*. But, on the other hand, she will also allow that she possesses the concept that is expressed by the word 'God' – that is, she, more or less, fully understands what would have to be the case if this term were to have a referent.

Ayer (1973:214) provides a nice expression of the position that is occupied by the fool.

I suppose that someone could insist on making it part of the sense of the term 'God', or indeed of any other term, that it carried an assumption of existence. For such a person, to say 'God does not exist' would be a misuse of language, because the attribute of non-existence would deny what the use of the subject-term had presupposed. But now it becomes clear that nothing is gained by this manouevre, since it remains an open question whether the subject-term has any use. Let it be written into the definition of perfect being that he is not imaginary. The question whether there is anything that has all the other properties of a perfect being and is also not imaginary can still significantly be answered 'No'. Thus, even if we allow to St. Anselm that to conceive of a greatest imaginable being is to conceive of him as existing, it will not follow that there actually is anything to which this concept applies.

Ayer's position is perfectly intelligible; so anyone who claims that it is foolish is making some kind of mistake.

Crawford (1966:122) claims that, when properly construed, St. Anselm's proof "at least silences the atheist, for it makes him aware that he just does not understand what he is saying." This is extremely implausible: Even if one thought that an ontological argument could demonstrate to theists that atheists do not understand their position, it is very hard to see how one could think that an ontological argument demonstrates to *atheists* that they do not understand what they mean when they say 'God does not exist'. In particular, if one denies that atheists have a concept of God, then how could one hold that atheists are in a position to learn from an ontological argument – that is, an argument that makes use of that very concept – that they do not have a concept of God?

McGill (1967:60n94) cites Barth: " 'Let us be clear: Anselm's proof was not made to convince the fool; it cannot do this. But it can show him the insufficiency of his criticism; it can make him see that his denial of God does not reach or touch and cannot break the faith of the believer'." I doubt that there is anything in the *content* of the proof that demonstrates any such thing to the fool – but, on the other hand, the *fact* that a believer espouses such a proof might lead one to conclude that there is nothing one can say to break the believer's faith. Of course, there are lots of other things that the believer could say that might produce a similar conviction – including lots of things that are not in the form of arguments. Given what Barth here claims for the proof, it is entirely insignificant that it is cast in the form of an argument.

Campbell (1976:195) discusses Anselm's reply to those who would say, "If any real thing is something than which a greater cannot be thought, then God is, but although the concept of such a thing entails that it exists, there still might not be any such thing."

It now emerges that the whole burden of his Argument is that such remarks are, strictly speaking, unintelligible. Anyone who makes them has not understood what he is saying. The whole realm of discourse which allows the believer to speak of God as something-than-which-a-greater-cannot-be-thought, he has argued, rules out the possibility of denying with understanding the existence of God. . . . They do not present live options for those who operate with the language we have and who are confronted with the phenomenon of the believer confessing his faith.

If this *is* what St. Anselm contends, then he is guilty of a clear confusion between (i) what is compatible with the presuppositions of the theistic user of the language and (ii) what is compatible with the presuppositions of the nontheistic user of the language. Moreover, he demonstrates a total failure to understand the position of the nontheist, a failure that need not be reflected in a failure of the nontheist to understand St. Anselm's view.

12.3. THE ABSOLUTE SECURITY OF THEISTIC BELIEF

Maloney (1980:13) suggests a position that many have found attractive, namely, to ensure the security of theistic belief by denying that nontheists have the same concepts: "The Augustinian and the Kantian differently evaluate the Augustinian's argument. They understand 'God' differently; their conceptual schemes are disjoint in their concepts of God. Unlike the conceptually deprived Kantian, the Augustinian understands 'God' by understanding God when he himself says 'I am who am'." This is a dangerous strategy. In particular, it requires us to say that those who lose their faith cease to understand what it is that they previously believed. But that is surely absurd: Anthony Kenny has the very same concept of God that he had when he believed; but he is no longer confident that there is anything that falls under the concept. Of course, the Kantian and the Augustinian disagree about which terms in their theories refer; and this could be called a divergence in conceptual scheme. But that does not entail that they have different concepts that they express with similar words. Maloney's ostrich strategy may successfully ward off doubt – that is, it may have practical success – but I do not think that it can be rationally justified.

Chubb (1973:345) defends the view that "the ontological argument," when properly construed, proves (i) that belief in God is rational, (ii) that belief that God does not exist is irrational, and (iii) that failure to believe in God reveals a positivistic conceptual impoverishment:

Just as there is no logical procedure for communicating the concept of God to a positivist . . . so there is no logical procedure for communicating a full and adequate ... concept of God to those whose religious sense is dormant. ... [The] true philosophical affiliation [of such people] is with those who do not doubt or reject the existence of God, but who reject the very concept of God as cognitively meaningless.

The insistence that possession of the concept of God requires belief in God is a gratuitous piece of linguistic imperialism, designed to deny atheists the means of expressing their position. Compare the position of someone who insists that he communicates telepathically with a particular gum tree, called Gummy, but who also insists that one can only understand what it is to communicate telepathically with Gummy if one communicates telepathically with Gummy. "Just as there is no logical procedure for communicating an understanding of communication with Gummy to a positivist ... so there is no logical procedure for communicating a full and adequate ... understanding of communication with Gummy to those whose telepathic sense is dormant." Surely even Chubb will concede that the mere availability of this argument does not show (i) that it is rational to believe that some people communicate telepathically with Gummy, (ii) that it is irrational to believe that no one can communicate telepathically with Gummy, and (iii) that failure to believe that some people communicate telepathically with Gummy reveals a (positivistic) conceptual impoverishment. Moreover, the availability of the argument does not show these things even to one who believes that he communicates telepathically with Gummy. This is not to deny that it might be rational to believe that one can communicate telepathically with Gummy; but it is to insist that no "internal" considerations can demonstrate that certain kinds of beliefs *are* rational, or that the denial of those beliefs *is* irrational.

CONCLUSION

One common view about ontological arguments that I have not discussed is that they present unresolvable conundrums or puzzles. Some works that exhibit a tendency toward this view include Diamond (1977), Ebersole (1978), Howe (1969), and Preuss (1980). Naturally, I think that this tendency is misguided: A proper examination shows that ontological arguments are just bad arguments.

I have also not considered work that seeks to provide debunking explanations of the acceptance of ontological arguments by some philosophers. Thus, for example, I have not discussed the contention of

Feuer (1968) (1969) that those who accept ontological arguments are "logical masochists" – compare the claim of Carmichael (1978) that the ontological arguer possesses "conative fixations" rather than reasoned beliefs. As earlier critics – for example, Watt (1969) and Sessions (1969) – noted, Feuer's claim is quite implausible and is only very weakly supported by the considerations that he adduces.

Finally, I have not discussed the view of Goode and Wettersten (1982:675) that the history of the ontological argument illustrates their thesis that "we learn from arguments by discovering new problems which are due to inadequacies in our arguments." It seems to me that their thesis is implausible; moreover, it is not at all clear that the "new problems" on which Goode and Wettersten focus – Leibniz's question about the consistency of the concept of God, Kant's suggestion that existence is not a predicate, Russell's theory of definite descriptions – really do point up *inadequacies* in the earlier arguments. At least in the case of Kant and Russell, it is plausible to suggest that what they took to be inadequacies in those arguments were not really inadequacies at all.

Bibliography

1. SOURCES ON ONTOLOGICAL ARGUMENTS

The following is a list of all the material on ontological arguments which I was able to read while this work was in progress. For references to some articles which I was not able to track down, see Miethe (1976) and the bibliographies in Brecher (1985), Dore (1984b), Hick and McGill (1967) and La Croix (1972). I note with regret that my confinement to a single language prevented me from surveying the vast non-English literature on ontological arguments.

Abelson, R. (1961). "Not Necessarily," *Philosophical Review* 70:647–84.

Abraham, W. (1962). "Is the Concept of Necessary Existence Self-Contradictory?" *Inquiry* 5:143–57.

Adams, R. (1971). "The Logical Structure of Anselm's Argument," *Philosophical Review* 80:28–54.

Adams, R. (1988). "Presumption and the Necessary Existence of God," *Nous* 22:19–34.

Allen, R. (1961). "The Ontological Argument," *Philosophical Review* 70:56–66.

Allinson, R. (1993). "Anselm's One Argument," *Philosophical Inquiry* 15:16–19.

Alston, W. (1960). "The Ontological Argument Revisited," *Philosophical Review* 69:452–74.

Anderson, A. (1990). "Some Emendations of Godel's Ontological Proof," *Faith and Philosophy* 7:291–303.

Anscombe, G. (1959). *An Introduction to Wittgenstein's* Tractatus. London: Hutchison University Library, p. 15.

Anscombe, G. (1993). "Russelm or Anselm?" *Philosophical Quarterly* 43:500–504.

Aquinas, St. Thomas. (1920/1272). *Summa Theologica*, Part 1 Questions 1–26, literally translated by Fathers of the English Dominican Province. London: Burns, Oates & Washbourne.

Armour, L. (1961). "The Ontological Argument and the Concepts of Completeness and Selection," *Review Of Metaphysics* 14:280–91.

Armour, L. (1986). "Newman, Anselm, and Proof of the Existence of God," *International Journal for Philosophy of Religion* 19:87–93.

Ayer, A. (1973). "The Existence Of God." In *Central Questions of Philosophy*, pp. 211–17. London: Weidenfeld & Nicolson.

Back, A. (1981). "Existential Import in Anselm's Ontological Argument," *Franciscan Studies* 41:97–109.

Back, A. (1983). "Amselm on Perfect Islands," *Franciscan Studies* 43:188–204.

Baier, K. (1960). "Existence," *Proceedings of the Aristotelian Society* 61:19–40.

Baker, J. (1978). "On a Classical Argument That Existence Is Not a Predicate," *Southwest Journal of Philosophy* 8:55–60.

Baker, J. (1980). "What Is Not Wrong with a Hartshornean Modal Proof," *Southern Journal Of Philosophy* 18:99–106.

Baker, J. (1983). "Religious Experience and the Possibility of Divine Existence," *International Journal for Philosophy of Religion* 14:225–32.

Ballard, E. (1958). "On Kant's Refutation of Metaphysics," *New Scholasticism* 32:235–52.

Balz, A. (1953). "Concerning the Ontological Argument," *Review of Metaphysics* 7:207–24.

Bandas, R. (1930). "The Theistic Arguments and Contemporary Thought," *New Scholasticism* 4:378–92.

Barnes, J. (1972). *The Ontological Argument*. London: Macmillan.

Barnette, R. (1975). "Anselm and the Fool," *International Journal for Philosophy of Religion* 6:201–18.

Barth, K. (1960). *Anselm:* Fides Quaerens Intellectum, translated by I. Robertson. London: S.C.M. Press.

Basham, R. (1976). "The 'Second Version' of Anselm's Ontological Argument," *Canadian Journal of Philosophy* 6:665–83.

Baumer, M. (1980). "Possible Worlds and Duns Scotus' Proof for the Existence of God," *New Scholasticism* 54:182–8.

Baumer, W. (1962). "Anselm, Truth, and Necessary Being," *Philosophy* 37:257–8.

Baumer, W. (1966). "Ontological Arguments Still Fail," *Monist* 50:130–44.

Beanblossom, R. (1985). "Another Note on the Ontological Argument," *Faith and Philosophy* 2:175–8.

Beard, R. (1980). "Is God's Non-Existence Conceivable?" *Southern Journal of Philosophy* 18:251–7.

Beckaert, A. (1967). "A Platonic Justification for the Argument A Priori." In J. Hick and A. McGill (eds.), *The Many-Faced Argument: Recent Studies on the Ontological Argument for the Existence of God.* New York: Macmillan, pp. 111–18.

Bedell, G. (1979). "The Many Faces of Necessity in the Many-Faced Argument," *New Scholasticism* 53:1–21.

Bednarowski, W. (1976). "The Riddle of Existence," *Proceedings of the Aristotelian Society*, Supplementary Volume 50:267–89.

Bibliography

Bencivenga, E. (1987). *Kant's Copernican Revolution.* Oxford University Press.

Bennett, J. (1974). "God." In *Kant's Dialectic,* Cambridge University Press, pp. 228–57.

Berg, J. (1961). "An Examination of the Ontological Proof," *Theoria* 27:99–106.

Bouwsma, O. (1984). "Anselm's Argument." In J. Croft and R. Hustwit (eds.), *Without Proof or Evidence: Essays of O. K. Bouwsma.* Lincoln: University of Nebraska Press, pp. 40–72.

Bradford, D. (1983). "Hume On Existence," *International Studies In Philosophy* 15:1–12.

Braham, E. (1932). "The Ontological Argument," *London Quarterly and Holbern Review* 157:522–9.

Brecher, R. (1974). " 'Greatness' in Anselm's Ontological Argument," *Philosophical Quarterly* 24:97–105.

Brecher, R. (1975a). "Hartshorne's Modal Argument for the Existence of God," *Ratio* 17:140–6.

Brecher, R. (1975b). "Pure Objects and the Ontological Argument," *Sophia* 14:10–28.

Brecher, R. (1985). *Anselm's Argument: The Logic of Divine Existence.* Aldershot: Gower.

Broad, C. (1953). "Arguments for the Existence of God." In *Religion, Philosophy, and Psychical Research.* London: Routledge & Kegan Paul, pp. 175–201.

Broad, C. (1975). "Theology." In *Leibniz: An Introduction.* Cambridge University Press, pp. 148–172.

Broadie, F. (1970). *An Approach to Descartes' "Meditations."* New York: Oxford University Press.

Brown, C. (1978). "The Ontological Theorem," *Notre Dame Journal of Formal Logic* 19:591–2.

Brown, P. (1964). "St. Thomas' Doctrine of Necessary Being," *Philosophical Review* 73:76–90.

Brown, S. (1984). *Leibniz.* Brighton: Harvester.

Brown, T. (1961). "Professor Malcolm on 'Anselm's Ontological Arguments,' " *Analysis* 22:12–14.

Brunton, J. (1970). "The Logic of God's Necessary Existence," *International Philosophical Quarterly* 10:276–90.

Buchanan, S. (1924). "Ontological Argument Redivivus," *Journal of Philosophy* 21:505–7.

Caird, E. (1899). "Anselm's Argument for the Being of God – Its History and What It Proves," *Journal of Theological Studies* 1:23–39.

Caird, J. (1880). "Proofs of the Existence of God." In *An Introduction to Philosophy of Religion.* Glasgow: James Maclehose, pp. 152–9.

Campbell, R. (1974). "Real Predicates and 'Exists,' " *Mind* 73:95–9.

Campbell, R. (1976). *From Belief to Understanding.* Canberra: ANU Press.

Campbell, R. (1979). "Anselm's Theological Method," *Scottish Journal of Theology* 32:541 62.

Campbell, R. (1980). "On Preunderstanding St. Anselm," *New Scholasticism* 54:189–93.

Cargile, J. (1975). "The Ontological Argument," *Philosophy* 50:69–80.

Carmichael, P. (1978). "The Ontological Argument at Work in Religion," *Philosophy and Phenomenological Research* 38:247–50.

Carnes, R. (1964). "Descartes and the Ontological Argument," *Philosophy and Phenomenological Research* 24:502–11.

Cassirer, H. (1954). "The Proofs of the Existence of God." In *Kant's First Critique*. London: Macmillan, pp. 312–19.

Chandler, H. (1993). "Some Ontological Arguments," *Faith and Philosophy* 10:18–32.

Charlesworth, M. (1962). "St. Anselm's Argument," *Sophia* 1:25–36.

Charlesworth, M. (1965). *St. Anselm's Proslogion*. Oxford: Oxford University Press.

Chellas, B., and Segerberg, K. (1994). "Modal Logics with the MacIntosh Rule," *Journal of Philosophical Logic* 23:67–86.

Chubb, J. (1973). "Commitment and Justification: A New Look at the Ontological Argument," *International Philosophical Quarterly* 13:335–46.

Clarke, B. (1971). "Modal Disproofs and Proofs for God," *Southern Journal of Philosophy* 9:247–58.

Clarke, B. (1980). "Beard on the Conceivability of God's Non-Existence," *Southern Journal of Philosophy* 18:501–7.

Coburn, R. (1963). "Professor Malcolm on God," *Australasian Journal of Philosophy* 41:143–62.

Coburn, R. (1966). "Animadversions on Plantinga's Kant," *Journal of Philosophy* 63:546–48.

Coburn, R. (1971). "Animadversions on Plantinga's Kant," *Ratio* 13:19–29.

Cock, A. (1918). "The Ontological Argument for the Existence of God," *Proceedings of the Aristotelian Society* 18:363–84.

Collingwood, R. (1933). *Philosophical Method*. Oxford: Oxford University Press.

Connelly, R. (1969). "The Ontological Argument: Descartes' Advice to Hartshorne," *New Scholasticism* 43:530–54.

Copleston, F. (1950). *History of Philosophy Vol. II: Mediaeval Philosophy – Augustine to Scotus*. London: Burns, Oates, & Washbourne.

Copleston, F. (1957). *Aquinas*. Harmondsworth: Penguin.

Copleston, F. (1958). *History of Philosophy Vol. IV: Descartes to Leibniz*. London: Burns, Oates, & Washbourne.

Copleston, F. (1960). *History of Philosophy Vol. VI: Wolff to Kant*. London: Burns, Oates, & Washbourne.

Cornman, J., Lehrer, K., and Pappas, G., (1987). "An *A Priori* Argument." In *Philosophical Problems and Arguments* (Third Edition). Indianapolis: Hackett, pp. 238–45.

Cosgrove, M. (1974). "Thomas Aquinas on Anselm's Argument," *Review of Metaphysics* 27:513–30.

Cottingham, J. (1986). "The Ontological Argument." In *Descartes*. Oxford: Blackwell, pp. 57–64.

Crawford, P. (1966). "Existence, Predication, and Anselm," *Monist* 50:109–24.

Crittenden, C. (1969). "The Argument from Perfection to Existence," *Religious Studies* 4:123–32.

Crocker, S. (1972). "The Ontological Significance of Anselm's *Proslogion*," *Modern Schoolman* 50:33–56.

Crocker, S. (1976). "Descartes' Ontological Argument and the Existing Thinker," *Modern Schoolman* 53:347–77.

Curley, E. (1969). *Spinoza's Metaphysics*. Cambridge, MA: Harvard University Press.

Curley, E. (1978). "God." In *Descartes Against the Skeptics*. Oxford: Blackwell, pp. 125–69.

Daher, A. (1971). "God And Factual Necessity," *Religious Studies* 6, pp. 23–39.

Dauenhauer, B. (1971). "Anselm's Universe Revisited," *Modern Schoolman* 49:54–9.

Davies, B. (1985). "The Existence of God and the Concept of God." In *Thinking About God*. London: Geoffrey Chapman, pp. 89–114.

Davis, S. (1976a). "Does the Ontological Argument Beg the Question?" *International Journal for Philosophy of Religion* 7:433–42.

Davis, S. (1976b). "Anselm and Question-Begging: A Reply to William Rowe," *International Journal for Philosophy of Religion* 7:448–57.

Davis, S. (1982). "Lopston on Anselm and Rowe," *International Journal for Philosophy of Religion* 19:219–24.

Davis, S. (1984). "Lopston on Anselm and Davis," *International Journal for Philosophy of Religion* 16:245–9.

Davison, S. (1991). "Could Abstract Objects Depend upon God?" *Religious Studies* 27:485–97.

Dazeley, H., and Gombocz, W. (1979). "Interpreting Anselm as Logician," *Synthese* 40:71–96.

Deane, S. (1962). (ed. and trans.). *Basic Writings of St. Anselm*. La Salle: Open Court.

DePaul, M. (1981). "The Rationality of Belief in God," *Religious Studies* 17:343–56.

Descartes, R. (1968/1637). *Discourse on Method and The Meditations*, translated with an introduction by F. Sutcliffe. Harmondsworth: Penguin.

Devine, P. (1975a). "The Religious Significance of the Ontological Argument," *Religious Studies* 11:97–116.

Devine, P. (1975b). "The Perfect Island, the Devil, and Existent Unicorns," *American Philosophical Quarterly* 12:255–60.

Devine, P. (1975c). "Does St. Anselm Beg the Question?" *Philosophy* 50:271–81.

Diamond, C. (1977). "Riddles and Anselm's Riddle," *Proceedings of the Aristotelian Society* (supplementary volume) 51:143–68.

Diamond, M. (1974). "The Ontological Argument: Perfection." In *Contemporary Philosophy and Religious Thought*. New York: McGraw-Hill, pp. 241–71.

Dicker, G. (1988a). "A Refutation of Rowe's Critique of Anselm's Argument," *Faith and Philosophy* 5:193–202.

Dicker, G. (1988b). "A Note on Rowe's 'Response To Dicker,'" *Faith and Philosophy* 5:206.

Doney, W. (1978). "The Geometrical Presentation of Descartes' *A Priori* Proof." In *Descartes: Critical and Interpretative Essays*, M. Hooker (ed.). Baltimore: Johns Hopkins University Press, pp. 1–25.

Doney, W. (1991). "Did Caterus Misunderstand Descartes' Ontological Proof?" In G. Moyal, (ed.), *Rene Descartes: Critical Assessments, Volume 2*. London: Routledge & Kegan Paul, pp. 344–53.

Dore, C. (1975). "Examination of an Ontological Argument," *Philosophical Studies* 28:345–56.

Dore, C. (1984a). "Reply to Professor Baker," *International Journal for Philosophy of Religion* 16:251–5.

Dore, C. (1984b). "A Modal Argument," pp. 49–61; "Is God's Existence Logically Possible," pp. 62–81; "Descartes's *Meditation V* Argument," pp. 83–103; "Two Arguments of St. Anselm," pp. 141–7. In *Theism*. Dordrecht: Reidel.

Dore, C. (1984c). "The Possibility of God," *Faith and Philosophy* 1:303–15.

Dore, C. (1986). "A Reply to Professor Rowe," *Faith and Philosophy* 3:314–18.

Dore, C. (1990). "More on the Possibility of God," *Faith and Philosophy* 7:340–3.

Downer, J. (1987). "Commentary on 'The Possibility Of God,'" *Faith and Philosophy* 4:202–6.

Downey, J. (1986). "A Primordial Reply to Modern Gaunilos," *Religious Studies* 22:41–9.

Doyle, J. (1974). "Saint Bonaventure and the Ontological Argument," *Modern Schoolman* 52:27–48.

Doyle, J. (1979). "Some Thoughts on Duns Scotus and the Ontological Argument," *New Scholasticism* 53:234–41.

Dryer, D. (1966). "The Concept of Existence in Kant," *Monist* 50:17–33.

Dummett, M. (1993). "Existence." In *The Seas of Language*. Oxford: Oxford University Press, pp. 277–307.

Duncan, R. (1980). "Analogy and the Ontological Argument," *New Scholasticism* 54:25–33.

Dupre, L. (1973). "The Moral Argument, the Religious Experience, and the Basic Meaning of the Ontological Argument," *Idealistic Studies* 3:266–76.

Dupre, W. (1975). "Anselm and Teilhard De Chardin." In H. Kohlenberger (ed.), *Analecta Anselmiana IV/I*. Frankfurt: Minerva GmbH, pp. 323–31.

Earle, W. (1951). "The Ontological Argument in Spinoza," *Philosophy and Phenomenological Research* 11:549–54; reprinted in M. Grene, (ed.) (1979), *Spinoza: A Collection of Critical Essays*. Notre Dame, Indiana: University of Notre Dame Press, pp. 213–19.

Earle, W. (1979). "The Ontological Argument in Spinoza: Twenty Years Later." In M. Grene (ed.), *Spinoza: A Collection of Critical Essays*. Notre Dame, Indiana: University of Notre Dame Press, pp. 220–6.

Ebersole, F. (1963). "Whether Existence is a Predicate," *Journal Of Philosophy* 60:509–24; reprinted, with some revision, in *Things We Know*. Eugene: University of Oregon Books.

Ebersole, F. (1978). "Everyman's Ontological Argument," *Philosophical Investigations* 1:1–15.

Elton, W. (1945). "Professor Hartshorne's Syllogism: Criticism," *Philosophical Review* 55:506.

Engel, M. (1963). "Kant's 'Refutation' of the Ontological Argument," *Philosophy and Phenomenological Research* 24:20–35; reprinted in R. Wolff (ed.), *Kant: A Collection of Critical Essays*. Garden City, New York: Doubleday, pp. 189–208.

Engel, M. (1964). "Reply to Dr. Schwarz," *Philosophy and Phenomenological Research* 25:412–13.

England, F. (1968). *Kant's Conception of God*. New York: Humanities Press.

Englebretsen, G. (1984). "Anselm's Second Argument," *Sophia* 23:34–7.

Esmail, K. (1992). "Anselm, Plantinga, and the Ontological Argument," *Sophia* 31:39–47.

Ewing, A. (1938). "Theology and the Ideas of Reason." In *A Short Commentary on Kant's Critique of Pure Reason*. London: Methuen, pp. 241–69.

Ewing, A. (1969). "Further Thoughts on the Ontological Argument," *Religious Studies* 5:41–8.

Ferguson, J. (1953). "Theistic Arguments in the Greek Philosophers," *Hibbert Journal* 51:156–64.

Ferguson, K. (1992). "Existing by Convention," *Religious Studies* 28:185–94.

Ferreira, M. (1983). "Kant's Postulate: The Possibility *Or* the Existence of God?" *Kant-Studien* 74:75–80.

Ferrera, V. (1975). "Hegel's Logic: A Dialectical Substantiation of Anselm's Ontological Argument." In H. Kohlenberger, (ed.), *Analecta Anselmiana IV/I*. Frankfurt: Minerva GmbH, pp. 261–74.

Feuer, L. (1968). "God, Guilt, and Logic: The Psychological Basis of the Ontological Argument," *Inquiry* 11:257–81.

Feuer, L. (1969). "The Autonomy of the Sociology of Ideas: A Rejoinder," *Inquiry* 12:434–45.

Findlay, J. (1948a). "Can God's Existence be Disproved?" *Mind* 57:176–83; reprinted in A. Flew and A. McIntyre (eds.) (1955), *New Essays in Philosophical Theology*. London: SCM Press, pp. 47–56; and in A. Plantinga (ed.) (1965), *The Ontological Argument*. New York: Doubleday, pp. 111–22.

Findlay, J. (1948b). "God's Non-Existence: A Reply to Mr. Rainer and Mr. Hughes," *Mind* 57:352–4.

Fitch, F. (1963). "The Perfection of Perfection," *Monist* 47:466–71.

Flimons, S. (1923). "Kant and the Proofs for the Existence of God," *American Catholic Quarterly Review* 48:14–48.

Follesdal, D. (1966). "Comments on Dr. Pollock's 'Proving the Non-Existence of God," *Inquiry* 9:197–9.

Forgie, W. (1972). "Frege's Objection to the Ontological Argument," *Nous* 6:251–65.

Forgie, W. (1974). "Existence Assertions and The Ontological Argument," *Mind* 73:260–2.

Forgie, W. (1976). "Is the Cartesian Ontological Argument Defensible?" *New Scholasticism* 50:108–21.

Forgie, W. (1990). "The Caterus Objection," *International Journal for Philosophy of Religion* 28:81–104.

Forgie, W. (1991). "The Modal Ontological Argument and the Necessary a Posteriori," *International Journal for Philosophy of Religion* 29:129–41.

Franklin, R. (1957). "Necessary Being," *Australasian Journal of Philosophy* 35:97–110.

Franklin, R. (1964). "Some Sorts of Necessity," *Sophia* 3:15–24.

Freeman, D. (1964). "The Ontological Argument," pp. 78–81; "Hume And Kant," 86–97. In *A Philosophical Study of Religion*. Nutley, N.J.: Craig.

Friedman, J. (1974). "Some Set-Theoretical Partition Theorems Suggested by the Structure of Spinoza's God," *Synthese* 27:199–209.

Friedman, J. (1978). "An Overview of Spinoza's Ethics," *Synthese* 37:67–106.

Friedman, J. (1979). "The Mystic's Ontological Argument," *American Philosophical Quarterly* 16:73–8.

Friedman, J. (1980). "Necessity and the Ontological Argument," *Erkenntnis* 15:301–31.

Friedman, J. (1982). "Was Spinoza Fooled by the Ontological Argument?" *Philosophia* 11:307–44.

Gale, R. (1986). "*A Priori* Arguments from God's Abstractness," *Nous* 20:531–43.

Gale, R. (1988). "Freedom Versus Unsurpassable Greatness," *International Journal for Philosophy of Religion* 23:65–75.

Gale, R. (1991). "Ontological Arguments." In *On the Nature and Existence of God*. Cambridge University Press, pp. 201–37.

Galloway, G. (1950). "The Theistic Proofs." In *The Philosophy of Religion*. Edinburgh: T. & T. Clarke, pp. 382–7.

Gardner, M. (1983). "The Proofs: Why I Do Not Believe God's Existence Can be Demonstrated." In *The Whys of a Philosophical Scrivener*. Brighton: Harvester, pp. 192–208.

Gaskin, J. (1978). "Being and Necessity." In *Hume's Philosophy of Religion*. New York: Harper & Row, pp. 59–73.

Gaspard, J. (1933). "On the Existence of a Necessary Being," *Journal of Philosophy* 30:5–14.

Geisler, N. (1973). "The Missing Premise in the Ontological Argument," *Religious Studies* 9:289–96.

Gellman, J. (1979). "On Arguing from God's Possibility to His Necessity," *Logique et Analyse* 22:525–6.

Gilson, E. (1955). *History of Christian Philosophy in the Middle Ages.* London: Sheed & Ward.

Gombocz, W. (1978). "St. Anselm's Two Devils but One God," *Ratio* 20:143–6.

Goode, T., and Wettersten, J. (1982). "How Do We Learn from Argument? Toward An Account of the Logic of Problems," *Canadian Journal of Philosophy* 12:673–89.

Goodwin, G. (1983). "The Ontological Argument in Neo-Classical Context: Reply to Friedman," *Erkenntnis* 20:219–32.

Gotterbarn, D. (1976). "Leibniz's Completion of Descartes' Proof," *Studia Leibnitiana* 8:105–12.

Gracia, J. (1974). " 'A Supremely Great Being,' " *New Scholasticism* 48:371–7.

Grant, C. (1957). "The Ontological Disproof of the Devil," *Analysis* 17:71–2.

Grant, C. (1989). "Anselm's Argument Today," *Journal of the American Academy of Religion* 57:791–806.

Grave, S. (1952). "The Ontological Argument of St. Anselm," *Philosophy* 27:30–8.

Gregory, D. (1984). "On Behalf of the Second-Rate Philosopher: A Defence of the Gaunilo Strategy Against the Ontological Argument," *History of Philosophy Quarterly* 1:49–60.

Grim, P. (1979a). "Plantinga's God," *Sophia* 18:35–42.

Grim, P. (1979b). "Plantinga's God and Other Monstrosities," *Religious Studies* 15:91–7.

Grim, P. (1981). "Plantinga, Hartshorne, and the Ontological Argument," *Sophia* 20:12–16.

Grim, P. (1982a). "In Behalf of 'In Behalf of the Fool,' " *International Journal for Philosophy of Religion* 13:33–42.

Grim P. (1982b). "Against a Deontic Argument for God's Existence," *Analysis* 42:171–4.

Gunderson, K., and Routley, R. (1960). "Mr. Rescher's Reformulation of the Ontological Proof," *Australasian Journal of Philosophy* 38:247–53.

Gutting, G. (1982). "Can Philosophical Beliefs be Rationally Justified?" *American Philosophical Quarterly* 19:315–30.

Haight, D. (1971). "The Predication of Existence: Another Footnote," *Idealistic Studies* 1:179–81.

Haight, D. (1974). "Devils," *International Journal for Philosophy of Religion* 5:152–6.

Haight, D. (1981). "Back to Intentional Entities and Essences" *New Scholasticism* 55:178–90.

Haight, D., and Haight, M. (1970). "An Ontological Argument for the Devil," *Monist* 54:218–20.

345

Hallett, H. (1957). "Proofs of the Existence of God." In *Benedict De Spinoza*. London: Athlone, pp. 24–7.

Hanson, N. (1961). "A Budget of Cross-Type Inferences," *Journal of Philosophy* 58:449–70.

Hardin, C. (1961). "An Empirical Refutation of the Ontological Argument," *Analysis* 22:10–12.

Hardin, C. (1962). "Cows and Unicorns: Two Replies to Mr. Resnick," *Analysis* 23:13–14.

Harris, E. (1936). "Mr. Ryle and the Ontological Argument," *Mind* 55:474–80; reprinted in J. Hick and A. McGill (ed.), *The Many-Faced Argument: Recent Studies on the Ontological Argument for the Existence of God*. New York: Macmillan, pp. 261–8.

Harris, E. (1972). "Collingwood's Treatment of the Ontological Argument and the Categorical Universal." In M. Krausz (ed.), *Critical Essays on the Philosophy of R. G. Collingwood*. Oxford: Oxford University Press, pp. 113–33.

Harris, E. (1973). "The Existence Of God." In *Salvation from Despair*. The Hague: Martinus Nijhoff, pp. 39–47.

Harris, E. (1977). "Kant's Refutation of the Ontological Proof," *Philosophy* 52:90–2.

Harrison, C. (1970). "The Ontological Argument in Modal Logic," *Monist* 54:302–13.

Hartman, R. (1961). "Prolegomena to a Meta-Anselmian Axiomatic," *Review of Metaphysics* 14:637–75.

Hartshorne, C. (1941). "The Necessarily Existent (Ontological Argument)." In *Man's Vision of God*. New York: Harper & Row, pp. 299–341; reprinted, in part, in A. Plantinga (ed.) (1964), *The Ontological Argument*. New York: Doubleday, pp. 123–35.

Hartshorne, C. (1945). "Professor Hartshorne's Syllogism: Rejoinder," *Philosophical Review* 55:506–8.

Hartshorne, C. (1950). "The Divine Relativity and Absoluteness: A Reply," *Review of Metaphysics* 4:31–60.

Hartshorne, C. (1961a). "Metaphysics and the Modality of Existential Judgements." In I. Leclerc (ed.), *The Relevance of Whitehead*. London: Allen & Unwin, pp. 107–21.

Hartshorne, C. (1961b). "The Logic of the Ontological Argument," *Journal of Philosophy* 58:471–3.

Hartshorne, C. (1962). "Introduction to Second Edition." In S. Deane (trans.), *Saint Anselm: Basic Writings*. La Salle, Ill.: Open Court, pp. 1–19.

Hartshorne, C. (1963). "Abstract and Concrete in God: A Reply," *Review of Metaphysics* 17:289–95.

Hartshorne, C. (1964). "What the Ontological Proof Does not Do," *Review of Metaphysics* 17:608–9.

Hartshorne, C. (1965). *Anselm's Discovery: A Re-Examination of the Ontological Proof for God's Existence*. La Salle, Ill.: Open Court.

Hartshorne, C. (1967a). "Necessity," *Review of Metaphysics* 21:290–6.

Hartshorne, C. (1967b). "Rejoinder to Purtill," *Review of Metaphysics* 21:308–9.

Hartshorne, C. (1967c). *A Natural Theology for Our Time.* La Salle, Ill.: Open Court.

Hartshorne, C. (1976). *Aquinas to Whitehead: Seven Centuries of Metaphysics of Religion.* Milwaukee: Marquette University Publications.

Hartshorne, C. (1977). "John Hick on Logical and Ontological Necessity," *Religious Studies* 13:155–65.

Hartshorne, C. (1991a). "Some Causes of My Intellectual Growth." In L. Hahn (ed.), *The Philosophy of Charles Hartshorne.* La Salle, Ill.: Open Court, pp. 3–45.

Hartshorne, C. (1991b). "Reply to Hubbeling." In L. Hahn (ed.), *The Philosophy of Charles Hartshorne.* La Salle Ill.: Open Court, pp. 664–69.

Hasker, W. (1982). "Is There a Second Ontological Argument?" *International Journal for Philosophy of Religion* 13:93–101.

Hegel, G. (1985/1831). "The Ontological Proof According to the Lectures of 1831." In P. Hodgson (ed.), *Lectures on the Philosophy of Religion, Vol. III.* Berkeley: University of California Press, pp. 351–58.

Hendel, C. (1925). *Studies in the Philosophy of David Hume.* Indianapolis: Bobbs-Merrill.

Henle, P. (1961). "Uses of the Ontological Argument," *Philosophical Review* 70:102–9.

Henry, D. (1955). "The *Proslogion* Proofs," *Philosophical Quarterly* 5:147–51.

Henry, D. (1967). "The Ontological Argument." In *The Logic of St. Anselm.* Oxford: Clarendon Oxford University Press, pp. 142–50.

Herrera, R. (1972). "St. Anselm's *Proslogion:* A Hermeneutical Task." In F. Schmitt (ed.), *Analecta Anselmiana III.* Frankfurt: Minerva GmbH, pp. 141–5.

Hick, J. (1961). "Necessary Being," *Scottish Journal of Theology* 14:353–69.

Hick, J. (ed.) (1964). "The Ontological Argument." In *The Existence of God.* London: Macmillan, pp. 23–70.

Hick, J. (1967a). "A Critique of the 'Second Argument.' " In J. Hick and A. McGill (eds), *The Many-Faced Argument: Recent Studies on the Ontological Argument for the Existence of God.* New York: Macmillan, pp. 341–56.

Hick, J. (1967b). "Ontological Argument for the Existence of God." In P. Edwards (ed.), *The Encyclopedia of Philosophy.* New York: Macmillan, pp. 538–42.

Hick, J. (1970). "The Ontological Argument: First Form," pp. 68–83; "The Ontological Argument: Second Form," pp. 84–100. In *Arguments for the Existence of God.* London: Macmillan.

Hick, J., and McGill, A. (eds.) (1967). *The Many-Faced Argument: Recent Studies on the Ontological Argument for the Existence of God.* London: Macmillan.

Hinchcliff, M. (1989). "Plantinga's Defence of Serious Actualism," *Analysis* 49:182–5.

Hintikka, J. (1969). "On the Logic of the Ontological Argument." In *Models for Modalities*. Dordrecht: Reidel, pp. 45–54.

Hintikka, J. (1981). "Kant on Existence, Predication, and the Ontological Argument," *Dialectica* 35:127–46.

Hinton, J. (1972). "Quantification, Meinongism, and the Ontological Argument," *Philosophical Quarterly* 22:97–109.

Hochberg, H. (1959). "St. Anselm's Ontological Argument and Russell's Theory of Descriptions," *New Scholasticism* 33:319–30.

Hocking, W. (1912). "The Ontological Argument For The Existence Of God." In *The Meaning of God in Human Experience*. New Haven, Conn.: Yale University Press, pp. 301–16; reprinted as "The Ontological Argument Reinterpreted," in J. Weinberg and K. Yandell (eds.) (1971), *Problems in Philosophical Inquiry*. New York: Holt, Rinehart, & Winston, pp. 509–13.

Hodges, H. (1979). *God Beyond Knowledge*. London: Macmillan.

Hoernle, R. (1922). "Notes on the Treatment of 'Existence' in Recent Philosophical Literature," *Proceedings of the Aristotelian Society* 23:19–38.

Hopkins, J. (1972). "Ontological Argument. "In *A Companion to the Study of St. Anselm*. Minneapolis: University of Minnesota Press, pp. 67–78.

Hopkins, J. (1976). "Anselm's Debate with Gaunilo." In H. Kohlenberger (ed.), *Analecta Anselmiana V*. Frankfurt: Minerva GmbH, pp. 25–53.

Hopkins, J. (1978). "On Understanding and Preunderstanding St. Anselm," *New Scholasticism* 52:243–60.

Hopkins, J. (1986). *A New Interpretative Translation of St. Anselm's* Monologion *and* Proslogion. Minneapolis, Minn.: Banning.

Hopkins, J., and Richardson, H. (eds. and trans.) (1974). *Selected Works of St. Anselm*. New York: Mellen.

Hospers, J. (1967). "The Philosophy Of Religion." In *An Introduction to Philosophical Analysis* (Second Edition). London: Routledge & Kegan Paul, pp. 425–92; especially "The Ontological Argument," pp. 427–9.

Howe, L. (1966). "Conceivability and the Ontological Argument," *Sophia* 5:3–8.

Howe, L. (1969). "Existence as a Perfection: A Reconsideration of the Ontological Argument," *Religious Studies* 4:78–101.

Howe, L. (1971). "The Necessity of Creation," *International Journal for Philosophy of Religion* 2:96–112.

Howe, L. (1972). "The Ambiguity of 'Perfection' in the Ontological Argument," *Proceedings of the American Catholic Philosophical Association*, 46:58–70.

Hubbeling, H. (1991). "Hartshorne and the Ontological Argument." In L. Hahn (ed.), *The Philosophy of Charles Hartshorne*. La Salle, Ill.: Open Court, pp. 355–76.

Hudson, W. (1964). "An Attempt to Defend Theism," *Philosophy* 39:18–28.

Hudson, W. (1974). "The Problem Of Objectivity: Conceptual Analysis." In *A Philosophical Approach to Religion*. New York: Harper & Row, pp. 26–40.

Huggett, W. (1961). "The *'Proslogion'* Proof Re-Examined," *Indian Journal of Philosophy* 2:193–202.

Huggett, W. (1962). "The Non-Existence of Ontological Arguments," *Philosophical Review* 71:377–9.

Hughes, G. (1948). "Has God's Existence Been Disproved? A Reply to Professor J. N. Findlay," *Mind* 57:67–74.

Hughes, G. (1970). "Plantinga on the Rationality of God's Existence," *Philosophical Review* 79:246–52.

Hughes, M. (1990). "Creation, Creativity, and Necessary Being," *Religious Studies* 26:349–61.

Hughes, R. (1975). "Descartes' Ontological Argument as Not Identical to the Causal Arguments," *New Scholasticism* 49:473–85.

Hugly, P., and Sayward, C. (1990). "Offices and God," *Sophia* 29:29–34.

Humber, J. (1970). "Descartes' Ontological Argument as Non-Causal," *New Scholasticism* 44:449–59.

Humber, J. (1974). "Causal Necessity and the Ontological Argument," *Religious Studies* 10:291–300.

Hume, D. (1948/1779). *Dialogues Concerning Natural Religion*, edited with an introduction by H. Aiken. New York: Macmillan.

Hume, D. (1978/1740). *A Treatise of Human Nature*, with text revised and notes by P. Nidditch. London: Macmillan.

Hutchings, P. (1957). "Necessary Being," *Australasian Journal of Philosophy* 37:201–6.

Hutchings, P. (1963). "God and Existence," *Sophia* 3:1–10.

Hutchings, P. (1964). "Necessary Being and Some Types of Tautology," *Philosophy* 39:1–17.

Imlay, R. (1969). "Descartes' Ontological Argument," *New Scholasticism* 43:440–8.

Imlay, R. (1971). "Descartes' Ontological Argument: A Causal Argument," *New Scholasticism* 45:348–51.

Imlay, R. (1986). "Descartes' *A Priori* Proof for God and the Second Set of Objections to the Meditations," *Modern Schoolman* 63:111–18.

Jacquette, D. (1994). "Meinongian Logic and Anselm's Ontological Proof for the Existence of God," *Philosophical Forum* 25:231–40.

Jarrett, C. (1976). "Spinoza's Ontological Argument," *Canadian Journal of Philosophy* 6:685–91.

Jarrett, C. (1978). "The Logical Structure of Spinoza's *Ethics*, Part 1," *Synthese* 37:15–65.

Joachim, H. (1901). "Reality as a Whole or God." In *A Study of the Ethics of Spinoza*. Oxford: Oxford University Press, pp. 36–64.

Johnson, C. (1973). "Why the Atheist Is Not a Fool" *International Journal for Philosophy of Religion* 4:253–8.

Johnson, G. (1977). "Hartshorne's Arguments Against Empirical Evidence for Necessary Existence: An Evaluation," *Religious Studies* 13:175–87.

Johnson, J. (1963). "The Ontological Argument in Plato," *Personalist* 44:24–34.

Johnson, O. (1965). "God and St. Anselm," *Journal of Religion* 45:326–34.

Kalin, M. (1982). "Is a Proof for God Still Possible?" *Philosophy Today* 26:76–84.

Kane, R. (1984). "The Modal Ontological Argument," *Mind* 93:336–50.

Kant, I. (1933/1787). *The Critique of Pure Reason* (Second Edition), translated by N. Kemp-Smith. London: Macmillan.

Kapitan, T. (1976). "Perfection and Modality: Charles Hartshorne's Ontological Proof," *International Journal for Philosophy of Religion* 7:379–85.

Kellenberger, J. (1970). "The Ontological Principle and God's Existence," *Philosophy* 45:281–9.

Kelly, C. (1986). "God's Knowledge of the Necessary," *International Journal for Philosophy of Religion* 20:131–45.

Kelly, C. (1994). "Circularity and Amphiboly in Some Anselmian Ontological Proofs: A Syllogistic Inquiry," *Nous* 28:482–504.

Kemp-Smith, N. (1952). "Descartes' Arguments in Proof of the Existence of God." In *New Studies in the Philosophy of Descartes*. London: Macmillan, pp. 295–307.

Kennedy, R. (1989). "How Not to Derive "Is" from "Could Be": Professor William Rowe on the Ontological Argument," *Philosophical Studies* 55:293–302.

Kenny, A. (1962). "Necessary Being," *Sophia* 1:1–9.

Kenny, A. (1968a). "Descartes' Ontological Argument," pp. 18–36; pp. 58–62. In J. Margolis (ed.), *Fact and Existence*. Oxford: Oxford University Press.

Kenny, A. (1968b). "The Ontological Argument." In *Descartes*. New York: Random House, pp. 146–71.

Kenny, A. (1968c). "Reply." In J. Margolis (ed.), *Fact and Existence*. Oxford: Oxford University Press, pp. 58–62.

Keyworth, D. (1962). "Cows and Unicorns: Two Replies to Mr. Resnick," *Analysis* 23:15–16.

Keyworth, D. (1969). "Modal Proofs and Disproofs of God," *Personalist* 50:33–52.

Kielkopf, C. (1978). "Duns Scotus' Rejection of 'Necessarily Exists' as a Predicate," *Journal of History of Philosophy* 16:13–21.

Kielkopf, C. (1984). "The Sense of the Holy and Ontological Arguments," *New Scholasticism* 58:24–39.

King, P. (1984). "Anselm's Intentional Argument," *History of Philosophy Quarterly* 1:147–65.

King-Farlow, J. (1982). " 'Nothing Greater Can be Conceived' (Zeno, Anselm, and Tillich)," *Sophia* 21:19–23.

Kiteley, M. (1958). "Existence and the Ontological Argument," *Philosophy and Phenomenological Research* 18:533–5.

Kiteley, M. (1964). "Is Existence a Predicate?" *Mind* 73:364–73.

Kneale, W. (1936). "Symposium: Is Existence a Predicate?" *Proceedings of the Aristotelian Society* (supplementary volume) 15:154–74.

Kondoleon, T. (1982). "Oakes' New Argument for God's Existence," *New Scholasticism* 56:100–9.

Kordig, C. (1981). "A Deontic Argument for God's Existence," *Nous* 15:207–8.

Korner, S. (1979). *Fundamental Questions of Philosophy.* Atlantic Highlands, N.J.: Humanities, pp. 226–30.

Krull, K. (1964). "The Existence of God: Scotus and Kant," *Duns Scotus Philosophical Association Convention Report* 28:142–77.

La Croix, R. (1972a). Proslogion II *and* III: *A Third Interpretation of Anselm's Argument.* Leiden: Brill.

La Croix, R. (1972b). "Malcolm's *Proslogion III* Argument," *Sophia* 11:13–19.

La Fleur, L. (1942). "The R-Being," *Philosophy of Science* 9:37–9.

Laird, J. (1941). "The Ontological Argument." In *Mind and Deity.* London: Allen & Unwin, pp. 29–56.

Laserowiz, M. (1983). "On a Property of a Perfect Being," *Mind* 92:257–63.

Laura, R. (1973). "God, Necessary Exemplification, and the Synthetic/Analytic," *International Journal for Philosophy of Religion* 4:119–27.

Leftow, B. (1988). "Anselmian Polytheism," *International Journal for Philosophy of Religion* 23:77–104.

Leftow, B. (1989). "Perfection and Necessity," *Sophia* 28:13–20.

Leftow, B. (1990). "Individual and Attribute in the Ontological Argument," *Faith and Philosophy* 7:235–42.

Leibniz, G. (1896/1709). *New Essays Concerning Human Understanding,* translated by A. Langley. New York: Macmillan.

Leslie, J. (1980). "The World's Necessary Existence," *International Journal for Philosophy of Religion* 11:207–24.

Lewis, D. (1970). "Anselm and Actuality," *Nous* 4:175–88; reprinted, with a postscript, in D. Lewis (1983), *Philosophical Papers* 1:1–25.

Lochhead, D. (1966). "Is Existence a Predicate in Anselm's Argument?" *Religious Studies* 2:121–7.

Locke, J. (1964/1690). *An Essay Concerning Human Understanding.* New York: New American Library.

Loewer, B. (1978). "Leibniz and the Ontological Argument," *Philosophical Studies* 34:105–9.

Lomasky, L. (1970). "Leibniz and the Modal Argument for God's Existence," *Monist* 54:250–69.

Londey, D. (1978). "Concepts and God's Possibility," *Sophia* 17:15–19.

Lopston, P. (1980). "Anselm, Meinong, and the Ontological Argument," *International Journal for Philosophy of Religion* 11:185–94.

Lopston, P. (1984). "Anselm and Rowe: A Reply to Davis," *International Journal for Philosophy of Religion* 15:67–71.

Lopston, P. (1986). "Conceiving as Existent: A Final Rejoinder to Davis," *International Journal for Philosophy of Religion* 19:123–5.

Losoncy, T. (1982). "Anselm's Response to Gaunilo's Dilemma – An Insight into the Notion of 'Being' Operative in the *Proslogion*," *New Scholasticism* 56:207–16.

Losoncy, T. (1990). "St. Anselm's Rejection of the 'Ontological Argument' – A Review of the Occasion and Circumstances," *American Catholic Philosophical Quarterly* 64:373–85.

Losoncy, T. (1992). "More on an 'Elusive' Argument," *American Catholic Philosophical Quarterly* 66:500–505.

Loughran, J. (1978). "Another Look at Mavrodes' 'Simple Argument,' " *New Scholasticism* 52:548–57.

Lucas, B. (1985). "The Second Epistemic Way," *International Journal for Philosophy of Religion* 18:107–14.

Lucey, K. (1986). "Theism, Necessity, and Invalidity," *Sophia* 25:47–50.

MacGregor, G. (1964). "The Ontological Argument." In *Introduction to Religious Philosophy*. London: Macmillan, pp. 102–8.

MacIntosh, J. (1991). "Theological Question-Begging," *Dialogue* 30:531–47.

MacIver, A. (1948). "A Note on the Ontological Proof," *Analysis* 8:48.

Mackie, J. (1976). "The Riddle of Existence," *Proceedings of the Aristotelian Society* 50:247–65.

Mackie, J. (1982). "Ontological Arguments." In *The Miracle of Theism: Arguments for and Against the Existence of God*. Oxford: Oxford University Press, pp. 41–63.

MacPherson, T. (1965). "The Ontological Argument." In *The Philosophy of Religion*. London: Van Nostrand, pp. 25–49.

MacPherson, T. (1974). "The Ontological Argument." In *Philosophy and Religious Belief*. London: Hutchinson, pp. 55–60.

Makin, S. (1988). "The Ontological Argument," *Philosophy* 63:83–91.

Makin, S. (1992). "The Ontological Argument Defended," *Philosophy* 67:247–55.

Malcolm, N. (1960). "Anselm's Ontological Arguments," *Philosophical Review* 69:41–62; reprinted in N. Malcolm (1963), *Knowledge and Certainty*. Englewood Cliffs, N.J.: Prentice-Hall, pp. 141–62; and in J. Hick (ed.) (1964), *The Existence of God*. London: Macmillan, pp. 48–70.

Malcolm, N. (1968). "Descartes' Ontological Argument." In J. Margolis (ed.), *Fact and Existence*. Oxford: Oxford University Press, pp. 36–43.

Maloney, J. (1980). "On What Might Be," *Southern Journal of Philosophy* 18:313–22.

Maloney, J. (1981). " 'God' Is a Term Than Which None Greater Can Be Used," *International Journal for Philosophy of Religion* 12:3–15.

Mann, W. (1967). "Definite Descriptions and the Ontological Argument," *Theoria* 33:211–29.

Bibliography

Mann, W. (1972). "The Ontological Presuppositions of the Ontological Argument," *Review of Metaphysics* 26:260–77.

Mann, W. (1976). "The Perfect Island," *Mind* 85:417–21.

Marion, J. (1992). "Is the Ontological Argument Ontological? The Argument According to Anselm and Its Metaphysical Interpretation According to Kant," *Journal of History of Philosophy* 30:201–18.

Martin, J. (1976). "Is Necessity Necessary?" *Religious Studies* 11:329–34.

Martin, M. (1990). "The Ontological Argument." In *Atheism: A Philosophical Justification*. Philadelphia: Temple University Press, pp. 79–95.

Martin, R. (1970). "On the Logical Structure of the Ontological Argument," *Monist* 54:297–311.

Mascall, E. (1949). "The Essentialist Approach To Theism." In *Existence and Analogy*. London: Longmans, Green, pp. 18–43.

Mascall, E. (1966). "The Traditional Approach." In *He Who Is*. London: Darton, Longman, & Todd, pp. 30–9.

Mascall, E. (1971). "God and Logic." In *The Openness Of Being*. London: Darton, Longman, & Todd, pp. 36–58.

Mason, P. (1978). "The Devil and St. Anselm," *International Journal for Philosophy of Religion* 9:1–15.

Matson, W. (1958). "Basson's Ontological Argument," *Review of Metaphysics* 12:316–20.

Matson, W. (1965). "The Ontological Argument." In *The Existence of God*, pp. 44–55.

Matthews, G. (1961). "On Conceivability in Anselm and Malcolm," *Philosophical Review* 70:110–11.

Matthews, G. (1963) "Aquinas on Saying That God Does Not Exist," *Monist* 47:472–7.

Mavrodes, G. (1966). "Properties, Predicates, and the Ontological Argument," *Journal of Philosophy* 63:549–50.

Mavrodes, G. (1970). "Some Recent Philosophical Theology," *Review of Metaphysics* 24:82–111.

Maydole, R. (1980). "A Modal Model for Proving the Existence of God," *American Philosophical Quarterly* 17:135–42.

McAllister, A. (1978). "Two Errors in Assessing the Ontological Argument," *International Journal for Philosophy of Religion* 9:171–8.

McGill, A. (1967). "Recent Discussions of Anselm's Argument." In J. Hick and A. McGill (eds.), *The Many-Faced Argument: Recent Studies on the Ontological Argument for the Existence of God*. New York: Macmillan, pp. 33–110.

McGrath, P. (1986). "The Modal Ontological Argument – A Reply to Kane and Morris," *Mind* 95:373–6.

McGrath, P. (1988). "The Ontological Argument Revisited," *Philosophy* 63:529–33.

McGrath, P. (1990). "The Refutation of the Ontological Argument," *Philosophical Quarterly* 40:195–212.

McGrath, P. (1994). "Does the Ontological Argument Beg the Question?" *Religious Studies* 30:305–10.

McKeon, R. (1928). *The Philosophy of Spinoza*. New York: Longman's, Green.

Mecklin, J. (1917). "The Revival of the Ontological Argument," *Journal of Philosophy* 14:124–35.

Mendelsohn, R. (1989). "Objects and Existence: Reflections on Free Logic," *Notre Dame Journal of Formal Logic* 30:604–32.

Miethe, T. (1976). "The Ontological Argument: A Research Bibliography," *Modern Schoolman* 53:148–66.

Mijuskovic, B. (1973). "Spinoza's Ontological Proof," *Sophia* 12:17–24.

Miller, B. (1979). " 'Exists' and Other Predicates," *New Scholasticism* 53:475–9.

Miller, B. (1982). "Existence and Natures," *New Scholasticism* 56:371–5.

Miller, P. (1961). "The Ontological Argument for God," *Personalist* 42:337–51.

Miller, R. (1955). "The Ontological Argument in St. Anselm and Descartes," *Modern Schoolman* 32:341–9, and 33:31–8.

Morewedge, P. (1970). "Ibn Sina Avicenna and Malcolm and the Ontological Argument," *Monist* 54:234–49.

Morreall, J. (1984). "The Aseity of God in St. Anselm," *Sophia* 23:35–44.

Morris, T. (1985). "Necessary Beings," *Mind* 94:263–72.

Morris, T., and Menzel, C. (1986). "Absolute Creation," *American Philosophical Quarterly* 23:353–62.

Morscher, E. (1986). "Was Existence Ever a Predicate?" *Grazer Philosophische Studien* 25–26:269–84.

Munitz, M. (1965). "Is the Existence of the World Necessary?" In *The Mystery of Existence*. New York: Appleton-Century-Crofts, pp. 160–173.

Nakhnikian, G. (1967). *An Introduction to Philosophy*. New York: Knopf.

Nakhnikian, G., and Salmon, W. (1957). " 'Exists' as a Predicate," *Philosophical Review* 66:535–42.

Nasser, A. (1971). "Factual and Logical Necessity and the Ontological Argument," *International Philosophical Quarterly* 11:385–402.

Nasser, A. (1979). "Divine Independence and the Ontological Argument – A Reply to James M. Humber," *Religious Studies* 15:391–7.

Nasser, A., and Brown, P. (1969). "Hartshorne's Epistemic Proof," *Australasian Journal of Philosophy* 47:61–4.

Nathan, N. (1988). "Explicability and the Unpreventable," *Analysis* 48:36–40.

Nelson, H. (1993). "Kant on Arguments Cosmological and Ontological," *American Catholic Philosophical Quarterly* 67:167–84.

Nelson, J. (1963). "Modal Logic and the Ontological Proof for God's Existence," *Review of Metaphysics* 17:235–42.

New, C. (1993). "Antitheism: A Reflection," *Ratio*, n.s., 6:36–43.

Oakes, R. (1972). "Logical Necessity, Self-Evidence, and 'God Exists,' " *Man and World* 5:327–34.

Oakes, R. (1974). "God, Electrons, and Professor Plantinga," *Philosophical Studies* 25:143–7.

Oakes, R. (1975a). "The Second Ontological Argument and Existence *Simpliciter*," *International Journal for Philosophy of Religion* 6:180–4.

Oakes, R. (1975b). "Containment, Analyticity, and the Ontological Argument," *Thomist* 39:319–31.

Oakes, R. (1980). "A New Argument for the Existence of God," *New Scholasticism* 54:213–23.

Oakes, R. (1984). "Reply to Professor Zagzebski," *New Scholasticism* 58:460–3.

O'Brien, A. (1964). "Duns Scotus' Teaching on the Distinction Between Essence and Existence," *New Scholasticism* 38:61–77.

O'Connor, M. (1969). "New Aspects of Omnipotence and Necessity in Anselm," *Religious Studies* 4:133–46.

O'Loughlin, T. (1989). "Who Is Anselm's Fool?" *New Scholasticism* 63:313–25.

Oppenheimer, P., and Zalta, E. (1991). "On the Logic of the Ontological Argument." In J. Tomberlin (ed.), *Philosophical Perspectives.* Vol. 5, *The Philosophy of Religion.* Atascadero, Calif.: Ridgeview, pp. 509–29.

Oppy, G. (1991). "Makin on the Ontological Argument," *Philosophy* 66:106–14.

Oppy, G. (1993a). "Makin's Ontological Argument Again," *Philosophy* 68:234–9.

Oppy, G. (1993b). "Modal Theistic Arguments," *Sophia* 32:17–24.

Oppy, G. (1994). "Weak Agnosticism Defended," *International Journal for Philosophy of Religion* 36:147–67.

O'Toole, E. (1972). "Anselm's Logic of Faith." In F. Schmitt (ed.), *Analecta Anselmiana III.* Frankfurt: Minerva GmbH, pp. 146–54.

Owens, J. (1979). "Existence as Predicated," *New Scholasticism* 53:480–5.

Pailin, D. (1969a). "Some Comments on Hartshorne's Presentation of the Ontological Argument," *Religious Studies* 4:103–22.

Pailin, D. (1969b). "An Introductory Survey of Charles Hartshorne's Work on the Ontological Argument." In F. Schmitt (ed.), *Analecta Anselmiana I.* Frankfurt: Minerva GmbH, pp. 195–221.

Pailin, D. (1975). "Credo Ut Intelligam." In H. Kohlenberger (ed.), *Analecta Anselmiana IV/2.* Frankfurt: Minerva GmbH, pp. 111–29.

Pailin, D. (1986). "The Ontological Argument." In *Groundwork of Philosophy of Religion.* London: Epworth, pp. 176–8.

Parkinson, G. (1954). "Justification Of The Method." In *Spinoza's Theory of Knowledge.* Oxford: Oxford University Press, pp. 36–56.

Patterson, R. (1970). "The Ontological Argument." In *A Philosophy of Religion.* Durham, N.C.: Duke University Press, pp. 479–513.

Paullin, W. (1906). "A Review of the Ontological Arguments," *American Journal of Theology* 10:53–71.

Paulsen, D. (1984). "The Logically Possible, the Ontologically Possible, and Ontological Proofs of the Existence of God," *International Journal for Philosophy of Religion* 16:41–9.

Pearl, L. (1990). "A Puzzle About Necessary Being," *Philosophy* 65:229–31.

Penelhum, T. (1960). "Divine Necessity," *Mind* 69:175–86.

Penelhum, T. (1961). "On the Second Ontological Argument," *Philosophical Review* 70:85–92.

Penelhum, T. (1968). "Descartes' Ontological Argument." In J. Margolis (ed.), *Fact and Existence*. Oxford: Oxford University Press, pp. 43–55.

Penelhum, T. (1971). "The Ontological Proof," pp. 11–18; "Some Recent Discussions of the Traditional Proofs – The Ontological Argument," pp. 365–72. In *Religion and Rationality*. New York: Random House.

Plantinga, A. (1961). "A Valid Ontological Argument?" *Philosophical Review* 70:93–101.

Plantinga, A. (1964). "Necessary Being." In A. Plantinga (ed.), *Faith and Philosophy*. Grand Rapids, Mich.: Eerdmans, pp. 97–108.

Plantinga, A. (ed.) (1965). *The Ontological Argument*. New York: Doubleday.

Plantinga, A. (1966). "Kant's Objection to the Ontological Argument," *Journal of Philosophy* 63:537–45.

Plantinga, A. (1967). "The Ontological Argument I," pp. 26–63; "The Ontological Argument II," 64–94. In *God and Other Minds: A Study of the Rational Justification of Belief in God*. Ithaca, N.Y.: Cornell University Press. The latter chapter is reprinted as "Alston on the Ontological Argument," in W. Doney (ed.) (1968), *Descartes: A Collection of Critical Essays*. London: Macmillan, pp. 47–63.

Plantinga, A. (1974a). *The Nature of Necessity*. Oxford: Oxford University Press.

Plantinga, A. (1974b). "The Ontological Argument." In *God, Freedom, and Evil*. London: Allen & Unwin, pp. 85–112.

Plantinga, A. (1975). "Review of Barnes (1971)," *Philosophical Review* 84:582–7.

Plantinga, A. (1976). "Existence, Necessity, and God," *New Scholasticism* 50:61–72.

Plantinga, A. (1979). "*De Essentia*," *Grazer Philosophische Studien* 7–8:101–22.

Plantinga, A. (1986). "Is Theism Really a Miracle?" *Faith and Philosophy* 3:109–34.

Platt, D. (1973). "What the Ontological Proof Can and Cannot Do," *New Scholasticism* 47:458–68.

Pollock, J. (1966). "Proving the Non-Existence of God," *Inquiry* 9:193–6.

Potter, V. (1965). "Karl Barth and the Ontological Argument," *Journal of Religion* 45:309–25.

Pottinger, G. (1983). "A Formal Analysis of the Ontological Argument," *American Philosophical Quarterly* 20:37–46.

Power, W. (1992). "Ontological Arguments for Satan and Other Sorts of Evil Beings," *Dialogue* 31:667–76.

Preuss, P. (1980). "Ontological Vertigo," *International Journal for Philosophy of Religion* 11:93–110.

Prior, A. (1955). "Is Necessary Existence Possible?" *Philosophy and Phenomenological Research* 15:545–7.

Puccetti, R. (1964). "The Concept of God," *Philosophical Quarterly* 14:237–45.

Purtill, R. (1966). "Hartshorne's Modal Proof," *Journal of Philosophy* 63:397–409.

Purtill, R. (1967). "Ontological Modalities," *Review of Metaphysics* 21:297–307.

Purtill, R. (1975). "Three Ontological Arguments," *International Journal for Philosophy of Religion* 6:102–10.

Purtill, R. (1976). "Plantinga, Necessity, and God," *New Scholasticism* 50:46–60.

Rabinowicz, W. (1978). "An Alleged New Refutation of St. Anselm's Argument," *Ratio* 20:149–50.

Rainer, A. (1948). "Necessity and God: A Reply to Professor Findlay," *Mind* 57:75–7.

Read, S. (1981). "Reflections on Anselm and Gaunilo," *International Philosophical Quarterly* 21:437–8.

Reardon, B. (1988). *Kant as Philosophical Theologian.* London: Macmillan.

Reichenbach, H. (1951). *The Rise of Scientific Philosophy.* Berkeley: University of California Press.

Reiss, L. (1971). "Anselm's Arguments and the Double-Edged Sword." *Philosophical Forum* 2:511–30.

Rescher, N. (1959a). "The Ontological Proof Revisited," *Australasian Journal of Philosophy* 37:138–48.

Rescher, N. (1959b). "On the Logic of Existence and Denotation," *Philosophical Review* 68:157–80.

Rescher, N. (1960). "A Ninth-Century Arabic Logician on: Is Existence a Predicate," *Journal of the History of Ideas* 21:428–30.

Resnick, L. (1962). "A Logical Refutation of Mr. Hardin's Argument," *Analysis* 23:90–1.

Resnick, L. (1963). "Do Existent Unicorns Exist?" *Analysis* 23:128–130.

Rice, V. (1964). "Necessary Being," *Sophia* 3:28–31.

Richman, R. (1958). "The Ontological Proof of the Devil," *Philosophical Studies* 9:63–4.

Richman, R. (1960). "The Devil and Dr. Waldman," *Philosophical Studies* 11:78–80.

Richman, R. (1976). "A Serious Look at the Ontological Argument," *Ratio* 18:85–9.

Robinson, D. (1951). "Hartshorne's Non-Classic Theology," *Philosophy and Phenomenological Research* 12:135–8.

Robinson, W. (1984). "The Ontological Argument," *International Journal for Philosophy of Religion* 16:51–9.

Rohatyn, D. (1982). "Anselm's Inconceivability Argument," *Sophia* 21:57–63.

Rosenberg, S. (1981). "On the Modal Version of the Ontological Argument," *Logique et Analyse* 24:129–33.

Rosenthal, D. (1976). "Possibility, Existence, and an Ontological Argument," *Philosophical Studies* 30:185–91.

Ross, J. (1969a). *Philosophical Theology.* New York: Bobbs-Merrill.

357

Ross, J. (1969b). "The Philosophical Arguments." In *Introduction to the Philosophy of Religion*. London: Macmillan, pp. 20–9, 50–71.

Ross, R. (1970). "A Form of Ontological Argument," *Harvard Theological Review* 70:115–35.

Rousseau, E. (1980). "St. Anselm and St. Thomas – A Reconsideration," *New Scholasticism* 54:1–24.

Rowe, W. (1976a). "The Ontological Argument and Question-Begging," *International Journal for Philosophy of Religion* 7:425–32.

Rowe, W. (1976b). "Comments on Professor Davis' 'Does the Ontological Argument Beg the Question?' " *International Journal for Philosophy of Religion* 7:443–7.

Rowe, W. (1988). "Response to Dicker," *Faith and Philosophy* 5:203–5.

Rowe, W. (1989). "The Ontological Argument." In J. Feinberg (ed.), *Reason and Responsibility*, 7th. edition. Belmont, Calif.: Wadsworth, pp. 8–17.

Ruf, H. (1975). "The Impossibility of Hartshorne's God," *Philosophical Forum* 7:345–63.

Ruja, H. (1963). "The Definition of God and the Ontological Argument," *Australasian Journal of Philosophy* 41:262–3.

Russell, B. (1985). "The Ontological Argument," *Sophia* 24:38–47.

Russell, B. (1900). "Proofs of the Existence of God." In *A Critical Exposition of the Philosophy of Leibniz*. London: Allen & Unwin, pp. 172–90.

Russell, J. (1993). "Tillich's Implicit Ontological Argument," *Sophia* 32:1–13.

Ryle, G. (1935). "Mr. Collingwood and the Ontological Argument," *Mind* 44:137–51; reprinted in J. Hick and A. McGill (eds.), *The Many-Faced Argument: Recent Studies on the Ontological Argument for the Existence of God*. New York: Macmillan, pp. 246–60.

Ryle, G. (1937). "Back to the Ontological Argument," *Mind* 46:53–7; reprinted in J. Hick and A. McGill (eds.), *The Many-Faced Argument: Recent Studies on the Ontological Argument for the Existence of God*. New York: Macmillan, pp. 269–74.

Ryle, G. (1951). "Systematically Misleading Expression." In A. Flew (ed.), *Logic and Language* (*First Series*). Oxford: Blackwell, pp. 11–36.

Rynin, D. (1963). "On Deriving Essence from Existence; or: How to Establish the Ontological Argument on a Firm Foundation," *Inquiry* 6:141–56.

Sagal, P. (1973). "Anselm's Refutation of Anselm's Ontological Argument," *Franciscan Studies* 33:285–91.

Salmon, N. (1987). "Existence." In J. Tomberlin (ed.), *Philosophical Perspectives*. Vol. 1, *Metaphysics*. Atascadero, Calif.: Ridgeview, pp. 49–108.

Saw, R. (1951). "Of God: That He Necessarily Exists." In *The Vindication of Metaphysics*. London: Macmillan, pp. 62–73.

Sayward, C. (1985). "God and Empty Terms," *International Journal for Philosophy of Religion* 18:149–52.

Schofner, R. (1974). *Anselm Revisited*. Leiden: Brill.

Schopenhauer, A. (1897/1813). *On the Fourfold Root of The Principle of Sufficient*

Reason, translated by Mme. Karl Hillebrand (Revised Edition). London: George Bell.

Schopenhauer, A. (1958/1844). *The World as Will and Representation* (Second Edition), translated by E. Payne. New York: Dover.

Schrader, D. (1991). "The Antinomy of Divine Necessity," *International Journal for Philosophy of Religion* 30:45–59.

Schufreider, G. (1977). "The Identity of Anselm's Argument," *Modern Schoolman* 54:345–61.

Schufreider, G. (1978). *An Introduction to Anselm's Argument.* Philadelphia: Temple University Press.

Schufreider, G. (1981). "What Is It for God to Exist?" *New Scholasticism* 55:77–94.

Schufreider, G. (1983). "Reunderstanding Anselm's Argument," *New Scholasticism* 57:384–409.

Schufreider, G. (1992). "A Classical Misunderstanding of Anselm's Argument," *American Catholic Philosophical Quarterly* 66:489–99.

Schwarz, W. (1964). "Professor Engel on Kant," *Philosophy and Phenomenological Research* 25:406–11.

Scott, G. (1966). "Quine, Modality and God," *Monist* 50:77–86.

Scriven, M. (1966). "The Ontological Argument." In *Primary Philosophy.* New York: McGraw-Hill, pp. 141–8.

Scruton, R. (1982). "The Logic of Illusion: Theology." In *Kant.* Oxford: Oxford University Press, pp. 51–4.

Scruton, R. (1986). *Spinoza.* Oxford: Oxford University Press.

Seeskin, K. (1978). "Is Existence A Perfection? – A Case Study in the Philosophy of Liebniz," *Idealistic Studies,* 8:124–35.

Sen, S. (1983). "The Ontological Argument Revisited," *Indian Philosophical Quarterly* 10:219–42.

Sennett, J. (1991). "Universe Indexed Properties and the Fate of the Ontological Argument," *Religious Studies* 27:65–79.

Sessions, W. (1969). "Feuer, Psychology, and the Ontological Argument," *Inquiry* 12:431–4.

Shaffer, J. (1962). "Existence, Predication, and the Ontological Argument," *Mind* 71:307–25.

Shedd, W. (1884). "The Ontological Argument for the Divine Existence," *Presbyterian Review* 5:213–27.

Sheldon, W. (1923). "Another Form of the Ontological Proof," *Philosophical Review* 32:355–72.

Sheldon, W. (1924). "Statistical Law and the Ontological Proof," *Philosophical Review* 33:286–9.

Sheldon, W. (1929). "Necessary Truths and Necessary Being," *Journal of Philosophy* 26:197–209.

Sievert, D. (1982). "Descartes on Theological Knowledge," *Philosophy and Phenomenological Research* 43:201–19.

Sillem, E. (1957). *George Berkeley and the Proofs for the Existence of God.* London: Longmans, Green.

Slattery, M. (1969). "The Negative Ontological Argument," *New Scholasticism* 43:614–17.

Smart, H. (1924). "Statistical Law and the Ontological Proof," *Philosophical Review* 33:73–82.

Smart, H. (1949). "Anselm's Ontological Argument: Rationalistic or Apologetic?" *Review of Metaphysics* 3:161–6.

Smart, J. (1955). "The Existence of God." In A. Flew and A. MacIntyre (eds.), *New Essays in Philosophical Theology.* London: SCM Press, pp. 500–509.

Smith, J. (1968). "The Ontological Approach." In *Experience and God.* New York: Oxford University Press, pp. 122–34.

Smullyan, R. (1983). "What Is There?" In *5000 B.C. and Other Philosophical Fantasies.* New York: St. Martin's Press, pp. 111–21.

Sobel, J. (1983). "Names and Indefinite Descriptions in Ontological Arguments," *Dialogue* 22:195–201.

Sobel, J. (1987). "Godel's Ontological Proof." In J. Thomson (ed.), *On Being and Saying: Essays for Richard Cartwright.* London: MIT Press, pp. 241–61.

Sontag, F. (1967). "The Meaning of 'Argument' in Anselm's Ontological 'Proof,' " *Journal of Philosophy* 65:459–86.

Sosa, E. (1969). "Comment." In J. Margolis (ed.), *Fact and Existence.* Oxford University Press, pp. 56–8.

Spade, P. (1976). "Anselm and Ambiguity," *International Journal for Philosophy of Religion* 7:433–45.

Sproule, R., Gerstner, J., and Lindsley, L. (1984). *Classical Apologetics.* Grand Rapids, Mich.: Zondervan.

Srzednicki, J. (1965). "The Ontological Proof and the Concept of 'Absolute,' " *Sophia* 4:28–32.

Stearns, J. (1970). "Anselm and the Two-Argument Hypothesis," *Monist* 54:221–33.

Steinitz, Y. (1994a). "Necessary Beings," *American Philosophical Quarterly* 31:177–82.

Steinitz, Y. (1994b). "Contradictions are Ontological Arguments," *Religious Studies* 30:505–9.

Stengren, G. (1975). "Malebranche's Version of the Ontological Argument." In H. Kohlenberger (ed.), *Analecta Anselmiana IV/1.* Frankfurt: Minerva GmbH, pp. 231–7.

Stone, J. (1989). "Anselm's Proof," *Philosophical Studies* 57:79–94.

Stove, D. (1978). "Part IX of Hume's *Dialogues*," *Philosophical Quarterly* 28:300–309.

Strasser, M. (1985). "Leibniz, Plantinga, and the Test for Existence in Possible Worlds," *International Journal for Philosophy of Religion* 18:153–9.

Streveler, P. (1976). "Two 'New' Critiques of the Ontological Argument." In

H. Kohlenberger (ed.), *Analecta Anselmiana V.* Frankfurt: Minerva GmbH, pp. 55–64.

Tapscott, B. (1971). "Plantinga Properties and the Ontological Argument," *Philosophy and Phenomenological Research* 31:604–5.

Tartarkiewicz, W. (1981). "Ontological and Theological Perfection," *Dialectics and Humanism* 8:187–92.

Tichy, P. (1979). "Existence and God," *Journal of Philosophy* 76:403–20.

Tillich, P. (1951). "The So-Called Ontological Proof." In *Systematic Theology,* Vol. 1. Welwyn: James Nesbit, pp. 227–31.

Tomberlin, J. (1970). "Prior on Tense and Time," *Review of Metaphysics* 24:57–81.

Tomberlin, J. (1971). "Existence Attributes: A Second Look," *Review of Metaphysics* 24:737–8.

Tomberlin, J. (1972a). "Malcolm on the Ontological Argument," *Religious Studies* 8:65–70.

Tomberlin, J. (1972b). "Existence and Existence Attributes," *Philosophy and Phenomenological Research* 32:535–42.

Tomberlin, J. (1974). "A Definition of 'God' Examined," *Sophia* 13:30–2.

Tooley, M. (1981). "Plantinga's Defence of the Ontological Argument," *Mind* 90:422–7.

Tully, R. (1980). "More on Moore on 'Existence,' " *Dialogue* 19:546–55.

Tweyman, S. (1992). "Some Reflections on Hume on Existence," *Hume Studies* 18:137–49.

Vallicella, W. (1983). "A Critique of the Quantificational Account of Existence," *Thomist* 47:242–67.

Vallicella, W. (1989). "A Note on Hintikka's Refutation of the Ontological Argument," *Faith and Philosophy* 6:215–217.

Vallicella, W. (1993). "Has the Ontological Argument Been Refuted?" *Religious Studies* 29:97–110.

van Inwagen, P. (1977). "Ontological Arguments," *Nous* 11:375–95.

Vaught, C. (1972). "Hartshorne's Ontological Argument: An Instance of Misplaced Concreteness," *International Journal for Philosophy of Religion* 3:18–34.

Verweyen, H. (1970). "Faith Seeking Understanding: An Atheistic Interpretation," *New Scholasticism* 44:372–95.

Wainwright, W. (1978a). "The Ontological Argument, Question-Begging, and Professor Rowe," *International Journal for Philosophy of Religion* 9:254–7.

Wainwright, W. (1978b). "On an Alleged Incoherence in Anselm's Argument: A Reply to Robert Richman," *Ratio* 20:147–8.

Wainwright, W. (1978c). "Unihorses and the Ontological Argument," *Sophia* 17:27–32.

Wald, A. (1979). " 'Meaning,' Experience, and the Ontological Argument," *Religious Studies* 15:31–9.

Waldman, T. (1959). "A Comment upon the Ontological Proof of the Devil," *Philosophical Studies* 10:49–50.

Walker, R. (1978). "God." In *Kant*. London: Routledge & Kegan Paul, pp. 165–92.

Walters, K. (1973). "Is the Non-Existence of Perfection Provable?" *Man and World* 6:390–6.

Walton, D. (1978). "The Circle in the Ontological Argument," *International Journal for Philosophy of Religion* 9:193–218.

Ward, K. (1982). "The Intelligibility Of Being," pp. 1–23; "The Necessarily Existent," pp. 24–48; "Perfection," pp. 49–68. In *Rational Theology and the Creativity of God*. Oxford: Blackwell.

Watt, E. (1969). "Feuer on Guilt and Logic," *Inquiry* 12:427–30.

Webb, C. (1896). "Anselm's Ontological Argument for the Existence of God," *Proceedings of the Aristotelian Society*, o.s., 3:25–43.

Webb, C. (1915). *Studies in the History of Natural Theology*. Oxford: Oxford University Press.

Webb, M. (1989). "Natural Theology and the Concept of Perfection in Descartes, Spinoza, and Leibniz," *Religious Studies* 25:459–75.

Weinberg, J., and Yandell, K. (1971). "The Ontological Argument." In *Problems in Philosophical Inquiry*. New York: Holt, Rinehart, & Winston, pp. 496–513.

Weiss, P. (1954). "Guilt, God, and Perfection I, II," *Review of Metaphysics* 8: 30–48, 246–63.

Werhane, P. (1985). "Existence, Eternality, and the Ontological Argument," *Idealistic Studies* 15:54–9.

Werner, C. (1965). "The Ontological Argument for the Existence of God," *Personalist* 46:269–83.

Werther, D. (1989). "Augustine and Absolute Creation," *Sophia* 28:41–52.

White, D. (1979). "God and Necessity," *International Journal for Philosophy of Religion* 10:177–87.

Wienpahl, P. (1979). *The Radical Spinoza*. New York: New York University Press, pp. 22–7.

Wilbanks, J. (1973). "Some (Logical) Trouble for Anselm," *New Scholasticism* 47:361–5.

Wild, J. (1950). "The Divine Existence: An Answer to Mr. Hartshorne," *Review of Metaphysics* 4:61–84.

Williams, B. (1969). "Comment." In J. Margolis (ed.), *Fact and Existence*. Oxford University Press, pp. 55–6.

Williams, B. (1978). "God." In *Descartes: The Project of Pure Enquiry*. Harmondsworth: Penguin, pp. 130–62.

Williams, C. (1981). *What Is Existence?* Oxford: Oxford University Press (esp. " 'Existence Is Not a Predicate,' " pp. 17–41, and "Kant's Criticisms of the Ontological Argument," pp. 333–44).

Williams, C. (1986). "Kant and Aristotle on the Existence of Space," *Grazer Philosophische Studien* 25–26:559–72.

Williams, C. (1992). *Being, Identity and Truth.* Oxford: Clarendon (especially Chapter 1, Section 13: "Philosophers' Muddles About Existence," pp. 20–2.

Williams, C. (1993). "Russelm," *Philosophical Quarterly* 43:496–9.

Wilson, M. (1978). "Immutable Natures And The Ontological Argument." In *Descartes.* London: Routledge & Kegan Paul, pp. 172–6.

Wilson, M. (1979). "Possible Gods," *Review of Metaphysics* 32:717–33.

Wippel, J. (1981). "The Reality of Non-Existing Possibles According to St. Thomas Aquinas, Henry of Ghent, and Godfrey of Fontaines," *Review of Metaphysics* 34:729–58.

Wolfson, H. (1934). "The Ontological Proof." In *The Philosophy of Spinoza.* Cambridge, Mass.: Harvard University Press, pp. 158–84.

Wolter, A. (1990). "Duns Scotus and the Existence and Nature of God," pp. 254–77; "Is Existence for Scotus a Perfection, Predicate, or What?" pp. 278–84. *The Philosophical Theology of Duns Scotus.* Ithaca, N.Y.: Cornell University Press.

Wolz, H. (1951). "The Empirical Basis of Anselm's Argument," *Philosophical Review* 60:341–61.

Wood, F. (1973). "The Relation of the Ontological Argument to Metaphysics," *International Journal for Philosophy of Religion* 4:92–104.

Woods, J. (1986). "God, Genidentity, and Existential Parity," *Grazer Philosophische Studien* 25–26:181–96.

Yates, J. (1986). "A New Form of the Ontological Argument," *Sophia* 25:41–3.

Yolton, J. (1961). "Professor Malcolm on St. Anselm, Belief, and Existence," *Philosophy* 36:367–370.

Young, J. (1974). "The Ontological Argument and the Concept of Substance," *American Philosophical Quarterly* 11:181–91.

Young, J. (1979). "Existence, Predication, and the Real," *New Scholasticism* 53:295–323.

Zabeeh, F. (1962). "Ontological Argument and How and Why Some Speak of God," *Philosophy and Phenomenological Research* 22:206–15.

Zagzebski, L. (1984). "Oakes' New Modal Argument for the Existence of God," *New Scholasticism* 58:447–59.

Zeis, J. (1986). "Ross's Antimony and Modal Arguments for God's Existence," *International Journal for Philosophy of Religion* 20:159–64.

Zemach, E. (1993). "Existence and Non-Existents," *Erkenntnis* 39:145–66.

(2) SOURCES ON RELATED TOPICS

The following is a list of other material referred to in this work, including some material on the general question of the analysis of existence. For more on Meinongian theories of objects, and so on, see the bibliographies in Parsons (1980) and Routley (1980), as well as the references cited in the various articles in Haller (1986). For more on free logics, see the bibliographies in Bencivenga (1986), Schock (1968), and the relevant articles in Spohn, van Fraassen, and Skyrms (1991).

Adams, R. (1974). "Theories of Actuality," *Nous* 8:211–31.
Anderson, A, and Belnap, N. (1975). *Entailment*. Vol. 1, *The Logic of Relevance and Necessity*. Princeton, N.J.: Princeton University Press.
Ayer, A. (1948). *Language, Truth, and Logic*. Second edition. London: Gollancz. First published in 1930.
Barker, J. (1976). "The Fallacy of Begging the Question," *Dialogue* 15:241–55.
Barker, J. (1978). "The Nature of Question-Begging Arguments," *Dialogue* 17:490–8.
Basham, R. (1977). "On Singular Attributions of Existence," *Philosophical Studies* 31:411–22.
Basson, A. (1957). "Unsolvable Problems," *Proceedings of the Aristotelian Society* 57:269–280.
Bencivenga, E. (1980). "Again on Existence as a Predicate," *Philosophical Studies* 37:125–38.
Bencivenga, E. (1986). "Free Logics." In D. Gabbay and F. Guenthner (eds.), *Handbook of Philosophical Logic*. Vol. 3. Dordrecht: Reidel, pp. 373–426.
Bertolet, R. (1984). "Reference, Fiction, and Fictions," *Synthese* 60:413–37.
Biro, J. (1977). "Rescuing 'Begging the Question,' " *Metaphilosophy* 8:257–71.
Biro, J. (1984). "Knowability, Believability, and Begging the Question: A Reply to Sanford," *Metaphilosophy* 15:239–47.
Brandom, R. (1984). "Reference Explained Away," *Journal of Philosophy* 81:469–92.
Bricker, P. (1991). "Plentitude of Possible Structures," *Journal of Philosophy* 88:607–19.
Bull, R., and Segerberg, K. (1984). "Basic Modal Logic." In D. Gabbay and F. Guenthner (eds.), *Handbook of Philosophical Logic*. Vol. 2. Dordrecht: Reidel, pp. 1–88.
Cargile, J. (1991). "Real and Nominal Definitions." In J. Fetzer, D. Shatz, and G. Schlesinger (eds.), *Definitions and Definability: Philosophical Perspectives*. Dordrecht: Kluwer, pp. 21–50.
Cartwright, R. (1960). "Negative Existentials," *Journal of Philosophy* 57:629–39.
Chellas, J. (1980). *Modal Logic: An Introduction*. Cambridge University Press.
Church, A. (1949). "Review of *Language, Truth, and Logic* (2nd. Edition)," *Journal of Symbolic Logic* 14:52–3.
Cochiarella, N. (1968). "Some Remarks on Second Order Logic with Existence Attributes," *Nous* 2:165–73.
Cochiarella, N. (1969). "A Second Order Logic of Existence," *Journal of Symbolic Logic* 34:57–69.
Copi, I. (1972). *Introduction to Logic* (Fourth Edition). New York: Macmillan.

Bibliography

Dauer, F. (1989). "Fallacy Of Begging the Question." In *Critical Thinking*. Oxford: Oxford University Press, pp. 261–6.

Dejnozka, J. (1982). "Frege: Existence Defined as Identifiability," *International Studies in Philosophy* 14:1–17.

Evans, G. (1982). *The Varieties of Reference*. Oxford: Oxford University Press.

Fetzer, J., Shatz, D., and Schlesinger, G. (eds.) (1991). *Definitions and Definability: Philosophical Perspectives*. Dordrecht: Klumer.

Field, H. (1986). "The Deflationary Conception of Truth." In G. MacDonald and C. Wright (eds.), *Fact, Science, and Morality*. Oxford: Blackwell, pp. 55–117.

Findlay, J. (1963). *Meinong's Theory of Objects and Values*. Oxford: Oxford University Press.

Fleming, N., and Wolterstorff, N. (1960). "On 'There Is,' " *Philosophical Studies* 11:41–8.

Flint, P. (1988). "Williams on What the President Knew," *Analysis* 48:61–3.

Forbes, G. (1985). *The Metaphysics of Modality*. Oxford: Oxford University Press.

Forbes, G. (1989). *Languages of Possibility: An Essay in Philosophical Logic*. Oxford: Blackwell.

Gale, R. (1966). "Existence, Tense, and Presupposition," *Monist* 50:98–108.

Geach, P. (1951). "Symposium: On What There Is," *Proceedings of the Aristotelian Society*, supplementary volume 25:125–36.

Geach, P. (1968). "What Actually Exists." *Proceedings of the Aristotelian Society* 42:7–16.

Gregory, R. (1966). *Eye and Brain: The Psychology of Seeing*. London: Weidenfeld & Nicholson.

Haller, R. (ed.) (1986). *Non-Existence and Predication*. (*Grazer Philosophische Studien* 26)

Hamblin, C. (1970). "Begging the Question." In *Fallacies*. London: Methuen, pp. 32–5, 73–7.

Hintikka, J. (1975). "Impossible Possible Worlds Vindicated," *Journal of Philosophical Logic* 4:475–84.

Hoffman, R. (1971). "On Begging the Question at Any Time," *Analysis* 31:51.

Hughes, G., and Cresswell, M. (1968). *An Introduction to Modal Logic*. London: Methuen.

Hughes, G., and Cresswell, M. (1984). *A Companion to Modal Logic*. London: Methuen.

Jackson, F. (1987). "*Petitio* and the Purpose of Arguing." In *Conditionals*. Oxford: Blackwell, pp. 100–14.

Jackson, F., Oppy, G., and Smith, M. (1994). "Minimalism and Truth Aptness," *Mind* 103:287–302.

Jacquette, D. (1994). "Logical Dimensions of Question-Begging Argument," *American Philosophical Quarterly* 30:317–27.

Jevons, W. (1895). *"Petitio Principii."* In *Elementary Lessons in Logic.* London: Macmillan, pp. 179–81.

Johnson, O. (1967). "Begging the Question." *Dialogue* 6:135–50.

Johnston, M. (1992). "Explanation, Response-Dependence, and Judgement-Dependence." In P. Menzies, (ed.), *Response-Dependent Concepts.* Working Papers in Philosophy, RSSS, ANU, pp. 123–83.

Joseph, H. (1916). *"Petitio Principii."* In *An Introduction to Logic,* Oxford: Oxford University Press, pp. 591–4.

Joyce, G. (1949). *"Petitio Principii."* In *Principles of Logic.* London: Longmans, Green, pp. 278–9.

Kripke, S. (1980). *Naming and Necessity.* Cambridge, Mass.: Harvard University Press.

Kuhn, H. (1959). "Existence in C. D. Broad's Philosophy." In P. Schilpp (ed.), *The Philosophy of C. D. Broad.* New York: Tudor, pp. 597–612.

Lambert, K. (1983a). *Meinong and the Principle of Independence.* Cambridge University Press.

Lambert, K. (1983b). "Review of C. J. F. Williams' *What Is Existence,*" *Philosophical Books* 24:103–8.

Leonard, H. (1956). "The Logic of Existence," *Philosophical Studies* 7:49–64.

Lewis, D. (1988). "Statements Partly About Observation," *Philosophical Papers* 17:1–31.

Linsky, L. (1967). *Referring.* London: Routledge & Kegan Paul.

Lotta, R., and MacBeath, A. (1956). *"Petitio Principii."* In *The Elements of Logic.* London: Macmillan, pp. 380–1.

MacKenzie, J. (1979a). "Question-Begging in Non-Cumulative Systems," *Journal of Philosophical Logic* 8:117–33.

MacKenzie, J. (1979b). "How to Stop Talking to Tortoises," *Notre Dame Journal of Formal Logic* 20:705–17.

MacKenzie, J. (1980). "Why Do We Number Theorems?" *Australasian Journal of Philosophy* 58:135–49.

MacKenzie, J. (1984a). "Begging the Question in Dialogue," *Australasian Journal of Philosophy* 62:174–81.

MacKenzie, J. (1984b). "Confirmation of a Conjecture of Peter of Spain Concerning Question-Begging Arguments," *Journal of Philosophical Logic* 13:35–45.

Menzies, P., and Pettit, P. (1993). "Found: The Missing Explanation," *Analysis* 53:100–109.

Mitchell, D. (1962). "Existence, Predication, and Identity." In *An Introduction to Logic.* London: Hutchinson, pp. 73–100.

Moore, G. (1936). "Is Existence a Predicate?" *Proceedings of the Aristotelian Society,* supplementary volume, 40; reprinted in A. Plantinga (ed.) (1964), *Faith And Philosophy,* Grand Rapids, Mich.: Eerdmans, pp. 71–85.

Nielsen, K. (1971). *Contemporary Critiques of Religion.* New York: Herder & Herder.

Bibliography

Noxon, J. (1967). "Question-Begging," *Dialogue* 6:571–5.

Oppy, G. (1990). *Attitude Problems: Semantics for Propositional Attitude Ascriptions.* Doctoral dissertation, Princeton University.

Oppy, G. (1992a). "Semantics for Propositional Attitude Ascriptions," *Philosophical Studies* 67:1–18.

Oppy, G. (1992b). "Why Semantic Innocence?" *Australasian Journal of Philosophy* 70:445–54.

Palmer, H. (1981). "Do Circular Arguments Beg the Question?" *Philosophy* 56:387–94.

Pap, A. (1946). "Indubitable Existential Statements," *Mind* 55:234–46.

Parsons, T. (1980). *Non-Existent Objects.* New Haven, Conn.: Yale University Press.

Passmore, J. (1952). *Hume's Intentions.* Cambridge University Press.

Pears, D. (1967). "Is Existence a Predicate?" In P. Strawson, (ed.), *Philosophical Logic.* Oxford: Oxford University Press, pp. 97–102.

Peetz, V. (1982). "Is Existence a Predicate?" *Philosophy* 57:395–401.

Purtill, R. (1973). "Deontically Perfect Worlds and *Prima Facie* Obligations," *Philosophia* 3:429–38.

Quine, W. (1953). "On What There Is." In *From a Logical Point of View.* Cambridge, Mass.: Harvard University Press, pp. 1–19.

Quinn, P. (1982). "Metaphysical Necessity and Modal Logics," *Monist* 65:444–55.

Rantala, V. (1975). "Urn Models: A New Kind of Non-Standard Model for First-Order Logic," *Journal of Philosophical Logic* 4:455–74.

Rescher, N. (1964). *"Petitio Principii."* In *Introduction to Logic.* New York: St. Martin's, pp. 85–6.

Robinson, R. (1950). *Definition.* Oxford: Oxford University Press.

Robinson, R. (1971). "Begging the Question, 1971," *Analysis* 31:113–17.

Routley, R. (1980). *Exploring Meinong's Jungle and Beyond* (Interim Edition). Canberra: Philosophy Department, RSSS, ANU.

Routley, R. (1982). *Relevant Logics and Their Rivals.* Atascadero, Calif.: Ridgeview.

Russell, B. (1905). "On Denoting," *Mind* 14:479–93.

Russell, B. (1918/1956). "The Philosophy of Logical Atomism." In R. Marsh (ed.), *Logic and Knowledge.* London: Allen & Unwin, pp. 175–281.

Russell, B. (1946a). *The History of Western Philosophy.* London: Allen & Unwin.

Russell, B. (1946b). "My Intellectual Development." In P. Schilpp, (ed.), *The Philosophy of Bertrand Russell,* (Second edition). New York: Tudor, pp. 1–20.

Salmon, N. (1986). "Reflexivity," *Notre Dame Journal of Formal Logic* 27:401–29.

Salmon, N. (1989). "The Logic of What Might Have Been," *Philosophical Review* 98:3–34.

Sanford, D. (1972). "Begging the Question," *Analysis* 32:197–9.

Sanford, D. (1977). "The Fallacy of Begging the Question: A Reply to Barker," *Dialogue* 16:485–98.

Sanford, D. (1981). "Superfluous Information, Epistemic Conditions of Inference, and Begging the Question," *Metaphilosophy* 12:144–58.

Sanford, D. (1988). "Begging the Question as Involving Actual Belief and Inconceivable Without It," *Metaphilosophy* 19:32–7.

Schock, R. (1968). *Logics Without Existence Assumptions*. Stockholm: Almqrusti & Wiksell.

Sidgwick, A. (1910). "Begging the Question." In *The Application of Logic*. London: Macmillan, pp. 201–19.

Smiley, T. (1960). "Sense Without Denotation," *Analysis* 20:125–35.

Sorenson, H. (1959). "An Analysis of 'To Be' and 'To Be True,' " *Analysis* 19:121–31.

Spohn, W., van Fraassen, B., and Skyrms, B. (eds.) (1991). *Existence and Explanation*. Dordrecht: Kluwer Academic.

Stace, W. (1959). "Broad's Views on Religion." In P. Schilpp, (ed.), *The Philosophy of C. D. Broad*. New York: Tudor, pp. 171–95.

Stebbing, L. (1948). *"Petitio Principii."* In *A Modern Introduction to Logic*. London: Methuen, pp. 216–21.

Stich, S. (1975). "Logical Form and Natural Language," *Philosophical Studies* 28:397–418.

Stirton, W. (1995). "The Logical Status of 'Exists,' " *Proceedings of the Aristotelian Society* 95:37–49.

van Fraassen, B. (1980). *The Scientific Image*. Oxford University Press.

van Inwagen, P. (1980). "Indexicality and Actuality," *Philosophical Review* 89:403–26.

Vision, G. (1993). "Fiction and Fictionalist Reductions," *Pacific Philosophical Quarterly* 74:150–74.

Wagner, S. (1982). "Arithmetical Fiction," *Pacific Philosophical Quarterly* 63:255–69.

Walker, J. (1969). "Existence, Time, and Properties," *Philosophical Studies* 20:54–61.

Walton, D. (1980). *"Petitio Principii* and Argument Analysis." In J. Blair and R. Johnson (eds.), *Informal Logic*. Inverness, Calif.: Edgepress, pp. 41–54.

Walton, D. (1985). "Are Circular Arguments Necessarily Vicious?" *American Philosophical Quarterly* 22:263–74.

Walton, D. (1987). "Longer Sequences of Argumentation." In *Informal Fallacies*. Philadelphia: John Benjamins, pp. 157–83.

Walton, D., and Batten, L. (1984). "Games, Graphs, and Circular Arguments," *Logique et Analyse* 27:133–64.

Whately, R. (1864). "Petitio Principii." In *Elements of Logic*. London: Longman, Green, Longman, Roberts, & Green, pp. 132–4.

White, R. (1978). "Wittgenstein on Identity," *Proceedings of the Aristotelian Society* 78:157–74.

Williams, C. (1969). "Baier on the Equivocal Character of 'Exists,' " *Mind* 78:212–28.

Williams, C. (1980). "Is Identity a Relation?" *Proceedings of the Aristotelian Society* 80:81–100.

Williams, C. (1984). "The Ontological Disproof of the Vacuum," *Philosophy* 59:382–4.

Williams, C. (1987). "Knowledge, Belief, and Existence," *Analysis* 47:103–10.

Williams, C. (1988). "How Much Did the President Know," *Analysis* 48:64.

Williams, M. (1967). "Begging the Question?" *Dialogue* 6:567–70.

Wilson, K. (1988). "Circular Arguments," *Metaphilosophy* 19:38–52.

Wilson, K. (1993). "Comment on Peter of Spain, Jim MacKenzie, and Begging the Question," *Journal of Philosophical Logic* 22:323–31.

Woods, J., and Walton, D. (1975). *"Petitio Principii,"* *Synthese* 31:107–27; reprinted in J. Woods and D. Walton (1989). *Fallacies*. Dordrecht: Faris, pp. 29–45.

Woods, J., and Walton, D. (1977). *"Petitio* and Relevant Many-Premised Arguments," *Logique Et Analyse* 20:97–110; reprinted in J. Woods and D. Walton (1989) *Fallacies*. Dordrecht: Faris, pp. 75–85.

Woods, J., and Walton, D. (1978). "Arresting Circles in Formal Dialogues," *Journal of Philosophical Logic* 7:73–90; reprinted in J. Woods and D. Walton (1989). *Fallacies*. Dordrecht: Faris, pp. 143–59.

Woods, J., and Walton, D. (1979). "Circular Demonstration and Von Wright – Geach Entailment," *Notre Dame Journal of Formal Logic* 20:768–72; reprinted in J. Woods and D. Walton (1989). *Fallacies*. Dordrecht: Faris, pp. 175–9.

Woods, J., and Walton, D. (1982a). "The *Petitio*: Aristotle's Five Ways," *Canadian Journal of Philosophy* 12:77–100.

Woods, J., and Walton, D. (1982b). Question-Begging and Cumulativeness in Dialectical Games," *Nous* 16, pp. 585–605; reprinted in J. Woods and D. Walton (1989). *Fallacies*. Dordrecht: Faris, pp. 253–72.

Wright, C. (1986). "Scientific Realism, Observation, and the Verification Principle." In G. McDonald and C. Wright (eds.), *Fact, Science, and Morality*. Oxford: Basil Blackwell, pp. 247–74.

Wright, C. (1989). "The Verification Principle: Another Puncture – Another Patch," *Mind* 98:611–22.

Ziembinski, Z. (1976). *"Petitio Principii."* In *Practical Logic*. Dordrecht: Reidel, p. 251.

Index